The author as a small boy sitting on the lap of Pietro, an Italian prisoner of war, on a farm at North Newton, near Bridgwater.

Mac Hawkins was born in Bridgwater, Somerset, in 1943 and educated at Christ's Hospital, Horsham. He began his career in the Royal Engineers, where he trained as a topographical surveyor, but in 1982 embarked on a full-time writing career. He is also the author of several best-selling railway books, which so far include *The Somerset & Dorset Then and Now, The Great Central Then and Now, Ivo Peters' Farewell to North-West Steam, LSWR West Country Lines Then and Now, Ivo Peters' Classic Steam* and *The Railway Paintings of Malcolm Root*. Returning to Somerset in 1966, he and his wife live on the Polden Hills; they have three grown up children.

1996 edition

Since this book was first published in 1988, the author has received numerous letters over the ensuing years; many of the correspondents offered new information and personal knowledge of episodes referred to in the book. Inevitably, however thorough the initial research, a few of the details had been recorded incorrectly, mainly due to errors of fact in the archive material used and although most were of a minor nature, the opportunity has now been taken to rectify these in this revised edition.

Sadly, with the passing of the years, some of the original contributors to this book have since died. This has proved that their testimony to the period between 1939 and 1945 was all the more important to have been recorded before it was lost forever.

Frontispiece
A 3.7-in gun manned and ready for action at Portbury. (S. Baker)

SOMERSET AT WAR
1939 – 1945

Mac Hawkins

HAWK EDITIONS

*This book is dedicated to all the people of the
county of Somerset, both civilian and military,
who lost their lives during the Second World War.*

THIS REVISION PUBLISHED BY HAWK EDITIONS IN 1996
First published in the UK in 1988 by The Dovecote Press Ltd
Stanbridge, Wimborne, Dorset BH21 4JD

Reprinted 1989, 1990
Paperback edition 1996

A catalogue record for this book is available from the British Library.

ISBN 0 9529081 0 7

Typesetting and reprograhics by Character Graphics, Taunton, Somerset
Printed in England by Biddles Ltd, Guildford and King's Lynn
for HAWK EDITIONS
PO Box 184, Cossington, Bridgwater, Somerset TA7 8YT

Contents

"Invasion troops". *Winston Churchill inspects troops of the 4th Battalion The Somerset Light Infantry, 12 May 1944.* (IWM)

Foreword

BY FIELD MARSHAL THE LORD HARDING OF PETHERTON, GCB, CBE, DSO, MC

As a native of Somerset with family roots in the county going back over several centuries I count it an honour to have been invited to write a foreword for Mac Hawkins' book on *Somerset at War 1939-45*.

I spent the first fifteen years of my life living in Somerset having been educated at Ilminster Grammar School and served in the county regiment, The Somerset Light Infantry. With many friends still living and working in the county, I have been a frequent visitor all my life and have a deep love for Somerset and take pride in calling myself a Somerset man. In consequence I, for one, am very glad that Mac Hawkins has placed on record the splendid way in which the people of Somerset faced up to the any problems, privations, dangers, sufferings and losses of war and played their full part over the six long years of war in the ultimate defeat of the Nazis.

Unfortunately, owing to failing eyesight due to my age, I have been unable to read the whole book myself, but extracts have been read to me and I have a good idea of the scope and most interesting content of the book, and I know the author has carried out prolonged and exhaustive research in arriving at his account of the events so the reader can be assured of its authenticity. He has captured the charm and the independence of the people who live in Somerset, with their distinctive dialect and readiness to give help to anyone in need, as witnessed by the welcome and care they extended to children evacuated in the early stages of the war to Somerset from other places and areas more vulnerable to air attack.

I commend this book most warmly to all Somerset folk, to those, like myself, with family roots in the county and to the many visitors who come to enjoy the beautiful countryside of Somerset, to visit the ancient buildings and places of historic interest.

LORD HARDING
Nether Compton, August 1988

Postscript
On 20 January 1989, a few months after writing this foreword, Lord Harding died aged 92; he was born on 10 February 1896.

Introduction

This book, commissioned in 1986 to document the events and record life in the county of Somerset during the Second World War, commenced with little idea how much work would be involved to try and cover the subject as comprehensively as possible and to keep within reasonable publishing limits. Once research had been embarked upon, it soon became clear that this was going to be no easy task. To gather information from a period half a lifetime ago and to select material has been difficult to achieve in the time available.

By good fortune, with help from many people who remember the war and by recording their memories, also studying the papers of the late Captain T.A. Bushell, who wrote an account of 'Somerset on Guard', latterly depositing them with the County Record Office, life was made somewhat easier. A debt of gratitude is owed to Captain Bushell for documenting so thoroughly many aspects of the military war in Somerset, particularly the Home Guard, which has enabled sections of his papers to be incorporated within this book. Without his diligent work it would have been impossible to regain the information that was readily available just after the war.

The war was essentially brought to Somerset from the skies and if this work tends to be biased towards aviation, it is true to say it was an air war as far as the county was concerned. Ask country people what they recall of the period, the first thing that they will probably tell you is that a bomb dropped in the vicinity, secondly, an aircraft crashed nearby. With the exception of those in towns, who suffered directly from the blitz, these are the things that made the most impression and are remembered best.

It has been difficult to achieve the right balance, particularly with regard to recording photographically the events in the county at a parochial level, partly due to the restriction of film which was not readily available to the general public, and of course it was a matter of security that one did not point a camera at militarily sensitive subjects. Aviation, however, is another matter and photographs were available to illustrate what in essence was Somerset's war. The only exceptions being that it proved impossible in the time available to locate contemporary photographs taken at either Merryfield or Weston Zoyland airfields. By way of a bonus, photographs to represent both British and German airmen who were in some way involved in the county's air war have been located, or lent by other authors and historians, are included.

The war holds bitter memories for many; loved ones lost, homes destroyed, long periods of separation, shortages of food and clothing, or perhaps the prospect of an uncertain future in a country overrun by a totalitarian régime, foreign to our democratic way of life. To others the war was the most challenging and exciting time of their lives, when ordinary men and women had a chance to do their bit, perhaps rescued by these events from a humdrum or routine existence, enabling them to be fulfilled. Often memories of the camaraderie bonded by a common cause in war will linger for a lifetime. The war had little effect on some people or their lives, who, maybe, had limited understanding of the events that surrounded them. This is perhaps best illustrated by a North Petherton cleaning lady who greeted her employer one morning with startling news she had just heard on the wireless: "Good news this morning ma'am - the Japanese have sunk two more American battleships!"

It is hoped that this book records a few of those memories between the years 1939 and 1945. A broad brush has been necessary to paint an overall picture, but inevitably there are subjects which, regrettably, have been left out, due to the fact it would have been impossible to include them within the confines of these pages.

MAC HAWKINS
Cossington, 1988

Acknowledgements

One of the great pleasures in the preparation of *Somerset at War*, is that it provided me with the opportunity to meet many interesting and charming people. The help that I have had from those interviewed has been of enormous value in being able to record just a little of what happened in Somerset during the war years. The assistance of the local press and media also has been tremendous in launching appeals on my behalf for anecdotes, information and photographs; to them I am most grateful. The response from the public was generally good and only one person who was approached, having in his possession a wonderful collection of wartime photographs taken in Somerset, failed to respond and regrettably felt he was unable to assist for 'copyright' reasons.

To single out individuals that have helped me enormously is difficult, but I feel special thanks go to both Ken Wakefield and Alan White, whose valuable assistance unflinchingly given enabled me to record the air war historically and photographically, particularly the Luftwaffe, and was indispensable. My old friend Ivo Peters unravelled the mysteries of the Royal Observer Corps and provided many anecdotes both of the Corps and the bombing of Bath - to him my special thanks. My interviews with Austin Hayter and Eric Westman were a joy.

The staff of the County Record Office, particularly Steve Hobbs, helped me beyond measure. David Bromwich of the Local History Library produced some fabulous photographs and answered, often patiently, many queries. Similarly to museum staff, reference librarians, archivists all over the (old) county; I could not have managed without their support. To them all, my gratitude.

Thanks go to all the following who responded to my appeals, gave interviews, material, lent photographs, documents and books: Freddie Ballam, Sergeant Keith Stout, Frank Welland, Ken Hodges, George Morley, Dave Benfield, Chris Ashworth, David Smith, Stephen Baker, Mary Ruau, Arthur Spender, Reggie Tongue, Peter Devitt, John Loosley, Sharon Poole, Jane Evans, H.H. Hole Esq, Bill Berry, Will Locke, Lt Col Ron Woodhouse, Gerald Little, Harald Penrose, John Penny, Ian James, John Winstone, Reece Winstone, Ken West, Colin Johnston, Arthur Knight, Jim Foster, Geoff Bell, Colin Church, Terry Temlett, Elizabeth Woods, Molly Hawkins, the late Mary Wallbridge, Douglas Allen, Cliff Tippetts, Wyndham Fry, Phyllis Wyatt, Mildred Matthew, Dr Ian Callow, Mike Tozer, Harry Foot, Reg Mack, Len Lovell, Anne Bell, Kit Houghton, the late Herbie Loader, Arnold Arnold, Nunzio Notaro, Billy Wontroba, John Sigmund, Ron Hansford, Reg Shattock, Bill Shattock, Michael Berry, Dick Vearncombe, Fritz Coles, Leonard Bond, Gladys Matthews, Alan Bye, Edith Simmons, Mrs M.W. Williamson, Irene Doble, Mrs M. Joyce, John Carpenter, Mr N.A. Perriman, Pauline Bland, Simon White, John Kirkham, Adrian and Rosemary Bawden, Colin Maggs, Chris Evelyn-White, Harry Routledge, Jerry Lock, Richard Cornish, Ted Stoyle, Phil Stoyle, Gordon Allen, Robert Dunning, Rene Cross, John and Jacy Kinross, Mrs N. Watts, Mrs B. Stockden, Hilda Otridge, Vera Thomas, Diana Chalk, Mrs E. Hucker, Mrs G. Stevens, Mrs R.F. Waddon, George White, Cyril Sparrow, Tim Lamacraft, Wendy and David Lamacraft, Cliff Sparkes, John Hellis, Monica Wyatt, Malcom Garrett, Ann Meade and to all the others whose names I either did not know or have mistakenly forgotten.

I could not have done without my wife's support; she is my best critic and helper, who spent many hours reading through draft manuscripts, endured my questioning or seeking advice - bless you. Thanks to my agent, Keith Hardy, who was responsible for my gaining this challenging commission.

Finally, I am greatly indebted to Field Marshal Lord Harding for kindly consenting to write the foreword to this book.

Glossary

AA	Anti-Aircraft	Instep	Fighter interception of aircraft attacking shipping
AACU	Anti-Aircraft Co-operation Unit	IWM	Imperial War Museum
A&AEE	Aeroplane & Armament Experimental Establishment	Ju	Junkers Flugzeugwerke-und Motorwerke GmbH (manfr Junkers a/c)
Ack-ack	Anti-aircraft fire	K	Killed
ADGB	Air Defence of Great Britain	LAA	Light Anti-Aircraft
AFS	Advanced Flying School/Auxiliary Fire Service	Luftmine	Aerial or land mine
AFU	Advanced Flying Unit	Luftwaffe	German Air Force
AGS	Air Gunnery School	Mandolin	Low-level strike against transport targets
AI	Airborne Interception (radar set in British a/c)	MT	Mechanical or Motor Transport
Anti-Diver	Patrol to destroy V-1 flying bombs	MU	Maintenance Unit
AONS	Air Observer Navigation School	NFS	National Fire Service
AOS	Air Observer School	NAFS	National Air Fighting School
ARP	Air Raid Precautions	NFS	National Fire Service
ATA	Air Transport Auxiliary	OADU	Overseas Aircraft Despatch Unit
AWOL	Absent without leave	OAP	Overseas Aircraft Preparation (Unit)
BAT Flt	Blind or Beam Approach Training Flight	OCU	Operational Conversion Unit
Bf	Bayer Flugzeugwerke GmbH (manfr Messerschmitt a/c)	Overlord	Code name for the invasion of occupied Europe
BG	Bombardment Group (eg 351BG)	(P)AFU	(Pilot) Advanced Flying Unit
BOAC	British Overseas Airways Corporation	PRO	Public Record Office
Bolero	Accommodation of US troops	PRU	Photographic Reconnaissance Unit
CAM	Catapult Aircraft Merchant (Ship)	PSL	Patrick Stephens Ltd
CD	Civil Defence	Q Site	Decoy airfield/factory site (QF, QL) to attract enemy
CO	Commanding Officer (or OC)	RA	Royal Artillery
(C)OTU	(Conversion) Operational Training Unit	RAAF	Royal Australian Air Force
CRO	County Record Office	RAE	Royal Aircraft Establishment
CU	Conversion Unit	Ramrod	Day bomber raid with fighter escort
DFC	Distinguished Flying Cross	RCAF	Royal Canadian Air Force
DMWD	Department of Misc. Weapons Development	RE	Royal Engineers
Do	Dornier Werke GmbH (manfr Dornier a/c)	Rhubarb	Low-level strike on targets in occupied Europe
DZ	Dropping zone	RNAS	Royal Naval Air Station
EFTS	Elementary Flying Training School	RNVR	Royal Naval Volunteer Reserve
E&RFTS	Elementary & Reserve Flying Training School	RNZAF	Royal New Zealand Air Force
FAA	Fleet Air Arm	ROC	Royal Observer Corps
FAAM	Fleet Air Arm Museum	Rodeo	Fighter sweep
FIS	Flying Instructors' School	RT	Radio transmitter
Flak	Fliegerabwehrkanone (German AA fire)	SAS	Severnside Aviation Society
Flammen-bombe	Oil incendiary bomb	SDF	Special Duty Flight
Flt	Flight	S&DJR	Somerset and Dorset Joint Railway
FPP	Ferry Pilots Pool	SFTS	Service Flying Training School
FTS	Flying Training School	Sqdn	Squadron
FW	Fighter Wing	Starfish	Dummy fire (QF) to attract enemy
GP	General purpose (bomb)	TCG	Troop Carrier Group (USAAF)
GWR	Great Western Railway	TCW	Troop Carrier Wing (USAAF)
HAA	Heavy Anti-Aircraft	TS	Training School
HCU	Heavy Conversion Unit	USAAF	United States Army Air Force
HE	High Explosive (bomb)	WRNS	Women's Royal Naval Service
He	Ernst Heinkel Flugzeugwerke GmbH (manfr Heinkel a/c)	W/T	Wireless telephony

PART I

WAR DIARY

The first major attack on Bristol occurred on the night of 24 November 1940. The ack-ack guns were in action all night. Seen here are those of 236 Battery at Portbury during such a raid. (S. Baker)

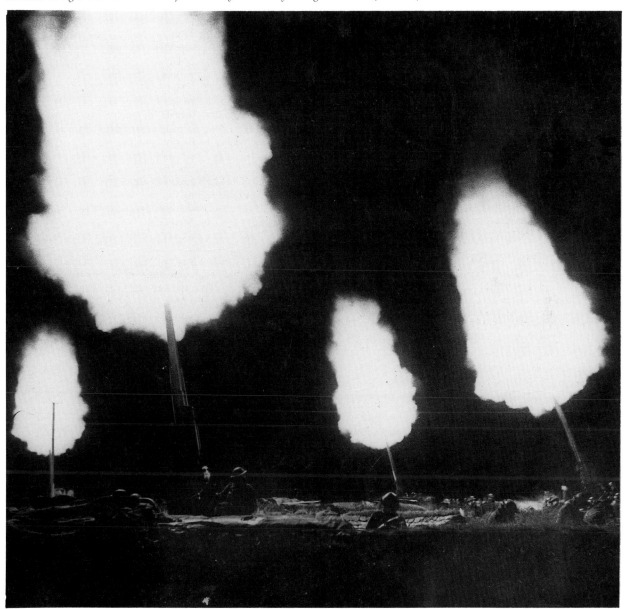

ONE

Somerset Prepares

In November 1938 there was a by-election in West Somerset. A 10,000 Conservative majority in Bridgwater had to be defended and the party chose 26 year-old Patrick Heathcoat-Amory, a member of a distinguished West Country family. He was challenged by a pugnacious broadcaster, journalist and diplomatic correspondent for *The News Chronicle* – attired in plus-fours and bow tie – Vernon Bartlett – who intended to stand as an Independent Progressive candidate. Both the Labour and Liberal parties, having no strong candidate to field against the Tories, put their weight behind him.

Bartlett fought solely on a foreign affairs ticket: "I want to get into Parliament to try and put a bit of guts into our foreign policy. The record has been one of humiliation, loss after loss, defeat after defeat". He had followed Chamberlain to Germany and reported on the three meetings with Hitler, gaining a valuable experience of the European situation at first hand. Heathcoat-Amory had no option but to stand solidly behind his leader and restated the policy of appeasement. The electors were forced to debate the Münich agreement. This was new and they liked it. Much to the annoyance of the Government – and reportedly to Hitler himself – the agreement was being debated in one of Britain's most rural communities. The German press vilified the constituency for allowing Bartlett to stand. The Conservatives soon latched on to this; a slogan was adopted: 'Hitler is watching Bridgwater'. Unruffled, Bartlett retorted: "Is he? Then we'll show him something".

Arguments echoed around the Quantocks and the surrounding villages; debates raged on in crowded halls. It was rumoured that Bartlett was about to pull out a trump card: Winston Churchill would speak on the Independent Progressive platform. The great man declined, but continued to issue dire warnings in the House of Commons about the German menace.

At the polling booths on 17 November, 36,748 electors voted – an 82.4 per cent turn-out – and gave Bartlett a comfortable majority. The Government was dismayed – Hitler was none too pleased either.

Bartlett's warnings were timely. Four months later, in March 1939, Germany invaded Czechoslovakia, forcing Chamberlain to abandon the policy of appeasement. In a famous speech made in his home city of Birmingham, he pledged that Britain would assist Poland if attacked by Germany. A complete about-turn of Government policy – the die was plainly cast for war. Hitler had made a mistake. He understood the worst motives of men, but not their feelings.

Conscription was introduced leaving five months to prepare for war. Local authorities set the wheels in motion: ARP lectures resumed, gas masks were issued and evacuation plans were finalised. Life went on as normal as possible in Somerset during that summer of '39. The usual round of fêtes, flower shows, bazaars and gymkhanas mirrored traditional country scenes as the county tried to set its troubles aside. The harvest still had to be reaped.

In August the crisis worsened. The Government reaffirmed its pledge to Poland on the 22nd – two days later the world was astonished to learn that a German-Soviet pact of non-aggression had been signed between two such enemies. The two powers had agreed to divide Poland: it was to be devoured between them. Parliament passed the Emergency Powers (Defence) Act, containing more than 100 regulations covering all aspects in defence of the realm. Reservists were called up the same day. The next day the treaty of alliance was signed with Poland. War was inevitable, and on 31 August it was announced that the evacuation of women and children from London would commence the next day. Somerset braced itself for the new arrivals.

On 1 September German tanks rolled into Poland. In Somerset the 101st Dunster Show was opened. The entry was a record, but the atten-

Throughout the war a watch was kept on the Somerset coastline. Coastguard Harry Cox is seen on Brean Down in 1943. Note the anti-aircraft and anti-landing craft obstacles placed on Brean Sands. (Weston Museum)

dance poor and the smallest in living memory. The worsening crisis would ensure people stayed at home listening to their wireless sets for news. Those that attended heard from a loudspeaker van the announcement that Germany and Poland were at war. Judging was suspended; the band stopped playing as the news sank home. At their tent surrounded by sheaves of corn, recruiting into the Women's Land Army was brisk. Around the county farmers were still gathering in the harvest.

Britain issued her ultimatum to Germany to withdraw from Poland. No such undertaking was received. And so at 11 am on the 3rd, Chamberlain gravely announced to the nation that a state of war existed between Britain and Germany. "Everything that I have worked for, everything that I have believed in during my public life, has crashed to ruins," he told the House of Commons. The barrage balloons rose in the sky once more and, for the second time in a generation, Britain was at war with Germany.

Sandbags had been delivered to various parts of the county. Children on the beach at Minehead had a new game to play: they stopped building their sand-castles and diverted their energies into filling sandbags. Precautions against possible air raids were hastily instigated all over the county. Householders busied themselves placing sticky tape on windows to lessen the effects of flying glass and suspended austere blackout curtains in place of colourful drapes. Whatever was in store, the people would be ready to meet it.

Months of stop-start preparations had come to an end. Surely things were about to happen fast? The British Expeditionary Force was despatched to France at all speed. They took up positions and waited...and waited. No sign of Hitler. The 'Phoney War', as the Americans dubbed it, was on. In Somerset the evacuation of women and children from London had started in earnest, but life remained much the same. The deprivations of rationing and hours of queuing at the butcher's shop or bakery were yet to have an impact on the housewife. ARP squads waited for the bombers to come, but they did not. It was the lull before the storm and was to last a full six months.

On 8 April 1940, the German Army occupied Denmark and Norway, meeting with valiant but little resistance. Norway's fall signalled the end of Chamberlain's career. Winston Churchill became Prime Minister on 10 May of a coalition government of all three main parties. That same day Hitler's armies launched 'Operation Yellow', the invasion of France, the Netherlands and Belgium. Dive-bombers blasted Rotterdam as they had Warsaw. The Germans by-passed the Maginot Line reaching the sea at Abbeville.

The French and British armies which had advanced into Belgium to stop a swing on Paris were cut off. For several weeks they tried to fight their way out. Short of ammunition and fuel, they could not continue the fight. Lord Gort, commander of the British Expeditionary Force, had no alternative but to disobey the French High Command and withdraw to the sea. He took his army to Dunkirk and the greatest evacuations in history of a fighting force was about to take place. 'Operation Dynamo' had begun on the 26th to evacuate troops from the beaches of Dunkirk. In the next eight days, a vast armada of ships of all sizes from destroyers to private motor cruisers rescued 338,226 men, two-thirds of them British, from the Dunkirk port and its adjoining beaches to English shores.

Only a narrow strip of blue sea separated Hitler from his final goal in the West. The white cliffs of Dover were within sight of a German army which had accomplished in seventeen days what its predecessor of the First World War had failed

Beating the INVADER

A MESSAGE FROM THE PRIME MINISTER

IF invasion comes, everyone—young or old, men and women—will be eager to play their part worthily. By far the greater part of the country will not be immediately involved. Even along our coasts, the greater part will remain unaffected. But where the enemy lands, or tries to land, there will be most violent fighting. Not only will there be the battles when the enemy tries to come ashore, but afterwards there will fall upon his lodgments very heavy British counter-attacks, and all the time the lodgments will be under the heaviest attack by British bombers. The fewer civilians or non-combatants in these areas, the better—apart from essential workers who must remain. So if you are advised by the authorities to leave the place where you live, it is your duty to go elsewhere when you are told to leave. When the attack begins, it will be too late to go ; and, unless you receive definite instructions to move, your duty then will be to stay where you are. You will have to get into the safest place you can find, and stay there until the battle is over. For all of you then the order and the duty will be : " STAND FIRM ".

This also applies to people inland if any considerable number of parachutists or air-borne troops are landed in their neighbourhood. Above all, they must not cumber the roads. Like their fellow-countrymen on the coasts, they must " STAND FIRM ". The Home Guard, supported by strong mobile columns wherever the enemy's numbers require it, will immediately come to grips with the invaders, and there is little doubt will soon destroy them.

Throughout the rest of the country where there is no fighting going on and no close cannon fire or rifle fire can be heard, everyone will govern his conduct by the second great order and duty, namely, " CARRY ON ". It may easily be some weeks before the invader has been totally destroyed, that is to say, killed or captured to the last man who has landed on our shores. Meanwhile, all work must be continued to the utmost, and no time lost.

The following notes have been prepared to tell everyone in rather more detail what to do, and they should be carefully studied. Each man and woman should think out a clear plan of personal action in accordance with the general scheme.

Winston S. Churchill

STAND FIRM

I. What do I do if fighting breaks out in my neighbourhood?

Keep indoors or in your shelter until the battle is over. If you can have a trench ready in your garden or field, so much the better. You may want to use it for protection if your house is damaged. But if you are at work, or if you have special orders, carry on as long as possible and only take cover when danger approaches. If you are on your way to work, finish your journey if you can.

If you see an enemy tank, or a few enemy soldiers, do not assume that the enemy are in control of the area. What you have seen may be a party sent on in advance, or stragglers from the main body who can easily be rounded up.

---

to achieve in four and a half bloody years. With the fall of France on 22 June the whole of the Channel Coast was in enemy hands. The invasion of England was imminent.

For the guidance of the civilian population the Government issued a leaflet entitled 'IF THE INVADER COMES'. It recounted the effect, seen in Continental Europe, of a population fleeing from their homes. "They crowded on the roads, in cars, in carts, on bicycles and on foot, and so helped the enemy by preventing their own armies from advancing against the invaders." Seven rules of conduct for the civilian population were laid down. The first was: "If the Germans come, by parachute, aeroplane or ship, you must remain where you are. The order is 'STAY PUT'."

How were the people to 'stay put' with the enemy in their midst? As a primary measure the Government was to be decentralised and full power vested in the Regional Commissioners. Should enemy infiltration isolate smaller areas of the country the functions of government would devolve upon special Invasion Committees capable of maintaining the life of the people and sustaining the defending forces in their own locality. These Invasion Committees roughly corresponded to the local government areas and included representatives of every Service, whether civil or military.

The Taunton Invasion Committee records were known as 'The Black Book'. On "Action Stations" one of the first functions of the committee would have been to provide some 400 civilians to undertake scheduled defence works at the orders of the Garrison Commander. Trees were felled, trenches and weapon pits dug. Mate-

FARM TRACTORS
PUT THEM OUT OF ACTION

All farm tractors in this area must be put out of action immediately.

To put your tractor out of action you must do the following :—

(1) **If it is a petrol driven vehicle —**

    (a) you must remove the distributor head and leads, and

    (b) in addition, you must <u>either</u> remove the carburettor <u>or</u> empty the petrol tank.

(2) **If it is a diesel engine you must** remove the fuel injection pump and connections.

All parts so removed and any similar spare parts must be hidden so that the enemy cannot find them.

Issued by Authority of the Regional Commissioner acting under Defence Regulation 16A.

(C44287—5) 27,500 3/42.

Opposite & above: *Leaflets: "Beating the Invader", "Stand Firm", "Farm Tractors": Instructions in the event of invasion were issued under the authority of the Regional Commissioner informing the population what to do, including directives to farmers on how to put their tractors out of action.*

Drives were launched to raise funds for the war effort. This 1942 march-past of troops in Weston-super-Mare was in aid of a campaign to sell National War Bonds 'to put more bombers in the air'. (Avon County Library)

rials were collected for an emergency bridge over the River Tone. Had the town bridge been destroyed these materials, which were kept handy, would have provided a temporary structure with a 10 ft wide carriageway and a narrow footway attached.

Home Guard casualties were to be handled by the Civil Defence Ambulance Service and the Emergency Hospital Service. Bishop Fox's School for Girls on the Kingston Road was scheduled as Taunton's No 1 Emergency Hospital. If further casualty accommodation was required, King's College, Queen's College, Taunton School and the Roman Catholic Convent would have been utilised in their turn. Members of the Home Guard were expected to provide their own rations for the first 24 hours, after which special 48 hour food packs were to be issued. Thereafter the feeding of the Home Guard would devolve on the Invasion Committee. Stores of food were accumulated in the town against such an emergency. The cooking was to be undertaken by the Women's Voluntary Services and in later years, by the Women's Home Guard Auxiliaries.

Communications with neighbouring areas would most certainly have been cut by the enemy in the event of invasion. Provision was made for this contingency by the setting up of short-range wireless stations at various points. One transmitter was sited in the Taunton sewage works. Its location was for long a closely-guarded secret: so also was the code by which the listeners would distinguish friend from foe. These secret transmitters went by the operational name of 'Beetle' and a continuous 'Beetle' watch was kept at all Home Guard headquarters during the critical

"Somerset was now ready for Hitler." Home Guard manning tank stop, Lyngford Lane, Taunton

days of 1940.

There were 48 members on the Taunton Invasion Committee; too unwieldy, it was said, for effective action. In practice this would not have been the case. In its preparations for the emergency, the Committee had the advice and assistance of almost every responsible officer in the town. In the event of invasion the greater number of them would have been at their posts 'in the field', leaving a small nucleus to carry on the essential functions according to plan.

The Garrison Commander was of course the senior military officer in each town. In the latter years of the war the British regular units in Somerset were all withdrawn, leaving the task of defence solely to the local Home Guard formations. Thus the North and South Somerset Home Guard Sector Commanders were eventually the Garrison Commanders respectively of the City of Bath and the town of Taunton. Elsewhere the Home Guard Battalion Commanders filled that rôle.

For the first time in its history, the nation was mobilised to counter the threat to its freedom. There were men on hilltops watching for parachutists, whilst others plotted the movement of enemy aircraft. The Civil Defence stood at their posts, awaiting the call for help – which would come soon enough. The post office, gas, electricity, and water services all had their emergency repair squads on standby.

Somerset was now ready for Hitler.

TWO

Battle of Britain Diary

"The Battle of France is over, I expect that the Battle of Britain is about to begin." Winston Churchill, 18 June 1940

The Air Defence of Somerset

The air defence of the county was the responsibility of No 10 Group, Fighter Command, whose headquarters were at Rudloe Manor, Box in Wiltshire – about two miles from the Somerset border. It covered the South West and South Wales areas, taking in Bournemouth, Salisbury, Andover, Oxford, Cheltenham, Brecon and to the Welsh coast at Cardigan.

Commanded by Air Vice Marshal Sir Christopher Quintin Brand No 10 Group became operational on 8 July 1940. At its disposal were No 87 Squadron (Hurricane), Exeter; No 92 Squadron (Spitfire), Pembrey; No 213 Squadron (Hurricane), Exeter; No 234 Squadron (Spitfire), St Eval, all of which operated through the Sector operations room at Filton, Gloucestershire. To protect Plymouth with its naval dockyard, six Gladiators of No 247 Squadron and their pilots were stationed at Roborough. These, with the Sea Gladiators of No 804 Squadron Fleet Air Arm, were the only biplane fighters to take part in the Battle of Britain. In August, Middle Wallop airfield and its satellite, Warmwell, were transferred to No 10 Group bringing in a further four squadrons: No 238 (Hurricane); No 609 (Spitfire); No 604 (Blenheim) and No 152 (Spitfire) at Warmwell.

A vital link in the county's air defence was provided by the Observer Corps: the southern area controlled by No 22 Group at Yeovil and the northern part by No 23 Group at Bristol.

During 1940 the airfields in Somerset did not come in for much attention from the Luftwaffe, save for the raids carried out on Yeovilton and Westland at Yeovil. The county had no front line fighter aerodrome during this period; both Weston Zoyland and Yeovilton were mainly used for

Spitfires of 92 Squadron, Pembrey, formed part of 10 Group defences. Seen with his aircraft and groundcrew is Flight Lieutenant A.R. Wright, who was soon to be in action over Somerset. (RAF Museum)

training purposes. In addition, anti-aircraft co-operation duties were carried out with Lysanders at the former and it was not until August the latter received its first operational squadron: No 827 with Albacores.

Weston and Yeovil airfields were primarily concerned with aircraft production. Whitchurch had been taken over by BOAC and No 3 Ferry Pilots Pool (ATA) were also located there with the task of ferrying aircraft from the production lines of the Bristol Aeroplane Company at Filton. Other airfields, such as Charmy Down, were either in the course of construction or remained to be planned; however towards the end of the war there were 13 airfields in use in the county.

Somerset – a backwater?

Although not directly in the front line for the

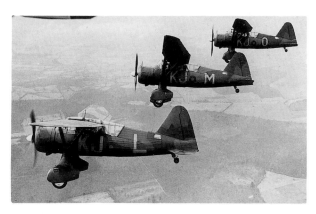

During this period Lysanders of 16 Squadron, Weston Zoyland were engaged in coastal patrols with the Army's Western Command. (IWM)

Battle of Britain itself, Somerset also suffered from the attentions of the Luftwaffe. The large-scale attacks on this country by German aircraft began on 10 July 1940, which is the generally accepted date of the beginning of the battle. On Somerset, however, attacks had begun within a few hours of the Prime Minister's June speech, two whole months before London's anti-aircraft guns first went into action.

The first bombs to be dropped, without any apparent objective, and due to enemy aircraft dumping their loads, had fallen at 09.15 on 18 June at Flax Bourton, near Bristol. A stick of four small bombs fell during the night of 19/20 June at Thornfalcon and West Hatch, two small parishes on the outskirts of Taunton. There were no casualties, but a woman later died from shock. However the Nag's Head public house on the Ilminster Road and some nearby cottages were damaged. On the same night bombs fell on the foreshore at Portishead. On 25 June the first bombs fell on Bristol and its immediate environs. A week later on 1 July, six bombs were dropped at Newton St Loe, Bath, damaging a bridge, putting both the main road and the Great Western Railway out of action until repairs could be effected.

From this time until mid-December there were few nights in which Somerset did not suffer from random bombing. Enemy aircraft were also over in daylight on a great many occasions. Part of the major air battles were fought over Somerset, although they did not approach either in number or in scale those which which took place over the south-eastern counties.

Large numbers of bombs fell in woods, marshes and on farms, as well as on towns. So widespread and apparently aimless was the bombing that it is quite impossible to list all the incidents, it must suffice to record only the more important, especially where loss of life was suffered. To highlight this fact, between 10 July and 12th, bombs fell at Congresbury, Redhill, Burtle, Huntspill, Mark, Edithmead, Bleadon and Edingworth, with no loss of life.

First strike – Yeovilton Airfield and Westland attacked

The Royal Naval Air Station at Yeovilton was attacked early on the afternoon of 15 July when part of a small force of Junkers Ju 88s from II/LGI, sent to attack Yeovil, bombed the airfield from 900 ft, causing damage to some buildings. Five service personnel were injured. The Ju 88s had suddenly appeared out of the low cloud and dropped 12 bombs on the Westland Aircraft Company's works and airfield at Yeovil, hitting the flight shed and pitting the grass runway, but fortunately missing the brand-new Whirlwind fighters parked on the aerodrome. One Ju 88 failed to return to its base – the crew of four were lost.

Harald Penrose, Westland's Chief Test Pilot at the time, described the raid in his autobiography:

It was too sudden for any air raid warning. Davenport was in my office. Came the startling crash of the first bomb, and he dived under my stout oak table. No room for me! I crouched against the wall. Then came another crump – and a great thump on my back. They've got me, I thought. I lay flat, listening to the succeeding detonations: then silence. I struggled to get up and found it was the overturned bookcase that pinioned my back.

Gerald Little recalls certain defensive measures employed by Westland in the event of an alert:

Enemy reconnaissance aircraft were often seen flying high overhead – they must have been photographing the works. New hangars were under construction at the time and they set up a light on Westland's main works, so that if it shone red, everyone working on the site knew when a warning was on. When there was a Jerry about the warning, which they called the '3 Gs', would go. The light would come on and a horn would sound and go *beep-beep-beep*, then everyone had to rush off and collect a corrugated sheet from a big pile, which they had stacked nearby and lay them down on the new concrete, which was then still white,

Forty-seven years after it dropped at Bankland Farm, North Moor, on 31 July 1940, the landmine crater is still in evidence. The size can be judged by the swan sitting on her nest. (Author)

to break up the symmetry of the floor near the hangars.

First casualties

On 18 July, Somerset suffered its first civilian casualties when bombs were dropped on Burnham-on-Sea, killing two people, injuring three and damaging 70 houses. During the same raid bombs fell at Mark, Cossington and Bleadon. At Wrington an enemy aircraft caught by a searchlight battery dived low and machine-gunned it, but failed to extinguish the beam and no casualties were reported.

On the 26th a Heinkel He 111 bomber from 1/KG4, which had been engaged in a minelaying sortie over the Bristol Channel, was attacked by Pilot Officer J.R. Cock in a Hurricane from 87 Squadron, Exeter, over East Portishead Point and brought down on the Blackdown Hills at Longfield Farm, Smeatharpe, between Churchingford and Upottery, a few yards over the Devon border. Four of the occupants were killed. One of the crewmen, Unteroffizier G. Strickstrock, landed at Middle Luxton Farm where he was captured by a member of the Churchstanton Home Guard Platoon, Sergeant Parsons. Despite the fact that the German had lost the tips from all his fingers on one hand, he was frog-marched several miles to the police station at Upottery.

Bill Berry, another member of the Churchingford Home Guard at the time, remembers the incident:

I heard an aircraft in trouble and could just make it out in the darkness – it fell just a ¼ mile or so inside the Devon border – near the road. The next day people came by car from miles around to look at the wreckage – scores of them. I went up to the site shortly before midday the next morning and remember seeing these bodies lying in the field which had been covered up; the police were on duty up there by then. Bits and pieces of the aircraft were scattered about. One of the airmen had fallen with his parachute unopened and he lay spreadeagled on the ground. When they lifted his body, he had made a perfect indentation in the field – you could actually see his finger imprints in the soil.

The last day of July brought a new weapon – an oil incendiary bomb fell at Kingston Seymour. Another new weapon was dropped from a Heinkel He 111 on the night of 1 August; in the early hours, Taunton and Bridgwater were shaken by a heavy, though distant, explosion. Daylight revealed an enormous crater 10 ft deep and 120 ft in diameter at Bankland Farm on North Moor. Nearby was a large unexploded magnetic mine. Fortunately details of the latest secret German weapon had been circulated to the Civil Defence authorities. The site was deep in the marshland and the Naval Bomb Disposal Party, which came up from Devonport, had to bridge three rhynes before commencing work.

When the landmine exploded that night, Jim Foster was fast asleep at Whites Farm, North Newton, and was rudely awakened by the blast which blew off his bedclothes. The next day he went to inspect the crater:

It was enormous – great clumps of earth as big as chairs were scattered about...in the trees as well; some had been blown more than a quarter of a mile from the site of the explosion. Eels which had been blasted out of the nearby rhynes, were also dangling from the surrounding trees – they remained there for several weeks afterwards.

At midnight on 1 August, 12 HE bombs were dropped in the Nether Stowey area, three of which fell in the grounds of Quantock Sanitorium, causing some damage to one cottage and overhead electricity wires. Leaflets containing Hitler's recent speech to the Reichstag: *A Last Appeal to Reason*, were found at Backwell and Axbridge.

Two parachute mines came down both at Sampford Brett on the night of 6th/7th, also at Curland near Taunton, causing damage to ceilings and windows, but fortunately with no casualties. On the night of 7th/8th HE bombs dropped at Yenston, Hewish, West Cross, West Coker and Oake near Taunton, also six HEs fell near Milborne Port. Some 30 enemy aircraft were active in the area, but none were intercepted.

Eight HE bombs fell at Bradney, near Bridgwater – one was of the whistling type – and further landmines were dropped on the night of 8th/9th at Tickenham and Kingston Seymour, again causing damage to ceilings and roofs of six houses.

For the next three years there were periods during which numbers of these mines were dropped: one or two per night, but they came down mostly in sparsely populated areas and did relatively little damage. Possibly those which fell in Somerset were intended for use against shipping in the Bristol Channel and elsewhere, but aircraft failing to find assigned targets through poor visibility or navigational errors dumped their loads as a matter of expediency. They might even have been under threat from nightfighter or ack-ack defences at the time.

There was a small raid carried out in the Yeovil area early hours on 9 August by a lone Junkers Ju 88: four HE bombs were dropped at Chilthorne Dormer, leaving craters of 32-36 ft in diameter. Its target was most probably the nearby airfield at Yeovilton, but on interception by Hurricanes of 'Blue Section', 213 Squadron, Exeter, who were on patrol in the area, had to dump its bombs in a hurry. The Ju 88 sustained damage in the attack

and the gunner was killed, but the aircraft managed to get back to its base. It was likely that the same crew member had been responsible for shooting down a barrage balloon at Yeovil which was completely destroyed and burnt out. There were no civilian casualties.

Practically every night during August HE bombs were dropped, but generally fell in remote areas, causing no damage of consequence. The first experience of unexploded HE bombs in large numbers was of 20 dropped at West Huntspill on 11 August, of which nine had failed to explode; and six dropped at Pill, of which four did not go off. There were two casualties on 16 August caused by delayed action bombs.

Battle over Sedgemoor

The first major air battle over the county took place in the late afternoon of 14 August. The enemy attacked a number of targets in the West Country, among them Cardiff, RAF Colerne and in Somerset RNAS Yeovilton was bombed by a lone Junkers Ju 88, which dropped six HEs, causing some damage to a runway and fuel bowser; a labourer was slightly injured.

At about the same time, a small force of Heinkel He 111 bombers from 9/KG27, on their way to bomb Cardiff Docks, were intercepted at 15,000 ft over the Street and Glastonbury area by Spitfires of 'Blue Section', No 92 Squadron, Pembrey. A running fight ensued and three of the enemy were shot down by the Spitfires within a period of 15 minutes. Flight Lieutenant Robert Stanford Tuck claimed two, with a third as being 'crippled & lost in cloud'. The other members of 92 Squadron responsible for the successful attack on the Heinkels were Flight Lieutenant A.R. Wright, Pilot Officers W.C. Watling, D.G. Williams and Sergeant Eyles.

The first Heinkel was brought down on the top of the Mendips with ground assistance from a Lewis gun. It made a forced-landing, demolishing a stone wall, on the road from Kingsdown to Charterhouse at a point between Gate and Velvet Bottom. The crew of five endeavoured to set fire to their machine but were prevented from doing so by members of the Charterhouse Home Guard who held them prisoner until soldiers from the Gloucester Regiment arrived from Yoxter camp and took them back there. Sentry duties were eventually handed over to the 1st Battalion

The first of three Heinkel 111s from 9/KG27 attacked by 'Blue Section' of 92 Squadron to be brought down on 14 August dumped its bombs and crash-landed at Charterhouse on the Mendips, demolishing a stone wall. (IWM)

Pilot Officer D.G. Williams of 92 Squadron who was partly credited with shooting down the Heinkel that fell near Toogoods Farm, Puriton. (RAF Museum)

Policemen and RAF personnel examine the wreckage of the KG27 Heinkel 111 at Toogoods Farm, the last to fall in Somerset on 14 August. Five aircraft of the 'Boelcke' Geschwader failed to return that day. Today a bungalow and a well-tended garden occupy the spot. (IWM)

Flight Lieutenant Robert Stanford Tuck of 92 Squadron claimed two Heinkels shot down with a third being 'lost in cloud'. (RAF Museum)

Coldstream Guards who were also in the area.

Farmer Hobbs, who was in the LDV, arrived at the scene first within five minutes of the aircraft coming down. He was closely followed by two colleagues, armed with a rifle and a shotgun, who legend has it, saw him with a fixed steely gaze leaning on his pitchfork near the aircraft and asked him: "Has anyone emerged from the plane?" "Arr" he replied, "but I vorked 'un back in agin!"

Within a few minutes a second Heinkel came down in flames at Puriton near Bridgwater, setting fire to Toogoods Farm, where a barn and hayricks were destroyed. The five occupants of this aircraft came down by parachute. The local Home Guard instantly turned out to guard the wrecked machine and to search for the airmen who were taken at East Huntspill. One of the Home Guard on seeing descending parachutes took a pot-shot at an unfortunate German dangling underneath one canopy. Luckily for him, Unteroffizier E. Flick was only slightly wounded in the neck. The other crew members were unhurt.

Cliff Tippetts, who was ten years old at the time, recalls the incident:

I had been sent by my parents to the Toby Inn up on the Polden Hills to collect pig swill, when I suddenly heard aircraft engines overhead and looked up to see this Jerry plane being chased by a Spitfire. I heard the

rrrrrrr of the fighter's machine-guns, then it broke off the attack and climbed steeply away. The next moment I saw parachutes open as the crew abandoned the aircraft, which was then on fire. To me they looked like dandelion seeds falling down. I didn't know where the plane crashed, but guessed it must have been over Puriton way.

Elizabeth Wallbridge was travelling down the A38 in a car and saw the Heinkel crash:

Approaching Dunball something made me look up and I noticed a plane in trouble, which stalled then crashed. I saw parachutes descending. We turned off the A38 to have a look and came across a very red-faced old woman running down the hill carrying what looked like a blunderbuss. She had obviously removed it from the mantlepiece and was making her way rapidly to the scene of the crash to do mortal battle with the enemy!

Eric Westman was working at the Bristol Wire Rope Company, Bridgwater saw one Heinkel, then noticed a pall of smoke rise from the direction of Puriton:

As I got onto the road there was a great phalanx of vehicles, mainly bicycles, coming out of Bridgwater – they spread across the whole width of the road...hundreds of them – it was if all the town was going to have a look. I nipped out to Puriton to have a look and saw a cottage chimney had been knocked off by the plane as it had come down. There were bullets exploding around – nobody dared get too close. A little while later, I saw the pilot and crew being taken away in a car to Bridgwater.

The third Heinkel fell in Bridgwater Bay, but because of cloud cover was not seen nor reported as having crashed by the ARP. Of the crew, only the body of Unteroffizier Hans Dolata, a gunner, was recovered from the mouth of the River Parrett on 12 September – nearly a month after being shot down; he is buried at Weston-super-Mare. No trace was ever found of the other crew members. Their aircraft was not recovered and lies somewhere in the bay to this day.

In addition to Yeovilton Air Station bombs fell that day at Cannard's Grave, Milborne Port, Weston-super-Mare, Banwell, Burnham, Berrow, Congresbury and Yatton. The railway was hit at Edington Burtle and also at Frome where the GWR loop was closed to traffic until an unexploded bomb could be removed. The ten HE bombs falling on Edington Burtle at 18.00 were probably dumped by Heinkels of 9/KG27 in their

Two of the five crew from the KG27 Heinkel that fell in Bridgwater Bay. Left: Only the body of gunner Unteroffizier Hans Dolata was recovered a month later and his remains buried at Weston-super-Mare. Right: Hauptmann Josef Riedl, pilot of the Bridgwater Bay Heinkel; he was a policeman before the war. (SAS)

panic to get away from the fighters which had intercepted them. A parachute mine exploded at Carhampton during the early hours of the morning but did no damage.

The night bombing continued. Due to the rural character of Somerset casualties were relatively few. On the 16th, nine HEs dropped in the Stringston/Doddington area and Shepton Mallet received a shaking on 20 August when 19 HE bombs dropped in the locality, causing slight damage to houses and telephone lines. From the outset a high percentage of enemy bombs failed to explode. Their guarding and subsequent removal caused much preoccupation on the part of the Civil Defence and Military authorities. The work was highly dangerous.

The same day a 1,000 kg bomb fell in the garden of a council house at Congresbury and failed to explode. It penetrated 25 ft into the earth, before being deflected sideways by a rock. Lieutenant Reynolds, Royal Engineers, was lowered head first into the hole and removed the three fuses. One was found to be of a time-controlled type set to explode the bomb within half an hour of removal. It was the first of its kind in a German bomb in this country. One of these went up at Camely near Clutton on 17th killing a Home Guard and a civilian. For this act of bravery Reynolds received a George Medal. On 20 September another party of these brave men was

less fortunate at Tintinhull, where an RE officer and two NCOs were killed instantly when a bomb they were defusing exploded.

Similar conditions prevailed in all the southern counties although at one time there were more unexploded bombs awaiting disposal in Somerset than in any other county in England.

Phyllis Wyatt lived at Edithmead during this period and can remember the bombs that fell in the area – many 'UXBs' amongst them:

When a stick of bombs were heard whistling down from an enemy aircraft, the personnel on duty at the post dived into what they thought was a dry ditch – it unfortunately turned out to be quite wet and they all got a thorough soaking! The unexploded bombs that came down on the farmland were dug out by the Royal Engineers who were billeted on householders in the village of East Brent.

During the last week in August there was increased night activity: in three nights, 23rd to 25th, about 320 HE bombs were dropped. Some 500 incendiaries were dropped in the Norton Radstock area during the night of 24 August and at Keynsham HE bombs demolished five shops without casualties. In the Cheddar and Wells district a large number of HEs caused damage to buildings, telephone wires and electric cables; around Yeovil 19 HEs killed farmstock.

Bridgwater bombed

There were seven fatal casualties and nine injured on the night of Saturday 24/25 August at Bridgwater. Three children were also killed and one man injured by stray bombs falling at Compton Martin.

After nightfall on the 24th the Germans attacked widespread industrial targets all over England. The sirens sounded in Bridgwater and soon enemy planes were heard passing overhead. In the early hours a raider, probably failing to find the designated target, dropped its load on the town, releasing at least 200 incendiaries across Cranleigh Gardens and into a brickyard at Colley Lane. Attracted by the fires, a second aircraft then dumped its load of HEs on Old Taunton Road.

The brickyard buildings were set alight, causing substantial damage. An HE bomb had fallen on Southgate Terrace of Old Taunton Road, severely damaging six houses and demolishing three. In one an ARP warden, Len Wilkins, who had been aroused by his warning bell, had got out of bed, dressed and was just in the process of putting on his boots when a bomb struck the house killing him, his wife Gladys and their 13 year-old daughter Margaret instantly. Other fatalities included a Mr and Mrs Collard.

Two of the victims' bodies were not found until the following Thursday when a memorial service was being held for the dead. In the debris of one house an old lady who had been sitting on a stool beneath the staircase, which had collapsed in the crater made by the bomb, was found clutching a bag of beans. After the sirens sounded she had obviously taken them with her to prepare for the Sunday lunch.

Despite the tragedy, there were lighter notes to this episode. One unusual survivor retrieved from the debris 36 hours later, a 100 year-old parrot, said to be much travelled having been round the world twice, was found a bit ruffled, but otherwise unhurt, in his battered cage. Previously talkative, he never uttered another word after the raid – not even to curse Adolf!

Hearing the sirens and seeing the 'fireworks' outside, Harry Rainey shouted to his wife who was upstairs in bed to hurry down to the Anderson shelter. "Me teeth...me teeth...I can't find me teeth," she cried, as she frantically looked for her false set. The exasperated Harry bellowed back up: "Don't worry about them, maid – they's chuckin' down bombs, not bloody sandwiches!"

Nine HEs fell in the Galmington, Bishops Hull and Norton Fitzwarren districts of Taunton on the 29th; the following night two HE bombs and an oil incendiary bomb dropped on Weston-super-Mare in Albert Quadrant, demolishing and damaging many houses, but causing only minor injuries. Demolition squads, rescue parties, highway, sewer, gas, electrical and water repair parties were put into operation for the first time.

Banwell hit

South Wales was heavily raided by the Luftwaffe during the first few nights of September and some of the bombs fell in Somerset. There were four fatal casualties at Portishead; three at Worle on the night of the 3rd/4th. The following night the village of Banwell was badly hit when an enemy bomber avoiding anti-aircraft defences dumped its load. A stick of bombs fell along the main street demolishing the Post Office and Telephone Exchange and damaging 100 houses and shops. Casualties had to be carried over fields

The Post Office in West Street, Banwell, after a stick of bombs fell on the village on the night of 3/4 September. (Somerset Local History Library)

and through hedges to waiting ambulances. Of the five persons killed two were policemen. Many other incidents were reported from all over the region that night. At Bath an AFS station was hit by incendiaries and caused a small fire. Livestock was not immune from enemy attack: two cows were killed at Beer Chael on the 7th.

Shortly before midnight on the 15th, 17 HE bombs exploded just 600 yd from Ham Green Hospital, but caused no damage. The same night a new type of weapon to the area exploded in mid-air and scattered its content of incendiaries over the village of Pill. This device became known to the British people as the 'Breadbasket': it was a container that could stow a variety of weapons from incendiary or anti-personnel bombs to para-flares designed to explode at any predetermined height. Nine houses were damaged at Pill on this occasion.

A Wellington bomber hit the balloon barrage at Yeovil during the night of the 18th. Three of the crew baled out, one of whom was seriously injured, but the remainder stayed in the aircraft which returned to its base safely.

Two Days In September

Day One: 25 September 1940

For Somerset the Battle of Britain reached its climax during the last week in September, when the German Air Force intensified its attacks on the aircraft industry, including manufacturers of aero-engines and ancillary equipment used in the construction of aircraft.

The first of two large-scale attacks occurred on the 25th – the airfield and the works of the Bristol Aeroplane Company at Filton were the Luftwaffe's major objective. At three airfields south-west of Paris, Dreux, Chartres and Villacoublay, a force of 64 Heinkel He 111 bombers from I, II and III/KG55 with an escort of 40 Messerschmitt Bf 110 fighters of ZG26 were prepared for the operation. The attack was to be led by the commander of II/KG55, Major Friedrich Kless.

At 11.00 the 'V'-shaped formation of 58 Heinkel bombers passed over Cherbourg at 16,400 ft; six had aborted during the take-off period. The escorting Me 110s followed them in a gentle weaving pattern slightly behind and above.

British radar picked up the raid at 11.04 which was designated as 'Raid 22'. Reported as a raid of ten aircraft heading for Portland, this caused no undue concern and a 'scramble' was not ordered immediately. However, the raid was amended to ten-plus and 609 Squadron was scrambled from Middle Wallop. At 11.09 No 152 Squadron was also ordered to take off and patrol Portland.

As radar plots improved the estimated number grew to 60-plus, which caused concern at Group Headquarters, as the raiders were now only 18 miles south-east of Portland – not one of 10 Group Squadron were airborne save two Spitfires of 152 Squadron patrolling the Isle of Wight. The Germans made several decoy raids, feinting one against Plymouth as well as attacking Portland at low-level with Messerschmitt Bf 110s. This caused confusion at 10 Group and the major raid went unmolested, reaching Portland Bill without incident. The spectacular formation passed over Portland at 11.23 and the AA guns opened up without success and the raid proceeded inland.

By the time the feints withdrew, the controllers

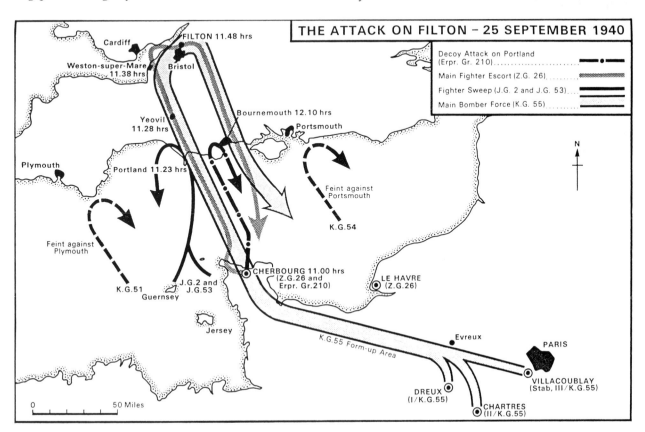

THE ATTACK ON FILTON – 25 SEPTEMBER 1940

Decoy Attack on Portland (Erpr. Gr. 210) ....
Main Fighter Escort (Z.G. 26) ....
Fighter Sweep (J.G. 2 and J.G. 53) ......
Main Bomber Force (K.G. 55) ....

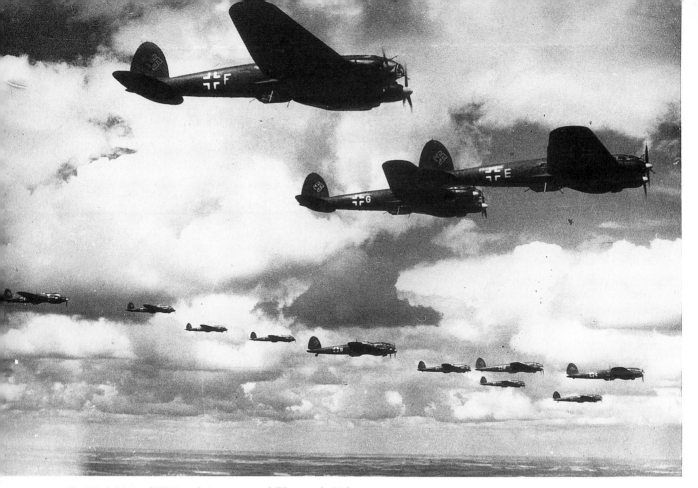

The Heinkel 111s of KG55 on their way to attack Filton on the 25th. Could this have been taken over the Somerset levels? (K.G. Wakefield)

at 10 Group realised the Westland Aircraft works at Yeovil could be the target. No 238 Squadron was scrambled from Middle Wallop with instructions to head for a point 10 miles south of Yeovil. All other 10 Group fighters were ordered to proceed to the town, but the bombers were only 16 miles from the Westland factory.

The raid approached Yeovil at 11.28 and further Squadrons in No 10 Group were brought to readiness, but the formation of bombers passed over the town and continued on towards Weston-super-Mare. A head-on attack was made just south of Yeovil by Pilot Officer R.F. Inness of 152 Squadron, flying a Spitfire. Bravely, he made a slicing pass through the enemy bombers, but the closing speed was so great he did not have time to observe the results. Further sections of 152 Squadron joined in but the attacks were inconclusive. One Spitfire was hit by return fire and Pilot Officer G.J. Cox had to return to Warmwell – he was the first casualty of the day. A man at Stoke-under-Ham was hit in the head

by a machine gun bullet and killed as the formation passed overhead.

The Heinkels and their escorts passed close to Weston Zoyland aerodrome and were reported by the RAF station, whose log recorded:

Approximately 70 enemy aircraft observed flying at about 16,000 ft in a north-westerly direction on a bearing of 045 degrees about five miles from the aerodrome. The aircraft were escorted by fighter aircraft; the number could not be ascertained. No bombs dropped in the locality.

A further attack by a Spitfire of 152 Squadron flown by Pilot Officer T.N. Bayles was beaten off by fire from the German gunners. His number two, Pilot Officer Eric 'Boy' Marrs, was fired on by some Bf 110s as he made his attack and forced to break away. Oberleutnant Hans Bröcker's Heinkel, attacked by Marrs, lagged behind the formation, having had the starboard engine damaged in an earlier encounter with fighters, dumped its load of oil incendiary bombs in order

The Portbury ack-ack crews gaze skywards at an incoming raid. Note the rangefinder and predictor. (S. Baker)

The 3.7-in mobile guns of 236 Battery, 76 HAA Regiment, Portbury, c. June 1940. (S. Baker)

to keep up with the formation. These fell harmlessly 2½ miles south-west of Street at 11.35.

Approaching Weston-super-Mare at 11.38 Major Kless ordered his pilot to alter course for Filton and all the bombers commenced a slow turn to the right. The escorting fighters did not see the main formation of Heinkels make the turn and continued on towards Cardiff before realising their mistake and then had to try and catch up with the bomber force, which were by now some five miles ahead.

As the Heinkels tightened up their formation in preparation for their bombing run they were attacked by a few Spitfires of 609 Squadron, who had joined those of 152 Squadron, some three miles to the south-west of the city. The crossfire from the bombers was effective enough to keep the fighters at bay.

Sergeant Hugh Rees of 609 Squadron attacked one of the Bf 110s, which he had mistaken for a Dornier Do 215, and saw the enemy aircraft dive down towards the sea off Portishead, apparently badly damaged. The engine of his own aircraft began to overheat and he glided down to make a forced-landing in a field half a mile south of Glastonbury Tor. Rees was not injured although his aircraft sustained undercarriage damage.

The four 3.7-in AA guns at the Gordano gunsite, belonging to 236 Battery 76th HAA Regiment, a Bristol Territorial regiment, opened fire and almost unbelievably a hit was observed on one aircraft, which went into a spiralling turn, its engines racing out of control and plummeted earthwards. The four guns at the Portbury site also engaged the enemy, but before further shots could be fired by either site the order came:

"Cease fire – fighters engaging!" much to the disappointment of all the gun crews.

The brief attack by Spitfires of 609 and 152 Squadrons and engagement by the AA guns seemed to disrupt the tight formation, as three aircraft broke away releasing their bombs prematurely, falling in various parts of the district: Nailsea, Abbots Leigh, Wraxall, Failand Lodge Farm, East End Farm, Tyntsfield, Chelvey, Leigh Court and other places. The bombs killed two pigs and four sheep besides badly damaging two cottages, a farmhouse and outbuildings at Home Farm, Tyntsfield.

The crew of the Heinkel, commanded by Oberleutnant G. Weigel, baled out successfully from the aircraft. The aircraft plunged into a ploughed field at Racecourse Farm, between Failand and Portbury, breaking up as it went, scattering wreckage over a wide area; its unarmed bombs, bouncing into a nearby wood, did not explode. The crew came down over Belmont Hill near Flax Bourton, landing near Abbots Leigh. One crewman, Oberfeldwebel G. Engel, suffered a fractured leg and was taken by ambulance to Clevedon Cottage Hospital.

Ex-Troop Sergeant Major Stephen Baker of 236 Battery at the Gordano gunsite saw the aircraft come down and the crew escape. One of them, Gefreiter Karl Greib, landed near Failand Church:

I ran out onto the road and commandeered a passing milkfloat and ordered the driver to make for Failand, where I noticed the parachutists coming down. As we approached the church I could see a German sitting on the wall, being held at bay by a one-armed farmer, who was wrestling with a 12-bore shotgun

Under new management. Hit by the 3.7-in guns of the Gordano ack-ack battery, Oberleutnant Weigel's Heinkel lies smashed in a field at Racecourse Farm, Failand. Wreckage still smoulders in the background. (BBC Hulton Picture Library)

Squadron Leader Peter Devitt, CO of 152 Squadron, who force-landed his Spitfire at Newton St Loe near Bath on the 25th, following damage received during the attack on Feldwebel Jürges' Heinkel. (via A. White)

under his stump trying to load with the other hand. The airman, terrified and resigned to his fate, was just sitting there shaking like a leaf. I said: "I'll take over." But the farmer was still menacing the poor devil: "Stand back! stand back!...I'll kill the bugger!" However I managed to get hold of the chap, loaded him onto the float and went back to the Battery, where the police came to take him away.

Meanwhile the rest of the formation made a perfect approach to the target. The 'raid imminent' warning was given out over the loud speaker system at the BAC factory and the employees made their way to the shelters as they had done so many times before.

Passing over the three main factory groups Kless gave the order: "*Bomben Los!*" Fifty-plus He 111s released their bombs in unison, which tumbled towards the complex 15,000 ft below, 350 falling in a box measuring one mile wide and ¾ mile deep; it was a classical bombing pattern and text-book attack. The time was precisely 11.48.

The works suffered severely; 900 houses in the Filton area were also damaged, many were flattened and the main railway line between Filton Junction and Patchway was blocked. There were many casualties: within the factory complex 72 were killed and 166 injured of which 19 later died from their injuries. Outside the factory 58 people lost their lives; 154 were seriously injured. Eleven soldiers were killed as they marched down the road between the Rodney and Patchway works. The high death rate among the employees was caused by a series of direct hits on six crowded air raid shelters.

Twelve Hurricane pilots of 238 Squadron were just too late on the scene and started their dive to attack the moment Kless gave the order to bomb. The bomber formation maintained its course for a short while and then made a gradual turn to the right; just as Squadron Leader Harold Fenton's Hurricanes hurtled down to attack the He 111s.

Fierce combat developed with the He 111s and Me 110s; the latter adopting their well-known tactic of forming defensive circles. Spitfires of 152 Squadron, led by the CO, Squadron Leader Peter Devitt, joined the fray shortly before the enemy reached Bath and made an attack on a Heinkel, closing to 20 yd. He saw the tracer bullets strike the enemy, but return fire from one of the Heinkels punctured his petrol tank, spraying the windscreen with fuel, causing him to break off the attack and make a wheels-up landing at Newton St Loe.

Peter Devitt recalls the incident:

I led the other aircraft down in echelon and attacked the Heinkel on the extreme left of the formation. I came in very close and was determined to shoot it down, but all I did was to silence the gunner in the upper position. Just as I turned away from the Heinkel at no more than 20 yards – only just missing him – there was a terrific bang...I found myself drenched in petrol and the windscreen of my Spitfire damaged. Realising the danger of fire, I switched the engine off. I think that if I hadn't done, the whole thing would have exploded. The Merlin engine used to 'spit fire' from the exhaust ports if you throttled back – the aircraft was well named! I pointed the nose straight down towards the earth and must have been doing some 400-plus knots. There were no enemy aircraft to be seen – it was peaceful and quiet as I looked for somewhere to land, but petrol was still dripping all over the place. I got down to 1,500 ft and saw what appeared to be a suitable field. I circled round it and to my dismay noticed electric cables right across, making it impossible to land. I picked another on the far side of a railway line and bordering a road junction...handy for getting the aircraft out! As the field was small, I raised the undercarriage for a belly landing. Coming in over the hedge, I saw there was another power cable spanning the field. I manoeuvred the aircraft quickly to avoid it and slid across the grass, coming to rest in a surprisingly short run without sustaining further damage. Relieved to be in one piece, I was amazed to see a woman, who had appeared from nowhere, with a cup of tea in her hand!

Elizabeth Wallbridge witnessed the Spitfire make an emergency landing alongside the main A4 road:

I was on the way up to Bath with my father and as we got nearer, we saw that there was a terrific dogfight going on overhead. We could see vapour trails in the sky and wondered whether it would be safe to continue our journey into the City. Approaching Newton St Loe we noticed a Spitfire in trouble, stopped the car, got out and watched the aircraft make a perfect belly-landing in a field. We cheered like mad when the pilot climbed out of his plane.

Ivo Peters was at his factory in Keynsham as the battle raged overhead:

The sirens had gone so I instructed my staff to go down to the air raid shelter to take cover. I could hear there was a tremendous aerial battle going on – instead of going down to the shelter myself I went outside to look. It was really quite fantastic – one minute there was a terrific amount of noise with planes twisting and turning in the sky – the next minute it was all over and really very quiet. I noticed a Spitfire in trouble – plainly it was losing height and realising that it was about to come down, jumped in my car and made off towards Bath. I got to Newton St Loe and noticed the fighter in a field to the left of the main road between the GWR and the Midland Railway lines. I went over to speak to the pilot whom I found perfectly all right. I offered him assistance and he said he would be grateful for a lift to Colerne airfield, which I gladly gave him.

Damage had been inflicted on several Heinkels and the formation began to spread out. Further running fights ensued and the British fighters went for the stragglers. But one of the leading Heinkels flown by the leader of 6 *Staffel*, Hauptmann Helmut Brandt, was attacked by Pilot Officer Dudley Williams of 152 Squadron. Smoke streamed from the engines of the bomber which curved downwards towards the patchwork of fields below and prepared to make an emergency landing, but four more fighters from 238 Squadron and 152 Squadron joined the fray; the pilots continued to attack the stricken bomber at very low level.

Observer/gunner Oberfeldwebel Rudolf Kirchoff died at his post whilst continuing to engage British fighters as his Heinkel plunged to earth. (SAS)

The wreckage of Hauptmann Brandt's Heinkel lies in a field at Church Farm, Woolverton. (IWM)

As the Heinkel made its final plunge towards the village of Woolverton, Brandt, the observer Oberfeldwebel G. Wittkamp and the flight engineer Unteroffizier H. Mertz, managed to bale out. Only Brandt's parachute deployed fully; the others did not have a chance: they had baled out too low and were killed. The bomber momentarily levelled out just missing the church. Radio-operator/gunner Oberfeldwebel R. Kirchoff stayed at his post continuing to engage the fighters and was still firing as the aircraft plunged into a field near Church Farm, exploding on impact. The air gunner, Gefreiter R. Beck had also stayed at his post and perished along with his colleague.

By a strange twist of fate, one bullet from those bursts of machine gun fire struck a Spitfire, penetrating the windscreen and killing the pilot, Sergeant Kenneth Holland of 152 Squadron. The aircraft crashed almost intact a short distance from the Heinkel.

Mrs Gladys Matthews lived at Church Farm, Woolverton:

I looked up and saw a bomber coming down followed by one of our planes which then did a victory roll. I could see the gunner in the German plane was still firing his gun on the way down. The bomber looked like it was heading straight for the village, but all of a sudden it veered away and crashed in one of our fields higher up. Both planes fell near the farm no more than a couple of hundred yards apart. The Spit-

fire broke its back as it crashed. I sent the gardener out to see if the pilot was all right – nothing could be for him – he had been shot right through the head. One of the German crew came down near Norton St Philip – he was the only one to get out alive, but was badly injured and when the ambulance came to take him away, they drove across the fields as fast as they could to give him a really rough ride – it was quite deliberate. There were a couple of the crew still in the plane when it crashed. The authorities removed the bodies of two airmen from the bomber the next day and when they passed through the yard, the stench of burnt flesh was dreadful.

Brandt showed considerable courage as he lay on the ground. He had suffered bullet wounds to the head, an eye injury, as well as fractures to his legs and the little finger on his right hand was almost severed. One of the first on the scene was Tom Meadway who made him comfortable, lit a cigarette and gave it to the wounded pilot. This action made some women in the crowd hostile accusing Brandt of bombing women and children, but he managed to explain in broken English that he was only doing his job. Brandt was alarmed when a member of the Home Guard arrived on the scene with a rifle but it was made clear to him that the British did not shoot their prisoners.

The main formation and their escorting fighters were heading back towards the coast continually being harried by British fighters: Hurricanes

Sergeant Pilot K.C. Holland of 152 Squadron killed by return fire from Brandt's Heinkel moments before it crashed. (Jon Falconer)

Memorial to Kenneth Holland erected where he fell a few hundred yards from the Heinkel. Ripley was the name of Holland's guardian, a serving RAF officer. (Jon Falconer)

of 601 Squadron attacked the enemy near Frome and the Germans lost a Bf 110, which made a perfect belly-landing at Well Bottom near Boyton in Wiltshire.

A crippled Hurricane from 238 Squadron was wrecked in a forced-landing at Charmy Down; the pilot, Sergeant F.A. Sibley, was unhurt. Another Hurricane flown by Pilot Officer D.S. Harrison made a forced-landing near the railway station at Mells Road, but later managed to fly back to Middle Wallop.

The battle left Somerset skies and continued on towards Bournemouth, where the Germans lost two more Heinkels: the first of which crashed into Poole Harbour, killing four of the crew, but one other was rescued from the water. The second Heinkel, that of Feldwebel Fritz Jürges, crashed-landed at Westfield Farm, Studland; one

crew member died, but the others were taken prisoner. The bomber, first hit by fighters over Bath and harried by others on the way, had managed to stagger towards the coast on one engine. Successive attacks and further damage forced the Heinkel to abandon its attempt to cross the channel. It was almost certainly the one attacked by Squadron Leader Devitt and other members of 152 Squadron. Further losses were reported: one Heinkel crash-landed at Caen and three more Bf 110s crashed, one ditched in the channel; all the crews were saved.

The camera catches a dramatic moment as a would-be rescuer runs to the downed Heinkel of Feldwebel Fritz Jürges at Studland. Members of the crew can be seen helping a wounded comrade away from the aircraft, whilst others arriving at the scene look on. Poole Harbour and Brownsea Island are seen in the distance. (Museum of Army Flying)

No. 152 Squadron, Warmwell, July 1940. L to R: P/O Warner, Sgt R. Walton*, P/O E.S. Marrs, Sgt E. Sheppard†, P/O R.F. Inness*, F/L E.C. Withall†, P/O Wildblood†, P/O C. Deanesly, P/O Jones†, F/L F.M. Thomas* (on back), P/O T.M. Bayles*, Sgt H.J. Akroyd† and Hon "P/O Pooch". *In action 25/27 September. †Killed before September 1940. (SAS)

Pilot Officer Eric 'Boy' Marrs of 152 Squadron. (SAS)

During the course of this day's fighting other bombs fell in Somerset at Portbury, Ashcott, Batheaston and Sandford near Weston-super-Mare.

Day Two: 27 September 1940

Following the events on 25th Air Chief Marshal Sir Hugh Dowding issued instructions for the air defence of the region to be beefed up, chiefly for the protection of the aircraft factory at Filton. No 504 (County of Nottingham) Squadron, equipped with Hurricanes, was sent down to Filton the next day. Hasty preparations were made and 17 aircraft, led by Squadron Leader John Sample, arrived at Filton in the afternoon of the 26th, followed by the groundcrews during that night.

The day of the 27th dawned bright and clear; the sirens sounding in Bristol repeatedly – another day in the air war was about to begin...

A Junkers Ju 88 of 3(F)/123, on a reconnaissance mission to photograph the western lock gates of the Manchester ship canal at Birkenhead, was plotted by Fighter Command's Operations Room as it approached the south coast.

The pilot, Feldwebel Helmut Ackenhausen, known to his comrades as 'Acki', was a veteran of many operations over Britain. Also on board were his observer, Oberleutnant Willi Rude; wireless operator Oberfeldwebel Erwin Riehle and Obergefreiter Wilhelm Ruehl, a replacement for Ackenhausen's flight engineer lost on a previous mission to Liverpool. This was to be Ruehl's first and last flight over Britain.

Three Spitfires from 152 Squadron, scrambled from Warmwell, caught up with the German over the Bristol Channel and attacked it: the Ju 88 dived steeply and headed towards the west. Pilot Officer Eric Marrs, who had been in action on the 25th, was one of those in pursuit and fired several bursts at the Junkers, but as he closed in his aircraft was hit by return fire: a bullet penetrated the cockpit, damaging the windshield. Undaunted, Marrs pressed home the attack and closed in from the port quarter. As the other Spitfires joined in the Junkers weaved from side to side, trying desperately to get away from its tormenters. With white smoke trailing from its engines, it headed towards the North Somerset coast.

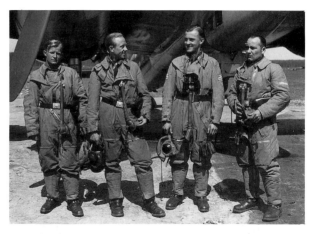

Feldwebel Helmut Ackenhausen (2nd left) and his crew stand in front of their Ju 88. With him on a photo reconnaissance mission to Liverpool on 27 September was wireless operator/gunner Oberfeldwebel Erwin Riehle (right). (K.G. Wakefield)

Arthur Knight was a young soldier who had recently joined the Somerset Light Infantry and was on detachment at Dunster at the time. He and his mates had a grandstand view of the action:

We were on parade along the seafront at Dunster doing routine weapon training when we heard the sound of aircraft approaching and noticed a Ju 88, going like hell, coming our way low over the Bristol Channel. Three Spits were having a go at him from behind and underneath – we saw the bullets strike the Junkers and bits fly off. The Jerry gunner was returning fire, but then stopped – he must have been hit. We watched the Ju 88 streaming white smoke from its motors go over the top of North Hill and disappear. We all cheered and clapped like mad, quite forgetting the rifle drill. One of the Spits came back and did a victory roll over our heads...it was smashing – then all three headed back up the Bristol Channel.

Reuhl, in the ventral gunner's position, was mortally wounded and had apparently been hit in the first attack. Both the Junkers engines stopped and Ackenhausen nursed the stricken aircraft down over Porlock Vale, scattering workers in the fields as the aircraft brushed the treetops, sending a great shower of leaves down from some poplars. Skimming the murky waters below, the Junkers came down to make a gentle crash-landing in the surf just off Porlock Beach. Riehle tried to pull the gunner from his position, but it was no good: the Junkers filled with water and Ruehl's body had to be left.

The three survivors came ashore where a re-

The Junkers Ju 88 lies wrecked off Porlock Beach. (SAS)

Arthur Knight of the Somerset Light Infantry witnessed the demise of the Ju 88 from 3/(F)123 that fell to the guns of 152 Squadron Spitfires. (A. Knight)

ception committee of the Home Guard was waiting. Ackenhausen disposed of his pistol, perhaps as a gesture of submission, throwing it over his shoulder into the sea. The Germans were taken by members of the 8th Battalion of the Somerset Light Infantry to Minehead Police Station for interrogation and, in the words of one local person, "a certain Mr Arkwright was called in to interpret because he spoke German."

Arthur Knight was posted as Guard Commander on the Junkers:

That evening I had to go out with a detail to guard the plane. When I arrived there was nothing to see – the tide had come in and covered the plane, but when it went out, there was the Ju 88! She was intact apart from the guns which had been removed and the starboard motor was out – the Germans had put an incendiary device in her but it failed to go off. I climbed in the cockpit and looked around...I had a great time. We were there to make sure that nobody pinched bits off it and were told the authorities were considering donating it to the Air Cadets at Minehead. But surprisingly we were called away fairly soon and the locals quickly made short work of picking the bones of it. There was not sufficient of it left to be worthwhile to the Cadets.

Reuhl was buried with full military honours and now lies in Porlock Cemetery. Ackenhausen returned to the area in 1972 and expressed a wish to meet the pilot responsible for shooting him down. Sadly this was not possible as Eric 'Boy' Marrs was shot down and killed over Brest on 24 July 1941 – a week after his 20th birthday. Poignantly, not long after his return home from Somerset, Helmut Ackenhausen died from a heart attack

The greatest events of 27 September were yet to come. It was the last occasion on which any comparable number of German aircraft crossed our coasts in daylight. There were in all four major attacks on Southern England in which the enemy used a record number of aircraft: about 850, of which 57 were lost; the RAF losing 28.

The first attacks were over Kent and made by fighters trying to clear the way for bombers. This did not entirely succeed, but later in the morning the Germans sent 300 aircraft to bomb London and others to Bristol. The target at Bristol was to be the aircraft factory of the Parnell Aircraft Company, who manufactured Fraser-Nash gun turrets. The Germans thought they would meet little resistance and were unaware that No 504 Squad-

34

504 Squadron pilots scramble from their crew room at Filton. (RAF Museum)

Flying Officer Michael "Scruffy" Royce prepares for another sortie. 504 Squadron, Filton 1940. (SAS)

ron had been moved to Filton the preceeding day.

Ten Messerschmitt Bf 110 fighter-bombers of Erprobungs Gruppe 210, each carrying two 500 kg bombs, took off from their base at Cherbourg at 10.40 to rendezvous with 42 Bf 110s from ZG26 as fighter escorts and in turn these were supported by 11 Bf 109Es of II/JG2. A further 29 Bf 109s from I and III Gruppen of JG2 and another seven aircraft from JG53 would cover the return of the attacking force – a total of 89 fighters to protect a force of just ten bombers.

British RDF stations picked up the raid as it left the Cherbourg Peninsula and plotted it as 'Fifty-plus'. There was some delay in despatching fighters to intercept the raid, but two Hurricanes of 238 Squadron were scrambled from Middle Wallop and told to patrol base. Hurricanes of 56 Squadron were airborne from Boscombe Down shortly afterwards with similar instructions.

609 and 152 Squadrons were scrambled from Warmwell just as elements of ZG26 and a few Bf 109s from II/JG2 flew abeam the airfield, but the British fighters were too late to intercept the enemy until they had passed some way inland.

Approaching Frome some of the Bf 110s left the formation to take up a defensive orbiting position above Portland hoping to draw off the British fighters from the bombers, thus the formation was reduced to 35 aircraft as it passed over Radstock.

Sirens sounded again in Bristol at 11.30 just as 504 Squadron were taking off in their Hurricanes from Filton, with Flight Lieutenant W.B. Royce in command of the 12 fighters, instructed to patrol base at 25,000 ft. The Bristol balloon barrage was a hindrance as the envelopes only seemed to be lowered very slowly and then only half way, the fighters having to thread their way carefully through them. At 10,000 ft 504 Squadron sighted the enemy to their rear.

Led by Hauptmann Martin Lutz, the fighter-bombers were going very fast as they headed towards Bristol in a shallow dive closely followed by their escort of 25 Bf 110 fighters. A Hurricane flown by Pilot Officer Murray Frisby, and still climbing, made a brave head-on attack opening fire on the leading German aircraft – that of Lutz – which banked sharply with white smoke streaming from its engines. This daring attack caused the German formation to break up in

35

chaos. Frisby was joined by other Hurricanes; a mêlée of twisting and turning aircraft ensued, each vying for position. The Germans tried to climb to 20,000 ft hoping that their superior speed would give them an advantage in a dive.

The dogfight was watched by hundreds of people on the ground and many clapped and cheered as the enemy scattered in all directions. Bullets, spent cartridge cases and shrapnel rained down on the streets below. Some of the hostile aircraft had been engaged by the AA guns around the city.

Molly Wallbridge, a Somerset girl in the Bristol ARP, saw the air battle going on whilst fishing from Keynsham Weir:

I was standing on the middle of the weir fishing for roach. The noise of the water drowned out all sound, but something made me look up...the sky was full of planes. I watched our fighters climb up into the formation, scattering the Germans in all directions. Dangerous to be caught out in the open because of the falling shrapnel and debris, I splashed my way over the weir as quickly as I could back to the bank to the shelter of an old mill, where I stood in the doorway to watch the air battle going on. I still couldn't hear anything of it for water going over the weir. The sky was full of vapour trails – it quite fantastic to watch.

The fighter-bombers jettisoned their loads and tried to make good their escape. Many of these bombs fell in open country around the northern outskirts of Bristol; some fell at Filton and others near Charlton, killing several people, including a man and two children who had been travelling along the road in a pony and trap.

One Bf 110 was hit in an attack by Pilot Officer B.E.G. White who had been climbing hard in his Hurricane and managed to get in a three-second burst, before stalling and falling away. The German crashed in flames at Fishponds, falling on the Stapleton Institution. The two crew, Oberfeldwebel Hans Tiepelt, the pilot, and his wireless operator, Unteroffizier Herbert Brosig were killed.

A second Bf 110 was in trouble. The Messerschmitt's pilot, Leutnant Joachim Koepsell, with his wireless operator Unteroffizier Johann Schmidt, was caught unawares whilst making a climbing turn before zooming down onto the British fighters, only to find they were at the same height and coming head-on towards them. Koepsell made a desperate attempt to bring his aircraft round into a firing position and, yawing

Leutnant Joachim Koepsell who was shot down at Radstock on 27 September. (K.G. Wakefield)

Unteroffizier Johann Schmidt in the rear cockpit of Koepsell's Bf 110. (K.G. Wakefield)

violently, fired at the closing fighters with little hope of achieving any success. It was too late: he had made a fatal mistake, becoming a victim himself and was hit by the guns of a Hurricane flown by Sergeant H.D.B. Jones.

Koepsell described in Kenneth Wakefield's

Above: *The "Flap" Room, 504 Squadron, Filton, September 1940. L to R: P/O Hunt, P/O Trevor Parsons, S/Ldr Johnny Sample, F/Lt Tony Rook, F/O Michael Royce, Sgt C. Haw. The latter three were in action on the 27th.* (SAS)

Right: *504 Squadron crew hut at Filton, September 1940. L to R: F/O Reggie Tongue, P/O Murray Frisby, F/Lt Tony Rook, Sgt Herbert Jones & P/O Mike Rook. The swastika-bedecked tail fin came from the Bf 110 shot down at Fishponds on the 27th.* (SAS)

book *Luftwaffe Encore,* what happened next:

Everything seemed to happen very quickly. My aircraft was badly damaged in the first encounter – the starboard petrol tank caught fire, my windscreen was shot up and from my comrade Schmidt, in the back, I heard a rattle from his throat over the intercom. A feeling of great calm came over me; I was still alive but in my mirror I could see blood running down over my face. The state of my aircraft ruled out any chance of getting home or even making a forced-landing – the forward petrol tank was now burning fiercely while the large tank situated behind it could explode at any moment...I no longer had any communication with Schmidt in the rear cockpit, but I caught sight of him slumped behind our inflatable rubber dinghy. With a certainty that a successful forced-landing was no longer possible I decided to try to catapult him out of the rear cockpit, through the open canopy, by rapid movements of the control column. I was hoping that his straps were undone and he would be able to open his parachute when clear of the aircraft. I then opened my own canopy roof exit, pulled myself up out of my seat and went out of the machine pulling the ripcord after a delay of five seconds.

Landing in some trees at Haydon Farm, Radstock, Koepsell was left dangling 15 ft in the air and confronted by what he assumed to be a Home Guard officer, but who turned out to be a member of the 1st Battalion of the Coldstream Guards, and instructed him to throw down his pistol. Koepsell again takes up the story:

He and his men were armed with a variety of guns, so I took it upon myself to explain to him that I was not hung in this fashion to become a sporting target of the English. To this the English officer responded dryly that neither was England a sporting target for German bombing practice.

The German pilot was helped down from the tree and then enquired about the welfare of his crewman, to be told that Schmidt had left the machine, but must have been knocked out or killed before doing so. He had landed with an unopened parachute close to the aircraft's dinghy.

The late Herbie Loader who worked at Kilmersdon Colliery wrote this eyewitness account shortly before he died in 1987:

During the war years I was a stoker at the colliery. I had been on night shift and while I was having my sleep, this daylight raid took place on Bristol. My wife shouted upstairs for me to get up quickly because a plane was coming straight towards our row of houses. when I reached our back door, I saw the pilot coming down on his parachute. He landed in a tree at a place called Hatchet Hill. The plane crashed in a field near the colliery, so decided I would take a stroll to the top of the railway incline to see what I could find. As I got about half way, I looked over the fence and saw something lying under the hedge, which I took to be a young cow. Climbing over to investigate I found it was the body of the plane's gunner. Walking on towards the incline I found the cockpit canopy from the plane. I made my way towards the colliery and had been there a few minutes when men the Coldstream Guards brought along the captured pilot. I heard him ask the officers if his crewman was all right. They told him he was OK, but of course they did not know until I told them what I had found. Later in the week Lord Nuffield's gang came to take the plane to pieces and remove it.

Sergeant H.D.B Jones of 504 Squadron wrote in his combat report:

Whilst at 10,000' enemy aircraft were sighted. We climbed to the attack and intercepted the enemy formation. I got in a beam attack on a Jaguar (5 second burst). I saw smoke coming from its port engine. I then made a frontal attack on another Jaguar (3 second burst) which turned over and dived straight down. It crashed to the south of Bristol, bursting into flames on impact.

The running battle continued, resulting in a complete rout of the German force. The Hurricanes of 504 Squadron pursued their quarry to the south coast and shot down further aircraft. They were joined by three other squadrons: 609, 56, 152 and a section from 238 Squadron. By midday the first returning Hurricanes landed back at Filton. Ten aircraft made it back there, but that of Sergeant M. Bush had to land at Weston short of fuel and Sergeant Haw forced-landed his Hurricane near Axminster, which was later salvaged.

There were further casualties: a Spitfire of 609 Squadron collided with a Bf 110 over Blandford, killing Pilot Officer R.F.G. Miller. The German pilot made a miraculous escape and parachuted to safety, but his wireless operator was killed. The leader of the attack on Yate, Hauptmann Martin Lutz, also lost his life when his aircraft was shot down, crashing at Tarrant Gunville, Dorset. Ten Bf 110s were lost, with a cost of 14 dead. The British lost just one Spitfire and its pilot.

Of those pilots from 504 Squadron who took part in the action on the 27th, five were killed on operations later in the war, including Pilot Officer Frisby and Sergeant Jones.

One of our Aircraft is Missing

While RAF Fighter Command were engaged in the air defence of Great Britain, British bombers were attacking the concentrations of ships and invasion barges in the Dutch, Belgian and French ports. Not all the bombers returned safely. In the early hours of the 27th a Hampden bomber from 106 Squadron, Cottesmore, had crashed in flames at West House Farm, Chilton Polden, setting fire to a wing of Chilton House, next door. Three of the crew lost their lives in this accident and only Sergeant Huggins, the pilot, escaped. The aircraft had been in trouble and apparently called up Weston Zoyland asking for the landing lights to be switched on. This request was refused due to enemy aircraft in the vicinity and the Hampden staggered on for a short while before crashing. Fragments from the aircraft and .303 ammunition were found at the site in 1987.

Several main roads in Somerset were closed to traffic for periods towards the end of September. On the 29th the A38 was closed at Taunton due to an unexploded bomb at the base of the tall chimney of the Galmington Brickworks; 300 people were evacuated from their homes for a short time due to this incident.

Target Westland

In the late afternoon on 30 September a force of 40 Heinkels from I and II/KG55 and Stab/KG55 escorted by Messerschmitt Bf 110s crossed the coast near Weymouth and headed for the Westland factory at Yeovil. Heavy cloud obscured the target and the Germans had to bomb blind. Nearby Sherborne took the full force of the attack: about 300 houses were damaged and 20 demolished; 18 people were killed and approximately 50 injured. Four Heinkels were shot down with a loss of 16 aircrew. One Hurricane of 504 Squadron was shot down and its pilot, Flying Officer J.R. Hardacre killed; four others were damaged in the combat: three forced-landed, two of which came down south of Yeovil and one landed back at Filton. A Spitfire from 152 Squadron, Warmwell, was shot down and its pilot, Sergeant L.A.E. Reddington, killed in the air battle that took place over the area.

A Wellington bomber crashed between Simonsbath and Challacombe on the night of the 30th, damaging the roof of a cottage. Five members of the crew baled out, but the sixth died in the crash.

Aerial view of the Westland Aircraft Company's works at Yeovil taken in 1942. Note the airfield has been camouflaged to represent fields. Careful study of the photograph will reveal 11 barrage balloons sited around its perimeter. Top right are Houndstone and Lufton Camps. (Westland Helicopters Ltd)

The Lone Raider

In the early morning of 1 October a lone Junkers Ju 88 was observed circling the village of North Petherton before heading towards Bridgwater, where it passed over one of two major road crossings of the River Parrett, without taking the opportunity to bomb it. The Junkers passed over the town, released its load of HE bombs and one oil bomb which exploded harmlessly on land owned by farmer Geoff Moate, near Church Path, Wembdon and did not cause any casualties or damage, but one of the three HE bombs failed to go off. An old gardener who had been tending his allotment up on Wembdon Hill later related the tale of his narrow escape to a small boy, who was all agog, and told him: "I saw 'un coming so I got down behind me beans an'out the way."

Wembdon was to suffer further that day when a Fairey Battle aircraft, from the Royal Aircraft Establishment, crashed in the orchard of Cokerhurst Farm, setting fire to a haystack and farm buildings. The aircraft, which had been involved in balloon cable-cutting experiments at Pawlett, is believed to have come to grief due to the photographer becoming fouled in the control wires as he leant out over the side to take pictures of the cutting equipment's effectiveness as the cable struck the wing. The photographer, Mr R.O. Tipple, was killed, but the pilot, Squadron-Leader C.H.A. Coleman, parachuted to safety.

Yeovil attacked

The target was the Westland aircraft works again: just after 3 pm on 7 October it was attacked by a force of 25 Junkers Ju 88s of II/KG51, escorted by about 50 Messerschmitt Bf 110s of II and III/ZG26. These were set upon by five squadrons of fighters from No 10 Group, who shot down seven Bf 110s and also one Ju 88, which crashed at Sidling St Nicholas, Dorset; the crew were captured unhurt. One Bf 110 crashed south of Yeovil, killing the crew, Oberfeldwebel Stahl and Unteroffizier Mauer.

The Germans aimed 80 HE bombs and six oil bombs at the target, but fortunately the damage caused to the works was slight; however an air raid shelter took a direct hit and a number of people were killed. Some property in the town was also damaged, including Montague Burton's shop which received a direct hit; in addition, a Wesleyan chapel, a canteen and an hotel were damaged. The overall casualties amounted to 15 persons dead and 30 injured. This was reported as the first concentrated raid on a Somerset town.

The raid was not without cost to the RAF: two Spitfires from 609 Squadron, Warmwell, were shot down with the loss of one pilot, Sergeant A.N. Feary, who, trying to save his aircraft, baled out too low. The other pilot was injured landing by parachute after abandoning his aircraft. Two further Spitfires from the squadron made forced-landings, as did a Hurricane of 601 Squadron south of Axminster and a Spitfire from 152 Squadron, at Sutton Scotney; a 56 Squadron Hurricane was shot down, but the pilot baled out.

Yeovil suffered three more attacks during this period; the second raid took place on 8 October when 39 HE bombs fell, resulting in eight more people being killed and 40 injured, with 'other sundry bits and pieces being found' of further bodies. The damage was confined to residential property on the northern edge of Westland's airfield. The dead were in an air raid shelter struck by one of the bombs. This night other bombs were dropped in the county, including 12 that fell near Yeovilton aerodrome but failed to explode; damage caused was slight.

A Vega Gull aircraft from 8 AACU, Weston Zoyland, exploded and broke up in mid-air at Fitzroy near Taunton, on 10 October, whilst giving a demonstration to troops based at nearby Norton Camp. The two crew, Sergeant V.N. Buchan and Aircraftsman L.C. Kell, were seen to fall from the aircraft and killed without any chance of their parachutes opening. Buchan lies buried at Middlezoy Church.

The "NAAFI"-type wagon at Whitchurch in 1943 refuelling BOAC pilots. An Anson and a Whitley can be seen in the background. (IWM)

Houndstone and Lufton Military Camps bombed

The next attack on Yeovil came on the 12th when four HE bombs fell on Houndstone Military Camp, killing five personnel and injuring 32 others. Damage was also caused by a further five HE bombs that fell in the centre of Yeovil, but without casualties.

Lufton Camp suffered on 14 October when it was attacked at low-level by a single aircraft, resulting in the death of 13 soldiers including the CO of 208 AA Regiment Royal Artillery, Lieutenant Colonel G.F.R. Wingate OBE, cousin of the legendary Major General Orde Wingate of the 'Chindits'. Three or four huts were destroyed by fire and 16 people were also injured in the attack. This incident had an ironic twist to it – Gerald Little who was at the camp explains:

The day after the attack, we pulled down any billets that were still dangerous. The MPs said half the identity discs found in the ruins were from people who had made themselves scarce and scarpered off home, going AWOL. They had chucked them in the debris hoping people would think they had been killed – possibly as many as 12 or 13 soldiers had done this! In succeeding months they were brought back as deserters. However, for the people that were actually killed in the raid, there is a section in Yeovil Cemetery especially set aside for dead from Houndstone Camp. Also trees to commemorate the dead were planted after the war and form an avenue near the hospital.

Weston-super-Mare also was hit on the 14th when 12 bombs dropped on the town causing damage to a few houses, a reservoir and pumping station in Ashcombe Park. Only one person was slightly injured. The next night bombs fell just short of the GWR loop line at Hutton on the northern boundary of Weston airfield, and according to reports, 'in an unsuccessful attempt to bomb a train'.

NAAFI to the rescue

Regular patrols were carried out by No 504 Squadron Hurricanes from Filton, and on 16 October they were airborne from their base when fog prevented them from returning. The Bristol balloon barrage was a constant hazard to aircraft, be they friend or foe. Not wishing to risk a landing back at Filton, several pilots elected to try for Whitchurch, an airfield just south of the city and wartime home for many aircraft of BOAC and Imperial Airways.

Pilot Officer Reggie Tongue, a pre-war racing driver, was one member of 504 Squadron who had joined the airfield circuit:

I circled the airfield several times along with others of the squadron before making my final approach. I touched down on the grass at quite a speed – hurtled past the parked passenger aircraft – charged over the perimeter fence – crossed the main Whitchurch Road (which must have alarmed motorists) and ended up in a pond on the other side. I was plied with tea before having a chance to get my feet wet! The fellow in the NAAFI waggon had seen me circling the airfield and happened to be in the right place when I came down. He got a ladder, placed it on the aeroplane, and I stepped out onto the wing over the ladder to the bank. The Hurricane wasn't badly damaged and was repaired in ten days. I've heard of good service, but I think that tops the lot!

On the night of 16/17 October, the enemy dropped more leaflets over the county. These were carried in small balloons of 10 x 20 ft and released by a clockwork device which operated a small explosive charge, causing the leaflets to scatter.

Flying Officer Reggie Tongue of 504 Squadron in the cockpit of his Hurricane. (SAS)

An RAF officer inspects wreckage of the Dornier Do 17Z from 2/KüFlGr606 at Maesbury Ring. (IWM)

The crew of the Maesbury Dornier. Top Left to Right: Fw Heinrich Faupel (pilot), Ogfr Wilhelm Schnake (wireless operator). Bottom L to R: Obltn z See Erwin Blanck (observer), Fw Gerhard Steppat (flight engineer). (SAS)

Dornier runs out of fuel and luck

Just before midnight on 16 October a Dornier Do 17Z from 2/Küstenfleigergruppe 606, on its way to bomb Liverpool Docks, crashed on Maesbury Ring at the summit of the Mendips. There was dense fog and visiblity practically zero. The aircraft was heard approaching from the Yeovil direction by a member of the Oakhill Home Guard, farmer James Maidment, who was on duty near his home. He could tell the aircraft was in trouble by the faltering engine note and a few moments later, heard the crash, but no explosion. He and his four colleagues were at a loss what to do and decided that nothing could be done until daylight.

Having milked his cows the next morning, Maidment set out to look for the aircraft. He soon came across the wreckage lying in the middle of Maesbury Ring and found the bodies of the four crew entangled in the wreckage; they were all severely mutilated. The aircraft's bombs had not exploded and were found lying nearby. The Dornier had apparently been hit by AA fire over the south coast or Yeovil and had run short of fuel, which resulted in the crash. The four crew members were taken to Wells and buried in the town cemetery, but after the war were removed to the German Military Cemetery at Cannock Chase.

A forest of guns

The anti-aircraft defence of Yeovil, positioned around the town mainly to protect the aircraft works, consisted of a balloon barrage, several light ack-ack weapons and a few 3.7-in guns. During the Battle of Britain there was an acute shortage of anti-aircraft guns in the country, which had to be strategically positioned around the major cities, airfields and along the South Coast. Houndstone Camp was a training centre for the Royal Artillery, but as yet had limited resources to offer in the defence of the town and its aircraft industry. The AA regiments responsible for the area were short of guns for a while and moved a wooden one from one gunsite to another to make the Germans think that there was a heavy concentration of ack-ack guns around the town.

Daylight battle ends

The final phase of the battle during October took the form of sporadic attacks by hit and run fighter-bombers and also an intensified night bombing campaign. Bombs continued to be dropped on the county at random.

The Battle of Britain had run its course: the enemy had failed to achieve air superiority over the English Channel or over English soil and the RAF had proved itself in the air, but at a great cost. The threatened invasion of England was called off, but the night blitz was about to begin...in earnest.

Pilots Flying Officer Trevor Parsons (left) and Flight Lieutenant Tony Rook of 504 Squadron, Filton, keep a lookout for incoming enemy aircraft, but the Battle of Britain was almost over and the daylight skies now empty. Date: 22 October 1940. (SAS)

THREE

Blitz Diary

Norton Fitzwarren Railway Disaster

In the early hours on the morning of 4 November, Taunton ARP Ambulance, First Aid and Rescue Parties were called to Norton Fitzwarren Station where they tended the unfortunate victims of a serious railway accident. Rescue work went on for hours in the blackout in very difficult conditions. The 9.50 pm express from Paddington, a time-honoured service of the GWR and on this occasion a heavily laden thirteen-coach train drawn by 'King' class locomotive No 6028 *King George VI*, arriving at Taunton 68 minutes behind schedule.

The train was signalled onto the down relief line to allow the 12.50 am newspaper express from Paddington, which was early, to pass. The driver of the 9.50 misread the signals and thought he was on the down main line, without realising he was actually on the down relief line. Approaching Norton Fitzwarren he received an adverse distant signal and a warning from the Automatic Train Control apparatus, only realising his mistake as the 12.50 overtook him at some 60 mph; his own train by then had achieved a speed of 45 mph after a smart get-away from Taunton. It was too late: the 9.50 was derailed at the catch points beyond Norton Fitzwarren station; the locomotive fell on its left side and the fireman was killed. The first six coaches were severely damaged, some being telescoped.

Twenty-seven people were killed and 56 seriously injured; many with appalling wounds, including loss of limbs. Thirteen of the dead were naval personnel returning to Plymouth. Amongst the fatalities were a doctor and his wife from Bromley whose house had been bombed and were on their way to visit their evacuee daughter in Helston. Other victims included the variety artist Archie Lewis and his wife.

Ray Comer heard the crash:

We lived about four miles away from the scene of the accident and were woken by the sound of a terrific

The scene of the railway disaster at Norton Fitzwarren on the morning of 4 November 1940. (Colin Maggs)

crash. The noise was such that we knew there had been a pile-up on the railway. I got on my bike and pedalled as fast as I could. When I arrived ten minutes later, it was like a battlefield – the devastation was terrible. Ambulances and rescue workers were already on the scene taking the injured and dead to hospital.

Ernest Poulson was a GWR driver at Taunton:

When I signed on duty the rosters were in disarray. We had to put goods engines on passenger trains and so on – the services were chaotic until they cleared the line at Norton. We heard afterwards that the driver of the train, an Old Oak Common man, was relegated to shunting duties at Paddington and never drove an express engine again.

Taunton machine-gunned

Just before daylight on 5 November a low-flying

enemy aircraft machine-gunned the streets of Taunton, believed to be aiming at a searchlight. One bullet smashed a bedroom window in Cleveland Street, broke ornaments in the room and spent itself in a bed without injury to the occupant. On the 6th the Yeovil raids claimed three further victims. An officer and two men of a bomb disposal unit were engaged on their perilous work 20 ft down a shaft when the bomb went off, killing them instantly.

Desultory enemy air activity continued all through November and the greater part of December. On 18 November there was a direct hit on the New Inn at Lulsgate Bottom (A38 road) killing two of the occupants and injuring four. On 10 December the enemy was again over Yeovil and shot down two barrage balloons.

On 12 December 1940 a Tiger Moth aircraft from 10 EFTS, Weston crashed into the sea at Brean whilst on a training flight. Will Locke, of the Somerset Light Infantry, was on coastal watch on duty when it happened:

The aircraft made several dives towards the sea, as if to practice dive-bombing, then dipped too low and crashed off shore a little way in front of us. The tide was coming in very fast at the time and some of our lads, who were from the Channel Islands, being strong swimmers, wanted to go out and rescue the crew, but were prevented from doing so, as it would have been too dangerous. We watched helplessly and saw the crew's heads bobbing up and down in the wreckage of the aircraft, which was most distressing. We had to wait for the tide to go out before the two men could be brought ashore. They were taken to a bungalow on the sand dunes and placed in the hall, where they were given artificial respiration for at least an hour, but it was no good – they had drowned.

The first great attack on Bristol occurred on the night of 24 November. Bombs fell in the county on a line between Chard and Bristol and at many places in a wide arc south of that city. In Bristol itself the shopping districts of Wine Street and Castle Street were entirely destroyed by fire, together with the ancient churches of St Nicholas, St Peter's, St Mary-le-Port and the Temple. Two-hundred people died in the city that night and 689 were injured. The second heavy raid followed on 2nd December when 156 of the citizens of Bristol were killed and 270 injured. Although 160 HE bombs fell in Somerset, mostly on a line from Templecombe towards Bristol, little damage was done and there were no casual-

ties. Four days later Bristol suffered again sustaining 288 casualties, 100 of them fatal.

Weston Bombed

The opening of the year 1941 saw an early resumption of the enemy's effort. Bristol was again the target on 3rd January. In a raid lasting a full 12 hours 149 persons were killed and 351 injured. The following night it was the turn of Weston-super-Mare where a good deal of damage was done: 33 people were killed and 69 injured. The raid started at 03.12 on the 4th, with hundreds of incendiaries and a few HE bombs dropping in the Blagdon and Redhill districts. The 'All Clear' sounded at 06.20 the next morning, but after several alerts the raiders returned at 21.25, dropping bombs in the sea at Brean.

Thirty-five minutes later a heavy attack developed over Sand Bay and ran parallel with the beach. A nursing home was damaged; bombs caused casualties when they fell near Grove Park and Glebe House. Damage was caused to a concert hall, shops and houses in the area. St Paul's Church was also hit and destroyed by fire, together with its Church Hall in Whitecross Road. A row of terraced houses in Rector's Way were damaged by a direct hit and many casualties occurred. Twelve houses on three sides of a square on the Bournville Estate were wrecked beyond repair when their fronts were sucked out by the blast. A number of bombs fell in the sand on the beach and did little damage. ARP reinforcements came from all over Somerset: Taunton, Minehead, Shepton Mallet, Wells and other areas. Rescue parties remained in the district for several days searching and clearing the debris; military assistance was also rendered. In the attack 430 buildings were damaged, 130 of them seriously.

Bombs were also dropped at many places south of Bristol from Clevedon eastwards to Bath. On the 16th Bath suffered a minor raid and 79 HE bombs fell in that part of the county during the night; 30 of them were unexploded and 10,100 incendiaries were also dropped. The following night attacks were widespread, including the district round Shepton Mallet, at Lyngford and Angersleigh, both on the outskirts of Taunton. On the 19th, 20th and 21st large numbers of aircraft crossed the county during three successive heavy raids on Swansea.

Wreckage of Leutnant Rusche's Heinkel from KG27 brought down on Portbury mudflats by ack-ack fire on 22 February 1941. (John H. Moreton)

February was a quieter month – nothing was reported for the first 13 days. The Luftwaffe introduced daylight hit-and-run raids the previous autumn, known as *Piratenflüge* (pirate attacks), they used crews chosen for their experience and skill. Targets earmarked were mostly connected with the aircraft industry.

Ack-ack claim a Heinkel

On the 22nd such a target was to be the Parnell Aircraft's factory at Yate. As yet previous attempts at bombing it had been unsuccessful: the debacle of September 27th being a notable example. The incoming raid was picked up by the south coast radar chain; plotted as 'Raid 128' it crossed the coast at Weymouth at 5,000 ft and was also tracked by the Observer Corps, but because of low cloud nothing much was seen of it until it reached Cheddar, where it was spotted by an air cadet.

The aircraft, in fact a Heinkel He 111 from II/KG27, emerged from the cloud at Clevedon and having got its bearings set course along the Somerset coast and flew up the Bristol Channel towards its target. As it approached Avonmouth just after 2 pm it was spotted by the gun crews of 236 Battery, 76 HAA Regiment, at the Portbury ack-ack site. They were greatly surprised to see the Heinkel suddenly loom out of the wintry haze over the Portishead power station and as it passed opened fire with a Lewis gun sited on the roof of the gun store, but it flew on before disappearing back into the cloud. The Lewis gun mounted on the end of Portishead Pier also managed to loose off a few rounds at it.

A few minutes later the sound of an approaching aircraft was heard by other members of 236 Battery at the Gordano gun site, who opened fire blind. The Portbury battery also claimed to have opened fire as it approached their site. The aircraft was hit by at least one AA shell also by machine gun fire; it also struck a barrage balloon cable before crashing and exploding at the water's edge, wreckage being strewn over the mud flats. According to eye witnesses, the gunner in the bola of the Heinkel was still returning fire as the aircraft plunged into the mud.

Of the crew, there was only one survivor, the pilot Leutnant Bernt Rusche. The other crew members were killed. Rusche managed to bale out from the stricken Heinkel from not much more than 300 ft. He and one other left the aircraft, but Feldwebel A. Hanke's parachute failed to open and he was killed on impact, landing in the mud near the wreck. The rescue party found two decapitated bodies, but could find no trace of two other crew members, Gefreiter E. Steinbach and Feldwebel G. Jankowiak. Some years later human bones were discovered in the filters of Portishead power station. Parts of the Heinkel and the balloon cable it hit are still in the mud today. The bodies of Hanke and Unteroffizier H. De-Wall were recovered; both are buried in the Greenbank Cemetery, Bristol.

The Gordano ack-ack site had been stood to following an alert with their 3.7s set to four points of the compass. The guns had been loaded and the rounds set with short fuses. It was common practice to combat low-level attacks by firing thus, with little chance of actually hitting the target. However public morale was a major consideration in adopting this strategy.

Troop Sergeant Major Stephen Baker was in charge of the guns:

We heard the aircraft come from the Clifton direction, but couldn't see it. As it drew nearer the order was given to fire, which all four guns did simultaneously. Just then a Heinkel 111 appeared from behind the cloud and we saw one of our rounds explode in front of it, which seemed to damage the wing. The aircraft staggered on for a bit then hit a barrage balloon cable over Easton way, knocking a wingtip off. It crashed and exploded at the water's edge at Portbury, wreckage being strewn over the mud flats. We went down to the site of the crash and got Major Harvey's 14 ft dinghy and used it as a sledge to get out to the wreckage some way off shore. We helped to get the pilot out, who was waist deep in mud, and tried to get the other crew member whose parachute had failed to open. I tugged at the lines, but couldn't haul it in and had to leave him as the tide was coming in. We could see at least two other bodies in the wreckage, but had to leave them as well. The flight bag was retrieved from the wreckage, complete with charts and information regarding the target. The pilot gave us the money he had in his pocket for souvenirs – he was quite an arrogant sort of fellow.

The Portbury battery also claimed shooting the aircraft down. Bill Bratt, an ex-member of the site, wrote this account of the incident:

We fired four rounds at it and many hundreds of rounds of tracer bullets from our Lewis gun. One of the shells exploded near the fuselage and blew the wing off. The bombs were released and exploded in the mud. One of the crew parachuted from the plane which crashed into the mud flats of the river opposite our site. We rushed to the scene with rifles rescued and captured the parachutist who was waist deep in mud. He made great point of raising his revolver high above his head and throwing it far into the mud. We took him to our Guard Room and to everyone's disgust was given bacon and eggs.

Although commanded by Major C.D. Harvey, the officer in charge of the action at Portbury on this occasion was Lieutenant J.I.P. Hunt. After this episode 236 Battery were given a barrel of beer by Georges Brewery. A propeller blade from the Heinkel was signed by 250 men and displayed for sometime outside the Portbury site, but were told to remove it after a dispute arose regarding the claim for shooting the bomber down. After the war it was displayed in an hotel at Portishead.

On the same day a Fairey Battle aircraft from Netheravon crashed into the face of the Town

Quarry, Weston-super-Mare, killing the pilot Flight Lieutenant T.P. De La Rue. The aircraft had dropped a passenger off at St Athan in South Wales and was returning when the accident occurred. The cloud base was no more than 300 ft and the pilot failed to clear the hill behind the town. The aircraft fell onto tar barrels in the quarry and immediately caught fire. This was just one of a number of fatal air accidents in the county around this time; there would be many more and some with far greater loss of life to both civilians and crew.

There were minor bombing incidents on the 26th. On the 27th Houndstone Camp was machine-gunned by a single German aircraft which flew low over Yeovil but no casualties were sustained. Other bombs fell on the 28th.

March 1941 brought many incidents, particularly during the first three weeks. On the 16/17th there was a further heavy raid on Bristol. Casualties were again heavy – 257 killed and 391 injured. Somerset was also to feel the weight of bombs during this raid, which fell in 26 different parishes on a broad line across the county northwest from Wincanton and Yeovil.

Bridgwater's landmines

Two magnetic mines exploded on the 20th on the south-western outskirts of Bridgwater, falling on soft ground in the Meads and near Durleigh Brook. Only one fatality was recorded, but 1,460 premises were damaged, 50 seriously, many were shops in High Street and Penel Orlieu that had their plate glass windows blown out. The craters left by the blast were said to be big enough to put two buses in each hole.

Eric Westman:

I cycled off to work the morning after and saw the damage in the town. There was broken glass everywhere, which I had to cycle over – windows were hanging loosely from houses – it was quite a mess. I saw two very old men coming up the road and one said to the other: "Aaah, so we've had it at last." The other one was agreeing with him: "Aaah, we've had it at last." They were talking as if Bridgwater had endured a terrible blitz!

Elizabeth Wallbridge lived three miles from Bridgwater:

I can remember all the noise starting – the sirens had gone. I didn't want to stay in the house during a raid and was standing at the front door with my mother waiting for father to come home, when suddenly there was an almighty flash and a couple of seconds later we felt a tremendous blast of hot air and were thrown back against the stairs like pieces of paper.

Harry Routledge was a soldier serving with the 4th Battalion, The Green Howards, billeted in Bridgwater, remembers the night the landmines came down:

The force of the explosion shattered a number of windows in the Cornhill. One of our lads happened to be glazing in a shop window of one establishment at the time, when the plate glass shattered, and thinking he would be accused of breaking it, left the scene in great haste and headed back for the billet at top speed!

Yeovil hit again

On the 26th a single Dornier made a daylight raid on Yeovil and dropped five HEs directed at the Westland Aircraft works; most of the bombs overshot the target and exploded in the nearby residential part of the town, killing eight people and injuring 36. Little damage was done to the factory, but 12 houses were demolished and about 90 damaged. The main water supply was also severed. One of the people injured in the raid was the Managing Director of Westland, Eric Mensforth.

It was during this raid that a tragedy occurred through a cruel twist of fate. On hearing the sirens a mother collected her five-year-old son from Huish Infant School at 11.45 am and took him back to their home in Westland Terrace, Yeovil. At 12 noon the house received a direct hit by a HE bomb. The little boy's body was never found and only parts of his mother's body were eventually recovered from the ruins of their home. The 'all clear' sounded at 1 pm...the school was untouched.

First Victim

Incidents occurred almost nightly during April: the 4th was a night of considerable activity in the north of the county. A Heinkel He 111 was shot down in flames by a Beaufighter from 604 Squadron, Middle Wallop flown by Flying Officer E.D. Crew, who with his radar operator Sergeant Guthrie, had made their first kill. The Heinkel, from Stab III/KG26, had been on its way to bomb Avonmouth Docks, fell near the White Hart Inn at Hewish. Three members of the crew

Flying Officer E.D. Crew's combat report following the action over Weston-super-Mare when he shot down the Heinkel He 111 from StabIII/KG26 on 4 April. (PRO)

parachuted to safety and survived. The pilot Oberfeldwebel Herbert Rose and the flight engineer Feldwebel Ernst Groschel, were taken prisoner near the Railway Inn at Congresbury; the third, navigator/bomb aimer Feldwebel Georg Fietzek, surrendered to a garage proprietor at Puxton, after unsuccessfully trying to give himself up to a driver of a lorry, who had promptly accelerated into the distance on seeing the German! Two others were killed: the airgunner Gefreiter Matthias Van Kaldenkerken was found in the wreckage of the aircraft with bullet wounds to the head; the radio operator, Oberfeldwebel Erich Blüher was found spreadeagled in the middle of the road at Puxton – his

Forty-six years after it was shot down, Arthur Knight displays wreckage from the Heinkel brought down at Hewish, including a tyre and inner tube. (Author)

Luftwaffe fallen: the graves of Matthias van Kaldenkerken, Erich Blüher, Hans Dolata, Werner Grothe and just hidden, Heinrich Schink at Weston-super-Mare, all of whom lost their lives over Somerset. (Author)

parachute having failed to open.

Geoff Bell, who lived in Weston, witnessed the action:

My brother and I were in the shelter under the table, when we heard aircraft in the vicinity and then a burst of machine gun or cannon-fire, so rushed into the back garden in time to see a Heinkel with one engine already on fire, then the whole front of the Beaufighter light up with another burst of cannon-fire. Both aircraft were in the direction of the Mendips at about 3,000 ft and virtually above Weston airfield. The Heinkel gradually veered round – you could see it very clearly in the moonlight – the whole wing was a mass of fire. We raced down the garden to see it vanish from view towards Hewish. The following day we cycled out there to have a look. When we got to the scene there were several policemen about and we noticed the wreckage some way behind the Woolpack Inn. It had been smashed to pieces and there was not a lot of it to be seen. The biggest part we could see was an engine and the main spar of the wing. Sergeant Mapstone was one of the Policemen on duty – a right old character – and a couple of RAF types who were there and told us to 'bugger off'. I could see pieces of wreckage about and of course, wanted a souvenir, hoping to get machine-gun bullets or something like that. Old Mapstone had a beady eye on us and knew what we were after, but then he suddenly said: "Go on – hurry up". We knew exactly what he meant and I grabbed a piece of tubular metal. I stuffed it into my pocket and off we cycled.

The Good Friday Raids

The night of Good Friday, 11/12 April 1941, was one of the worst of the war so far as Somerset and Bristol were concerned. Bristol suffered what was to prove the last of the major attacks upon the city. There were two distinct raids, causing the deaths of 180 people and injuries to 382. At Frome there were two fatalities and six persons injured caused by ten HE bombs, resulting in 150 houses being damaged. Four bombs fell at Yeovil in the centre of the town, completely demolishing the WVS Headquarters, the Evacuee Canteen and four shops. Many houses and business premises were damaged, including International Stores, Messrs Clements the grocers, and also the Corn Exchange, in which troops were billeted. Of the troops, four were killed and three wounded. The civilian casualties were nine people injured, four seriously. At Long Ashton five were killed and one injured. Portishead and the Gordano district had one fatality and nine persons injured.

Bombs also fell at Chedzoy, Chewstoke, Croscombe, Norton Malreward, Peasedown St John, Portbury, Publow, Stanton Drew, Stockwood, Shepton Mallet, Whitchurch, Whatley and Winscombe. Both Taunton and Yeovil sent fire pumps to Bristol. In addition, Weston-super-Mare, despatched 3 first aid parties, 3 ambulances and one rescue party; Frome sent 3 first

Flight Lieutenant Hugh Speke DFC, 604 Squadron, descendant of the famous Somerset explorer John Hanning Speke, now lies in the family vault at Dowlish Wake near Ilminster. (SAS)

aid parties, 3 ambulances and 2 rescue parties, Bridgwater despatched one rescue party to the city.

Nightfighter successes

May was notable for the successes of our night fighters over Somerset. Five enemy bombers were brought down within four days. The first of these was at Corton Denham near Yeovil on the 3rd, when a Heinkel 111 of 9/KG27 was shot down by a Beaufighter from 604 Squadron. This was the ninth victim of Squadron Leader John 'Cat's-eyes' Cunningham, Britain's top-scoring night fighter pilot. Three of the Heinkel's crew, survived and were captured, but Feldwebel A. Amode, the flight engineer, was killed. Less than an hour later a Junkers Ju 88 from 1/KGr806 was shot down and crashed in flames at Moon Hill near Stoke St Michael; all four crew members were taken prisoner. A Beaufighter flown by Flying Officer Woodward and Sergeant Lipscombe of 600 Squadron from Colerne near Bath claimed this victory – their first kill.

At 01.00 on the 4th the third victim of that night, a Heinkel 111 of 1/KG26, which had bombed Bristol, crashed in Binford Wood, Crowcombe Heathfield. Three of the crew were killed; one being found impaled upon a tree. The wireless operator, Unteroffizier Herbert Muller, survived and was captured by the Home Guard. The aircraft caught fire, setting alight the wood which burnt for three days.

The aircraft was shot down by Flight Lieutenant Hugh Speke of 604 Squadron, a descendant of the Somerset explorer John Hanning Speke. This was Hugh Speke's first victory, but tragically he was to lose his life in a flying accident when his aircraft flew into Oare Hill, Pewsey, a few weeks later on 25 July. Hugh Speke is interred in the family vault at the church of St Andrew, Dowlish Wake, near Ilminster.

Bombs fell that night at points near Compton Martin, East Brent, Keynsham, Mells, Radstock, Wincanton Racecourse, Shepton Montague, Wootton Courtenay, Whitchurch and Rode.

Heinkel by Royal Command

Two Heinkels were brought down on May 7th between 11.00 pm and midnight, one at Weston Zoyland and the other at Langford, Churchill, near Weston-super-Mare.

King George VI had visited Middle Wallop fighter station that evening and was invited to meet members of 604 Squadron, who had been so successful in bringing down a considerable number of German aircraft over the region. Amongst those to whom the King was introduced were Squadron Leader John Cunningham and his radar operator Sergeant Jimmy Rawnsley. The King asked Rawnsley what was his 'score', who told him it was nine. "Nine eh?" the King replied, "will you get another one for me tonight?" Rawnsley, not knowing quite what to say, answered sheepishly: "Well Sir, I'll do my best."

Cunningham and Rawnsley took off and were soon vectored onto a 'contact', which had been picked up approaching the south coast at 23.26. Not wishing to be silhouetted against the sea in the moonlight, they stalked their prey until over land. Rawnsley wrote this account of the combat in his book, *Night Fighter*:

We were right below our target, a great fat prima-donna of a Heinkel. John started pulling up behind it and the long, long wait was even more agonising than usual. But the enemy crew showed no reaction. We were right behind and there came the final moment of tension with the sharp little lurches as John brought the sight to bear. Still there was no response from the Heinkel. Then came the blessed relief of the crash of the guns and the sudden surge upwards to get out of the way of the hurtling wreckage. A wicked orange glow appeared inside the fuselage of the Heinkel and the wheels fell down in a most forlorn way. As we flew alongside, watching, the glow burst through the skin and the flames took over. The whole aircraft trembled and broke into a violent pitching and with a plume of flames streaming out behind it the Heinkel went down in a headlong plunge to earth. The show was over.

Their victim was a Heinkel 111 from 7/KG27 on its way to bomb Liverpool Docks. The pilot, Oberfeldwebel Heinz Laschinski, a veteran of

His Majesty King George V1 meets Squadron Leader John Cunningham DFC of 604 Squadron at Middle Wallop on 7 May 1941. (IWM)

some 120 missions over Britain, had participated in the major attacks on many British cities and ports, including Liverpool, London, Cardiff, Bristol and Birmingham.

He and his crew had taken off from Rennes taking up action stations shortly after: Feldwebel Fritz Klemm to the gun position in the belly, known as *Das Sterbebett*, or Death Bed; Feldwebel Heinz Schier sat next to the pilot to assist with the navigation and Feldwebel Otto Willrich, the wireless operator, taking the seat above the bulkhead door to the bomb bay, looking to the rear.

They flew over the South Coast and successfully penetrated the searchlight belt. Laschinski was acutely aware of the ack-ack defences around Bristol and Cardiff, making sure that he avoided them on this bright moonlit night. Approaching the Bristol Channel, Laschinski had just started to transfer fuel from the outer to inner tanks, when he suddenly felt the impact of cannon and machine gun fire rake the fuselage followed a split second later by a blinding flash. The cockpit was now awash with petrol. Heinz Schier slumped forward dead. Laschinski ordered the other two to bale out. Having felt the impact of shells, Willrich clambered down to the lower gun position and saw that Klemm had died instantly in the hail of cannon-fire, then

Oberfeldwebel Heinz Laschinski (left) poses under the nose of his Heinkel with the two crew that lost their lives over Somerset on the night of 7 May: Feldwebel Fritz Klemm (centre) and Feldwebel Heinz Schier (right), who are buried at Bridgwater. (SAS)

made a rapid exit from the open bomb bay, parachuting to safety.

At the moment Laschinski ordered the crew to abandon the stricken aircraft the petrol ignited. With flames all around him Laschinski reached for the emergency exit handles above his head, but they were already enveloped in flame. He grabbed them, but his hands instinctively recoiled with pain. This was his only chance of escape so he grasped them once more and disregarding the excruciating pain, managed to release the hatch. Having undone his harness he stood on the seat, but his parachute became snagged on the edge of the exit and in desperation to free himself of the flames which now engulfed him, pulled the ripcord of his parachute.

Laschinski lost consciousness but awoke to see his white canopy deployed above him in the night sky and the ground beneath him drawing nearer before blacking out again. He came to and found himself lying flat on his back in a meadow, which was damp with dew. After some time and now in great pain, he freed himself from his parachute harness, struggled to his feet and made off across the field. He found a drainage pipe in which to deposit his Luger pistol and the

maps he was carrying, before continuing along a lane where he came upon a farmhouse near Weston Zoyland. Laschinski roused the elderly occupants and asked them in broken English to send for the police. His wounds were tended and hands bandaged. Finally overcome with pain and fatigue he slumped on the grass to await the arrival of the police, who eventually came along with members of the Home Guard and took him off to Bridgwater Hospital.

Willrich was captured as he walked along a lane near Moorland and only slightly injured, but his ordeal was not quite over. Next to New House Farm on the Huntworth/Moorland boundary lived Sam Gamblin, a huge man of over 23 stone - his family could not ascertain how heavy he was, because they did not have enough weights for the scales to balance him...he was a giant. Gamblin saw Mr Barrington, a neighbour, escorting Willrich along the lane and went to investigate. Noticing the throat microphone's cord around the German's neck and thinking he was being strangled by a piece of flex, took out his lambsfoot pocket knife to cut whatever it was. Being confronted by such a huge man armed with a lethal looking knife was too much for Willrich, terrified that his throat was about to be cut the German's screams rent the night air. The police were telephoned from Huntworth and a sergeant came out in his Ford Prefect car from Bridgwater to collect the German.

Wyndham Fry who farmed at Fowlers Plot, Chedzoy saw the aircraft crash:

I looked out of the window to see a mass of flame in the sky - it came down a little way off towards Andersea. My brother was travelling along the Weston Zoyland road in his car and was frightened to death, as he thought the thing was going to crash on him. He came to the farm and we decided to go and have a look. We got to the site and saw the burning wreckage and noticed one of the crew slumped in the nose section, which was all smashed to pieces. We did not get too close, because of the intense heat and flames.

Cunningham and Rawnsley landed back at Middle Wallop shortly after midnight to be told that the King had witnessed the action. The King heard the two aircraft fly overhead, had seen the combat from the Ground Control Interception (GCI) station at Sopley, near Bournemouth, to where he had motored and watched the burning Heinkel fall from the sky. It crashed in

51

fields near Andersea belonging to Bert Bawden, who still farms there today and uses a torque tube salvaged from the aircraft to strengthen the handle of a cider shovel.

Laschinski's stay in Bridgwater Hospital is remembered by many of the townspeople. There he was known to all and sundry as '57' - after the Heinz variety - named by Sister Jessie Dalling. He endeared himself to many by his charming manner. Many people sent him chocolates, sweets and flowers, but others were not so kindly disposed towards him. He was eventually transferred to the RAF hospital at Locking, before being 'put in the cage'. He spent most of the remaining war years in Canada, following a short spell at Bury, where he met up with Willrich.

Sadly, Heinz Laschinski died in 1980 two weeks before a planned visit to Bridgwater to meet some people who befriended him all those years ago. Fritz Klemm and Heinz Schier were buried together in the Wembdon Road Cemetery, Bridgwater, where their remains lie to this day. The mens' families pay occasional visits to the grave.

Jack Kitch of Fordgate remembers the aftermath of the crash:

The plane came from the south-east direction and shed a wing just before it crashed, which fell in one of my father's fields of wheat. It was like a fair up there - people came in droves to have a look at it, but so much damage was being caused by all the spectators who trampled over the crop to have a look at the wreckage that my father, Fred, decided to drag the wing to a place where less damage would result and attached one of his farm-horses to it and hauled it to the headland of the field.

Second Heinkel

A few minutes after the demise of Laschinski's aircraft, another Heinkel bound for Liverpool of StabsSt/KG27 was brought down at 23.55 near Wrington and completely burnt out. The five crew all baled out from the aircraft. Four were captured near the Bell Inn, Congresbury by members of the Home Guard and the fifth near the Star Inn on Rhodyate Hill by another Home Guard of the Congresbury Platoon. Flying Officer G. Howden and his A1 radar operator, Sergeant Fielding, from 600 Squadron, Colerne, were credited with shooting down this Heinkel.

Bombs also fell during the night of the 7th/8th

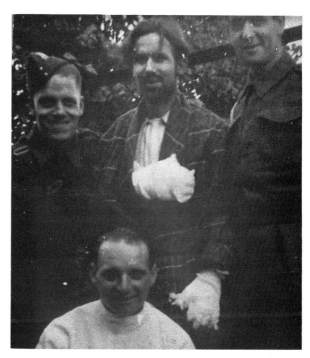

Heinz Laschinski, his hands bandaged, stands with his guards outside Bridgwater and District Hospital, May 1941. (Sister J. Dalling via K.G. Wakefield)

in districts around Taunton, Minehead, Woolavington, Kilmersdon and on Sedgemoor, causing slight damage to some cottages. Incendiaries dropped on the Woodleigh Vale Estate at Whitchurch, causing damage to nine houses, but no casualties, 1,000 fell at Easton-in-Gordano and a further 1,000 in the Long Ashton area, but damage was negligible. A raiding aircraft had a fright on the following night when it struck a balloon cable at Yeovil, cutting the balloon adrift. The aircraft released its bomb causing slight damage to the balloon site and some nearby buildings. Two of the bombs failed to explode and landed near the GWR line at Yew Tree Close Farm, Yeovil around midnight on the 9th.

Dogfight over Taunton

During the early evening of Sunday 11 May an air battle developed over Taunton. Two Messerschmitt Bf 110 fighters first appeared flying north-west at no great height. Almost immediately a larger number of aircraft were sighted as silver specks in a clear blue sky. They were too high up to be identified with any certainty from the ground. More silver specks came out of the blue astern of the first and a general mêlée ensued. A Hurricane of 504 Squadron at Exeter came spiralling down with a smoking engine crash-landing at Pinkmoor Lane, Rockwell Green, near Wellington. The pilot, Flying Officer B.E.G. White, known as 'Crasher' to his colleagues, though wounded in the legs, was successfully extricated. Several of the enemy were brought down in this sortie and a number of parachutists were reported seen south of Willet Hill.

There were scattered incidents on the night of the 12th at Yeovilton. A lone Junkers Ju 88 made a low-level bombing attack on the airfield, but no casualties were sustained. At Fiddington some cattle were killed and buildings damaged at New Barn Farm. Bombs also fell at Barrow Gurney and Stogursey. The village of Old Cleeve was machine-gunned and bullets came through the roofs of the houses. On this night six small HE bombs fell within Taunton. Some houses in Eastleigh Road were rendered untenable and others were damaged. Although all these houses were occupied, the inhabitants escaped with minor injuries.

Throughout this period, it was not only the Germans who were losing aircraft, but many British aircraft and their pilots were lost as well, chiefly through training accidents. A Hurricane pilot from 759 Squadron, RNAS Yeovilton was authorised to carry out aerobatics in the early afternoon of the 12th. The pilot got into difficulties because of engine trouble and tried to make a forced-landing in a field near Langport. Sub-lieutenant J.N.W. Parish succeeded in putting the aircraft down, but because his windscreen was obscured by oil, failed to see the River Parrett into which his aircraft toppled and inverted. Trapped in the cockpit, Parish could not be freed in time and drowned. Another Hurricane from 759 Squadron crashed at Hazelgrove House, Sparkford on the following day and the pilot, Lieutenant J.P. Eustace was killed. The engine was seen to emit white smoke then the aircraft inverted and spun into the ground.

Yeovil received more hits on the 9th, 16th and 25th. On the 25th around midnight, a single enemy aircraft flew three times over the town before dropping 14 HE bombs from very low level, with five persons killed and seven injured. Three houses were demolished, 20 badly damaged and a further 110 slightly damaged. On the

The Hurricane of Pilot Officer B.E.G. White on patrol over the Somerset coast. (SAS)

Pilot Officer B.E.G. 'Crasher' White, 504 Squadron. (SAS)

31st isolated bombs and mines were dropped over the greater part of the county: Fitzhead, Radstock, Duddlestone, Corfe, Williton, Weston-super-Mare, Clevedon, Nailsea, Kingston Seymour, Clapton-in-Gordano, Mudford Sack, Nether Stowey, West Bagborough, Redhill, Kewstoke, Long Ashton, Weston Zoyland and Wellington. At Weston Zoyland a 'G' mine that had dropped on the 29th and was buried about ten feet in soft ground, exploded at 13.05 on the 30th leaving a crater some 60 ft wide and 20 ft deep, causing the road to be partly blocked. Two other 'G' mines fell at Kingston Seymour, killing a number of cattle. An HE landed on the promenade at Weston, fracturing and setting fire to the gas main. One HE bomb fell at Shoscombe damaging the communication lines of the Somerset and Dorset line at Paglynch Farm. The only casualties in this night of activity were the cattle; many were killed or injured across the county.

June and July saw a slackening of the enemy's effort. Isolated incidents occurred on 1 June ranging over the county, but no casualties were inflicted, save damage to several cottages and farm buildings. A pilot was killed when his Spitfire crashed at Shiplate Court Farm near Bleadon on the 10th. On the 12th a Hampden bomber from 106 Squadron, Finningley, crashed into the sea off Brean. All four occupants were killed. The aircraft's wreckage was never recovered.

On 28 June an unusual number of parachute mines came down in a wide arc east, south and west of Taunton. The village of Wrantage lost its school and hardly a house escaped damage. Other mines fell at Stoke St Mary, Thurlbear, Churchstanton, Churchingford, Halse and Lydeard St Lawrence. The same night a barrage balloon broke away at Devil's Bridge near Weston and fouled electric cables causing a power failure. Golfers at Minehead had a surprise on the afternoon of the 30th and a good excuse to retire to the 19th hole when a Spitfire made a forced-landing on the links. The pilot was unhurt.

More mines dropped on the Mendips on 1 July. Bombs fell on the 4th/5th near Frome and also at Curland, Pitminster and Rowleigh – all near Taunton.

Austin Hayter remembered the effects of a landmine.

Enemy planes often came over the Templecombe area and I recall that on the night that Coventry was bombed, we were on full alert – that was quite a night – Jerry was going over in droves. I had been on duty with the Home Guard that evening and remember one of the planes dropped a landmine in the area causing quite a bit of damage. On another occasion I was busily milking away in the shed and heard a plane go over, but took no notice of it, when suddenly the whole place shook – the cows jumped out of their skins and I rushed outside as the whole place lifted off the ground and settled back down again. The galvanising rattled like hell – it frightened the life out of me, let alone the cows. I didn't bother to milk the remaining four – I was off home. I had gone several hundred yards up the road in my car – I was driving without lights – and saw a figure...it was Mother. She

had come down to see if I was all right. That landmine had dropped about 150 yd from where I was milking. It blew a huge hole in the clay – I had been very lucky.

Heinkel down at Frome

At 01.07 on the 5th, a Heinkel He 111 from 7/KG26 was brought down by a nightfighter of 604 Squadron at Murdercombe Hill near Frome. One German, Obergefreiter Edward Köppl was killed; the other three, Leutnant Siegfried Baden, Feldwebel Ernst Witt and Gefreiter Ludwig Kugel baled out. One was injured and sent to Bath Hospital. Ludwig Kugel slept under a tree that night and surrendered to the police at Frome in the morning. He wrote a propagandized account of this episode that was featured in the Sunday Dispatch on 20 July. Köppl's body was not found until 29 August, recovered from a field of corn which had concealed him – he had been thrown clear of the wreckage as the Heinkel crashed.

Also on the 5th gunfire was heard and an enemy aircraft was seen to fall in flames by Bill Berry of the Home Guard, who was on duty that night on Staple Hill, near Churchingford. The aircraft was a Heinkel He 111 from 3/KG4 was shot down over Somerset and crashed at Oakford near Bampton.

This was to be the last attack for a period of three months.

A present from the Reichsmarschall

Lightning struck a barrage balloon at Weston-super-Mare on the night of the 20th damaging the Borough Arms Hotel. The only other incident of note during the next thirteen weeks was a gift to this country of a Junkers Ju 88A-5 bomber from 3/KG30 – and of the latest type. The relief landing ground at Lulsgate Bottom, then called Broadfield Down, was in process of enlargement to meet the requirements of a fighter station. The work was being pushed on at high speed and a large gang of men were employed laying out the new runways. Just after 06.00 on 24 July these men had hardly started work when, to their surprise, an aircraft was heard coming in low through the mist from the Bristol Channel. It taxied along the partially completed runway and stopped near a group of workmen. Four airmen jumped out, walked over to one of the men, a driver of a mechanical digger, and began to ask

The Junkers Ju 88 of 3/KG30 seen at Lulsgate shortly after it landed by mistake on 24 July. (Ken West)

questions. They soon discovered their mistake: the workman, who remained calm and answering the questions in the broadest Doric, signalled to his mate to fetch the guard. Meanwhile the military guard from the King's Own Royal Regiment had given the alarm: it was the dawn "stand to" and within a few seconds a truck full of men was racing across the airfield. The German airmen, running hard to regain the aircraft, were intercepted by the troops in the nick of time. They were outnumbered and taken prisoner. Thus four more German airmen were captured and the RAF received a present in the form of a new Junkers 88 bomber.

The explanation given to the interrogating officer was simple: the Luftwaffe men had mistaken the Bristol Channel for the English Channel and thought they had landed on an emergency airfield in France. They had become confused by a British radio beacon working on the same frequency as Beacon 173 at Audierne. In the early morning mist that covered South Wales and Somerset, also seeing a balloon barrage in an appropriate position, the upper part of the Bristol Channel looked like Brest Roads.

The Germans, Unteroffizier Wolfgang Hosie (pilot), Feldwebel Paul Zimmermann (observer), Obergefreiters Franz Sander (wireless operator) and Robert Riemann (gunner), were an inexperienced crew who had taken off from Lanvaoc in France at 23.35 to attack Birkenhead. They made a flight west of the Scillies, out over the Irish Sea and had become confused on their return journey. They were to spend the rest of the war as guests of the British in a PoW camp!

Hurricane down – another statistic

Although there was a lull in German activity during this period, the RAF and Fleet Air Arm were continually training young men for combat against them. The costs continued to prove high in both men and machines. An incident occurred on 2 September when several Hurricanes from 759 Squadron, RNAS Yeovilton were airborne during a late summer's afternoon. Two aircraft had been detailed to make mock attacks on one another and to record their efforts with the use of camera guns.

Nineteen year-old Midshipman J.F. Williams was flying Hurricane P2953 accompanied by Sub-lieutenant T. Milne in another aircraft. They had taken off at 17.00 and headed for the Bridgwater area to carry out their exercise. Milne made an attack on Williams satisfactorily and informed him over the R/T that he had done so and instructed him to do likewise. Milne looked into his rear-view mirror to see Williams' Hurricane making a shallow dive to port. Milne called him on the R/T, but got no reply, so informed Williams that he was returning to base and he would have to map read home.

Williams was observed flying low around the village of North Petherton. He made several circuits of the village at ultra low-level before pul-

55

Wrens service a Hurricane of 759 Squadron at Yeovilton, 1941.
(FAAM)

ling up to avoid an oak tree and at the same time attempted to roll his aircraft in a show of *joie de vivre*, but failed to recover completely, his aircraft hit a bank and then somersaulted before bursting into flames. He was spotted by Observers Vickery and Clatworthy of the K1 Observer Corps Post at Dancing Hill, close to the location of the crash at Hulkshay Farm. They summoned the Fire Brigade and informed 22 Group HQ at Yeovil before rushing to the scene, but could not do anything for Williams due to the intense heat of the fire and exploding ammunition.

Several people witnessed the accident, including farmer Leonard Bond in whose field the Hurricane crashed:

I was in the same field doing a bit of hayraking, then noticed this plane was heading straight towards me at a terrific speed – I jumped off the rake and put the reins into the old horse and told him to go on down towards the hedge, which he did. I lay flat on my face thinking that both the horse and I were going to cop it, but the plane crashed in the bank on the far side of the field and went through the hedge, tipped over and exploded. It took the bank clean out between the fields. The horse was very frightened and became wedged behind a hayrick on the far side of the field. Part of the engine flew off in the explosion and landed not more than ten yards in front of him.

Michael Berry lived at Boomer, North Petherton:

The Hurricane circled Boomer Farm about three or

four times and was so low we could look up the machine gun barrels on the wings – as he passed you could feel the prop wash. There was a puff of smoke from the engine as he did a victory roll just before the crash. I was quite distressed because I was sure it was someone who knew us at the farm.

Arthur Spender, a member of the Observer Corps, went to the scene of the crash:

I was just going off duty, when we were alerted by a plane flying erratically. By the time I got there the plane was burnt all up one side. The ammo in the wings was exploding. One of the first people to get there was an RAF armourer, who ran down to the plane and knew exactly what to do. He clambered up on the other wing, opened the panels up and jerked the ammo out and threw it out of the way. We could not get near the pilot because of the flames. The Fire Brigade arrived and they dammed up the stream with an old barn door to obtain more water. They found the pilot with his arm raised as if to protect himself – we could see he was burnt to a cinder – you couldn't recognise him as a man at all. A lot of people came up to see the crash – which was natural really.

Whirlwind collisions

On 9 October Whirlwind fighters of 263 Squadron from Charmy Down near Bath were on an exercise involving flight formation practice and were returning to their base, when the last two aircraft in an echelon of six collided. One pilot, Flight Lieutenant H.StJ. Coghlan, baled out at

Standing in front of his twin-engined Whirlwind fighter at Charmy Down is Flight Lieutenant H. StJ. Coghlan of 263 Squadron, who baled out of the aircraft following a mid-air collision on 9 October. (IWM)

Squadron Leader Johnny Sample DFC, CO of 137 Squadron, who lost his life when his Whirlwind was in collision with another on 28 October. (IWM)

5,000 ft, landing in the main street of Weston village near Bath; the aircraft crashing at Kelston. The second Whirlwind, that of Pilot Officer J.H. Hoskins, crashed in the yard of the GWR station at Saltford, exploding on impact. The aircraft embedded itself into the weighbridge pit and there was nothing that could be done for the pilot – he had been killed instantly.

Almost unbelievably, on 28 October a very similar accident befell another Whirlwind unit based at Charmy Down, No 137 Squadron. The commanding officer, Squadron Leader John Sample DFC, a veteran of the Battle of Britain and ex-CO of No 504 Squadron which had been based at Filton during the latter part of the battle, was killed in this accident. Three aircraft took off from Charmy Down on a mock combat exercise. Sample instructed one of the trio, Sergeant J.F. Luing, to make a practice attack on him and the other aircraft flown by Sergeant M.J. Peskett. It was whilst Luing was making a second attack, he noticed Sample's Whirlwind go out of control, having struck that of Peskett from underneath, shearing off the rudder. The aircraft spun from a height of 7,000 ft. Sample baled out too low for his parachute to open and plunged through the roof of a cow shed at Manor Farm, Englishcombe,

as did the aircraft itself, bursting into flames. The other two Whirlwinds landed safely back at Charmy Down.

In the previous few days there had been further flying accidents, one of which occurred on the 25th, when a Magister from No 8 AACU crashed at Impens Farm, North Newton, killing the crew, Flight Sergeant T.A. Maslen and Sergeant R. Bedowski. The aircraft was seen to be flying low, stalled during a turn and crashed to the ground. It is believed that one of the crew had relatives in the nearby village and was 'buzzing' them.

That night bombs and mines fell in an area to the north of the Quantocks: Elworthy Barrows, Nettlecombe and Spaxton, where two mines caused damage to Hawkridge Farm. Unexploded parachute mines were found at Little Clay Hill Farm near Wembdon, where a German aircraft had crashed after being brought down. The aircraft was a Junkers Ju 88 of 7/KG30. The gunner, Gefreiter Hubert Mayer, aged 21, was killed, but the other three members of the crew parachuted to safety and were taken prisoner; one being apprehended as far away as Thornfalcon by a Home Guard. The aircraft was shot down by a Beaufighter of 604 Squadron, Middle Wallop, which had claimed so many victories during this period.

The Watcher on the Hill

The action was witnessed by a young man who lived at Woolavington. George Morley often used to climb the hill overlooking the village of Woolavington to watch air raids that took place on Bristol, Avonmouth, Swansea and Cardiff. The raiders would pass overhead night after night on their way to their targets.

Being bright moonlight, 28 October was ideal for a raid, so he made his way to the top of the hill to see what developed and did not have to wait long before he heard the haunting throb of 'Jumo' engines – the Luftwaffe was on cue. The drone faded and in a little while he saw searchlights probing the sky over Bristol. Star shells and AA bursts twinkled in the distance. He could hear the faint rumble of explosions from bombs being dropped on the city – there was an ominous red glow in the sky – a perfect beacon for other raiders.

Soon he heard a returning bomber. George Morley describes what happened next:

I scanned the sky to see if I could see the plane, but a large cloud passed in front of the moon making it impossible to do so. Suddenly the air was rent by a burst of cannon fire – I could see a vivid red glow blossom from behind the cloud and heard engines go beserk, revving out of control. Then out from the cloud came a flaming mass with glowing cinders trailing behind. I watched in awe as the plane plunged to earth some five miles away in the direction of Wembdon – I heard and felt the impact as it hit the ground. I also heard another plane circling for a little while before heading off east – this must have been the plane that shot the Jerry down.

Joseph Cooper who was a lieutenant in command of a searchlight battery near Wembdon at the time, described the incident in his autobiography, *Face the Music*:

The blitz on the major cities had started. One night searchlights had got clearly in their beams what looked like a Ju 88. It went right overhead and our fighters went in for the kill. A copy-book exercise. The plane came roaring down out of control, directly over us. The screeching of its engines came so near that we lay on our stomachs, waiting for the end. But suddenly, an almighty crash – then silence! It was somewhere very near. I went with my second-in-command, Sergeant Ingrams, to investigate. We were met by two Home Guard officers. They pointed the position of the plane and warned us that unexploded bombs were scattered around. However, Ingrams and I, with torches (and revolvers), approached the wreckage. I saw the bombs, positively identified it as a Ju 88, but saw no sign of life. I telephoned this information to BHQ on our return to site. Apparently, three of the crew had baled out, but the gunner in the fuselage gun-turret had been trapped. Bits of his body were found by the bomb-disposal crew the next morning. The three other Germans had given themselves up at various farms and were given a good breakfast.

Cliff Sparkes recalls how people had tried to supplement their petrol rationing at German expense:

There were pools of petrol left in ruts made by the crash. The locals tried to scoop it up in saucepans, bowls and anything that they could lay their hands on for use in their cars. I don't think they had much success though – their cars wouldn't run on it at all!

Mary Wallbridge had gone into the Bridgwater Gas Company's shop specifically to pay her bill. They had on display several items of clothing in the window and some wreckage from the aircraft and had put flag notices on Mayer's flying suit pointing to 'Blood':

I went up to the man behind the desk to pay my account and wondered what the crowds were looking at outside the shop window, so I enquired. The man said: "Haven't you seen our window display?" "What display," I asked. "We've got the German's uniform in the window – the one from the plane that was brought down at Wembdon and killed – isn't it marvellous," he replied. I was absolutely furious and said to him didn't he realise that the airman was somebody's son and that he died fighting for his country which was more than he was doing sitting on his backside behind that desk – I stormed out of the shop. It was not until I got home that I realised that I had completely forgotten to pay the gas bill.

Unwelcome guests?

The following night was also noisy with the reverberating thunder of exploding mines at Crewkerne, Charterhouse, Nettlecombe, Petherton Park, Kilve, North Newton and Thornfalcon.

Jim Foster and Clifford Lavis were returning from Bampton Fair, when an enormous blast threw them into the hedge. Picking themselves up, Lavis indicated he was going back home to

Petherton to get some beer from his house and, if all was well at home, return to Foster's farm at North Newton with the ale to round off the day. Jim Foster remembers the incident well:

When I got home my father and grandfather told me that a landmine had exploded in Parker's Field, North Petherton way, but another had come down on our land and had not gone off. So Father, Grandfather and myself went to look for it and we searched the nearby fields. It was a bright moonlight night and a low mist hung over the fields. We went into the ploughed ground – a turnip field – when we saw what looked like parachute lines and, thinking that we had stumbled across an airborne invasion of German parachutists, approached cautiously – just at that moment Grandfather saw a figure appear through the mist and called for Father, who had his shotgun with him, to 'shoot the bugger'! We hollered at him – it was only poor old Clifford who had come back with the beer! Mind you, he wore a funny cap and talked a bit strange – he wasn't a proper local, not like we. We approached the parachute cautiously then noticed, to our horror, we were staring at an unexploded landmine! We immediately reported this to the authorities and two or three days later the bomb disposal squad came up from Plymouth. We were evacuated from the farm and couldn't go back till they had defused it.

Dornier in Channel

At 22.15 on 1 November an aircraft was seen in flames over the Bristol Channel. It plunged into the sea three miles north-east of Watchet. The Minehead lifeboat was launched and a search was made over a wide area but no trace could be found, either of the plane or of any survivors. Some days later pieces of an aircraft, including oxygen cylinders, were washed ashore, together with a German military cap and boot. The words 'Werck Dornier' found on some of the wreckage established its identity: it was a Dornier 217 and had been shot down by a nightfighter. The crew of four were killed.

Scattered mines were dropped in the southern parts of the county on 2nd November and on every night from the 24th until the end of the month, but remarkably little damage was done. One mine fell in the sea at 20.32 on the 24th between New Pier and the Knightstone Baths, Weston-super-Mare, causing slight damage to 37 houses. An unexploded mine was found 500 yd north-east of the Atlantic cable pole, Weston-

super-Mare, which had dropped at the same time.

An air action was witnessed by the Churchingford Warden Service at 20.00 on 25th who reported seeing an aircraft fall in flames towards Honiton. That night a JU 88 was attacked over the Churchstanton area by a fighter from 307 (Polish) Squadron, Exeter but they succeeded only in damaging the German who managed to return to base.

December was quiet, but started with another fatal air crash. A Beaufort from 5 OTU, Chivenor, crashed on Court Hill, Exford. The four crew, Pilot Officer R.W. Hopkins, Sergeants Smart, S.G. Boyle and R. Masters were killed. Towards the close of the month, on the 28th, there was a non-fatal aircraft accident when a Whitley bomber from Honeyborne crashed behind the electricity works at Weston-super-Mare, but the crew all escaped unhurt.

Tragedy at Blue Anchor

The only incident reported to County ARP Control throughout the month was on the 19th when two men were killed while tackling a mine in the sea off Blue Anchor beach. Two objects were observed the day before and one was reported as being like the wingtip of an aeroplane protruding 6 ft out of the water about a half to three-quarters of a mile off shore with about half a mile separating them. Admiral Casement, the Resident Naval Officer, requested that the Minehead lifeboat be launched to investigate. Mr J.S. Lawrence, the Honourable Secretary of the Minehead lifeboat, refused this request because he could not justify launching the lifeboat to investigate 'aircraft wreckage', but agreed to send a member of the crew out in his private fishing boat as soon as practicable.

Thomas Escott, an auxiliary fireman, shore signaller and member of the lifeboat crew, owned the fishing boat 'Monette'. He and his cousin, John Slade, went out the next day on a fishing trip having also agreed to investigate the reported wreckage. The boat was observed through binoculars near the most easterly object by Alfred Hobbs, a coastwatcher. He saw the two men stand in the bow and stretch a boathook or rope to it. By then the boat appeared to be on mud – the tide having gone out. A few minutes later there was a violent explosion: the boat, and the two men vanished in a cloud of black smoke and debris. A rescue party was sent out, but all they could find was a large mud crater and just a few specks of white paint from the boat's hull. Thomas Escott's body was recovered on the 27th at Blue Anchor; no trace was ever found of John Slade. The objects that they had discovered were parachute mines. The second one was found at the next low tide. It is conceivable that they could possibly have been jettisoned by the Dornier that crashed into St Audries Bay on 1 November.

The enemy's sustained night bombing attack had now petered out. There can be no doubt that the whole of his resources were being absorbed on his eastern front. Germany's assault on Russia was at its height and it stood almost at the gates of Moscow – a goal never to be reached.

But for Somerset, 1942 would be a year in which more civilian lives were lost due to enemy bombing than for the rest of the war put together...it was to be the year of the notorious Baedeker raids.

The large RAE barrage balloon hangar at Pawlett still stands today.
(Author)

FOUR

1942: *Year of the Baedeker Raids*

No bombing incidents of any kind were reported in Somerset during the first three months of 1942. The attack upon the Soviet Union was clearly absorbing the whole of the enemy's strength.

There were a few incidents of note involving aircraft. A bomber manned by a Czech crew returning from a raid on the night of 7/8 February was badly damaged. The pilot ordered the crew to abandon the aircraft; three baled out and landed at Cossington, one of whom was killed when his parachute failed to open. The aircraft managed to land safely at an airfield in Gloucestershire with the other three members of the crew on board. Cliff Sparkes remembers a strange fact about the incident:

The body of the airman whose parachute had not opened was found near Cossington Quarry beside the railway line – it made a hollow in the ground and the uncanny thing was that nothing grew on that spot for three years afterwards.

On the 8th, a Hurricane from 87 Squadron, Charmy Down crashed at Naish Farm, Clapton in Gordano, killing the pilot Sergeant J.R. Keith. Another Hurricane crashed at Dead Woman's Ditch, Crowcombe on the 13th; the pilot was killed, and on the 23rd a Magister training aircraft crashed on Wincanton Racecourse killing Pilot Officers D.G. West and E.G. Bright. An aircraft engaged in bombing practice over the Pawlett Hams range on 11 February accidentally dropped some of its bombs which fell at East Brent, Bridgwater and Woolavington.

Balloon cable cutting trials

The development of adequate balloon cable cutting devices, which could be incorporated on wings of aircraft, was of paramount importance if the chances of survival were to be improved should an aircraft accidentally run into a balloon barrage. Trials were conducted to test such equipment. The duty was extremely hazardous and it took men of immense courage to fly deliberately into a barrage balloon cable in order to test untried cable cutting equipment.

The Royal Aircraft Establishment needed a site which was safe to conduct such experiments and chose the flats adjacent to Bridgwater on the Pawlett Hams. A large balloon hangar was built on the western edge of Pawlett Hill with a small camp to house a unit of men needed to tend the balloon.

Trials commenced at the site in 1940 and continued for the best part of the war. Various types of cutting gear were tried on cables of different strength and thickness. The pilot would have to aim the aeroplane at a suspended cable which was denoted by red flags attached thereto. The tethered cable was without flags and woe betide the pilot who got this wrong, resulting in a lost balloon. Small boys in the neighbourhood used to delight in running after the cut cables which would be festooned with these bright red flags.

One aircraft had already crashed during these trials: the Fairey Battle that had come down at Cokerhurst Farm, Wembdon on 1 October 1940. In March a Vickers Wellington bomber was sent from the RAE at Farnborough on detachment to Churchstanton to conduct trials at Pawlett. On the 24th, Squadron Leader C.R.J. Hawkins DFC, the aircraft's pilot and sole occupant, took off from the airfield to carry out a cutting trial over Pawlett Hams. The propeller of one engine became fouled in the cable causing the Wellington to become uncontrollable. Squadron Leader Hawkins had no option but to abandon his aircraft which crashed one mile west of Pawlett Church; he escaped unhurt.

Accidents involving cable cutting experiments were surprisingly few, but there were numerous others during this period. On the 25th a Hampden bomber from 455 Squadron crashed at Watchfield, killing Pilot Officer A.H. Metcalfe and his crew of three. A Hurricane from 87

Squadron came down at Dundry on 1 April; the pilot, Sergeant R.W. Marshall was killed. Another air tragedy occurred on 6 April when a Hampden bomber from 16 OTU, Upper Heyford in Oxfordshire, crashed on Air Ministry property at Locking, near Weston-super-Mare. The aircraft was seen to go into a flat spin following violent manoeuvres over the RAF camp. The four crew, Sergeants A.B. McKeith, W.B.M. Wilson, H.G. Stalker and F.A. Dann, were killed instantly

Lübeck and Rostock bombed

Incensed by the bombing of Lübeck and Rostock and the loss of these German mediaeval landmarks, Hitler ordered retaliatory attacks upon historic English cathedral cities and towns resulting in the Baedeker raids, so named because the targets were well known on the Continent to users of the Baedeker guide books and timetables. The fury of the enemy fell in turn upon Exeter, Bath, Canterbury, Norwich, York and Weston-super-Mare. Why Weston-super-Mare was included is uncertain for it was not on the German's Baedeker list, but it has been suggested that publicity given to a military demonstration on the seafront to 'munitions and aircraft workers' was excuse enough to launch a stinging fire attack on the town.

Bath had thus far escaped the bombing. Situated so near to battered Bristol the city was accustomed to grim sights brought about by bombing – her Civil Defence workers had many times gone to the aid of the neighbour city, but were unprepared for an attack – Bath had no anti-aircraft guns to defend it. General Sir Frederick Pile's resources of AA Command had to be stretched and Bath was not considered a prime target for bombing, therefore no guns could be spared for its defence. Throughout the weekend of 25 – 27 April 1942 much of Bath was to be reduced to dust and ashes, and many of its citizens were to be killed and wounded.

Bath's refugees: the Admiralty

The city had become a centre for evacuation and over 4,000 arrived by train at the outbreak of war. In addition various departments of the Admiralty had moved to Bath, taking over a number of buildings in the city, including the Pump Room Hotel which housed the main body of the Design and Naval Construction Department. The Admiralty also took over the Pulteney, Spa and Empire Hotels; hutments were built at Foxhill and they also requisitioned schools in the area in order to perform all the functions necessary of such a large department. With the influx of these 'refugees' Bath's population increased by an estimated 10,000. The essential nature of the work carried out by these Admiralty departments made Bath potentially very vulnerable, for any attack on them involving disruption of their work, or indeed their destruction, would be deemed catastrophic.

Bombers assemble

At Luftwaffe bases in Northwest France 163 bombers of Luftflotte III were marshalled for the attack – it was to be their biggest effort over Britain in nearly a year. Units from KG2, KG30, KG4, KG55 and the newly-trained 1/KG2 equipped with Dornier Do 217s, plus units equipped with Junkers Ju 88s from KG3; the Ju 88s of KGr106, which would act as pathfinders, were assembled. The bombers would be preceded by the veteran (F)123 Gruppe, a skilled reconnaissance wing, to photograph the target. This mixed bag of Dornier

Luftwaffe target photograph of Bath. Note the Admiralty hutments at Fox Hill are highlighted, as are the gasworks. (Bath City Council)

Do s, Do 217s, Heinkel 111s and Junkers Ju 88 were to wreak havoc on one of Britain's finest architectural jewels. Exeter had already been attacked the night of the 24th, causing heavy damage to the historic cathedral city, now it was to be another target – Bath.

At about 22.15 a force of 40-plus German bombers appeared on the radar screens along a broad front of south and west England – from the Isle of Wight to Seaton in Devon. Portland's AA guns opened up at 22.27, but without effect. The raiding force passed over Dorset and Somerset making their way towards Bath. The two RAF night-fighter Squadrons, 87 and 125, based at Charmy Down and Colerne respectively, put up their aircraft in readiness.

Raid one

The first blows fell on Saturday 25 April. The alert sounded at 22.59. Already the western sky was pricked with the shell bursts of the Bristol barrage – a situation which had occurred so many times before as to lull the people of Bath into a false sense of immunity. The city was at the enemy's mercy.

At 23.15 enemy aircraft came in low over the lip of the hills. Chandeliers hung in the moonlit sky illuminating the peaceful city. The flares were followed by thousands of incendiaries and Bath became a bowl of smoke and fire. Wave after wave of bombers roamed the skies above the city. Unopposed, the attackers were able to fly so low as to circle the amphitheatre at a few hundred feet, firing at will with machine-guns at the Civil Defence workers and fire-fighters below to discourage their efforts. A warden running home to alert his wife found her lying dead on the cobbled street outside their home. Ambulance drivers, mostly women, were shot up as they tried to reach St Martin's Hospital with the injured.

With the target now pinpointed by the stab of fires, the enemy began to drop HE bombs. One of the first narrowly missed the Report and Control Centre at Apsley House, blew in a wall and put all the telephones out of action as the first calls were coming through. A gasometer was struck and set ablaze, illuminating large parts of the city.

Ivo Peters was home that night at 9 The Royal Crescent:

The sirens sounded and I went outside to have a look. The whole city of Bath was bathed in silver moonlight. There was an absolutely deathly hush – no aircraft...nothing. Suddenly I heard the sound of a twin-engined aircraft coming from the north behind me. I expected to see a Beaufighter come over the top of the Crescent making a wide circuit for Colerne. To my astonishment it was a Junkers 88. The next moment I could see the glint of its bombs in the moonlight as they dropped. They just missed Queen Square Station and landed in Green Park. These were the first to drop and caused a huge fire – it could have been incendiaries – most probably the aircraft was a Pathfinder. Other aircraft appeared in no time at all. Some flew below the height of Lansdown and friends of mine who lived there said afterwards that they could look down onto their wings as they flew over the city – they must have been at about 300 ft. There was just time for me to usher staff and family into the basement. The bombs were consistently falling short – theoretically the Crescent should have been obliterated, but in fact it was Julian Road behind that suffered. Bombs straddled the Crescent and hit houses at the rear. Two in the Crescent were burnt out with incendiaries, some of which bounced on our roof. Stick after stick of bombs fell, one landed about 30 yd short of the back of Royal Crescent – all the windows at the back went – there were shattered window frames and glass was everywhere. Julian Road was on fire – the wind must have been from the north as it was carrying burning debris from St Andrew's Church, which was an inferno, into our windowless house. We went around the house and stamped on the smouldering embers that we found, including those right at the top of the house. It was all a very frightening experience.

The local nightfighter squadrons were having no success: No 87 put up 16 operational patrols during the course of the raid and individual fighters were assigned to a searchlight box, but their simple radar sets were saturated with information preventing the pilots from determining any one contact long enough to be able to track it. A Hurricane of 87 Squadron ran short of fuel; the engine cut out whilst the pilot was switching tanks. Being pursued by what he took to be a JU 88 and not being able to restart the engine, Pilot Officer McNair was forced to abandon his aircraft, which crashed near Charmy Down.

Mrs N. Watts' home was badly damaged in the attacks; she and her family were injured and lucky to escape with their lives:

I was living at the Hollow in Southdown at the time. Considering we were not near any sort of target pos-

Above: *The roofless arches of St Andrew's stand silent witness to the previous night's devastation.* (CRO)

Above: *St Andrew's Church in Julian Road ablaze.* (Wessex Newspapers)

Below: *The extent of the damage to Julian Road is evident. Gaunt walls are all that remain of people's homes.* (CRO)

Nothing remains of Burlington House which once stood next to St Mary's Roman Catholic Church in Julian Road. The church was also badly damaged. (Wessex Newspapers)

Emergency services are on the scene, but fires still rage in Upper Bristol Road, where a house has received a direct hit. Note the 'Dig for Victory' poster. (Wessex Newspapers)

Standing opposite the Assembly Rooms the Regina Hotel received a direct hit cutting it almost in two and a number of guests lost their lives. (Bath Reference Library)

Francis Hotel in Queen Square lost half its front after suffering a direct hit. (Wessex Newspapers)

fourth had the cylinder head of his machine smashed by a flying fragment, but found a deserted autocycle which he commandeered. One rider saw a colleague dash up a street, but just as he swerved round a house fell on him with a great roar, burying him under mountains of masonry. He was found dead in the rubble the next morning. All were severely handicapped by glass and debris, but communications were maintained.

The difficulties of the night were further increased by the enforced evacuation of the Casualty Service Headquarters in St James' Parade. A bomb tore its way down a chimney, burst into a room and came to rest quietly upon a mattress. It did not explode, but its presence necessitated the removal of personnel and ambulances, at the time their services were in greatest demand.

Mrs B. Stockden belonged to the Civil Defence and was attached to the Church Hall at Bear Flat for First Aid and casualty work:

My brother James and I, having heard the sirens warning for an air raid, made haste from our home at Millmead Road to reach Bear Flat. En route via the Scala Cinema, bombs started to fall, so we had to dive quickly into the gutter, as the wall above us was strafed with bullets – the scars remain there to this day. We ran up the streets until we stopped, petrified, at the turning to Bear Flat and saw that Bath was burning. It was like one huge flame spread right across the city. We arrived at the Church Hall and had not been long in changing when we were shaken by bombs falling. My brother was supposedly on his way home, but instead, about half an hour later, returned driving an ambulance with casualties in it. The casualties from Oldfield Park came in and we knew so many of them. After they were moved to hospital and we had managed a cup of tea, my brother came back for us to return home together, but we had not been long gone when the siren went again and we had just got into the shelter when a bomb fell at the end of Ringwood Road. I left the shelter and ran up the road quickly. The garage owner opened up for us to put casualties inside – one of whom was a very great friend of mine and not badly injured, but a friend of

ition, we had a very severe attack with direct hits on two houses; in one a mother and child were killed and in the other a husband and wife. A lot of high explosive and incendiary bombs fell close by and the bungalow, where I lived with my husband, two children and my mother, was extensively damaged. My husband was injured and one of the children badly bruised. Our home was also machine-gunned by the raiders and the bullets made holes through the doors and skirting boards. We decided to take the children and go up the garden under a hedge but my mother would not move from her bed and though surrounded by bricks and debris was miraculously untouched. I was very badly bruised with climbing over the piles of rubble to get up the garden and was expecting my third child. We had to leave what was left of our home, and went to stay with relatives in Wiltshire. My husband's place of work, a butcher's shop in Julian Road on the other side of the city, was also destroyed. I shall never forget seeing the man, whose wife and child had been killed, coming up the road later the next day. He had been on fire watch in the city that night and returned to find everything in his life gone. The way he looked is imprinted on my memory for ever.

Deprived in one blow of the principle means of communication, the defenders had to rely entirely upon their despatch riders and messengers. One rider, blown off his machine, secured another from the shattered window of a nearby cycle shop and on this continued his duties throughout the night. Another had a steel girder fall in front of him which he crossed at high speed, the machine staying behind! A third ran into the tail fins of an unexploded bomb and a

my younger brother was unfortunately killed. We had to wait many hours before an ambulance could get through to take the casualties to hospital. After all that my parents and family had to walk through the devastated city to get to Bathford to stay with a married sister and her husband, as our home had a large hole in the roof.

Raid 2

Following a lull lasting just a few hours the attack resumed. Some of the bombers, having refuelled and rearmed set off again on their second mission of the night. An estimate of at least 40 or more crossed the coast and reached Bath at 04.35 – the same time as a 'Raid Imminent' warning was given. Again the local RAF squadrons, Nos 87 and 125, took to the air in defence of the city, but neither had any better success than before. The last raiders left, crossing the coast at the first light of dawn.

Daybreak found the city shrouded in a pall of smoke. Fires were still raging but the National Fire Service had prevented a major conflagration. Streets were piled with debris and rescue squads toiled ceaselessly in the extrication of the dead and injured. Timely and much needed help came in from all sides. There were Civil Defence squads from Bristol, Cheltenham, Coventry, Devizes, Gloucester, Keynsham, Swindon and Weston-super-Mare.

Raid 3

In the small hours of the following morning, Monday 27th, the enemy returned to Bath with 65 or more bombers. Flying at roof-top height, they added to the devastation of the previous night in a 90 minute raid of great intensity. The Admiralty had managed to acquire a Bofors gun which fired a few rounds from Foxhill, where it had been sited, but scored no hits. Nearly 10,000 'trekkers', as they were called, fled their homes in the city and slept under hedgerows in the surrounding countryside, their faces covered with clothes to avoid being seen by the German aircrews. This third raid was completely unanticipated by the hard-pressed General Pile and he had to spread his AA defences the length and breadth of southern England, trying to guess where the enemy would strike next, and admitted later: "Unfortunately, though excusably, we were waiting in the wrong place".

Enemy losses

The enemy did not escape unscathed: of the 50 or so aircraft employed on the first night the RAF shot down five – on the second, the numbers were fewer and four were destroyed. None came down on Somerset soil or were brought down by local fighter squadrons. Other squadrons, some equipped with Bristol Beaufighters with more sophisticated radar, were used to good effect. Amongst the German losses on the first night was an errant Ju 88, brought down over Hereford way by a Beaufighter from 255 Squadron at Higher Ercall that was on a training sortie. The Junkers crew were inexperienced and had strayed off course. A Do 17 on its way home was shot down into the sea by a Beaufighter up from Tangmere, also airborne on a training mission and a Do 217 was brought down at Wimborne, but whether by ack-ack or a nightfighter from 307 Squadron is uncertain; they also claimed others destroyed on the Sunday.

Rescue and valour

Rescue work went on for several days. The Civil Defence services of Bath, together with the reinforcements sent to them, worked as a great team, to which were joined men of the Welsh Guards, the Royal Engineers and the city's two Home Guard battalions. Eight members of the Bath Special Constabulary and nine members of the Civil Defence services were killed. The casualties of the 5th (Bath City) Home Guard Battalion numbered nine killed on duty and seven wounded. By reason of its constitution the Admiralty Home Guard Battalion was able to offer sustained and very substantial assistance to the Civil Authorities. As many as 400 men were employed daily for a week or more. They were directly responsible for saving over a hundred lives, one boy being rescued alive as late as on Wednesday 29th. They were also able to give material assistance in the restoration of the gas supply and other public utilities.

Mrs Hilda Otridge helped the homeless after the raids:

The Schoolroom at Walcot Methodist Church was quite large one and in late April opened to receive anyone who was made homeless through the raids. My husband I offered to take over the care and attention of these unfortunate people. We were told to expect about 200 people but we ended up by having 500. This was a problem. We kept the schoolroom open for five days with the help of others who came forward to help feed and bed down on the floor on blankets. The next problem was to find homes for a good many of these poor folk. We had a schoolmaster living and teaching in the area, so he and I canvassed around to find people who were willing to house them pro tem. Some were quite amenable to receive hospitality, but we had some who didn't want to be split up. This became a problem and we then decided to ask the Council to do something for us. They did by providing a coach so that we were able to send the families who were a bit awkward out into the countryside around Bath. The country people were most kind and accepted families until they were able to return to proper accommodation.

A helping hand is given to an elderly couple in Bridewell Passage. (Wessex Newspapers)

An airman helps refugees, many of whom left the city and slept out in the countryside at night, following the attacks. They became known as the 'Trekkers'. (Wessex Newspapers)

There were many awards for bravery: Mr R.N. Willey of Keynsham, the leader of 2/6 Rescue Squad, received the George Medal for his outstanding work of rescue at the Circus Tavern. Willey had constantly put himself at risk by tunnelling his way to victims that had been buried under the table, when their house had collapsed on them.

A George Medal was also awarded to CSM (later Lieutenant) T.A. Leslie of the 6th Somerset (Bath Admiralty) Home Guard. The citation shows that while the raid was still in progress he effected an entry into the basement of the Regina Hotel by means of an aperture through the debris, permitting only one man to enter at a time. A woman, trapped by falling masonry and hanging by the knees, was supported by Leslie for hours while other men tried to release

The King and Queen visited the city in the week following the raids. They are seen here inspecting a line-up of Special Constables, who did such good work during the blitz. (CRO)

her. The danger was so great that they were covered by a sheet so that they should not see the falling blocks if they were hit. At one time the danger of fire was very great and Leslie had to be doused with water to prevent his clothes from catching fire.

Of the other members of 6th Home Guard Battalion working in the ruins of the Regina Hotel, three received the BEM. They brought out 25 people from the wrecked hotel, only five of whom were found to be alive. The spectacle of seeing a few people slumped in their chairs – some still clutching a book or newspaper they had been reading when the hotel was struck, or were found in their bedrooms with little apparent injury, but covered in dust, must have been an eerie sight and a difficult situation for the rescue squads to deal with.

Many other acts of bravery were performed during that calamitous weekend in April 1942. Mrs J.M. Woolmer of the city's Casualty Service, Private G. Cheeseborough of the Pioneer Corps and Sergeant B. Brown of the 5th Somerset (Bath City) Home Guard, all received the BEM. Seven members of Bath's Civil Defence services received awards.

The human and material cost

The total number of people killed is said to have been 417, but this could include all raids in the area throughout the war. 357 people were seriously, and 515 slightly, injured in the raids.

The centre of the city escaped the worst that might have befallen it. The Abbey lost much of its stained glass but suffered little structural damage. The Roman Baths were undamaged. The most serious architectural loss was that of the famous Assembly Rooms. Built by John Wood the Younger in 1771 they had first witnessed all the gaieties of Regency England, then fallen to a lower estate only to be restored again as recently as 1938 to their former magnificence. HRH Marina, Duchess of Kent, had danced at the reopening charity ball. The original chandeliers and some furniture, moved to a place of safety early in the war, remained unharmed.

Other places that were affected included the Royal Crescent, the Mineral Water Hospital, the Circus and Catherine Place. In addition the churches of St James, Holy Trinity, St Andrew and St Bartholomew were destroyed by fire. Seven other churches, including St John's and St Michael's, chapels, and six schools, were seriously damaged. Over a thousand other buildings, most of them dwellinghouses, were damaged beyond repair. The Francis Hotel in Queen Square was also badly damaged and lost 26 yd of its frontage. The Victoria Works of Messrs Stothert and Pitt were hit on the Saturday night and the Newark Works suffered on the Sunday.

Stotherts made tank turret mountings and midget submarines. In the early part of the war they had received publicity for building a colossal trench digger nicknamed 'Nellie'. Winston Chur-

Many victims of the Bath raids were buried in mass graves. Seen here is such a plot in the Haycombe Cemetery, Bath. (Author)

'Nellie' the trench digger manufactured by Stothert & Pitt photographed on 25 July 1941 at Clumber Park during a demonstration for the benefit of Winston Churchill. (IWM)

chill inspected this contraption and was photographed in 1940 beside it – the machine was never used.

Among the 16,883 other buildings which suffered damage, to a greater or lesser degree, were the Abbey Church House, the Masonic Hall (formerly the old Theatre Royal), the offices of the Bathavon Rural District Council, the Royal National Hospital for Rheumatic Diseases, and other well-known hospitals and hotels. Over 250 HE bombs (one list puts the total number as high as 323) and thousands of incendiaries were dropped in the three raids. On the nights during which Bath was under bombardment, bombs fell elsewhere in Somerset at Ansford, Coat near Martock where one child was killed; Combe Hay, Keynsham, Spaxton, Staple Fitzpaine, West Hatch, Wookey Hole, Whitchurch and Wincanton. There was further desultory bombing on the 29th without human casualties.

The night of Monday 27 April was Norwich's turn. Throughout the rest of the war Bath would have no more raids. In Somerset the last few days of April 1942 were quiet and so was May. The only incident that occurred was a daylight raid in which five HE's were dropped on Thornfalcon, near Taunton.

Aircraft accidents continued unabated. A Spitfire crashed near Axbridge railway station on 27 April, killing the Czech pilot, Flight Lieutenant Rohacek. A Wellington of 57 Squadron crashed into Kewstoke Bay on 3 May but all the crew managed to bale out. On 5 June Yeovilton lost a Hurricane and its pilot, Lieutenant J.C. Luke, only to lose another pilot a couple of days later in a landing accident involving two Fulmar aircraft.

Weston-super-Mare's big raids

Why Weston was attacked has caused much debate: whether it was one of the Baedeker raids, just an opportunity target, or was brought to the attention of the German High Command by publicity given to a military display in April on the seafront, are among the reasons proffered. There were, however, military targets in the area, namely the shadow factories for the Bristol Aeroplane Company situated at the western end of the airfield at Old Mixon, also between Hutton and Banwell at Elborough, which were protected by a balloon barrage. From the nature of the attack, carried out at low-level in the east-west direction, leaving little doubt to the German bomber crews of their actual location, it can be assumed that the town itself was the target and thus fits into the Baedeker category. German tactics corresponded closely to those employed in the other raids, a moonlit night, low-flying aircraft, thousands of incendiaries to fire the town, followed by heavy HE bombs to weaken the defence.

The Luftwaffe strength was heavily depleted in the west by the time Weston was attacked, and to muster a sizable force of bombers to carry out an effective raid was no easy task. Like the Bath raids, the enemy force was made up from several, including training, units. Thought to be amongst those that took part were KG2, KG6, KG100, 7/KGr100 and possibly 4/KG55; the pathfinder force was again KGr106.

The raids occurred on the nights of June 28th and 29th. The first raid began at 01.20, just before the sirens sounded. Double Summer Time meant that it was not very long after nightfall. There were many big fires. Casualties from the HE's were severe. The National Fire Service and the Fire Guard, with stirrup pumps aquitted themselves well. The RAF Initial Training Wing at Locking Air Station sent parties who assisted in the fire fighting and rescue work.

Amongst the buildings damaged were Uphill Church, Kewstoke Emergency Hospital, two laundries, Tivoli Cinema and the New Inn at Worle. One of the worst affected areas was the corner of Moorland and Devonshire Road, where three separate sticks of large HE bombs met.

The Tivoli Cinema destroyed. Fire hoses still cross the street the morning after the raid as rescue workers clear up the mess. Small boys gaze at the ruins of a place that once entertained them. (Woodspring Museum)

Other incidents were reported in Stradling Avenue, Eatonhurst School, Sunnyside Road and the railway station, where unexploded bombs were found. An UXB was found in the Guards Armoured Division School on the seafront and a canister of incendiaries landed in a narrow shopping centre, scattering its contents over the street, but failed to explode.

Mrs Edith Simmons lived in Argyle Avenue:

On the Sunday night houses were burnt out in this road. I was standing at a bedroom window and saw a plane very low, then watched as the bomb doors opened. A bomb flattened the grocer's shop at the corner of Moorland Road, killing the owner and his

Once a popular shopping centre, Lance's Corner lies in ruins. It was Weston's only real departmental store of wartime. (Author's collection)

daughter, also a house was hit in this road and two people were killed. The planes returned the next night and houses were bombed and twelve people lost their lives, two of them school children. My children and I were in a shelter and we heard the bomb whistling overhead and as it dropped the whole shelter seemed to lift and then come down again. After that night we went over the fields and were crouching in a ditch when Hutton village was bombed with more loss of life. Every window was lost in my house as well as a few personal belongings.

Geoff Bell was a boy living in Weston with his parents at the time of the raids and states that Weston had the most number of bombs drop per capita in the country:

Some of the first bombs to fall in the area were in our road – Grove Road, Milton – and we were evacuated because of explosive incendiaries. We had a whole string of 'breadbaskets', which were large canisters of incendiaries, drop in the area and burn out two bungalows opposite us, also setting fire to a friend's property across the way. When we saw flames come from there, my brother and I went to help him. The next minute our friend said: "Hey, Geoff! you'd better get back over to your house – it's on fire!" Two incendiaries had gone through the roof and we saw flames come out from the top – the whole thing was a greenish glow. By the time we got back, my father was there filling buckets of water and had a step ladder up to the loft – we used to keep a bath full, just in case of such raids – the water was splashing about all over the place as he was getting up into the roof. As he opened the trap door a great sheet of flame shot

Above: *Prospect Place and Orchard Street were badly hit resulting in many lives being lost. This scene shows the extent of the devastation in the area.* (Author's collection)

Below: *Moorland Road was badly hit and many buildings destroyed, including the Moorland Laundry. The gentleman in the bowler hat is the late Dr Dennis Clarke who several times, at considerable risk to himself, crawled through to reach trapped survivors in order to administer morphia. He was later awarded the BEM. Just behind Dr Clarke is Mrs G. Stevens, who is seen searching through the wreckage of her parent's home.* (Author's collection)

across his head sending him backwards causing him to slip and hit his head on the opening to the attic. He shouted: "Damn and blast!" It was the only time in my life I heard him swear! My brother was severely reprimanded for kicking a complete 'breadbasket' which failed to open, back over to the Police Station down Walliscote Road.

On the night of the 29th the siren sounded at 01.50, giving a full 30 minutes warning of what was to be expected. The first bombs therefore found the Civil Defence services at the ready. The second night's raid was again heavy and aircraft were overhead for about 50 minutes. Groups of bomb craters were found round five of the six road-rail bridges within the Borough, none of which was actually hit. A large bomb

crater and an unexploded bomb at the railway caused the suspension by the Regional Commissioner of the issue of railway tickets to the town for a short time, although the station was never quite out of action and the main line continued to function.

The shopping centre suffered severely. The heaviest casualties occurred in the Orchard Street district. Rescue work was complicated by the fact that the destroyed houses contained newly arrived visitors. The wardens often could not tell how many persons were trapped beneath the wreckage. One example of this was a house in the road which had received a direct hit and the rescuers were only able to find "sufficient human remains to fill two coffins". Two of the

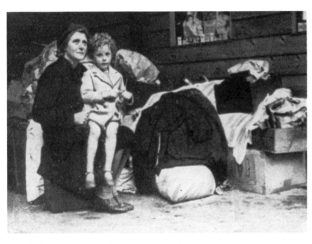

Bewildered survivors sit dazed amongst salvaged possessions.
(Author's collection)

casualties included a woman and her lodger. She had seen her soldier husband off to London at the station earlier that evening, but he returned to try and identify her, which he did by one of her pink shoes found nearby. The lodger's daughter was called to try and identify her father, but the only way she was able to do was by his tobacco pouch and grey flannel trousers found in the debris. This was a problem peculiar to a seaside resort in the summer months. Ninety-seven high explosive and an estimated 10,000 incendiary bombs fell in Weston-super-Mare on those two nights. The ironical feature of the two

What appears to be a German SC500 drum-type bomb has been defused and is winched to the surface on the Bournville Estate, Weston. (Pauline Bland)

raids was that the identical figure of 47 tons of bombs fell on both nights. The raids caused 102 deaths with 338 people injured, 170 seriously.

All branches of the Civil Defence services were brought into action. Rest Centres were opened; emergency feeding and clothing schemes came into this operation. Reinforcements came in from Bristol, Bath, Taunton and indeed from all parts of Somerset.

Mr H. Cox received the George Medal and Mr W.J. Tye the BEM for hazardous rescue work at Prospect Place; both came from Bristol. To Weston's own Civil Defence personnel were granted one MBE, one BEM and two Commendations, one of the latter going to a boy messenger for continuing on duty at a first aid post whilst injured.

As the King and Queen had visited Bath after the April raids, so the Duke of Kent now came to Weston-super-Mare to encourage and comfort the inhabitants on Wednesday 15 July. His Royal Highness toured the badly damaged districts and continued on foot among the people to the Beach Lawns, where he inspected the Civil Defence personnel and talked to a great number of them.

Wellington machine-gunned

During the first of these two raids on Weston-super-Mare there was a minor incident when an enemy aircraft shot up and damaged Wellington School and some houses in South Street with cannon fire. On the second night there was a similar incident at Shoreditch Road, and also Holway, Taunton, when an aircraft was reported flying overhead at no more than 50 ft spraying the area with machine-gun fire, but fortunately without casualties.

A few incendiaries were dropped on the 29th at Cannington and Otterhampton, but caused no damage. A Mustang from 16 Squadron Weston Zoyland, engaged on live-firing practice, crashed on the foreshore of Stolford on 30 June, killing Pilot Officer G.P.D. Young, who had made several successful dives onto the target, but on the last occasion was thought to have hestitated and failed to pull out.

Bombs were dropped at Churchstanton on 2 July. A Blenheim aircraft from 13 OTU Bicester, crashed at the edge of the Pawlett Hams bombing range on the 5th; all four crew perished. The aircraft was seen to dive at great speed into the ground from several thousand feet. Only a few fragments of clothing were found, including sergeant's chevrons from a tunic; virtually nothing was recovered of the crew themselves. Weston Zoyland suffered another tragedy on 4 August, when a Defiant aircraft was pushed beyond its safe limits, stalled and crashed after 'buzzing' the control tower; the two crew, Flight Lieutenant M.W. Hamlyn and Corporal C.H. Odle, did not survive.

Focke Wulfs over Yeovil

Just before dusk on 5 August, two Focke Wulf 190 fighter-bombers carried out a 'hit and run' attack on Yeovil, causing damage and casualties at Gordon Road and Dampier Street. The aircraft dropped two 500 kg delayed action bombs from a very low altitude; one of the bombs hit the ground and bounced for over 200 yd, clearing a number of houses before exploding in Dampier Street. Three people were killed and a further 27 injured, of which 13 were detained in hospital. Enemy aircraft machine-gunned barrage balloons at Yeovil during the evening of the 8th, but no damage was reported. On 18 August bombs fell at Spaxton and at Cannington, damaging houses but causing no human casualties.

High casualties in Bristol

On 28 August Bristol was taken unawares by a lone enemy raider who crossed the county of Somerset at extreme height on a fine clear summer morning. Soon after 09.00 the faint drone of aircraft engines could be heard by some, which continued for ten minutes or more, but those among the noise and bustle of the city heard nothing. There was no siren, no balloons rose and not a shot was fired until after the event, and then only in intermittent fashion. The attacker was far up out of reach. A single bomb fell with an echoing crash at Broad Weir; unhappily it was in use that morning as a temporary bus terminus. Three buses were hit and caught fire. Forty-eight persons were killed and 56 injured – the heaviest casualty list for any single incident in all the raids on Bristol.

A barrage balloon was reported adrift at high altitude over Milton, Weston-super-Mare on 18 August. It was the usual practice for the RAF balloon squadron to contact their flying counterparts of the RAF who would often send a fighter or any suitable aircraft, such as a Lysander from Weston Zoyland, to shoot it down.

Hit and run attacks

There now occurred four daylight incidents in Somerset, widely spaced in time, but the work of a single enemy machine flying very low to escape detection by radar. The attacks showed considerable skill on the part of the German pilots, who struck their targets with precision. In each case the attacker flew at roof-top height and dropped four bombs. The targets were all railway junctions or milk factories, or both.

Castle Cary bombed

The first of these daytime attacks occurred at 09.15 on 3 September on Castle Cary Station and, being the junction for Weymouth line, was a prime target. The first bomb wrecked a locomotive and eight trucks of a goods train, damaged five other trucks, brought down the telephone wires and blocked the main line. The second bomb demolished the signalbox, goods shed and parcels office (all small buildings) and damaged further trucks. The third destroyed the Railway Hotel and damaged Prideaux's milk factory and three cottages. The fourth fell in the River Brue. The four 500 kg bombs had been dropped with deadly accuracy. Unfortunately the German crew used machine-guns thereby raising the casualties to three killed, one of whom was a signalman, and ten injured. All links were restored and normal working resumed at 23.00, except there was only single line working between Castle Cary and Sparkford over the Weymouth permanent way.

Templecombe hit

The second of these attacks came on 5 September. Templecombe Junction was the target. The attack was probably made by a lone Junkers Ju 88. The aircraft flew so low that the first bomb travelled laterally 52 yd before exploding. The second bomb similarly passed clean through three cottages. The third fell on the Somerset & Dorset line and the fourth on the Southern Railway, blocking both. The Wincanton road was also temporarily blocked, two houses were demolished, nine badly and 46 slightly damaged. Two churches and two hotels were also dam-

The effects of a hit and run attack. This is Castle Cary Junction following the raid of 3 September 1942. The signalbox has been completely demolished; its lever frame lies amongst the ruins. (Colin Maggs)

aged. Casualties were high for so small a place: 13 were killed and 17 injured. Traffic by road and rail was restored the following day.

Austin Hayter, who lived on a farm near the station, gives this graphic account of the raid:

I had been out harvesting and got home about 9 o'clock. The back door was open and suddenly we heard an aeroplane rev up – throttle wide open as he went away, and with the same there was a BANG...BANG...BANG...BANG! The house shook – the ceilings came down upstairs. We dived outside to look if we could see anything and we noticed a lot of smoke and dust come up from the station. I slipped on my Home Guard tunic and went straight on down there. They had really made a job of it. The first bomb that dropped fell in front of the School House garden – pitched off there and into a row of cottages. The Coombes' lived in the first one, the Howes in the second, the Matthews' in the third and the Miltons in the end one. The bomb pitched right in the end house and exploded in the grate, which literally dismantled it, depositing the people in the Howes house into the fireplace. The Matthews had two rooms: kitchen and dining room come sitting room. The father had gone down to have a drink with the Howes next door and had left his wife and three daughters there. They had gone into the other room to play the piano and couldn't get out because their house was pushed right in and blocked the door behind them. Everybody else there was killed except young John Howe, who was in bed and still there on top of a pile of rubble

when they got him out. The baby beside him was suffocated by the dust. The next bomb landed on the church steps and exploded, blowing the front out of a big four-storey red-brick house nearby. The lady who lived there died from blast injuries later on that night. The third bomb pitched on the 'Dorset' line. The Bath train was just on its way out of the station and the blast blew the Guard's van window out. The fireman of the train thought that detonators had gone off, but was told by the driver: "Detonators be buggered – them's bombs!" Opposite the school a reading room with a couple of snooker tables disintegrated. The fourth pitched over on the siding by the parcels office at the station. Dart, a wheeltapper; Hillier, a ganger; Bert Ray the Head Porter and Pat Gawler a greaser, were on the station platform and all killed. One of them was stood up against the wall and all that was holding him up was his backbone. We took the injured to the Royal pub and did what we could for them. The ambulance driver lived in South Cheriton, so it was nearly an hour before he arrived on the scene and we could send people off to hospital. The police wanted an HQ to direct operations and since we had the nearest phone to the station, we let them use our dining room. The sergeant from the Yeovil police asked me to compile a list of who was missing, since I knew everyone and spent all night trying to sort this out. Because people had been evacuated, some of whom had gone to relatives, it was difficult, but I had to make sure people were all right. The next morning the local bobby came to the farm and said he wanted my help and told me the dead were placed in the old United Dairy's building and would I come up to see that they were all correctly labelled. Three evacuees were also amongst the dead – they were in the big house next to the station. Also there was a mother, baby and a little girl of three that were in bed in the house. The mother and baby had been killed, but we found the little girl standing on the edge of the room – where the whole of the front of the house had been blown out. The 13 dead were buried in the churchyard at Templecombe.

Somerton Milk Factory

The third raid to occur was at 08.20 on 29 September, when a single aircraft aimed four bombs at the 'Cow and Gate' milk factory, Somerton, which was a conspicuous building marked for many miles around by its tall chimney. The factory received a direct hit and was largely destroyed. Ten houses in the vicinity were badly damaged. Nine people were killed and 37 injured, nine seriously.

Chard Milk Factory

The fourth raid took place at 16.20 on 23 October at Chard Junction on the county border. Once again a milk factory, the Wilts United Dairy, was the target, but the bombs were released so low they bounced clean over the factory which escaped serious damage. One person was killed, five seriously injured and 28 others hurt, some suffering from shock. Three bombs fell in Somerset; the fourth bomb fell over the border in Dorset.

The same day an enemy aircraft was reported over Yeovil at 16.15 flying south-east, but dropped no bombs; it was engaged by ack-ack fire. Also Yeovil barrage lost two balloons that day, one of which grounded at Glenthorne Avenue, Yeovil and the other was last seen drifting in an easterly direction. Machine-gunning by an enemy aircraft was reported at Cudworth, which caused considerable damage to two factories, and ten cottages were slightly damaged.

These four daylight raids demonstrated what a resourceful enemy pilot could do. The authorities stepped up defensive plans. Light anti-aircraft troops were formed, mostly from the railway Home Guard units at the principal junctions and stations. This type of raid was not repeated in Somerset, neither were there any further incidents during 1942.

The only other incidents of note were further aircraft crashes. A Wellington bomber crashed at Holford on 29 October in which one of the crew was killed and four were injured. The same day a USAAF B-24 Liberator bomber struck the top of North Hill, near Minehead, in bad visibility, crashing on the foreshore of Porlock Beach. Eleven of the crew were killed, but apparently the rear gunner escaped after the turret in which he was sitting was knocked from the aircraft as it hit the hill, depositing its occupant on the ground. A memorial to those killed in the crash has been erected at the spot where they died.

There were at least 18 other air accidents in the year, some of which were fatal. The most horrific involved a naval pilot engaged in a night-flying exercise. He took off, but his aircraft failed to gain sufficient height to clear some trees, which clipped the port wing. The aircraft came down at the back of a farm house, but the pilot was still alive. Hearing a terrific crash, the occupants went outside to see the inverted aeroplane in their back yard. They extricated the pilot and took him inside the house. They telephoned the emergency services and ushered the young man, who was complaining of the cold and an injured back, into the front room, where they had a roaring fire going. They laid him flat on the hearth to try and warm him up and massaged his hands to get the circulation going. This seemed to do no good as the pilot asked for the fire to be stoked up, so he could get warm. The couple said they could not put any more on the fire, as they already had a grate full of coal. The young man then sat up and put his hands over the fire and started to rub them together, but as he did so, he suddenly burst into flames. Petrol vapour had impregnated his thick serge uniform and flying clothing. He leapt up and ran through the house a human torch. The elderly couple tried to smother the flames with coats – but all to no avail: the pilot ran from the house only to collapse in a heap over the wing of his aeroplane in the back yard. The emergency services arrived soon afterwards and he was taken by ambulance to hospital, where he later died from his burns.

Two Hurricanes of 759 Squadron from Yeovilton that were involved in a 'tail-chase' exercise collided and crashed on Godney Moor on 5 December, but both pilots were unhurt. Three crew of an Oxford training aircraft from 286 Squadron were killed when it crashed at Durbin's Farm, Nailsea on the 17th. A Wellington from Harwell came down at Beckington on the 30th, the crew were injured, two seriously.

FIVE

Towards D-Day

The year 1943 brought ever increasing allied air activity over Somerset. New airfields were built from which squadrons operated day and night. Other airfields were constructed for the United States Air Forces. As allied air strength grew the enemy's incursions over Somerset became fewer; only six, all at night, being recorded. Only 38 HE bombs were recorded as having fallen during the year, of which 15 were unexploded. Bombs fell at West Coker on 9 January, at Bleadon on 12 March and at Kingsdon on 24 April. These were isolated incidents.

The night of 17/18 May brought more widespread activity with machine-gunning both at Chard and Highbridge; at the latter the night goods train from Exeter to Cardiff was attacked but not damaged. Two parachute mines fell near Wellington damaging the highway and nearby Nowers House, but causing no casualties. These were the last parachute mines to come down in the county. Bombs were also dropped that night at Fordgate, on moorland near North Petherton. Machine-gunning was reported at Langport, but again with no casualties. A stick of nine HE bombs just missed the village of West Pennard, doing little damage save to overhead power lines and orchards. 1943 was remarkable in the fact that no civilians were reported killed or injured by enemy action in the entire year.

Corporal Frederick Alfred Duke BEM

There were some notable air accidents in 1943, but mercifully fewer than the preceeding year. A Wellington bomber from 15 OTU, Hampstead Norris crashed at 19.00 on 23 January near RNAS Yeovilton. Extraordinary heroism was shown by Corporal Frederick Alfred Duke of the 3rd Somerset (Yeovil) Battalion Home Guard. Duke was off duty and cycling home when he heard an aircraft flying very low and in difficulties, then an explosion followed by a crash. He ran towards the crash, but 30 yd from the scene he was thrown to the ground by another explosion which blew him for some distance along the grass. Stunned, he came to and found himself crawling on hands and knees away from the crash, but realising what had happened, got up and went towards the Wellington which was now burning fiercely. Hearing screams coming from the rear gunner who was trapped in his turret, Duke could just see the airman's outline through the flames struggling to get out.

Duke battled to reach the rear of the aircraft and grabbed a machine gun to swing the turret round, but was badly burnt on the hands as he did so. He was joined by both H.R. Bartholomew, a Warrant Writer from nearby RNAS Yeovilton, and a local farmer, Mr E.C. Elford. They succeeded in swinging the turret enough to be able drag its occupant out. This was done in spite of the intense heat and exploding small-arms ammunition and not knowing if the aircraft carried bombs. One of the gunner's rubber boots was burning and Duke managed to remove it despite the molten substance sticking to his hands, swinging the airman's legs free shouting to Bartholomew and Elford to support them, whilst he stuck his head inside the turret to release the man's equipment.

As they dragged the airman out there was another violent explosion. They all threw themselves on the ground, Duke across the airman's face to protect him. The three men managed to carry the gunner about 30 yd from the aircraft to safety, where he was attended to by others that arrived on the scene. Duke returned to the burning Wellington to see if others could be helped, but to no avail and he could see there was no hope for the rest of the five-man crew. He then made his way to the Lamb and Lark Inn where he received first aid for his burns. From there he was taken to the Sick Bay at Yeovilton and detained until 29 January. For his outstanding bravery Duke was awarded the British Empire Medal.

B-17 Flying Fortress "Thumper" of the 303BG crash-landed at Lulsgate after suffering battle damage over Lorient on 23 January. (Smithsonian Institution)

Thumper down

Besides its training function Lulsgate was designated an emergency landing ground. Earlier in the day of 23 January a B-17 Flying Fortress, *Thumper*, from the 303BG, Molesworth, had made an emergency wheels-up landing on the grass after having its hydraulic systems and two engines damaged over Lorient. Lieutenant John Castle and his co-pilot made a safe landing, but the bomber would never fly again as the fuselage was twisted in the landing through the ball turret suspension frame being pushed up into the spine. The rest of the crew of ten had baled out, but one was killed when his parachute failed to open.

Recommended for the Victoria Cross

On 23 February Bomber Command launched their heaviest attack yet on Lorient naval base; 464 aircraft taking part. This was to be the sixth operational sortie of Flight Sergeant George Ashplant and his crew from 166 Squadron, Kirmington, who were among those detailed to attack the target.

The attack was successful and Ashplant was on his way home and flying at about 8,000 ft when the Wellington was struck by another aircraft from underneath. The other aircraft, a Halifax from 158 Squadron, Rufforth, with a seven-man crew, tore off a large part of the Wellington's nose section, including the bomb aimer's parachute stowage and contents. Both propellers on the Wellington were smashed and sent spinning into space.

Ashplant was unable to maintain control of the stricken bomber and soon found he was losing height: 2,000 ft had been lost before he regained some measure of control. He gave his own parachute to the bomb aimer and ordered the crew to abandon the aircraft, having no option but to stay with the aircraft, hoping to effect a safe landing. Somehow he managed to put the aircraft down in the darkness landing in a ploughed field near Kingsbury Episcopi. He climbed out of the wreck to find that not only the nose section and propellers, but incredibly both engines had been torn off as well.

The crew of the Halifax were not so lucky: the aircraft was sent spinning out of control and crashed on flooded moorland near Langport. The crew did not stand a chance of escape and all perished.

Farmworker and Home Guardsman Dick Vearncombe lived in The Avenue, Langport and witnessed the collision. The Halifax crashed near his home:

It was my daughter's birthday – February 13th – and we had promised that she could stay up late and listen to Lord Haw-Haw for a treat. We had a few fowls in the lane and I went down to shut them up and also to tighten the aerial to get a better reception on the radio. All of a sudden I heard an aircraft in trouble and looked up to see this plane coming down in circles making a whirring sound as it spun down. I lay flat on the ground and cover my head. It pitched some distance from me – I didn't know where. I looked up and saw a bright light some way off and thought it was the plane, but a Special Constable came along and said it was not, but was an incendiary that had fallen from one. He said the actual plane had come down nearby in the flooded fields at the end of the lane. The bright light appeared to be at Newtown and eventually we found out that it was where an engine from one of the planes had dropped between the garage and a bungalow in the village.

The next morning Royal Air Force recovery crews

The aftermath of the tragedy at Downside Abbey. The remains of McCraken's Hurricane lie at the foot of the embankment on the boundary of the cricket pitch. Recovery vehicles have arrived from Yeovilton to remove the wreckage. (CRO)

had the difficult task of trying to recover the crew and the wreckage of the Halifax. The only practical means of achieving this was to cast drag lines into the flooded moorland in hopes of recovering wreckage from the aircraft.

Three of the Halifax's crew, Sergeants E.W. King, K.W. Scott and C.W. Steadman, were taken to Bridgwater for burial. For his outstanding courage and act of selflessness in giving his parachute to the bomb aimer, George Ashplant was awarded a Conspicuous Gallantry Medal, although he had been recommended for the Victoria Cross.

Tragically George Ashplant and two of the crew that had been with him did not survive long. He was on his 22nd operation on the night of 24/25 July, when his Wellington was hit by flak over Hamburg – the eighth aircraft out of 12 lost that night, during the first of the attacks on what became known as the Battle of Hamburg. He and his five-man crew were buried in Hamburg Cemetery.

The Downside Tragedy

The most tragic air accident to occur in Somerset during the entire war happened on 15 May, and involved a Sea Hurricane that crashed onto the cricket pitch of Downside Abbey whilst play was in progress, killing nine boys, severely injuring 11 others and with the loss of a young New Zealand pilot from 759 Squadron, Yeovilton. Four other boys were slightly injured.

Sub-lieutenant A.C.H. McCraken and his instructor Sub-lieutenant J. Birch were detailed for exercises involving 'follow the leader' training. The two Hurricanes took off from Yeovilton at 14.30 and flew in the direction of Shepton Mallet. They were observed flying in the vicinity of Downside Abbey at heights estimated to be between 2,000 down to 500 ft or less during the aerobatic manoeuvres performed whilst these exercises were in progress. The two aircraft passed the playing fields several times at fairly low altitude and from different directions.

Birch's aircraft led that of McCraken and then made an approach from the west, pulling up over the playing fields in the process. McCraken failed to do so and his aircraft hit the ground at a slight angle, but not at great speed. The pilot struggled to regain control: the aircraft bounced back into the air, but crashed down again and burst into flames, skidding along the ground towards the cricket pitch. Boys sitting at the boundary, on the edge of an embankment near the pavilion, scattered in a desperate attempt to get out of the way of the careering aircraft. The Hurricane cut a swathe through a number of boys, who could not escape in time, before coming to rest at the bottom of the slope, leaving the dead, injured and dying in its wake. In spite of the danger from exploding ammunition, players and spectators rushed to help the casualties. McCraken was hurled from the aircraft and onto the pitch in front of the pavilion.

There is a memorial tablet in the cloisters at Downside to the boys who lost their lives in this tragedy. Their names are inscribed thereon. They are:

B. L. Patrick (16), D. M. Jennings (10), P. H. P. Rose (14), K. E. C. Stokes (15), L. J. McNabb (15), G. N. Lettes (13), D. H. Lownes (16) and H. G. Dearlove (14). The remains of Sub-lieutenant A.C.H. McCraken RNZNVR are interred at Downside Abbey.

Don't tell I, tell 'ee

At 03.25 on 18 May a Junkers 88 of 1/KG6 was brought down by a nightfighter of 151 Squadron at Bougham Farm, Timberscombe, narrowly missing the attractive village on the borders of Exmoor, before crashing into a willow tree plantation and catching fire. The pilot Leutnant Horst Hahn and observer Obergefreiter Fritz Sagemüller were killed. The other two crew members, wireless operator Unteroffizier Albert Wurtz and flight engineer Feldwebel Otto Bök escaped by parachute, descending near Slowley, between Roadwater and Luxborough.

Witnesses to the crash sent out a search party and came across a neatly folded parachute together with evidence that one of the airmen had eaten some butter and cheese from his emergency pack. They also found a turret and machine guns cast from the aircraft in a field at Styles Farm, Rodhuish. Bök and Wurtz were eventually picked up and taken to the Police Station at Minehead. They had been wandering around until daylight, when one of them came across a member of the 1st (Minehead) Home Guard Battalion and tried to surrender to him. It was then 06.00 and the Home Guard informed his would-be prisoner that he had finished soldiering for the night, his cows would not wait for anybody – not even Germans – so if the airman wished to surrender he had better climb to the top of the hill where he would find a searchlight battery only too pleased to receive him! The Home Guard's response to the German is now Exmoor folklore and reported to have been: "No, I can't be bothered wi' 'ee…I be late fur me work as 'tis."

Dorniers collide over Channel

In the early hours of that same morning a Dornier 217 of 2/KG2 and a Dornier 217 of 3/KG2 collided over the Bristol Channel near the Somerset coast at Woodspring Bay. Detailed to attack Cardiff, an incoming aircraft collided with a returning one. There was only one survivor from the two crews of four men. Unteroffizier Joachim Tröger, the pilot of the 2/KG2 aircraft, managed to swim ashore at Clevedon, being picked up at 05.00. Three days later one of the wrecked aircraft was found on its back and practically submerged on some quicksands about one mile offshore at Woodspring Bay. The wreckage was visible for no more than half an hour at low tide. On 24 May the body of Unteroffizier Werner Grothe (2/KG2) was washed ashore at Burnham-on-Sea and that of Unteroffizier Willie Petzke (3/KG2) at Portishead on 4 June. The body of Unteroffizier Wilhelm Schmidt (2/KG2) was washed ashore at Greenbank, Portishead on 30 June. Unteroffizier Erich Gratz (2/KG2) was found at Woodspring Bay on 19 June, Unteroffizier Fritz Richter (3/KG3) at Llantwit Major on 5 July, Leutnant Emil Holthaus (3/KG3) was not recovered and Unteroffizier Heinrich Schumacher (3/KG3) was eventually recovered and originally buried at Boverton, South Wales before being moved to Cannock Chase.

Spitfire hits train

On 4 June 1943 a Spitfire of 313 Squadron from Churchstanton, practicing a mock attack, hit the second coach of a passenger train on the GWR

A Dornier Do 217E-4 identical to the aircraft from 2/KG2 and 3/KG2 which collided over the Bristol Channel on 18 May. (SAS)

Flying Officer Jaroslav Čermák of 313 Squadron, Churchstanton, was killed when his Spitfire collided with a train on 4 June. (John Sigmund)

main Line at Hillfarrance near Taunton. The Czech pilot Flying Officer Jaroslav Čermák, lost his life and a woman passenger, slightly injured, was taken to Taunton Hospital. Čermák is buried in Wellington Road Cemetery, Taunton.

Bombers down

A Halifax struck the side of Ashley Combe at Porlock Weir, which was shrouded in thick mist, on 11 June and crashed into the wooded hillside. Four of the crew were killed and two injured. Three local men, H.J. Pollard, T.J. Cook and J. Ridler, who had heard the aircraft circling, were on the scene within minutes and rescued the surviving members of the crew, one of whom was found badly injured in some bushes near the wreck but died later. The pilot was rescued under the wing of the Halifax by Cook and Pollard, who also removed a body from the wreck. The three men had difficulty in breathing as the atmosphere was laden with petrol vapour. As Ridler was assisting a completely dazed airman from the scene, the vapour ignited and the force of the explosion swept the two men down the hillside. Ridler, who had no jacket and his shirt sleeves rolled up, suffered third degree burns, but returned to help the injured airman down

the hillside, handing him over to the others, before making his way home, where he collapsed. He was taken to Minehead Hospital and detained for exactly a month. All three men were recommended for a gallantry award and received commendations for bravery.

On 20 August a Wellington, laden with depth charges, unaccountably struck the top of the Quantocks at Buncombe Hill in broad daylight, only one member of the crew surviving, who was attended by two people on the scene, a messenger, Miss E. Brashflower and a warden, Mr H.H. Sweet-Escott. Five of the crew were killed.

The only other incidents during 1943, apart from further air crashes, were on 1 November when there was machine-gunning reported at South Brewham and HE bombs at West Pennard and in Marston Woods near Nunney.

On 31 December a B-17 Flying Fortress of the 351st Bomb Group, Polebrook, returning from a raid on Cognac and Chateaubernard airfields crash-landed at Burnham-on-Sea. The Fortress was seen flying low over the town, passed over the church and flopped down on the mud not far from the lighthouse. The crew of eleven escaped unhurt. The aircraft was apparently recovered by a series of winches attached to a number of tracked vehicles. However, the engines were ripped from the B-17 in the process and the bomber never flew again.

In January 1944 there were two other serious bomber crashes. A Wellington came down at Shapwick on the 21st, killing all four crew and on the 27th a Stirling from 1660 CU Swinderby, crashed at Bridgetown on Exmoor. All eight of the crew, including the pilot, Sergeant R.A. Partridge, lost their lives. A Liberator of the US Navy crashed at Hazel Manor Farm, Compton Martin on 14 March. Five of the crew survived, but five others died.

The Baby Blitz

The Luftwaffe made a last ditch attempt to mount an offensive against Britain; this was the so-called "Baby Blitz" that the Germans coded *Operation Steinbock* and was to last from 21 January to 29 May 1944. As far as Somerset was concerned an isolated incident occurred at Beckington on 5 February followed by two heavier raids.

The night of 27/28 March was curious. There was a widespread blanket of low cloud or mist, so that little could be seen by watchers on the ground. The primary target was evidently Bristol, but Weston-super-Mare was also hit. Powerful anti-aircraft batteries sited there since the last raid immediately went into action and claimed a number of hits. The number of 3.7-in AA guns around Weston-super-Mare had been increased to 21 by this date. Large phosphorous oil incendiary bombs were dropped on the town, but mostly fell in gardens and on railway embankments; some failed to explode in the soft earth. In the meantime a report to Fighter Command brought the nightfighters upon the scene within a few minutes. The enemy scattered and were chased all over the south Somerset. As they turned tail they released their remaining bombs, most of which fell in the area between Weston-super-Mare and Highbridge. At Charlton Mackrell incendiary bombs set light to a hayrick, cottages and one of the many roadside ammunition dumps that had been stockpiled in preparation for D-Day. Ten NFS pumps were involved in trying to control the fire. There were no casualties.

Four hostiles down in a few minutes

The first success of the evening was achieved by an aircraft of No 456 Squadron, Royal Australian Air Force, operating from Ford. A Junkers Ju 88 of 3/KG54 was intercepted at 15,000 ft by Wing Commander Keith Hampshire DSO and his operator, Flying Officer T. Condon, in a Mosquito. The Ju 88 was brought down at Westport, near Isle Brewers at 23.50. All four occupants baled out, but the parachute of 23 year-old wireless operator, Unteroffizier Robert Belz, failed to open. His body was to lie undiscovered in a water-filled ditch at Hungry Mead, Braden Farm until 13 April. A carter from a neighbouring farm noticed something amiss when he let his carthorses out into the field. They kept shying and reared up when passing a certain place. Upon investigation, Belz was discovered.

The other crewmen were all unhurt and taken PoW, one by a member of the local fire brigade. Two of the airmen wandered around until daylight when they walked into Broadfield Farm next to the American aerodrome at Merryfield. They greatly surprised farmer's wife Mrs Ruby Brown, who was milking the cows at the time. She thought the two men were Americans and were drunk having slept rough. She told them

that they were out of bounds and to clear off. Only when they greeted her with "Morgen, Morgen", and on seeing the insignia on their lapels, it dawned upon her that they were Germans. They had deposited their flying kit and parachutes under a bridge before making their way to the farm. Mrs Brown finished the milking, then took the men to the house and gave them some coffee. She sent one of her sons to fetch the police, who came in due course and took the men to Taunton.

At 23.55, a Junkers Ju 88 from Stab/KG54 was brought down on Tadham Moor, near Wedmore. This machine was accredited to the AA gunners at Weston-super-Mare. The aircraft fell on peaty soil and buried itself deeply. Three members of the crew managed to parachute from the aircraft. The wireless operator Unteroffizier Heinrich Schink was found dead the next day; evidently his parachute failed to open. He was buried with full military honours in Ashcombe Road Cemetery, Weston-super-Mare. Parts of the aircraft were dug up from the moor in 1986 and found to be in a remarkable state of preservation. The engines could not be recovered as they were buried too deeply below the 30 ft hole already dug. When items from the Junkers were dug up, petrol poured from some fuel pipes and was able to be ignited with a match – some 42 years later.

At the same time as the crash at Wedmore, the sound of cannon-fire was heard over Taunton and at 00.05 another Junkers Ju 88, this time of 2/KG54, crashed in the drive of Hestercombe House, then occupied by the US Army. The machine burned for some time. Pieces were later found at Flyboat Farm, Pitminster, and on the playing fields of Queen's College, Taunton. The victor in this encounter was a Mosquito of No 219 RAF Squadron from Colerne; Squadron Leader H.V. Ellis and Flight Lieutenant J.M. Craig the crew. The pilot of the Junkers, Leutnant Friedrich Kerkoff, was killed in the attempt to extricate himself from the aircraft; his parachute was found snagged on the canopy. The other three crew members had all baled out successfully.

A Junkers Ju 188 of 5/KG2, the fourth aircraft to be brought down in Somerset that night, fell to Flying Officer Robert Russell and Flight Lieutenant Walter Weir in a Beaufighter of No 68 RAF Squadron from Fairwood Common in South Wales. It came down near the Post Office at Cox-

ley, on the outskirts of the City of Wells at 00.10. The pilot Leutnant Werner Siebert and his crew of four all made safe exits from the stricken aircraft.

Mrs Rene Cross had a lucky escape as the Junkers crashed near her farm:

I heard this plane making a terrible noise and rushed downstairs and pulled the curtain back to have a look. It was heading straight for us, but luckily hit a solitary tree in the middle of Cloverclose Field – no more than 50 yd away – which saved us. There was a mass of flame – bullets and incendiaries were exploding and pinging on the corrugated iron along the edge of the field. We had a horse known as 'the black mare' and three cows in the field – none of them suffered a scratch! The children were terrified. The neighbours and their children came to the house – we had nine kids sleeping in the front room, but none of us adults could sleep, so I made tea all night. In the morning the field was covered in mist and there was a lone policeman sitting on a stile guarding the wreckage. He was frozen and was very grateful for a cup of my tea.

The nightfighters of the RAF brought down 15 enemy aircraft in the western counties that night out of an estimated force of 50. By early morning Taunton Police Station was uncomfortably crowded with German airmen held there awaiting RAF escort.

Although HE bombs fell over such a wide area, casualties were remarkably few. Five civilians were killed, four of whom lived in bungalows that were destroyed on the Oldmixon to Hutton road near Weston-super-Mare, and one other person was injured. A serviceman was also killed

The burial of wireless operator Unteroffizier Heinrich Schink at Weston-super-Mare after his Junkers Ju 88 was brought down on Tadham Moor by AA fire from Weston's guns on 27 March. The firing party was provided by RAF Locking. (Norbert Uhlenbrock)

Mervyn Sweet displays the rear fuselage section of the Junkers Ju 88 dug up on Tadham Moor 43 years after it was shot down. (Author)

in the Weston-super-Mare area and two people injured. One other person was killed that night at Lower Milton, near Wells, and a man injured at Bridgwater. Ten houses were seriously damaged at Cannington by one HE bomb and incendiaries; 28 others were slightly damaged.

Bombs were reported to have been dropped, some of which caused fires, at Beckington, Bleadon, Cannington, Edingworth, Masbury, Milton near Wells, Over Stowey, Radstock, Weare, West Sutton, Windwhistle, Winford and Wrington. Incendiaries fell at Bridgwater, Burnham-on-Sea, Chilton Polden, Chewstoke, East Huntspill, Highbridge, Isle Brewers, Keynsham, Leigh on Mendip, North Petherton, Sharpham, Taunton and Wookey Hole.

Many of the bombs dropped on this raid failed to explode, providing the bomb disposal squads of the Royal Engineers and of the Home Guard with one of the biggest jobs they had had during the war. Roads were closed and traffic diverted for considerable periods while this work was in progress. The phosphorous bombs were poisonous to cattle and great efforts were made to clear the farmlands as soon as possible. Two weeks later there were still 122 UXBs to be dealt with and the last was not cleared until the end of the year.

The last two German aircraft to be shot down in Somerset fell at 02.30 on the 15 May. Wreckage of the Junkers Ju 188 from 2/KG6 that crashed at Inwood House, Henstridge is lifted by crane during salvaging operations. (PRO)

Flight Lieutenant John Hall (left) and Flying Officer 'Jock' Cairns of 488 (NZ) Squadron, seen with their Mosquito, were responsible for shooting down the Ju 188 at Henstridge. (SAS)

The other aircraft to be brought down on the 15th, a Dornier Do 217K of 7/KG2, fell near Camel Cross. Another crew from 488 Squadron, Flying Officers Ray Jeffs and Ted Spedding, seen here, claimed this victory. (SAS)

The weapon: Ray Jeffs' Mosquito ME-Z at its home base, Colerne 1944. (Ray Jeffs)

Luftwaffe's last effort

On 24 April bombs were dropped at Batheaston, Stoke-under-Ham and Wrantage and then on 15 May came the enemy's last effort over Somerset. The intended target is unknown but bombs fell in such widely separated places as Bicknoller, Buckland Dinham, Combe St Nicholas, near Milverton, near Rode, Whatley and Wincanton.

The Royal Air Force was active: a Mosquito of 488 (RNZAF) Squadron, Zeals, crewed by Flying Officer J.A.S. Hall and his radar operator, Flight Lieutenant J.P. Cairns, engaged a Junkers JU 188 of 2/KG6 and shot it down at 02.30 in the grounds of Inwood House, Henstridge. This machine, whilst being chased, dropped two bombs in South Street, Wincanton. One struck the Westminster Bank where one person was killed and four injured. These were the last civilian casualties by enemy action in Somerset. Sixty-three buildings were damaged in Wincanton, including a church, five hotels and four halls. Three of the Junkers' crew survived and two were killed. The pilot Leutnant Gerhard Wentz, Unteroffiziers Karl Fritz and Karl Hoyer were taken prisoner, one had walked up the main railway line to Templecombe and was captured at the station by a member of the Home Guard. Unteroffizier Hilmar Korf and Gefreiter Büttner were buried in the Haycombe Cemetery, Bath.

Half an hour later another Mosquito from the same squadron, piloted by Flying Officer R.G. Jeffs RNZAF, with his A1 operator, Flying Officer E. Spedding, brought down the last enemy aircraft to fall in Somerset. It was a Dornier 217 of 7/KG2 and came down at Camel Cross near Yeovilton. Three of the crew survived, but the pilot, Leutnant Johannes Domschke was killed. He was buried in Bridgwater, but moved to Cannock Chase in 1963. The survivors were taken prisoner. The aircraft was completely burnt out – it was seen from Zeals airfield by other members of No 488 Squadron, picked out in a searchlight diving towards the ground with one engine on fire and smoking badly.

There was no further enemy activity over Somerset during May 1944 and indeed, for the rest of the war. A total of 668 people had been killed due to enemy action, 665 seriously and 943 others injured. In addition, nearly 35,000 buildings had been destroyed or damaged.

The county was almost bursting at the seams, laden with men and equipment ready to use it as a springboard for the biggest invasion to be launched on occupied territory in the history of man. D-Day was about to begin.

SIX

D-Day to Victory

"These are great days; they are like the days in Lord Chatham's time, of which it was said you had to get up early in the morning not to miss some news of Victory."
Winston S Churchill

Somerset was one of the bases from which the attack on Hitler's Fortress Europe was mounted. Thousands of troops, aircraft and equipment were gathered in the county for the assault that would lead to final victory.

The plan for mounting that invasion was unfolded during a secret conference in the Judge's Dining Room at the Shire Hall, Taunton, on 22 March 1944. There was no mention of a date – it was simply 'D-Day'. It was explained that Southern England was to be divided into 'Concentration' and 'Marshalling' areas. Troops – in the case of Somerset, almost wholly American – were to be concentrated in the first-named areas, moving gradually into the latter, which were immediately behind the actual embarkation points.

Somerset on Guard

Amongst those who gathered were Brigadier-General C.L. Norman and Colonel G.H. Rogers, commanding respectively the South and North Somerset Home Guard Sectors; the commanders of all the southern battalions; Superintendent White of the Somerset Constabulary; staff officers from Somerset sub-district of Southern Command and from South Sector Headquarters. To these people would fall the responsibility guarding vital areas and the movement of troops through the county.

In the marshalling areas it would be impossible to provide sufficient camps for the waiting troops. Whole areas would be set aside and completely cut off from public access. There was to be no contact with the outside world once the men had been briefed on their invasion duties.

The position of Somerset, leading to the western ports, made it a potential focal area for possible enemy attacks. Protection of essential lines

Members of the Langport Home Guard set up communication links at Somerton Tunnel prior to D-Day. (CRO)

of communication from any interruption, whether open attack or minor sabotage, was discussed at the Taunton conference.

Plans were drawn up for reception centres to receive Home Guard and American Army casualties in the event of such an attack, which would have been Doniford Camp, Watchet; Middleway Camp, Taunton; Houndstone Barracks, Yeovil; Edgarley Hall, Glastonbury; Brent Knoll; Highbridge; Sunnyside Road, Clevedon and Camerton Court, Bath. The last two were intended for casualties from Anti-Aircraft Command.

It was agreed that certain bridges and tunnels would be guarded in South Somerset and that there should be a watch on a stretch of the West

Somerset coast. The particular locations concerned were Somerset Bridge, Bridgwater; Cogload Flyover; the railway tunnels at White Ball; Somerton; the viaduct at Venn Cross and parts of the Southern main line near Yeovil. The 1st (Minehead) Battalion Home Guard would take responsibility to provide a coastal watch between Glenthorne and Porlock. The Military Police were to take up duty at selected vulnerable points by day to be relieved by the Home Guard, in greater strength, from dusk to dawn. To the Police fell the task of road diversions for civilian traffic.

On 20 April security restrictions were enforced on coastal regions and on the 24th operational orders for the defence of the railway lines took effect. Taunton 'A' and 'C' Company Home Guard protected White Ball Tunnel each evening, where an old railway coach was used as a guardroom. Each end of the tunnel was connected by a telephone line installed by the railway company. Both the Cogload Flyover and the railway bridge at Norton Fitzwarren were the responsibility of 'B' Company of the 2nd Somerset Battalion Home Guard. The Langport Home Guard Company mounted guard at both ends of the Somerton Tunnel, with communication links between the companies.

A minor case of sabotage occurred during the precautionary period. A Home Guard company reported from White Ball that telephone wires connecting them with the 3rd Devons had been cut. Simultaneously came the information that a convict had escaped from Dartmoor and was known to be making his way eastwards dressed as a Home Guard sergeant. All guards and patrols were warned. The convict, who exchanged his Home Guard uniform for grey flannels and a tweed jacket, managed to make his way to London; he was apprehended a few months later. An inquiry into the wirecutting incident produced no results.

The build-up

As the weeks wore on, the ammunition dumps by the main roads and farm lanes of Central Somerset grew bigger by the day. Jeeps and lorries began to appear with vertical flexible pipes from their exhaust systems – part of waterproofing devices whereby they could be driven off landing craft. Tanks had long been a familiar sight; rescue launches, landing barges, steam

tugs and other strange craft were added. One one occasion a seagoing tug was seen in an enormous conveyor on the top of the Blackdown Hills, shepherded fore and aft by police motorcycles, to avoid going under any bridges whilst it traversed Somerset.

Elizabeth Wallbridge remembers her father had a laborious task to perform prior to D-Day:

I helped my father measure every bridge in the county on all major roads. The reason was never disclosed at the time, but subsequently it was known that it was for the movement of Mulberry Harbour sections to the coast, and also other bulky equipment that was needed for the Normandy landings.

USAAF Troop Carrier Wing moves in

During the last week in April, the 50th Troop Carrier Wing of the IX Troop Carrier Command USAAF, started to move to its allocated air bases in the South West. These were at Exeter, Upottery, Merryfield and Weston Zoyland, and excepting the latter, 400 gliders would take off from these airfields in the assault phase of 'Overlord'. Four Squadrons, the 99th, 100th, 301st and 302nd of the 441st Troop Carrier Group moved into Merryfield with their Douglas C-47 Skytrains and Waco gliders, although some construction work was still going on - it did not prevent the base becoming operational. Advanced elements of the 442nd Troop Carrier Wing arrived at Weston Zoyland on 23 April and on 20 May, the first of their gliders flew in.

Training got underway at both Somerset airfields, where 6,000 ft main runways had been laid in preparation for an aerial armada of gliders and tugs. Local residents became used to seeing massed formations of C-47s towing their gliders around the sky. Nights were busy too, with simulated troop-drops taking place. By the end of May, the 441st and 442nd TCGs were proficient in marshalling their gliders and tugs, enabling rapid hook-ups and take-offs to be achieved from the runways. No troops were actually dropped over Somerset during these preparations.

To these groups would fall the task of dropping élite pathfinding elements of the 82nd and 101st US Airborne Division to their designated dropping zones (DZs), on D-Day. This was to be near Ste Mère Église in order to seize road/rail bridges and other strategic points around the River Mer-

A familiar scene before D-Day: Troop Carrier wings of the USAAF practised towing their gliders across Somerset skies. A C-47 Skytrain of the 53rd TCW takes off "somewhere in England" with a Horsa. (IWM)

deret in preparation for the main assault with glider-borne troops that would follow.

Armies on the move

The movement of troops to the marshalling areas began on 15 May. Somerset, for the most part, was a concentration area; transport and armour collected on little-used roads and gradually moved off into Devon and Cornwall, where 17 special camps and 12 areas had been set aside for the concentration of troops.

D-Day

Embarkations began on 31 May and were completed by midnight of 2 June. Delayed by bad weather for 24 hours, the assault on Normandy was launched on 6 June. The only troops to sail from Somerset shores were part of two divisions which sailed from Portishead. The initial attack on both the British and American sectors of Normandy was made by parachute and glider-borne troops.

Residents in the Vale of Taunton who were awake in the first hour of the 6th saw the massed squadrons of the 50th TCW with their C-47 Skytrains (Dakotas) rising from the brightly-lit aerodrome at Merryfield, near Ilminster, at an average of ten-second intervals. This was the first of two serials of *Albany* (the parachute assault) which

carried the vanguard made up of the 1st Battalion, part of the 2nd, and Regimental Headquarters of the 501st Parachute Infantry Regiment. In the lead aircraft were Lieutenant Colonel Theodore Kershaw, the Group commander, and Colonel Howard R. Johnson, the regimental commander.

The second serial would take most of the 2nd Battalion of the 501st, half an engineer company and some medical personnel. A total of 91 aircraft took off from Merryfield this night. The sky over Taunton was temporarily filled with twinkling lights, for in addition to the normal navigation lights of peacetime, each aircraft carried recognition lamps on the leading edge of the wings. The sight would never be forgotten by many who witnessed it, for it was truly spectacular. Each Skytrain carried 18, sometimes more, fully-equipped paratroopers. Some men weighed as much as 325 pounds when loaded and had to be boosted to board their aircraft, rather like knights of old hoisted onto their horses!

Similar activities were going on in other adjoining counties: a third serial of 45 aircraft was flown by the 440th from Exeter. The 441st reached its DZs with relatively few losses, but had encountered cloud over France and broke up. The first

Paratroops of the 501st Infantry Regiment, 101st US Airborne Division, pose briefly by the aircraft of Colonel Theodore Kershaw, Group Commander of the 441st TCG at Merryfield, shortly before take-off in the first hour of 6 June...D-Day. (Dave Benfield)

serial started its drop at 01.26, the second serial at 01.34. Between them 1,475 troops were carried, of which at least 1,429 were dropped. Amongst those returned were one soldier who fainted, plus 12 who had slipped on vomit and became entangled with each other. The 440th began their drop at 01.40 and managed to put down 719 out of 723 carried: flak wounded one man and he blocked the exit of the other three.

All three waves lost less than five per cent of their aircraft. One aircraft blew up before reaching the DZ, another crashed after dropping its load. A third hit by AA fire forced-landed near Cherbourg, but the crew eventually managed to make their way back to Allied lines. One aircraft returned to its base damaged and was only fit for scrap. Another 14 aircraft of the 441st were damaged in the course of the operations. Many stragglers from the first serial of the 441st and some from other waves had to make two or three passes over the DZs to orientate themselves. Only one aircraft gave up and returned without dropping its load. Most had returned to Merryfield by dawn.

D-Day plus one

Another serial of the 441st TCG commenced take off from Merryfield at 07.17 on 7 June; this time with 50 aircraft and 50 Waco gliders. They carried 363 troops, mostly service personnel of the 325th and 401st Regiments (82nd Airborne Division); 18 tons of equipment, including twelve 81 mm mortars; 20 Jeeps; 9 trailers and 6 tons of ammunition. A pathfinder aircraft, piloted by Colonel Julian M. Chappell, commander of the 50th Wing, and Lieutenant Colonel Kershaw of the 441st, guided the aircraft to their zone.

Some of the troop carriers had been seriously overloaded, making them difficult to handle. The sky was leaden and the air so turbulent that spectators on the ground could observe the gliders pitching, sometimes quite violently. The C-47s with their charges made their way across the channel with a reassuring escort of fighters to LZ 'W'. The release of the gliders commenced at 08.51. The 441st lost no aircraft, but eight were damaged by small-arms fire. All C-47s arrived back at around 10.25. Throughout the day a shuttle-service was operated with varying numbers of aircraft, mainly on supply drops.

Of the men and materials dropped on the first mission, 25 gliders landed on the zone, another 19 were within one mile of it and the remaining six were not far off it. Although eight Wacos were

destroyed, there was only one death among the airborne occupants and 15 people injured; whilst 18 out of the 20 Jeeps and eight out of the nine trailers came though unscathed. One glider pilot was killed and five injured.

Warrant Officer Gordon Allen, an ex-Beaufighter RAF pilot, was amongst the aircrew who flew from Merryfield:

I had been transferred to the Americans to gain some experience in handling C-47s with gliders and posted to Merryfield. It was like a holiday camp compared to an RAF station. There was very little formality like saluting – all very casual really. We had extra rations; much more food than we had been used to and of infinitely superior quality. We practised day and night flying in formation, with and without gliders in tow. We eventually became very proficient at it. I made several round trips to Ste Mère Église – I forget how many it was exactly – possibly five or six – on supply missions and with troops. We landed, refuelled, checked the aircraft and off again – it was quite hectic. I also towed gliders on at least three or four occasions – all of which were laden with men. The first time I landed in France, sometime after D-Day, it was at Lille on a metal mesh surface.

The 442nd

The bulk of the 2,200 USAAF personnel of the 442nd Troop Carrier Group started to move into Weston Zoyland on 10 June and during the next few days 76 C-47 Skytrains and 100 gliders also moved in. They too had taken part in the operations during this period and managed to deliver their troops without suffering too many casualties and had operated on D-Day from Fulbeck in Lincolnshire. Their destination was DZ 'T', some two miles south of Ste Mère Église. Forty-five C-47s were involved and they took the 1st Battalion 507th Parachute Infantry Regiment together with the Regimental Headquarters, dropping them at 02.40. Three aircraft were shot down and 28 received minor damage. The following day 56 aircraft took part in *Memphis*, the re-supply mission for the American 101st Airborne Division. Some 21 aircraft were damaged by small-arms fire, but only two persons were injured. The 442nd TCG operated four squadrons, the 303rd, 304th, 305th and 306th and stayed at Weston Zoyland until October.

Royal Observer Corps

An active rôle was played by No 22 Group Headquarters of the Royal Observer Corps, Yeovil. On the night of 5 June more than 5,000 aircraft operated over the Group. Sixteen Somerset members

Opposite: *'B' Company of the 2nd Battalion Home Guard on duty at Cogload flyover on D-Day. (CRO)*

Right: *The fighters from RAF Culmhead were kept busy during the first week in June 1944, with many raids over occupied Europe. (PRO)*

OPERATIONS RECORD BOOK

Page N

K.R. and A.C.I. chapter XX. and

of (Unit or Formation) R.A.F. STATION, CULMHEAD.

No. of pages used for da

SECRET.

Date	Time	Summary of Events	
1.6.44.		In the morning, 8 aircraft of 131 Squadron, operating in two sections of four, carried out Rhubarb No.265. The first section, flying to Guingamp, Morlaix and Landernau claim 1 locomotive damaged. P/O. Atkinson (aus) was hit by flak and failed to return. The second section damaged 3 locomotives and a small camouflaged lorry. In the evening, 8 aircraft of 616 Squadron carried out Rhubarb No.266. The first fighter sweep claim 1 locomotive damaged. The second fighter sweep damaged 6 railway wagons and destroyed a motor lorry. They also attacked a concentration of railway trucks and engines, claiming 1 locomotive and many trucks damaged.	
		S/Ldr. A. E. R. Gilligan and Plt/O. D. H. Fletcher, Area Welfare Officers visited the Station. F/Lt. J. T. Craig, arrived from Colerne, for Intelligence duties.	
2.6.44.		8 aircraft of 126 Squadron carried out Rhubarb No.267. The operation was not completed owing to bad weather, and the aircraft returned early. 6 aircraft of 616 Squadron carried out an A/S/R patrol for a pilot of 41 Squadron off N.E. of Guernsey. The dinghy was located and patrolled until relieved by 131 Squadron. 4 aircraft of 126 Squadron escorted a Warwick to the scene and later saw the pilot picked up by lifeboat from Herm.	
3.6.44.		A section of 126 Squadron, detailed to carry out an early morning shipping recco to St. Peter Port and Lezardrieux had to abandon the mission owing to bad weather. 1 aircraft crashed soon after take off, but the pilot (F/Lt. Owen) is safe. The other three aircraft landed at Exeter. In the afternoon, 8 aircraft of 126 Squadron operating in two sections, carried out Rhubarb No.270. The first section claim 1 locomotive, 1 6-ton van and 4 camouflaged lorries damaged. The second section sighted a train but did not attack.	
4.6.44.		Bad weather restricted activity apart from a convoy patrol by 126 Squadron and standing patrols by 616 squadron.	
5.6.44.		4 aircraft of 131 Squadron on patrol S. of Lyme Bay, sighted a line of objects thought to be possible shipping, but afterwards identified as rocks. A further 2 aircraft of the same Squadron investigated the report but sighted nothing. Instructions received confining all personnel to camp until further notice. Easily identified markings painted on aircraft.	
6.6.44.		131 squadron led by W/Cdr. Brothers, D.F.C. formed the first fighter sweep in Rodeo No.156. 616 Squadron formed the second fighter sweep. 131 squadron claim 2 locomotives, a goods train, 3 staff cars, 4 military vehicles, and lorries damaged. 1 aircraft of 616 returned early, and the rest attacked and damaged a goods train and a locomotive, and destroyed 4 military trucks. Information received that the Allies had made several landings on the French coast in the Le Havre area. The operation proceeded according to plan with very little enemy air opposition.	

of the Corps went to sea as aircraft identifiers, attached to the Royal Navy during D-Day and subsequent operations and remained afloat until the attacks of the Luftwaffe no longer offered a serious menace to cross-channel shipping. In due course they were awarded the France and Germany Star, being probably the only members of the Somerset Defence Forces to earn that distinction while so serving.

Flow of men and materials

Units of the American V Corps, whose headquarters had been at Norton Manor, Taunton, landed on the western Normandy beaches, where due to the presence on manoeuvres of an additional German division, greater resistance was met than anywhere else during the initial stages.

It has been estimated that during the height of the attack the flow of American men and materials from the South Coast ports in western England was at the rate of 45,000 men and 6,000 vehicles daily. In Somerset the great depots worked at feverish speed. The piles of ammunition stacked along the roads began to diminish

rapidly. There was a constant flow of military vehicles, particularly on the Fosse Way, and in the reverse direction came the Red Cross trains and ambulances, bringing casualties to the six American General Hospitals situated within the county.

In the following few weeks the presence of the US troops would diminish to a significant degree. As the Allied armies swept on, the backup operations would be gradually transferred to Europe. Things were to become much quieter in the county as the war in Europe drew to a close. The climax was past – life began to return to something like normal.

Two more Fortresses down

There was still great aerial activity – some of which resulted in aircraft coming down in the county. A B-17 Flying Fortress crashed in an orchard at Higher Ilbere, Kingston on 25 June and burst into flames. The aircraft had been abandoned by its crew, but not over Somerset. Another B-17 crashed on the same day at Snag Farm, Wincanton. The aircraft from the 91st

Bomb Group had been battle-damaged and the nine crew were killed. Another American aircraft, a UC 64A Norseman, crashed on 10 July at South Brewham with the loss of three lives. Six lives were lost when a Wellington of 12 OTU Chipping Warden crashed at Uplands Lane, Keynsham on 26 August.

Arnhem's first Casualties

Operation Market – the plan for the British 1st Airborne Division to hold the bridge across the Rhine at Arnhem had begun. At 10.00 on Sunday 17 September 1944, Stirling bombers began towing Horsa gliders off from Keevil airfield in Wiltshire. Gradually these and other aircraft assembled over the Bristol Channel into a great aerial armada, passed over Weston-super-Mare and set course for Holland.

The massed formation approached Paulton when suddenly and without warning tragedy struck: a glider flying 1,500 ft in the middle of the stream broke up in mid-air, shedding its complete tail section, which fell in the Farringdon Road. The stricken Horsa plunged vertically towards the ground, carrying its two crew and 21 men of the 9th Airborne Field Company, Royal Engineers to their deaths.

It crashed in a field known as Double Hills. Those on board never had a chance and were fated to be the first casualties of the Arnhem campaign. The Stirling towing the glider immediately broke out of the formation in a diving turn, heading back against the oncoming stream of aircraft in order to take stock of the situation on the ground before flying back with all speed to Keevil, where the pilot jumped in a Jeep and immediately returned to the scene.

People had come out of their houses to watch the once-in-a-lifetime spectacle of the massed formation of Stirlings and Halifaxes towing their charges across Somerset skies. Amongst those who witnessed what happened was 15 year-old Ron Hansford, who lived nearby:

The sky was black with gliders and other aircraft – we all stood open-mouthed in awe at witnessing such

Stirlings of 299 Squadron and Horsa gliders marshal at Keevil on the morning of 17 September in preparation for operation 'Market'. (IWM)

The Horsa crash at Farringdon Gurney has produced these artefacts retrieved over recent years, including belt and webbing buckles, fly buttons, .303 bullets, cartridge cases, cordite sticks, penicillin ointment tubes, a razor handle and perspex from the aircraft's canopy. (Author)

a sight. Suddenly we saw a glider break up into several pieces and plunge down to earth – it all seemed so unreal and none of us grasped what was happening for a moment or two. Other bits of the plane were fluttering down to earth like confetti. Several of us ran as fast as we could to the field where the wreckage lay. We got there in a few minutes to find a scene of total devastation....the aircraft was on fire – explosive charges were detonating and ammunition was exploding sending the bullets flying everywhere. We then saw, to our horror, that there were bodies of soldiers in the wreckage. They were in one big pile – all on top of one another – although some had been blown to pieces and parts of them were scattered all over the field. We tried desperately to free the men who remained tangled together and I grabbed the leg of one of them – he was still on fire, but it was no good. There was nothing more that could be done for them and we had to wait for the Paulton Fire Brigade who arrived about an hour later and put out the fire; they removed the bodies from the wreckage and carried them to a big oak tree a few yards away under which they laid them out and covered them up until the ambulances arrived and took them away to Weston-super-Mare.

The Royal Engineers on board had been carrying explosive charges, hand-grenades and various types of ammunition; also included in the cargo were several 'Corgi' miniature motor-cycles which had full tanks of petrol, all of which contributed to the catastrophic results of the crash. These were scattered about the field together with other items of equipment and bits were still being picked up months later. There has never been proof of what caused the disaster to Horsa RJ 113.

There was a twist to this episode as the crew of the Stirling, LK 148 of 299 Squadron, went on a supply dropping mission in their aircraft to Arnhem two days later and were shot down behind British lines. The co-pilot was badly wounded and had to have his leg amputated by a British Medical Officer. He was eventually taken prisoner by the Germans and spent considerable time in hospital.

Two years after the crash, Ron Hansford and his brother went 'nutting' under a hedge in the field and found a piece of a human nose and part of a jaw with three teeth and a complete .303 rifle bullet, which had not gone off, was lodged in the bone. Fragments of wreckage have been recovered over recent years including webbing buckles, tunic and fly buttons, ointment tubes, pieces of perspex and fabric covering.

The 23 victims were buried with full military honours and now lie interred at the Milton Road cemetery in Weston-super-Mare:

Glider Pilots
Sgt Fraser R.A.; L/Sgt Gardner L.J.
Royal Engineers
Sgt Oakey A.F.; L/Sgt Allen R.H.; Cpl Clampitt A.L.; L/Cpl Pickburn E.V.; L/Cpl Burrow W.H.; Spr Beale J.C.; Spr Cuthbertson A.; Spr Calvert C.W.; Spr Carney R.; Spr Davis F.A.S.; Spr Fernyhough J.; Spr Evans J.; Spr Godfrey E.J.; Spr Hall A.; Spr Holtham D.E.; Spr Street A.R.; Spr Sheppard E.E.; Spr Turner G.; Spr Westfield J.; Spr Watt A.G.; Spr Williamson J.S.

A memorial to the men was recently erected at Double Hills, where an annual parade and service is held as near to 17 September as possible to commemorate the men killed. The parade is organised by the Double Hills Arnhem Committee.

The memorial at Double Hills in the field near the crash site. (Author)

Halifax crash at Long Ashton

There was a serious accident involving a Halifax bomber of 1662 Heavy Conversion Unit, Blyton, on 23 November, when it crashed at Parsonage Farm, Long Ashton. The seven Polish crew all lost their lives. A memorial to the crew has been erected in recent years at the site of the crash. This was the last crash involving serious loss of life in Somerset during the war.

The final curtain

There came the stand down of the Home Guard and the relaxation of Civil Defence duties in December. The month saw countless farewell dances, suppers and concerts. The camaraderie was obvious amongst those that had served together: bonds of friendship between all those that were united in a common cause would not be equalled. Now peace was near the ties would be broken, but never forgotten.

The Surrender

23 April saw the blackout end in Britain – the lights were begining to shine all over the land. Hitler died by his own hand on 30 April – the Russians were entering Berlin. On 3 May at Lüneburg Heath, Field Marshal Montgomery received the unconditional surrender of all the German forces opposing him in Northwest Germany, Holland, the Islands, Schleswig-Holstein and Denmark. Two days later Admiral von Freiberg met General Dwight D. Eisenhower at Rheims where he took the surrender of all German forces on the western front. Finally, the total unconditional surrender of all German forces was signed at 02.41 on 7 May, with effect for all hostilities to cease at midnight on 8 May: the war in Europe was at an end.

Celebrations

The day was marked by celebrations held county-wide. In Taunton on the evening of VE Day hundreds of people gathered in the church of St Mary Magdalene where the clergy conducted a spontaneous service. For hours the congregations came and went, crowds pressing in as others left, until in the small hours of morning and with yet a full church, the clergy were forced

The war in Europe is over and time to celebrate. Street parties are held all over the county. This one is in Stradling Avenue, Weston-super-Mare. (N.A. Perriman)

by sheer exhaustion to bring this remarkable service to a close. On the following Sunday a great Drumhead Service was held in Vivary Park, attended by British and American Forces and all the uniformed organisations in the town. Burning of blackout curtains on bonfires in the streets, and on the beach at Minehead, exploding thunderflashes, marked the celebrations. A Union flag fluttered from the top of Dunkery Beacon. The last train loads of evacuees were going home – the danger over.

VJ Day was celebrated on 15 August. A feature of the evening at Taunton was the number of bonfires in the streets and the vast crowds which assembled. One particularly remembered the long procession of Americans carrying their national flag and firing endless volleys from Very pistols from which the bluish lights floated down gracefully, each beneath its tiny parachute.

Thus ended V Day 1945 and so the curtain fell on the story of Somerset at War – it was again at peace. Now it was time to remember those lost in the struggle: the loved ones who would not return to the fold or to the county that was theirs...

PART II

WAR MACHINE

This superb photograph taken shortly before the outbreak of war shows the ack-ack range at Doniford with troops engaged in firing practice. (Kit Houghton)

SEVEN

Fortified and Prepared

SOMERSET'S PILLBOXES

Ironside's plan

Following surveys carried out by the various Army Commands, who sent out teams to survey the countryside, General Sir Edmund Ironside, Commander-in-Chief Home Forces, and his staff devised a plan that would involve the construction of defence lines by which London and the Midlands were protected with the GHQ Line and a series of command, corps and divisional stoplines. The country was thus divided into defence lines with strong points centred on various villages and towns. This plan was completed by 12 June, put to the Chiefs of Staff and Winston Churchill on the 25th and given qualified approval. The Fortification and Works Branch of the Royal Engineers, together with others, was given the responsibility of the construction of defences and the distribution of stores.

With enemy occupation of the Channel and Biscayan coasts of France it became clear that the West of England was vulnerable to attack, both from the north and south. If the enemy occupied Ireland, however unlikely, the Bristol Channel would be wide open and an obvious point from which to attempt a landing in conjunction with one made on the South Coast. The narrowness of the West Country from the South Coast to the Bristol Channel across Somerset seemed to invite attack. Its loss would have cut off the western naval ports and opened a way to the industrial Midlands and across to London. The leg of Britain would therefore have been amputated and could play no further part in the war.

Therefore it was decided to erect a chain of forts between the Bristol and English Channels. Hinged to the northern end of the line was another extending eastwards across the county and a third running south again to make a defensive 'box', including parts of Somerset, Devon, Wiltshire and Dorset. In addition, the northern Somerset coast was partly fortified from Porlock to the Parrett estuary and beyond.

This mammoth task required an army of workers and vast quantities of cement, sand and other materials. The pillboxes were usually octagonal with a massive central pillar supporting the roof, which, like the walls was three feet thick. This was thought to be proof against the heaviest aircraft bombs and also against the largest calibre guns which an invading force could bring to bear.

The pillboxes were sited for all-round defence although the anti-tank ditches and defensive wiring of the north to south line were constructed to meet an attack from the west. Pillboxes in open country were high enough to give a wide field of fire. The embrasures were small and suitable only for rifle and machine gun fire, although where they commanded roads or railways they were large enough for mortars and anti-tank weapons. This type was mostly sunk well into the ground.

The largest pillboxes were constructed to take the 2-pounder anti-tank gun and in some case a 3-pounder or even a 6-pounder, the latter two of which were naval weapons dating back to the First World War. Considerable doubt remained whether there was ammunition available for the latter in sufficient quantities. However, the 2-pounder was an effective anti-tank weapon for its day and could be used to good advantage against the early marks of Panzers, but would be outclassed by the end of the war. The design and construction of the 6-pounder type of pillboxes left a lot to be desired: they had enormous apertures in the front to give a wide arc of fire; because of this they were extremely vulnerable to shell, grenade or flame-thrower attack. Having no rear entrance the only way that manning crews could gain entry was through the front, offering no chance of escape in the event of a sustained frontal attack.

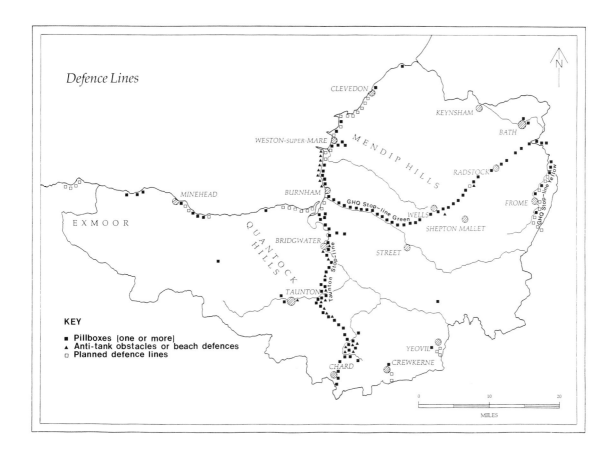

Defence Lines

KEY
■ Pillboxes (one or more)
▲ Anti-tank obstacles or beach defences
□ Planned defence lines

The Stop Lines

The Taunton Stop Line, from the estuary of the Parrett to the English Channel at Seaton on the mouth of the Axe, consisted of 355 pillboxes; the GHQ 'Green' Line from Highbridge eastwards to Freshford on the Wiltshire boundary, which followed natural and artificial waterways using topographical features where possible, had 107; the 'Yellow' Line from the confluence of the rivers Avon and Frome near Bath to the Wiltshire boundary, had 46. In addition, the Somerset coast defences contained 233 and the airfield defences 112 of these forts. Twenty-six of the pillboxes in the Taunton Stop Line were in Devon, so the total within Somerset was 828. If one added the smaller type erected to cover road blocks in the towns and the approaches to certain factories, the total in Somerset probably exceeded one thousand.

The first scheme provided for continuous lines of forts, mostly sited on the banks of rivers and canals. Efforts were made to deepen the River Isle near Ilminster, but the river silted up as fast as it was excavated. Where there were no natural barriers, artificial ditches were dug. At intervals there were strongly fortified areas which could be held whether the lines were pierced elsewhere or not – a principle adopted by the Germans two years later in Russia and known then as 'hedgehogs'.

Construction at all speed

Construction of the pillboxes was undertaken by private contractors. Early in June 1940 a meeting was held at the County Hotel, Taunton, under the chairmanship of Mr Stansell of Messrs Stansell and Son of Taunton, a leading firm of local builders. A general also attended and told the assembled builders exactly what the War Office wanted. Absolute priority was given to the supply of necessary materials.

Work began immediately and was greatly

View looking south-west from a pillbox designed for a 6-pounder ex-naval gun on the Taunton Stop Line at Curry Mallet. Note the gun mounting still in situ and the magazine area underneath the apron of the aperture. This position would have been lethal for the defenders. (Author)

Typical of the brick-faced Type 24 pillbox is represented by this example on the Taunton & Bridgwater Canal near Fordgate. On the opposite bank are 'pimple' anti-tank obstacles. (Author)

aided by the remarkably fine summer that year. Civilian labour was supplemented by the Pioneer Corps; even the maintenance staff of British Cellophane were employed in the construction of pillboxes. The most serious obstacle was the very soft subsoil encountered in many places, resulting in a few of the pillboxes starting to lean at odd angles before they could be completed. They weighed hundreds of tons, so this was difficult to remedy, but these problems were overcome with little delay. As invasion was expected from hour to hour speed was essential. Many 'fiddles' were perpetrated by some workmen, who often found favour with farmers by 'selling' them bags of precious cement at knock-down prices. Many of the pillboxes were in remote areas making it almost impossible to get heavy equipment like cement mixers on site, so this had to be done by hand.

Master of disguise

Many of the forts were in exposed positions and

Line of anti-tank blocks on the east bank of the old Taunton/Chard canal near Curry Mallet. (Author)

The clever camouflage used on this pillbox at Minehead is self evident. Natural materials were used to good advantage on the north Somerset coast. (Author)

an effective disguise was imperative. So skilfully was it done that it was possible to pass within a few yards of these structures without being aware of their true identity. It is said that much of this camouflage was carried out to the designs of Mr Oliver Messel, then an officer at 8th Corps Headquarters. Mr Messel was widely known as a theatrical designer and for the sets of many famous films.

The fundamental axiom of the work was that it should be indistinguishable from or natural to its surroundings. Thus the pillboxes on Porlock beach were faced with pebbles; those on Minehead and Blue Anchor promenades appeared as seaside shelters, newspaper kiosks or beach cafés. At Watchet, where some of the backs of the houses are towards the sea, the forts were pseudo washhouses and lavatories. The coast defences extended eastward from Porlock Bay and were erected wherever the beach was considered suitable for enemy landing. At Minehead two 4-in guns and searchlights were mounted on the old stone quay. The Victorian iron pier was removed to give a clear field of fire down the Bristol Channel. A forest of poles stretched away along the beaches as far as the Steart Flats to discourage landings by glider-borne troops. Arthur Wallbridge, a senior officer from the County Council Planning Department, had the task of surveying the whole of Somerset to see where such poles should be sited. The contractors nearly caused a disaster at Dunster where they breached the sea wall. As the tide rose the sea came near to flowing in and might have flooded the flats to the foot of Dunster Castle, but the breach was filled in just in time.

The Taunton Stop Line began on Pawlett Hams where pillboxes were dotted about the marshy area north of the Parrett Estuary. At Bridgwater that part of the town between the river and the railway was turned into an anti-tank 'island'. Across every entering thoroughfare was a road block. Cemeteries or gardens were studded with blocks of concrete enfiladed by pillboxes. One of the latter, a mock water tank, was a prominent feature on the Great Western main line. The Stop Line continued along the east side of the Taunton-Bridgwater Canal where the blockhouses were spaced at five to the mile. In open country on the borders of Sedgemoor concealment was difficult. There were 'cowsheds,' 'poultry houses,' and an occasional 'bathing station' suit-

ably labelled, but it is not known whether a German translation was also given!

The railway junction at Durston was heavily fortified, as was Creech St Michael village. One pillbox was entirely constructed within a house without disturbing the structure. The permanent hump back bridges over the canal were provided with anti-tank obstacles, some of which still lie alongside these bridges today. The swing bridges were hurriedly dismantled and their component parts removed during the invasion scare on 7 September. This drastic action provoked a minor crisis – those farmers not possessing boats found that they had to walk miles to the nearest remaining bridge in order to reach their cows on the opposite bank. Since the cows had to be milked, even in wartime, the Army had to build temporary bridges, many of which survived until recently. These were built at Glastonbury in prefabricated form. Some of these bridges have been removed during the current restoration of the canal to a navigable waterway.

At Creech St Michael the Taunton-Chard canal, derelict for nearly a century, was carried upon an aqueduct. Here was an excellent anti-tank obstacle. Trees and undergrowth growing in the bed of the old canal provided natural concealment for forts erected there. Where the canal crossed the Taunton road, two motor cars were filled with concrete to form anti-tank obstacles. The wheels, however, would not stand so great a weight so the cars remained immobile to the end. The branch railway to Chard runs parallel to the old canal. This provided excellent scope for the concealment artist. There was a convincing new 'signal box' at Creech and near it a 'gangers' hut' complete with brick chimney, tarred roof and sides. At Ilton there was a 'water tank', somewhat over-sized for a single-line railway. Here also was a large fortified area with a dug anti-tank ditch and a pillbox constructed to look like a bus shelter, complete with a clock-face on the wall and timetables of buses that never ran!

Ilminster fortified

Ilminster was completely surrounded by forts, scarping, ditches and wire, which, on plan at least, were strongly reminiscent of mediaeval days. The pillbox at the junction of the Ilminster and Dowlish Wake roads was a Gothic tollhouse,

The ingenuity of Mr Oliver Messel is highlighted by this 'pillbox' on the GWR line at Ilton, near Ilminster. (CRO)

The only known photograph showing a pillbox manned. Troops of the Green Howards oblige for the camera. (IWM)

conforming in design to the nearby entrance of Dillington House. There were isolated pillboxes at Dowlish Wake, Ilford and at Whitelackington. Forts standing on arable land were disguised as straw stacks: the straw being cleverly woven onto an enclosing frame of wire netting. The flaps over the firing apertures were detachable. When they were in position the illusion was complete.

The railway, provided with 'dragons' teeth' of steel rails and concrete posts, formed an outer defensive screen. At Chard the Stop Line crossed the border into Devon where it followed the windings of the River Axe to the sea.

Across the Levels and over Mendip

The Somerset section of the 'Green' Line began at the mouth of the River Brue near Highbridge, followed the river past Bason Bridge to its junction with the Division Rhyne near Meare and continued along the rhyne to Upper Godney where it turned north and east to Coxley. Skirting Wells the Line continued through wooded country eastward to the Somerset and Dorset railway line at Masbury to the Somerset coalfields around Radstock, then following Wellow Brook to the Wiltshire border at Freshford. The 91 mile-long Line, which extended to a point six miles southwest of Gloucester, was also called the Bristol Outer Defence Line. The work did not proceed as rapidly as on the Taunton Stop Line with the result that it was abandoned before it could be completed. The 'Yellow' Line had its northern end at the junction of the Rivers Avon and Frome at Freshford and followed the latter river through Farleigh Hungerford southward to Frome town turning south-east into Wiltshire at a point near Witham.

Home Guard mans the Line

'A' Company of the 2nd Somerset (Taunton) Battalion of the Home Guard took over a section of the Taunton Stop Line between Thornfalcon and Creech St Michael in September 1940, by which time the whole sector was completed. Exercises in attack and defence were held, but the heaviest weapons then available to the defenders were Lewis guns.

The building of the pillboxes went on apace but exercises showed that while the fortified lines might stop the enemy infantry, they would be ineffective against tanks. The anti-tank ditch, where artificially dug, was too small and did not seem to exceed six feet either in breadth or depth. Landing craft were gradually increasing in size and it became obvious that if tanks came at all they would be of the heaviest. For this reason in the Spring of 1941 the Stop Lines were, for the most part, abandoned.

COASTAL DEFENCES

Plans for defending the mouth of the Avon were implemented in Napoleonic times to deny a water-borne invader a safe anchorage: gun batteries were constructed at Portishead and across the river at Avonmouth. During the 1860s the defence of the Severn Estuary itself was tackled with vigour. Fortified gun batteries were built at Brean Down, Steep Holm, Flat Holm (north and south), Portishead and on the Welsh coast at Lavernock Point, Cardiff, Newport, Nells Point. The batteries scribed an arc of fire right across the channel with adequate overlap to provide maximum coverage utilising the natural features of the topography.

These battery sites were used for the defence of the Bristol Channel and served as positions from which ex-naval guns could be located, giving some degree of protection from an invasion force and the possibility of marauding destroyers or 'E' boats causing havoc with shipping in the narrow confines of the channel. The lessons learnt in the First World War when enemy warships bombarded Yarmouth would provide the need to protect the busy shipping channel with its vital ports on either side of the coast.

Brean Down

Brean Down was re-garrisoned and two ex-naval 6-in Mark VII CP coastal guns located there, together with at least one Lewis gun for anti-aircraft protection. It was manned by 366 Coast Battery, 571 Coast Regiment. Numerous accommodation huts were erected which survived until 1958. During the war a detachment from HMS *Birnbeck*, Weston-super-Mare, from the Admiralty Department of Miscellaneous Weapons Development kept the Royal Artillery company, testing their weird contraptions designed for undersea warfare. The rocket ramp used during their 'Expendable Noise Maker' trials is still extant. Today Brean Down is owned by the National Trust who are restoring part of the Garrison.

Steep Holm

A similar battery was installed on the Victorian fortifications at Steep Holm, where four 6-in Mark VII CP guns were installed together with four searchlights as late as April 1942. 188 and 189 Coast Batteries of 571 Coast Regiment manned this site. 189 Battery was also responsible for anti-aircraft defence and had at least six Lewis gun positions on the island in 1941.

Flat Holm

Although not strictly in Somerset, save for an outcrop of rock on the south-east tip of the island, Flat Holm was heavily armed and equipped with two batteries of twin dual-purpose 4.5-in guns and two searchlights for anti-aircraft and anti-shipping duties. Nos 146 and 205 Coast Batteries of 570 Coast Regiment were later supplemented by 351 HAA Battery who took over responsibility for the anti-aircraft rôle after objections had been raised by the other batteries to whom this task had fallen. 351 was also equipped with two 20mm Bofors guns, one twin Lewis gun and four single Lewis guns for anti-aircraft duties. The 4.5-in guns on the south side were mounted by 23 September 1941 and soon became operational, although emplacements were not built for them until a year later. The north side became operational in December 1942 and was used in the close defence rôle. The batteries became non-operational on 18 December 1944.

Portishead

The fort at Battery Point, Portishead, protected the approaches to the mouth of the River Avon and Avonmouth Docks. The battery was equipped with two ex-naval 6-in Mark VII CP coastal guns and was manned by 365 Coast Battery, 571 Coast Regiment.

ACK-ACK DEFENCES

Guns on the cliff-tops

Since 1925 the cliff-tops at Doniford on the West Somerset coast had been used for anti-aircraft gunnery practice. In the 1930s a larger and more powerful gun was heard: the ear-splitting crack of the 4.5-inch guns that could hurl a half-hundredweight shell to a height of eight miles in 50 seconds was the latest in modern technology. Something else was new: not only were the normal types of target-towing aircraft plying their trade, but a novel derivative of the Tiger Moth, called the Queen Bee, was being used as a remote-controlled drone for live firing practice.

In July 1939, 15 years of summer practice camp culminated in a visit being made by the top brass and 'bowler hat brigade' to see ack-ack training in progress. General Sir Frederick Pile, chief of AA Command, accompanied by Lieutenant General W.D.S. Browning, Director General of the Territorial Army; Leslie Hore-Belisha, War Minister and 16 mayors of the London boroughs, plus 50 or so Members of Parliament, watched firing demonstrations of the AA guns sited along the cliff-tops.

Training intensified by day and night and throughout the war thousands of gunners were trained at Doniford near Watchet, where a permanent camp was built. So vital was the co-operation of the RAF, that they established a permanent airfield at Weston Zoyland from where No 1 Anti-Aircraft Co-operation Unit operated their Hawker Henley and Miles Martinet target-towing aircraft. The Watchet ranges were used until the late '50s.

Latterly only Bofors guns of the RAF Regiment were fired from there. Today only the concrete base remains of the gun park and is the range's sole visible reminder of more than 30 years use.

Anti-aircraft defences near Bristol

Shortly before the outbreak of war a number of mobile AA sites were placed around Bristol and Avonmouth for their defence. The guns, strategically placed around the northern semi-circle of Bristol, mainly for the protection of the aero works at Filton and the docks at Avonmouth, initially were 3-in 20-cwt, 3.7-in Mark I mobiles.

Six sites were to become static before May 1941, when the numbers increased around Bristol to 20. Those located on Somerset soil were at Sheep-

way near Portbury and Easton-in-Gordano, and by early summer 1940 were equipped with 3.7-in Mark II static guns.

On 24 August 1939 76 HAA Regiment was deployed to man both the Portbury and Easton-in-Gordano sites along with others around Bristol. Initially 237 Battery manned the Portbury site and remained there until 17 March 1940, being posted to Moreland and Hythe, when 236 Battery took over. A temporary site with two 3.7-in mobile guns was established by 236 Battery in August 1939 at Haberfield near Pill, but moved their guns to the new site at Gordano on 18 December. By June 1940 four concrete octagonal gun pits were in the process of being built at each site together with semi-underground magazines, command posts and a large billeted area with all the facilities of a normal army camp.

By September 1941 236 Battery had left to go to North Africa. No 411 Battery, 104 HAA Regiment was then located at Portbury and at Gordano 349 Battery of 76 HAA Regiment had moved in.

Portbury received four 4.5-in static guns in 1942, but in May 1944 were re-equipped with 3.7-in Mark VI guns. In addition to these weapons both sites were equipped with a number of LMGs and had Lewis gun positions located on top of the gun stores for close AA work.

Weston-super-Mare and Yeovil's AA sites

In 1941 a number of AA sites equipped with 3-in semi-mobile guns were established around Weston to protect aircraft factories on the outskirts of the town. By September batteries were established at Uphill and Hutton, manned by 418 Battery, 55 Regiment. A number of Bofors guns were eventually located at these sites and manned by the Home Guard. The strength of Weston's AA defences increased steadily and by 1943 the number of 3.7-in guns had risen to 21. A similar measure of defence was afforded Yeovil, which only had four 3.7-in guns during the Battle of Britain. These increased over the next year or two and the numbers closely corresponded with those of Weston.

103

There were hundreds of searchlights sited all over Somerset. This one was located in the Portbury area. (S. Baker)

SEARCHLIGHTS

Searchlights not only provided some measure of defence against hostile bombers, but were of considerable help to friendly aircraft that might have been lost and disorientated. Literally dozens of searchlight batteries were sited all over Somerset during the war and widely dispersed – even on Exmoor. Searchlights were also placed near potential targets around towns and cities or airfields and often adjacent to ack-ack batteries.

Austin Hayter, serving in the Home Guard, remembers the batteries at Charlton Horethorne.

We went to a dance one night in the pony and trap, which was then put in the stable behind the pub. The dance was over, we had got the pony and trap out and were just hitching it into the trap when a searchlight went off at ground level. The pony was so frightened that I had to walk it around the village triangle six times to quieten it. I stood up in the cart to try to gain better control and wrestled with the reins all the way home. The pony was still shaking like a leaf when we got there!

Many batteries were formed by locally raised TA regiments. So widely dispersed were they, that a definitive list of sites would be impractical to compile. One such Territorial Army unit was 66 Regiment (formerly the 4th City of Bristol Gloucester Regiment TA) who deployed No 448 Battery on 24 August 1939 to various sites around the Weston-super-Mare, Clevedon and Portishead districts. Their headquarters were set up at the Churchill crossroads. In addition they had a number of batteries on the Mendips, including No 449, at Higher Pitts Farm. They also had batteries in other parts of the county; 447 Battery at Galhampton between Sparkford and Castle Cary was one. 76 Searchlight Regiment had batteries on Exmoor, including No 493 at Elworthy Barrows, Brendon Hill. 'N' Troop, 2nd Searchlight Battery RA, were also known to be manning sites in the South Brewham area during the summer of 1940.

Cyril Sparrow served with 485 Battery, 66 Searchlight Regiment, and was posted to Sutton Mallet, near Bridgwater:

We had one light with a mobile lorry-mounted generator set up on land owned by George Warren and used his farm buildings for cooking and so on – although we were under canvas for our sleeping accommodation. Our battery often picked out German planes that were heading for Bristol and Cardiff. It was terrifying when some used to follow the searchlight beam in a steep dive in order to swerve out of the light. We had an establishment of ten men led by a corporal. Searchlight batteries were usually placed in a ring in order that planes could be coned. Others in our group included Woolavington, Wembdon and Cossington.

Ivo Peters explains how searchlight batteries, working with the Observer Corps, helped lost aircraft:

In the King 1 area of the West of England on a good night we used to get hordes of planes, especially trainers, swarming like gnats, in the area. Inevitably some would get lost. Often they wouldn't have a clue where they were and their instruction if lost, was to circle, which would indicate such to an observer on the ground. On the balcony overlooking the plotting table at Group there would be liaison chaps from the RAF and Army – some were in charge of the searchlight batteries and would instruct their units in the area to help get an aircraft down. Instructions would go out to the adjacent searchlight batteries at an airfield, say Colerne, to which the lost aircraft was to be guided. One light would point vertically in the air; surrounding ones, maybe four or more, would angle their lights at 45°, raise and lower them several times, ending by pointing towards the vertical light at Colerne, the pilot who was lost would then follow the searchlight path back to the airfield.

BARRAGE BALLOONS

As a further measure of defence to protect vital areas from air attack, particularly dive-bombing, was the deployment of barrage balloons. The LZ (Low Zone) Kite Balloons were hydrogen/air filled envelopes with a capacity of about 19,150 cu ft. Overall length was 64.2 ft, maximum diameter of 25.2 ft, overall height 31.8 ft and an overall width of 33.7 ft. These were designed to fly at heights of 5,000 ft, but were often placed at an operational height of 6,500 ft and had three stabilising fins which helped to make the balloon controllable.

Somerset had two barrages, comprising of 24 envelopes each, to protect vital aircraft factories located at Yeovil and Weston-super-Mare. Both barrages were sited by July 1940. The value of such defensive measures to protect isolated installations was doubtful. These shining silver objects in a clear blue sky would indicate to an enemy force where the target was, rather than to deter attacks in daylight. Bristol had a substantial number of balloons deployed to protect vital industries and docks. A number of these for the protection of Avonmouth Docks were flown on the Somerset side of the Avon, centred around Pill, Portbury and Easton-in-Gordano.

The balloons came under the control of No 32 (Balloon Barrage) Group, No 11 Balloon Centre, Bristol. The 24 envelopes at Weston-super-Mare were in the charge of No 955 (Balloon) Squadron, who had four Flights; their HQ was at Banwell Castle, Banwell.

Considerable aggravation was caused by the balloons which hampered flying training from local airfields. Several 'hot' memoranda flew between the RAF Commands concerned and as a result of a trial it was decided from February 1942 No 11 Balloon Centre would hand over control of the barrages to 10 Group. Inland balloons would either be grounded or close-hauled (500 ft) if flying was in progress. Because of reduced enemy activity ample warning could be given, sometimes as much as 15 minutes, if hostile aircraft were approaching the area. This allowed sufficient time for the balloons to be lofted.

Barrage balloons were vulnerable to lightning strikes and on 20 July 1941 several were struck and destroyed at Weston-super-Mare and at Bristol. This happened on a number of occasions. Occasionally they broke free from their moorings and drifted off, often causing havoc to power supplies when the suspended cables would foul overhead lines. On occasions some were machine-gunned by enemy aircraft and shot down.

In February 1943 the barrages at both Weston and Yeovil were reduced to 20 envelopes apiece

and by two Flights at each. WAAFS were in predominant control of the barrages by this date and 880 were on the strength of No 11 Balloon Centre. Often rough and ready, living conditions were far from desirable for women and had to be improved.

Both barrages were sent to the south coast on 21 June 1944 as part of the *Anti-Diver* measures in combating the V1 menace. In September 1944 the Hydrogen and Silicol factories in the Weston area closed.

DECOYS

Since the begining of the war various ruses to confuse enemy bombers had been debated. A meeting was convened at Bomber Command on 17 September 1939, to discuss the feasibility of constructing decoy or dummy airfields. The idea was to make them convincing enough to lure the enemy away from the intended target, so that bombs would be dropped harmlessly on the decoy, with obvious saving of life and material. The idea was deemed practical and plans were drawn up in October for the construction of two sites: one for daylight using the code-name 'K' and one for night-time coded 'Q'.

Construction and design of these was entrusted to Colonel John Turner, who established a department at Shepperton film studios. By January 1940 one example of each was completed. The country was divided into four 'K' areas containing a total of 36 sites. These were gradually increased and by the beginning of 1941 there were 42. Each site had a complement of one sergeant, three corporals, 15 aircraftsmen, one driver and a 3 cwt lorry.

Several 'Q' sites were constructed in Somerset, taking the form of lights set out in open ground to simulate the flare path and landing lights of an active aerodrome, which would remain lit until the enemy was known to have seen them, then dowsed. A 400 yd cable carried the power to the lighting system from a splinter-proof shelter, which in turn was connected to Control by telephone. One man would be stationed outside the shelter to listen for aircraft.

Not only airfields were decoyed but strategic civilian targets had to be protected, namely munitions, chemical and aircraft factories, so 'QL' and 'QF' sites were contrived for night protection. The 'L' stood for lighting and the 'F' for fires;

Remains of the splinter-proof blast shelter at the Stawell decoy 'QL' site. (Author)

the lights would be extinguished in a similar manner to those of a dummy airfield on the approach of bombers. The decoy fires of a 'QF' would be lit only when bombs fell on or near the intended target, as the real fires were being extinguished, in the hope that the attack might be diverted. The 'K' and 'Q' sites proved their worth: between June and December 1940, there were 30 attacks on the former and 174 on the latter, plus 23 against dummy factories.

These successes burgeoned into the far bigger 'Special Fires' or *Starfish* sites, developed after the disastrous raid on Coventry on 14 November 1940. These were built around cities including Sheffield, Derby, Birmingham, Coventry, Crewe and Bristol. The latter had six *Starfish* sites – all in Somerset. These were on Kenn Moor near Clevedon; one mile west of Kingston Seymour; just west of Redhill adjacent to Lulsgate Bottom airfield; on Dundry Hill; between Whitchurch and Keynsham; the last on the Mendips just north of Cheddar Gorge, which could also be used for Weston-super-Mare, if threatened. There were two *Starfish* sites near Bath: to the south and south-east of the city; one of which was located in Somerset near Hinton Charterhouse. Four other *Starfish* sites were built in Somerset; one on Great Downs just south of Milverton; the second south-east of the A38 near Bradford-on-Tone between Wellington and Taunton; the third, to protect Yeovil and the Westland factory, between Brympton and West Coker on Camp Hill; the last on Queen's Sedge Moor between Glastonbury and Wells.

Various 'QL' sites were constructed for the protection of airfields and associated aircraft factories. Filton had four 'QL' sites, two of which

were located in Somerset: at Portbury and Leigh Woods. Further south on the Mendips, others were constructed for the protection of the airfield and Bristol Aeroplane Company's shadow sites at Old Mixon and Hutton at Weston-super-Mare. These 'QL' sites were at Dolebury Warren, south-east of Churchill; between Charterhouse and Blagdon; the last was located near Yoxter Range, south-east of Charterhouse. Another 'QL' site for Weston airfield was constructed on Bleadon Level. A 'Q' site for Yeovilton was set up on King's Moor, some five miles west of the base.

The Royal Ordnance Factory at Puriton had a 'QL' decoy built near Stawell at the north foot of Pendon Hill, two and a half miles south-east of the factory. This doubled as protection for the Bridgwater factories, chiefly British Cellophane, and also Weston Zoyland aerodrome. It also had 'QF' facilities.

The 'QF' and *Starfish* sites were more dramatic. A typical *Starfish* decoy comprised a building-like structure of timber and metal frame covered in hessian on the sides and roof. Inside were two rows of drums filled with highly combustible material. Asbestos would be packed around the whole in order that it could be used several times. The sites, in groups of three, would usually be positioned within four or five miles of the Key Point and were to be ignited when the real target came under attack. Telephone communications were linked to Control, No 80 Wing, who would actually give the order to fire; the decoys would then be electrically ignited from a concrete post some 600 yd distant. Basket-type fires had a duration of about one hour and were fired in relays. The site at Stawell had the Boiler Fire-type of decoy, which were tanks elevated on towers;

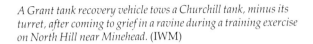
A Grant tank recovery vehicle tows a Churchill tank, minus its turret, after coming to grief in a ravine during a training exercise on North Hill near Minehead. (IWM)

some were filled with combustible material and others water which was pumped into a trough. When the water was added to the burning material it had the effect of an explosive burst to simulate the dropping of an oil bomb.

The first *Starfish* were fired on 2 December 1940 during an attack on Bristol, when two of the decoys between them attracted 66 HE bombs and a number of incendiaries. The site near Lulsgate Bottom attracted a number of bombs on the night of 5 April 1941 and two UXBs caused some disruption to the flying at the adjacent airfield.

The Bleadon 'Q' site was the scene of bravery by an airman on the night of 2/3 January 1941. During a heavy raid on Weston, it was activated, but the ignition switches failed to operate. AC2 Bright went out of the bunker and lit the dummy buildings by hand. The attack immediately switched to the site and hundreds of incendiaries as well as high explosive bombs fell, which heavily cratered the area. Bright was awarded the Military Medal. The site proved its value again on the night of 19 May, when 14 HE bombs dropped on the dummy gooseneck flare-path. The only casualties were several unfortunate cows killed, but no damage was caused either to Weston or the aerodrome.

SOMERSET: A TRAINING GROUND FOR WAR

The topography in certain parts of the county made it ideal to train troops for all kinds of warfare. The hills of Exmoor were used widely for infantry and artillery training. The Royal Artillery had a range on Dunkery; the crack of guns firing and the thud of shell was often heard in those parts of Somerset.

North Hill, also known as Camp Hill, near Minehead had been used as a summer training ground for local volunteers and regiments since 1890. From 1942 until the end of the war it became a tank training ground. A gunnery range consisting of a movable target was constructed on the north face and operated along a short railway track cut into the side of the hill. Firing practice was therefore reasonably safe as only the Bristol Channel lay before the guns. Concrete roads, marshalling areas and a tank loading ramp were also constructed.

Many hundreds of tank crews, British, Canadian and American trained here, firing thousands of shells, and in 1946 some 600 live rounds of all descriptions were gathered up then made safe. Towards the end of the war a Guards battalion used the area for mortar practice.

There were a number of serious training accidents, sometimes involving children, who had trespassed onto the ranges in the quest for souvenirs. This often had lethal consequences. Four small children were killed when one of them kicked a rifle grenade along a path at Pitminster. Three of the children were from one family. Three other children were killed after finding 2-in mortar rounds on the Mendip ranges. One was a 13 year-old boy who picked up two and banged them together to see if they would explode...they did. Five soldiers from the 4th Battalion, Royal Northumberland Fusiliers were killed in April 1945 during a mortar demonstration near Shepton Mallet, when one of the rounds exploded just after leaving the tube.

There were numerous ranges, used for rifle, grenade and mortar practice, scattered all over the county. Many were on the Mendips, including the biggest at Yoxter, where a sizable camp was built, which is still used by cadets and Territorial units today. Other ranges included the old Roman lead mines at Charterhouse; Langport; Dulberrow Bottom; Quant's Reservoir, Pitminster.

EIGHT

The Wheezers and Dodgers

Somerset's first encounter with the Department of Miscellaneous Weapons Development (DMWD), run by the Admiralty, came during the development of the Parachute and Cable Anti-aircraft device – known as the PAC. This was a powerful rocket that carried a length of steel cable up to a height of 500 ft at which point a parachute would deploy allowing the cable to be temporarily suspended in the air. The idea was to employ this device as an emergency balloon barrage which would be set up around the perimeter of an aerodrome. If the airfield was attacked by a low-flying aircraft, at the touch of a button the PAC could be fired in its path, hopefully ensnaring the attacker with the cable and bringing it down.

The Admiralty soon realised that the device might easily be used at sea. Once fitted on merchantmen, it would force enemy aircraft to bomb from greater heights, thereby reducing the risk of ships being hit. A variant known as the 'Type J', which had a bigger parachute, a more powerful rocket than the standard PAC and incorporated a 5-ton cable which the rocket could haul to 600 ft, was tested in a remote part of the Somerset coast, near Woodspring Bay. When the Type J was triggered, it fired with a brilliant flash, accompanied by a noise like giant sheets of calico being torn asunder. On one occasion it so panicked two horses pulling a reaper that they instantly broke into a full gallop, careered across the field with the madly whirring implement in tow, then charged over a bordering bank sustaining mortal damage to the machine's cutters. In due course the Director of Naval Accounts received a large bill for repairs, which was appropriately offset against scientific research! It was not the first time such a claim was made against the Wheezers and Dodgers – nor was it to be the last.

The outcome of the trials appeared to have been successful for when the PAC was taken off the Secret List in 1943, the DMWD were able to

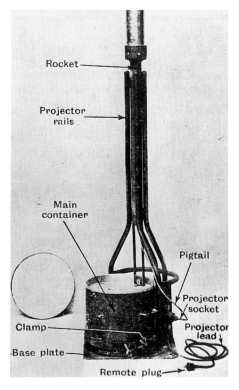

The type 'J' Parachute and Cable device as tested at Woodspring Bay. (IWM)

tell the workers in the Surrey factory, where it was made, that it had accounted for nine enemy aircraft confirmed as having been destroyed, plus the odd item of agricultural equipment. In addition an estimated 35 ships were reported saved from destruction following the weapon's use during attacks made on them.

His Majesty's Pier: HMS *Birnbeck*

By the spring of 1941 the need for a suitable site to develop the 'Hedgehog' was paramount. The Hedgehog was a forward firing anti-submarine weapon mounted on a ship which would encircle a submarine with multiple mortar charges set to explode at a pre-determined depth.

A site with a high rise and fall of tide, was required to retrieve experimental projectiles fired into deep water. Birnbeck Pier at Weston-super-Mare was perfect. Since the outbreak of war it had seen few visitors, was reasonably isolated, which was a definite security advantage, and had the added bonus of suitable buildings that could easily be converted into workshops.

The pier master was amazed when approached by a Sub-lieutenant Francis, who asked if he could set up a mortar at the end of the pier to fire a few Hedgehog rounds into the sea. Soon development of the weapon was in full swing and various trials were carried out on its ability to penetrate submarine plating and the best bomb pattern that would give a U-boat the least chance of escape. Much thought was given to this problem, but eventually a solution found and by May 1941, the Hedgehog was ready for sea trials; it entered service soon afterwards.

Although the pier still officially preserved its civilian status, the Admiralty realised a Sub-lieutenant, with no official authority to acquire real estate on their behalf, was requisitioning more and more of the pier. This was too much for the powers-that-be and within a year the Admiralty descended on Weston, acquired the whole of the pier and named it HMS *Birnbeck*, thus it became one of His Majesty's naval shore establishments.

The acquisition of the pier enabled the DMWD to expand their operations considerably. It soon proved an ideal testing ground for underwater projectiles and either side of the bay stretched miles of lonely headland: Brean Down and Sand Point – also vast expanses of empty beaches...the location could not be better.

The 'Hedgehog' anti-submarine device being fired 200 yd ahead of a corvette. Notice the circular pattern of fall in the water, which is 140 ft in diameter. It was one of the most successful weapons to be deployed against the U-Boat. (IWM)

The 'Hedgerow' weapon was similar to the 'Hedgehog', but was used to clear beach defences and minefields. Some of the 180 rounds are seen here installed in a tank landing craft. (IWM)

Research at Birnbeck embraced every aspect of war. From the difficulties envisaged crossing mined beaches and scaling cliffs; clearing jungles; to dealing with enemy submarines. Many unusual experiments were soon taking place at Brean Down and at Middle Hope Cove: two high-speed catapult tracks were laid there for testing missiles – the like of which had never been seen before in the history of modern warfare.

Birnbeck was to play host to a variety of people who would arrive with mysterious packages containing jelly bombs and other weird devices that they wanted to try out: all hours of the day and night loud explosions and blinding flashes of light came from the island upon which the pier was anchored. Such was the quantity of bombs and other contraptions being despatched from Paddington for Weston, that after a little while they aroused no more than passing interest amongst the railway staff. However, Wheezers and Dodgers' fellow passengers on such trains never felt quite at ease on finding they were also sharing a compartment with some lethal-looking object that would be unceremoniously dropped on the floor with a thud and shoved under a seat, with the accompanying remark, "You did remember the fuse, didn't you?"

In the autumn of 1941, James Close was amongst other officers posted to Birnbeck for full-time duty and he was to direct operations for 18 months until succeeded by Lieutenant Commander C.N. Boswell, RNVR. Boswell had helped to develop the PAC device and had also been involved with the task of producing a new type of anti-submarine flare. Although answerable to the DMWD, HMS *Birnbeck* came under the local control of the Naval Officer-in-Charge, Appledore – a retired rear admiral serving in the rank of captain. This was complicated by the fact that their immediate superior was the Resident Naval Officer, Watchet – a retired Vice Admiral, John Casement, serving in the rank of Commander. The latter was a man of great charm and wit; however he was one of the old school and a strict disciplinarian, so he was somewhat disconcerted by the unorthodoxy of the pier's inhabitants at first, but soon realised the organization worked well and generally left them to their own devices – literally!

Eventually Admiral Casement moved his headquarters to Weston, where he found that life was full of surprises. Amongst the devices undergoing trials at the time was the 'Expendable Noise-maker', which was designed to foil the enemy's acoustic torpedos. This was fired from a mortar, rather like the Hedgehog bombs, and on sinking supposedly caused a series of rhythmic detonations.

The Army had been entrusted with the first trials of this gadget and prepared to fire the rounds into shallow water just off the beach.

Although they went to enormous trouble to take careful measurements of the range, they completely overlooked the fact that the mortar was some 40ft above sea level when mounted on the end of the pier. The first round was duly fired: it soared majestically over the water and exploded with an almighty bang in mid-air right outside a cliff-side café, which emptied with great alacrity! A hasty conference ensued... the baffled soldiers made some adjustments to the elevation of the mortar and fired again. The second round dropped a yard short of Admiral Casement's office – the explosion of wrath emitting from therein was almost as cacophonous as the one outside.

A more advanced type of Noise-maker came up for trial. This was a formidable affair consisting of a rocket-propelled container which burst open scattering a variety of exploding objects. It was decided to test this at Brean Down, as the stability of this contrivance was somewhat suspect having no fins to stabilize it in flight. The first round was fired directly out to sea and gave no hint of deviation from its course, so Boswell and Jesse Wyllie, an RNVR lieutenant, decided to give the recovery party a better chance and aimed the second round along the water's edge. All went well for the first few hundred yards, when to their astonishment, the projectile made a ninety-degree turn and headed inland at great speed. They heard a loud explosion in the distance which appeared to be uncomfortably close to a farm and with some trepidation set off to look for it. Before long they came across a man, puce with rage, carrying a mass of blackened and twisted metal.

"Where did it land?" they tentatively asked.

"In me chickin run...that's where the bugger landed," the farmer snorted.

"Phew – what a lucky thing," said Wyllie with a friendly sigh of relief, "and where were you at the time?"

"Where was I?" bellowed the angry farmer, "in the bloody chickin run – that's where I was to!"

It was concluded that the trials would have to be continued in an area even more remote, due to the unpredictability of the weapons now being tested. Middle Hope Cove, just over the brow of a hill behind Woodspring Priory, was deemed suitable. The Burrough brothers who farmed the land stoically endured the most startling inconveniences, their cattle and horses stampeding with fright regularly – especially when the advanced version of the PAC was being tested.

Various other projects were examined at Birnbeck, including a 'Water Hammer': a device for absorbing a weapon's recoil at sea. Development of the 'Weasel' tracked vehicles for use in snow and mud was carried out and one of these overturned on the way to Brean killing the driver and trapping Lieutenant Ritchie in a waterfilled rhyne, where he very nearly drowned. Other projects undertaken by Ritchie included a method of distilling water for ships' lifeboats and the evolution of a new anti-submarine star shell invented by Richardson, one of the team. Dummy silhouettes of submarines were made and at night team members would fire star shells from Flat Holm, the illumination being measured with special instruments on the pier.

Although the Wheezers and Dodgers had their own workshops on the pier, they were very fortunate in acquiring the services of a local hotelier and engineer, a man in his fifties by the name of Dick Crowe, who also ran a small engineering firm in the town. He undertook all sorts of tasks from the welding of Hedgehog rounds to the making of rocket trolleys and catapults. He was so resourceful that he even made a slipway out of masts salvaged from a derelict ship. Despite doubts cast on his calculations, it was so successful that it remained in use for the rest of the war.

It was Crowe's association with the Auxiliary Fire Service that stood him in good stead on one occasion and got a DMWD party out of trouble. A 200-ton mine recovery vessel was left high and dry in a meadow after trying to get to its moorings in the River Axe on the highest tide of the year. The next spring tide fell some five feet short of the vessel, so Crowe borrowed Weston's biggest fire engine and used its hoses to cut ground away from under the ship and at the same time carving a channel right back to the river bed. She was duly refloated but leaked like a sieve and could only be kept afloat with a trailer fire-pump that had to be manned constantly.

Gradually the emphasis shifted from defensive weapons to offensive types, particularly with the advent of a second front in Europe. Ways of clearing underwater obstructions and blockships, were examined. The hulk of the steamer *Fernwood* was filled with reinforced concrete and sunk off Weston and various charges were tried out on its submerged hull.

The next problem that had to be tackled was the disposal and clearing of enemy mines laid on beaches. A scientist, Dr Guggenheim, invented an apparatus which he had given the code name of 'Hedgerow'. It was designed to be carried in converted landing craft and when fired would drench the beaches with a salvo of bombs which exploded just above the ground – in principle it was very similar to the 'Hedgehog'. Trials were conducted on Berrow beach and hundreds of German Teller mines, lifted from the Western Desert, were used in the experiments. Sixty of these would be laid out in mathematically precise patterns then a Hedgerow device would detonated in the centre of the field. It could be hazardous work as the Teller mines became unstable after six months or so and the Birnbeck party were using some that were at least two years old.

Considering the dangers, there were very few accidents. There was one notable occurrence which involved a prominent member of the team, Dr H.S. Hatfield, a talented physicist and inventor, who had set up a workshop in the confectionery shop. One dark night he absentmindedly turned to lean on the pier's railings to gaze out to sea, but he had chosen a spot where they had been removed to enable the Hedgehog mortar to be fired. He plunged 40 ft onto the rocks below. It was not until later that night somebody noticed his bed had not been slept in and a search for him was made. Miraculously they found him alive, although unconscious and badly injured, just before the tide covered the rocks upon which he lay. He soon made a full recovery, but to this day the place of his misadventure is known as 'Hatter's Leap'.

Nautical Bouncing Bombs

At the end of 1942, the DMWD became interested in pilotless aircraft that might be used for laying smoke screens across invasion beaches. Lieutenant Commander L.M.H. Lane, a leading member of the Wheezers and Dodgers team, visited Dr Barnes Wallis, chief designer at Vickers Aircraft. He soon was talking to Wallis about a totally different and exciting project upon which he was currently working – a revolutionary earthquake bomb, which he had designed to destroy the great Ruhr dams: the Möhne, Eder and Sorpe. Barnes Wallis had, however, achieved little support in getting his 'bouncing bomb' idea accepted in high places.

As a result of the final success of the Dambusters Raid, the Admiralty became interested in developing a seaborne version that could be used against naval targets launched from motor-torpedo boats. A catapult track was laid at the northern end of Birnbeck pier, down which it was planned to launch a rocket-propelled trolley with the projectile mounted on top. Serious doubts about the pier's ability to take the stress of the trolley were cast and eventually it was decided that it would be unsafe to proceed with the trial there; also it presented a security risk – too many prying eyes. Although not an ideal site, the project moved to Brean Down where a level stretch was hewn out of the rocky ground and a new ramp built, so that trials of the trolley could be carried out. A large wall of sandbags filled with cement was built up at the back of the buffers at the seaward end by way of reinforcement.

With the construction of the new launch site now complete, a small firing party gathered on the ridge behind the trolley loaded with its twelve 2-inch rockets and waited apprehensively for the signal to fire. The results were dramatic to say the least: with a shattering roar the trolley, enveloped in flame, hurtled down the track at a terrific speed and drove straight through the buffers, scattering the blast wall to the wind, filling the air with a whirring mass of sandbags, hawsers and pieces of sheet steel. The trolley, with its rockets still spewing yellow flame, vanished rapidly from view over the cliff edge and into the sea. A rather alarmed and chastened group of individuals were left staring open-mouthed from their vantage point at the spectacle they had just witnessed.

This failure was a sobering experience for the team who decided that no hydraulic mechanism would stand up to the stresses imposed by the speed necessary to catapult the bomb from the trolley. Further trials incorporating a wall of sand to halt the trolley were conducted at Middle Hope Cove, which proved entirely successful. Two new tracks were laid at the cove: one at sea level and the other ten feet higher, to allow for tide variation. The giant ball could now be fired more or less in line with the shore and a course was set out with marker posts set at 20 yd intervals.

A long series of tests were conducted, which were filmed with high-speed cameras, but the rockets continued to be a constant hazard, due to their unpredictable nature. The steel balls weighed more than 70-pounds, and sometimes had to be recovered from mud 13ft deep, but although it was exhausting work, things generally went well. The missile achieved most encouraging results and its speed across the surface of the water was far more impressive than the torpedo, and due to its idosyncrasies, made it much more difficult for countermeasures to be employed against such a weapon. The lower track proved a problem, for every time it was used tons of shingle and seaweed had to be removed from it. On one occasion two dead sheep were revealed as the track was being cleared.

Vice Admiral Wake-Walker had a chance to see the missile in action and authorised sea trials to commence, but at this point the weapons development was slowed down due to more pressing requirements.

However, some progress was made with trials of the missile, which continued, but difficulties remained in achieving the range required. To increase the velocity of the projectile, they stepped up the explosive charge far beyond the safe limit of the tube. The result was even more alarming than the first trial undertaken at Brean, for the missile screamed past the end marker post, swerved sharply towards the shore, jumped a sea wall, then plunged across the headland at the end of the cove, stampeding Boroughs' terrified cattle once again, and was last seen heading out towards the Atlantic at terrific speed.

Catapult trials were also conducted with another missile, invented by a Norwegian naval officer, before the Wheezers and Dodgers left Birnbeck, but further events overtook the DMWD who had to embark on a wide range of other tasks in preparation for the invasion of Europe. Some of the projects they worked upon were designs of rocket landing craft; Mulberry Harbour; Pluto, the giant pipeline; explosive motor-boats; various beach clearance devices; cliff climbing; incendiary floats; magnesium flares of half a million candle-power attached to balloons were tested in the Bristol Channel; radar buoys for guiding the invasion fleet and numerous other things including the 'Helter Skelter' which helped speed up disembarkation of troops from ships.

Project Hajile

Towards the end of 1942, the DMWD was asked to look at a project which had been originated by the Army, who saw a need to drop heavy loads such as vehicles, guns and stores, from aircraft. It was considered that parachutes would be inadequate for the high speed of fall which was deemed essential to reduce the risk of drift and damage from enemy ground fire, and the DMWD eventually hit on the idea of using the blast from a nest of rockets to cushion the impact just before touch down. The object to be dropped was fitted with a harness upon which was girdled a candelabra of rockets; these would be triggered when only a few feet off the ground. The spectacular trials commenced on Salisbury Plain and Jock Davies, typically armed with suitable Biblical quotations, suggested a code name for the project. "Look at it!" he exclaimed as he watched one of the first trials, "it's Elijah in reverse." Henceforth the project was known as 'Hajile'.

Soon it was decided that over-water trials should be conducted and the team loaded all their gear and drove down to Birnbeck. The first trial over water commenced: a Lancaster bomber was loaded with a large block of concrete and set course for Birnbeck. The pilot made his run in, but dropped it too far out to sea for it to be filmed. Not to make the same error of judgement again, the pilot was now on his mettle and was determined to give the team a good show. He

made a couple of dummy runs and then released the huge concrete block and its girdle of rockets, from 2,000 ft with alarming accuracy. The watchers on the pier stared open-mouthed as this huge object hurtled towards them. It suddenly dawned that the pilot was about to score a direct hit on them. The pack scattered for their lives and the concrete 'bomb' sheared through DMWD's workshop roof, and then demolished the covered way of the steamer jetty. The rest of the trials proceeded without hitch and by March 1943, had almost perfected the system.

Weston: the town of trials

In addition to the Wheezers and Dodgers, a small workshop set up behind the Playhouse Theatre was used by a Commander Varley, of Varley Pumps, and his small team, to develop a variety of equipment including breathing apparatus and propulsion units for use on and with midget submarines and human torpedos. Midget submarines were observed off Birnbeck pier from time to time.

The area of Sand Bay and Sand Point was used as an aircraft gunnery range. Four steel targets were set up on scaffolding poles along the point and when firing began red cones were hoisted on a large pole adjacent to a manned RAF hut located a quarter of the way along the headland. A variety of aircraft used the air to ground firing range and cannon shells can still be found on Sand Point to this day.

It is only in recent years that the area around Birnbeck Island was cleared of explosive objects left in the sea since the war. The Admiralty still maintain a facility at Middle Hope Cove for the occasional testing of underwater devices.

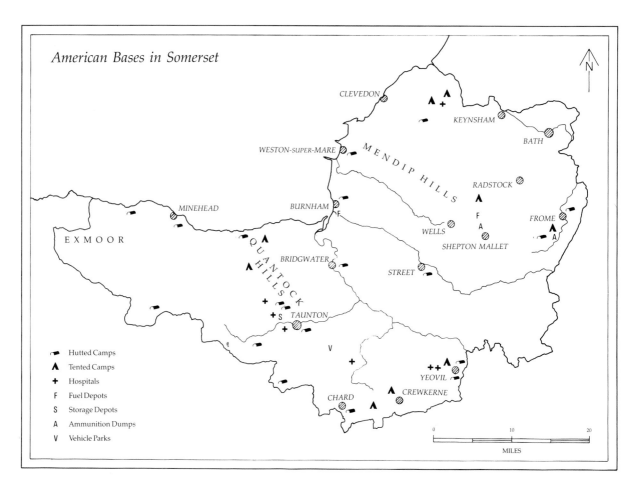

American Bases in Somerset

🛏	Hutted Camps
▲	Tented Camps
+	Hospitals
F	Fuel Depots
S	Storage Depots
A	Ammunition Dumps
V	Vehicle Parks

MILES

NINE

The Americans

One of the biggest impacts of the war to befall the people of Somerset was the influx of thousands of US troops. The South West had been designated an area from where the Americans would launch their part of the planned invasion of Europe. The well-worn cliché of 'Over paid, over sexed and over here' was generally applied to the American GI. However, their presence was, for the most part, welcomed and Somerset played glad host to many thousands of them.

At one time it was said that the number of US troops in the county almost outnumbered the local inhabitants and that the Americans had even mooted evacuating the entire civilian population from the South West! Somerset would ultimately benefit from the their stay in the county and they left a number of hospitals built in preparation to receive wounded back from France, one of which is still in use today: Musgrove Park serves as the county's major hospital some 45 years after it was built – as a semi-permanent structure.

Preliminary arrangements for the accommodation of US Forces in the South Western Counties were begun by Headquarters of 8th Corps at Pyrland Hall, Taunton, towards the end of 1942. The scheme, which was known as *Bolero* was continued by South Western District Headquarters when 8th Corps moved away in January 1943; by then British Forces in this area were few.

US Corps Headquarters

The *Bolero* scheme provided for the establishment of a US corps headquarters in the vicinity of Taunton, with three divisions based on Tiverton, Tavistock and Cannington. At the end of May 1943 the US 29th Division moved to Tavistock in relief of the 55th British Division, the last remaining Regular British Army unit in the West Country. Other US divisions followed as planned. The US 5th Corps Headquarters was set up

at Norton Manor. In July 1943 the XIXth District Headquarters of US Services of Supply was established at Hestercombe House, residence of the Portman family and situated a short distance to the east of Pyrland Hall. The principal British and US Headquarters were thus in close proximity.

Depots

The Americans took over a part of the huge stores depot which, since 1940, had risen from a greenfield site on the eastern side of the village of Norton Fitzwarren. The building of this vast depot was a gigantic operation, and a complete network of railways was installed to serve the storage sheds. Known as 'G 50' and soon too small for their needs, it was soon extended northward to include Cross Keys Camp and eastwards along the main Great Western Railway towards Taunton Station. At Walrow, near Highbridge on the Somerset and Dorset railway line, there was a vast fuel dump and extra sidings were laid to facilitate the unloading of equipment.

Billets

Large numbers of men were billeted on the civilian population, particularly in the towns. This did not cause too much friction and in the main, good will abounded. With D-Day approaching, the Americans were widely dispersed, particularly in South Somerset.

The police were responsible for locating billets for American troops and they scoured the county looking for suitable accommodation. Mary Ruau's parents lived in Taunton Road, Bridgwater; she remembers the Americans they had to stay:

The first of them arrived just before Christmas 1943. The requirement was to give them accommodation from 10 o'clock at night until the morning, but in our home they could come in at anytime they wanted.

US troops were glad of a good second home. Seen here is Mary Ruau (née Kemp) outside her parents' house in Bridgwater with Staff Sergeant Sewell from Port Allgheny, Pennsylvania. (Mary Ruau)

Albany, N.Y. November 13th., 1944.

Dear Mrs. Kemp:-

      Your letter dated Oct. 17th. just reached me to-day Nov.10th. I wish I just could express in words how grateful I am for your very kind letter and the happiness it brought into our home.

      Alan had already told us of his new found "home" so very far away, the kindness that has been extended by you and your family on his occasional visits and remarked that he did'nt think there could be another family like the "Bourque's" for really before this terrible war started, we were so devoted to our two boys and I am sure Alan misses his home atmosphere but keeps it all to himself and never complains and I likewise when I write let on we are not worrying, but he will never know how we miss him and our home is not the same since he went away. He is a very good and genuine boy and loves music, yes I can imagine he does play a lot when he gets the chance and the old "Boogie Woogie" is still going strong.

      His little brother Gene who will soon be fourteen is growing quite tall and is a decided blond and a great lover of sports such as fishing and hunting. I am alone this afternoon as his Dad took him in the woods hunting and he left so happy, he misses Alan so and remarks many times "gee I wish my brother could come home" we are going to give him lessons on the saxaphone as he wants to surprise Alan when he comes home.

      You must be glad that you have daughters they can't take them away from you. It just seems such a short while ago when Alan was a wee boy and I try so hard to be brave but many times I smile but with a heavy heart.

      Christmas is near and it will be the first one Alan is spending it away from us and I am so pleased to think he will be in your home and with such kind people. I hope I can repay that doubly so some day. You British are wonderful and we admire your great courage. Mrs.Kemp, you probably know that we are at heart Canadians because I was born there and naturally have a deep feeling for our "Mother Country". Alan has no doubt has told you that my husband was in the first world war. Little did we think our Alan would be following in his foot steps. Fate weaves strange patterns in our lives does'nt she?

      I do wish you could write me again and I hope your daughters like my son whom I know they will find genuine solid moral boy and can be trusted.

      Mr.Bourque and I want to assure you of our deepest appreciation for the kindness extended to Alan and wish you and your husband and daughters God's blessing and a quick ending of this terrible war. Please when you next see Alan give him a great big hug and kiss for me.

      Very sincerely yours,

(mrs) Lola Bourque.

Many American mothers were grateful to Somerset people for providing accommodation for their sons, who were a long way from home, highlighted by this letter. (Mary Ruau)

Often those that couldn't get into their own billets would come to our house and lay their heads down somewhere. There was a preference for officers, as most people wanted to have them, but my father didn't mind enlisted men at all. I think they received 10d a night for the Americans which was 4d better than that paid for British troops! This was for accommodation only – no meals had to be provided, but we would give them supper at our house. The Americans had canteens in the town: one was at Blake Hall and the other near Cranleigh Gardens and they used to go there for most of their meals.

Camps

Enormous camps were built for the accommodation of troops, some of semi-permanent structure and in addition, other encampments were set up of canvas. These large square tents had a chimney pot protruding through the roof and were the envy of British troops. Gerald Little was a British soldier stationed at Houndstone Camp near Yeovil and remembers the first Americans to arrive in the area:

In 1942 the American black labour battalions were sent over to help finish with the construction of various camps in the area – Houndstone was one of them. They were not allowed to sleep in the camp, as it also housed women, but were shipped out at night by big lorries and back the next day. There was a large tented camp not far away which they had made their base.

Will Locke was an NCO in the 8th (Holding) Battalion Somerset Light Infantry and stationed at Sherford Camp in Taunton, where he was on the staff of 114 Military Convalescent Depot, which was opposite an American camp:

The American negro troops lived in pretty primitive conditions in their camp. They had utility-type portable lavatories and we used to see them standing on the seats of these in order to wash themselves down with buckets of water. They had big dixies in which to prepare their food and we were absolutely amazed by the fact that the food was all stirred together – custard, prunes and potatoes...the lot! If ever there was trouble during a night out in Taunton their MPs were very tough with them – they really walloped them with truncheons...seeing was believing. The Americans were very popular with the local girls and were free and easy in their manner. I was later posted to an isolated camp up on the Blackdowns and there were more American negro troops based near Churchstanton. They would do anything to get hold of a bike. One of our chaps on the staff, who used to drive a lorry, went down to a depot somewhere, gave the quartermaster a back-hander, and got hold of a load of old bikes to flog them to the Yanks. It was a racket – he used black paint to cover up the rust and tinkered with them a bit to make them half presentable. He made so much money...it was unbelievable.

The GIs meet Dad's Army

When the US 29th Division took over at Tavistock they had to assume the operational rôle of their predecessors and the British South Western District, through liaison officers, had to acquaint the newcomers with the Defence Scheme of a country still threatened, although to a rapidly lessening degree, with enemy invasion. The peculiar character of the Home Guard – civilians by day and soldiers by night had to be explained; the functioning of the civil defence services and the plans for aid by the military to the civil power in the event of heavy air attack; the immobilisation of vehicles and of petrol; in fact the whole inter-related plans of a nation besieged had to be assimilated.

In August 1943, 'Exercise Hay' was staged for the purpose of testing the co-operation between the two armies. The Americans found it difficult to appreciate the character and rôle of the Home Guard, of which they did not have the direct equivalent. Unaware of their static rôle, several US commanders endeavoured to move whole battalions across the region to meet tactical requirements. The exercise was not the success it might have been.

Fraternisation

By the Spring of 1944, the county was bulging with American troops. In some towns the press of human beings was so great that it made the going extremely difficult. Smart in their appearance; free-spending, free-drinking and generous, the Americans soon won the hearts of many local girls, some of whom were out to fleece them for all they could get. A few were wives or girlfriends of British soldiers who might have been away fighting in some part of the world. This inevitably caused many incidents which eventually resulted in broken homes. German propaganda

was quick to seize the opportunity and produced leaflets in which they depicted such situations. Other unions were more happy – some local girls became GI brides and went to live in the States.

Private First Class Donald Hall was stationed at the 185th (US) General Hospital at Sandhill Park near Taunton and recalls the effect of English ale on some of his colleagues. Inns often had to display 'No beer' notices outside and it was not uncommon for six nights out of seven, such was its popularity:

They would take a swallow, look around at each other, putting on expressions of total satisfaction and complete enjoyment of what they were tasting. But, eventually they had to break down, gasp, shudder and shake from the effects of the bitter brew going down. They braved it out though, until they had eventually consumed their drinks. Most of them were sick that night from the effects.

The Americans soon developed a penchant for the local brew – scrumpy. A great many cider houses and farms were frequented by troops, some of whom paid very generously for the privilege of drinking it – as certain farmers could have verified!

Ron Hansford remembers his association with the Americans stationed in the Midsomer Norton area – and on one occasion, learnt a very painful lesson that was suffered by other children, sometimes fatally, in other parts of the county where there were practice ranges:

Some Americans were encamped in Pows Orchard – up past Church Lane, Midsomer Norton – quite a big camp with wooden huts, built at the beginning of war. They used to swim in the claypits nearby and they also used to go up there practising with smoke bombs, grenades and all sorts. A gang of us boys used to play with what they left behind. We found that the grenades were safe in water but exploded once exposed to air. A lad had his boot set on fire kicking a phosphorous grenade and I landed up in hospital for five weeks after one went off in my hand. There often used to be fights at dancehalls – between the Yanks – black and white...right old punch-ups – again usually over the local girls! Paulton Football Club, was a recreation centre in those days and the Yanks used to be welcomed there and join in any fun or dance that happened to be going on. Clark Gable was stationed at Midsomer Norton for a time – even though he was a flier. There was a photo of him with his bomber. He often could be seen at a football match. Joe Louis gave an exhibition of boxing at the Welton Football Ground – he was in uniform and sparred with another Yank.

Various dances were organised for the entertainment of troops in all parts of the county. Mary Ruau attended and helped at such functions:

There was a canteen at the YMCA in Bridgwater called the Welcome Club, which was organised and staffed by volunteers, who would provide entertainment and food for the troops. On occasions dances were held and I can remember one British Cellophane had organised. Invitations had been sent out to some Americans and when they arrived, they turned out to be coloured. This caused horror in certain quarters, but I got the girls from the lab where I worked to come with me and asked them to dance. This helped break the ice a bit.

Congested roads

The roads in the county, almost devoid of civilian traffic, became increasingly congested with military transport. Signposts, removed after Dunkirk, appeared once again in strange and unfamiliar forms at cross-roads and junctions. The Americans found the narrow country roads a trial, which led to many an accident. A truck crashed through the parapet of Dulverton town bridge into the river 14 ft below, also a runaway coach

Not all Americans intended to stay in Somerset. This B-17 Flying Fortress 'The Bearded Beauty - Mizpah' forced-landed at Yeovilton on 18 November 1942, following a mid-air collision during a raid on the U-Boat pens at St Nazaire. Seen here are the crew with the pilot, Lieutenant John T. Harding (5th from right) standing next to the CO of the air station, Captain M.S. Thomas DSO RN, and to his right is Lieutenant Robert Arnold RNVR. (IWM)

loaded with GIs crashed on St Andrews Hill at Dulverton, severely injuring 23 soldiers and killing a local child.

Jeep demonstrations were often put on for the benefit of the local children...proving, they said, that a Jeep 'can do anything a horse can do, except eat oats'. David Milton remembers one such episode:

Crates of jeeps were unloaded at Glastonbury Station, where my father worked, and they were all complete save wheels which were bolted on. Petrol was put in and they were just driven away. A Texas sergeant was responsible for the job of unloading them and boasted that the Jeep could do anything a horse could. He gave me a ride in the passenger seat of one to show its prowess, including driving over the railway lines. I asked him if it could rear up on its hind legs like a stallion – he was most put out and promptly handed me back to my father.

A chance in a million

Most formidable of all American vehicles were the large tank transporters, which usually moved in convoy, each with its flashing red and white lights to warn other road users.

Two incidents of note involving these transporters occurred in the build up to D-Day. In March 1944, an American driver tried to take his laden tank transporter under the Hanging Chapel at Langport, blocking the arch completely. Happily the damage was not too severe and only some of the mediaeval masonry was brought down, however the ancient monument survived and was eventually restored to its former glory.

The second incident was much more serious and involved considerable loss of life. The concentration of troops in the area was to reach great proportions in the months prior to D-Day and the railways took their fair share of transporting military personnel to holding areas along the south coast. On one such occasion, Monday 13 March 1944, one of many southbound troop trains which traversed the Somerset and Dorset line was running behind schedule, due to the severe gales which it had encountered over the Mendips.

The double-headed train, made up of ten coaches, was approaching Henstridge and just passing under the A30 road, when an American tank transporter negotiating the narrow bridge above demolished the parapet and crashed down onto the two locomotives, severing the coupling between them. The pilot locomotive, enveloped with wreckage from the transporter, remained upright and carried on down the line for some distance before the driver managed to stop it. The other engine was struck by the remainder of the transporter and its load, crushing the locomotive's smokebox in the process. The engine careered off the rails and ended up on its side some way from the track in a field. As the stricken train lurched past the platform of Henstridge Station, some debris knocked a signal post, up which Porter William Jackson was tending the oil lamp, sending it crashing to the ground. Jackson was lucky – he managed to escape unhurt and dropped into a field as the signal tilted over.

Though suffering from shock, Driver Harold Burford and his mate managed to put out the

A familiar scene in the Somerset skies around D-Day were massed formations of C-47 Skytrains from Merryfield and Weston Zoyland. (IWM)

fire in their engine's boiler and then proceeded to administer first aid to some of the wounded. Someone noticed that the rear of Burford's overalls were smouldering, but fortunately managed to extinguish them before the driver became a casualty himself. Considerable damage was sustained to the first five coaches, causing many casualties: at least six soldiers were killed and many more injured in the first coach. The total number of fatalities has never been revealed.

The USAAF in Somerset

Three airfields in Somerset were transferred to the United States Army Air Force in preparation for the airborne assault on Europe. In November 1943, Charmy Down, near Bath, became the 4th Tactical Air Depot (Station 487) and stored many aircraft prior issue to operational units. Assigned to the 9th Tactical Air Force on 1 February 1944, it became the home of the 422nd Night Fighter Squadron, USAAF, equipped with the mighty P-61 'Black Widow' twin-boom fighter. The Americans had little liking for the exposed windswept site and the location was none too popular! The USAAF vacated Charmy Down on 15 October 1944.

Another casualty of the air war. A B-17 Flying Fortress at Henstridge following the loss of a propeller. (FAAM)

This C-47 Skytrain of 99th Squadron, 441st TCG, 50th TCW, was based at Merryfield near Ilminster. (IWM)

Merryfield, near Ilton and Weston Zoyland, near Bridgwater, were assigned to the IXth Troop Carrier Command. Merryfield opened on 9 February 1944 to the four squadrons of the 441st Troop Carrier Group, 50th Troop Carrier Wing, equipped with Douglas C-47 Skytrains and Waco Hadrian gliders. Training for D-Day commenced immediately and by the end of May they were proficient in marshalling their gliders and tugs on the runway. Weston Zoyland was transferred to the USAAF in April 1944 and the first gliders were flown in during May. Paratroops exercises ensued before the arrival of some C-47s from the 442nd Troop Carrier Group which moved in just after D-Day. The truly spectacular sight of massed formations of aircraft towing gliders across the Somerset skies will be imprinted in many a memory for a long time to come. Night operations were equally dramatic – seeing the twinkling navigation lights of aircraft formations practising for night paratroop drops will also not be forgotten.

On one occasion Nunzio Notaro, an Italian PoW working on a farm near the village of Greinton, witnessed the spectacular crash of a glider from nearby Weston Zoyland:

I looked up to see a plane towing a glider which was corkscrewing wildly behind it. The tow was cast. The glider crashed down hitting the ground not far from Lower Nythe Farm, bounced over Eighteen Feet Rhyne, before coming to rest on the far side of King's Sedgemoor Drain. The cable sliced through a cow which was grazing in a nearby field, killing it instantly. The Police were called and they contacted the Americans at Weston Zoyland, who came out to the scene within ten minutes or so. The pilot of the glider was quite unhurt, although badly shaken by his ordeal.

The Americans used light aircraft for courier and

liaison duties and most divisional, brigade or corps headquarters had facilities to operate them. In the main, Piper Cub and Stinson aircraft were used. It is known they operated from Hestercombe House, near Taunton; at Watchet near the Doniford ack-ack gunnery range; in the grounds of Redlynch House, near Bruton, where the 3rd Armoured Division was located; the Ashton Court Estate, near Bristol and also from an airstrip north of Frome.

Prisons

Early in 1940 Shepton Mallet Prison was leased to the British Army to house defaulters. The job of refurbishing it was entrusted to the Royal Pioneer Corps. In 1942 the Americans took it over to house their many defaulters, run by the 6833rd Guardhouse Overhead Detachment. The prison régime was very severe and strict discipline was the order of the day. The Americans built a substantial execution house, which was attached to the main accommodation block and was incongruous as it was constructed in red brick, whereas the prison was built of grey stone. Twenty-one soldiers are known to have been hanged during the American occupation and two others shot by firing squad. The latter were believed to be of Red Indian descent; hanging would have been against their religious principles.

Hospitals

Meanwhile US Army hospitals, either specially built or in converted mansions, were established in various parts of the district. In Somerset, the 801st Hospital Centre was located at Hestercombe House; the 67th General Hospital was at Musgrove Camp, Taunton; the 74th was at Tyntesfield, near Bristol; the 101st at Norton Camp, near Taunton; 185th at Sandhill Park, Bishops Lydeard; the 121st at Lufton Camp and the 169th at Houndstone Camp both near Yeovil. A large blood bank was set up at Chilton Polden near Bridgwater.

The 61st Field Hospital was established at Merryfield in July 1944 to cope with the air-evacuated wounded and there was a large tented area with an ambulance park close to the technical site at the airfield.

Following D-Day, the casualties were flown back to the area, usually into Merryfield by C-47 (Dakota) aircraft. The roads between the aerodrome and the hospitals in the Taunton area were crowded with ambulances operating a shuttle service with the wounded.

Ike pays a visit

The gradual build up of forces into the area reached its climax in May 1944. Freight and troop trains were arriving in the area on a daily basis, laden with men and equipment. In a single day, 15 troop trains arrived at Dulverton each carrying a thousand men and vast stores of food. One train, however, held a surprise for the many men stationed in the area – and indeed for some of the local inhabitants. General Dwight D. Eisenhower, Supreme Commander Allied Expeditionary Forces, arrived by train at Dulverton to visit his troops in the region. A horse was hired to provide transport for his tour of inspection and he rode across the moors to Winsford, thence to Withypool, where he had a drink at the Royal Oak before returning to the station. General Eisenhower had been to Somerset before when he came by air, landing at RAF Culmhead in a Dakota transport aircraft on the afternoon of 18 March 1944. He was on an informal visit to a fellow general in the Taunton area and flew back to London the next day.

After D-Day the American presence gradually diminished in Somerset. The great invasion armies, of which they formed a major part, swept across Europe to final victory. Some of the men who had spent time in the county, never returned – or to their homeland. Others did, and have renewed their associations with Somerset in more peaceful times, to sample the tranquillity and charm of a county they once knew at war.

TEN

Key Points

Production of war materials in many of Somerset's factories, often totally different from their peacetime rôles, meant that they were potential enemy targets, designated by the authorities as Key Points.

The war production in the region was predominantly concerned with the aviation industry. Both Westland Aircraft and the Bristol Aeroplane Company had major factories in the county. Westland were centred at Yeovil, but BAC built two sub-sites near Weston-super-Mare at Hutton and Old Mixon; in addition, each had dozens of sub-contractors all over the county. Tomahawk aircraft were assembled in a shed off Locking Road, Weston-super-Mare after being shipped over from the USA in component form; Avimo Ltd at Taunton made optical gun sights; Butler and Tanner's factory at Frome was used as a machine-shop making components for Bristol Aero Engines. Swarf from the lathing operations remains embedded in the Canadian maple floor to this day.

The diverse nature of wartime production was highlighted by factories located at Bridgwater: Trojan Ltd made shell cases; the Light Buoyant Company's factory at Saltlands constructed landing craft and when completed these were craned into the River Parrett at West Quay; Electro-Dynamic Construction Co Ltd designed and manufactured electric motors, some of which were used in tanks and aircraft. From 1941 a quarry at Cliff Road, North Petherton near Bridgwater was used for the extraction of red sand and sent to Messrs Denning's foundry in Chard for the casting of idler wheels for tanks, which were produced by the thousand.

Mary Ruau worked in the Physical Test Laboratory at British Cellophane in Bridgwater:

Due to shortage of materials film was restricted to certain applications: cigarettes going abroad to soldiers; wrappers for army biscuits; for plasma or blood and as an anti-rust covering for a type of bullet used in humid places like Burma. They experimented with the film to see which sort was best. Later it was used with dehydrated foods. The War Office wouldn't order exclusively from one firm so Rayophane, Sidac and Diaphane shared orders. The film was tinted with a special colour – pink, pale green, yellow and Cellophane's blue to distinguish between the suppliers. Father worked in the Engineering Section and was involved in building Bailey bridges. He had to go to the Admiralty at Bath for meetings. When they announced about Mulberry Harbour father said: "that's what we were making!" – it was one small component.

Besides the aircraft industry, two of the largest employers of local labour and skill were the Admiralty Hydrographic Supplies Department at Taunton and the Royal Ordnance Factory at Puriton, near Bridgwater.

The Hydrographic Supplies Department

The large buildings of the Hydrographic Supplies Department at Taunton have been a well-known landmark in the town since 1940/1. The older building still has a trace of camouflage on it, which signifies its heritage and vulnerability as a potential target in time of war.

William Ewart Llewellyn, a civil servant and running the Hydrographic Department at Cricklewood, decided to disperse operations, realising that if the Department was bombed none of the ships would have a chart. After much consideration it was decided to look for suitable sites for the various functions performed by the Department.

Whilst heading by train for Exeter, looking for a suitable location for the printing department, Llewellyn spotted a potential site near Taunton, and a 32-acre site at Creech Barrow was purchased, being ideal for the erection of one large building to house the printing machinery. The first sod was cut in 1939 and in 1940 the building started in earnest. The various other operations were to be widely dispersed: Exeter, Armadale

and Ironside in Shropshire. However plans were shelved to centralise all the supplies departments at Taunton. The building was occupied in about 1941 and was then known as 'Creechbarrow House'; this became known as the Hydrographic Supplies Department.

The importance of the work carried out at the site during the war is almost immeasurable, for without charts the Navy would have been unable to operate. The thousands of charts printed at Taunton were a major contribution to the allied war effort. Throughout the war the post of Chief Hydrographer was held by Vice Admiral Sir John Edgell.

The Royal Ordnance Factory, Puriton

The siting of the Royal Ordnance Factory at Puriton proved to be of great benefit to Somerset and has provided much employment to this day. It also enabled a major drainage scheme of the levels to be financed.

There was a need to build a new factory to produce Cyclonite, Hexogen, T4, or RDX, as it became known. The Royal Arsenal, Woolwich, began studying the value of RDX as a military explosive shortly after the 1914-18 war, and by 1939 it had been decided to begin production. A potential location for the plant was eventually found at Huntspill on a site offering several advantages: the methanol, TNT and anthracite required for production could be obtained from

South Wales; transport facilities were favourable, a rail link could be provided via the GWR line and seaborne coal could be unloaded at Dunball Wharf. A supply of water was available from Durleigh Reservoir, and because it was remote, the factory was unlikely to warrant undue attention from enemy bombers.

Once the site had been selected, it was decided to build the plant in two parts, each capable of producing 120 tons per week. By mid-1940 work was well advanced, but a shortage of resources had reduced intended production to a weekly average of 60 tons.

It soon became apparent that Durleigh Reservoir's capacity of 21,000,000 gallons was not going to be sufficient to meet the needs of the factory, so alternative sources of water had to be found. The surrounding levels were the obvious choice, for they held considerable resources of raw water that would be suitable for the plant's needs; this helped persuade the Ministry of Agriculture and Fisheries to fund a new cutting, which once dug became known as the Huntspill River. The Somerset River Catchments Board had contemplated a drainage scheme but lacked the financial resources to implement it before the war. The new river connected the Glastonbury Canal and River Brue to the estuary of the River Parrett giving the main factory an estimated supply of 232,000,000 gallons of process water, in addition to which, a further 38,000,000 gallons was available at the southern side of the Poldens from the King Sedgemoor Drain.

Delays were experienced in the building of the plant. The marshland proved difficult: some piles sunk to 80 feet failed to find hard rock and were lost, resulting in the resiting of some buildings.

With invasion and air attack a real possibility, camouflage instructions were issued in July 1940 and put into effect. The buildings were unscathed when 14 HE bombs fell in the area between the plant and Highbridge during September. Many failed to explode and buried themselves to a depth of over 40 ft and had to be abandoned by the bomb disposal teams.

By November 1940 enough of the plant had been built to allow some of the machinery to be installed. In the next few months experienced staff were recruited from other plants and 500 local men were transferred from building and construction. The factory went into production of RDX in August 1941 following months of preparation and setbacks. Demand soon increased, and in November 1941 it was decided to employ female process workers on the RDX section for the first time. All other sections except the tetryl plant followed suit. The factory employed 374 people in May 1941 and peaked at 2,816 in March 1943. The demand for RDX continued and by May 1945, the plant was producing 200 tons per week.

Over 40 years later the plant is still in production and a major source of local employment.

The withy trade at war

Arthur Spender tells of the revival in the withy weaving trade during the war, when a new use was found for locally made 'hampers':

At the turn of the century basket wicker work employed over 100 workers in the village then a decline set in mainly due to the Netherlands flooding the market with cheap wicker which had been grown in raw sewage. By 1925 the industry was dying, but the war brought a revival in its fortunes for there was a need for baskets that could be dropped easily by air. At one period a lorry load would be despatched daily to the Air Force. They were expendable baskets, so much work was created in making these. For the first time in history women played a major part in making them. Previously they had been employed in boiling the withies and stripping their skins off. A purpose-built hostel for women was built in 1940 adjacent to Cemetery Road, North Petherton which had a dormitory, kitchen and dining hall.

PART III

THE SERVICES

In February 1943 a booklet was prepared to illustrate the work of signallers in the field. A Division of Signals from the Guards Armoured Division at Templecombe was enlisted to help and this scene shows a field telephone being used in an 'advanced' position. (IWM)

ELEVEN

The Home Guard

An Army is born: the Local Defence Volunteers

Somerset, like all the counties of Britain was ready to meet the call when it came. The news from the Continent was not good: the English Channel just a small obstacle to invasion. On 14 May 1940 – the day on which Rotterdam was heavily bombed and Dutch resistance was crumbling – Anthony Eden, Secretary of State for War broadcast an appeal:

"We want large numbers to come forward now and offer their services. The name of the new force will be the 'Local Defence Volunteers.' When on duty you will form part of the Armed Forces and your period of service will be for the duration of the war."

Anthony Eden had hardly finished his appeal before the first volunteers began to gather at police stations. Volunteers who responded to the call early on the following morning hoping to be among the first to enrol found themselves well down the list. Within a few days the numbers went into hundreds of thousands and later passed the million mark.

Six days were sufficient time for the initial organisation of the LDV in Somerset. The county was constituted a sub-area under Southern Command with Colonel W.O. Gibbs, ADC of Barrow Gurney, as the county organiser. In the early days organisation was into sections, platoons and group companies conforming to the appropriate Police Divisions.

Until the Army could be reorganised and re-equipped following the evacuation from Dunkirk, England seemed defenceless. The LDV were already guarding beaches, aerodromes, landing strips, fields, roads and railways. There was an urgent need of arms which were pitifully small in number due to the loss of equipment suffered by our forces at Dunkirk: so few that the initial allocation of rifles to Somerset was set at two hundred – 200 rifles and 2,000 rounds of ammunition – for the 6,000 men enrolled during the first week! An appeal was made for sporting guns, revolvers, indeed any kind of weapon. These were collected by the Police with the assurance that they would be returned to their owners once the danger had passed.

The original War Office instruction was that six Volunteers should be enrolled for each rifle. In Somerset more than five times the permitted number of men had come forward, and it was ordered that those without a rifle should arm themselves with an axe or heavy stick.

Other orders soon followed:

If a parachute landing is taking place by day, every volunteer will rush to the scene at once and kill the enemy as they land...remember that they often land holding their hands up as if in surrender and in each hand they hold a grenade. At night the principle should be to close in from all sides, moving silently and then rush in with club and axe.

It sounded all so naïve and overlooked the fact that the LDV would, in all probability, be faced by Hitler's crack paratroopers. A certain amount of good natured cynicism crept in and the LDV was soon nicknamed the 'Look Duck and Vanish Brigade'!

At this stage the War Office issued the famous pikes. A few were received in Somerset and, despite an order for their return, are preserved that future generations may see the state to which England had come in the year 1940.

Recruiting went on apace; volunteers were accepted between the ages of 17 and 65. As no birth certificates were demanded there was no upper age limit. In the same way the requirement of 'reasonable physical fitness' was very liberally interpreted. The loss of a limb was rarely a disqualification and many men so disabled readily offered their services and were often accepted.

Following the fall of France, invasion became more probable. Signposts were taken down; the name boards of every railway station disappeared; place names on factories, offices, shops, vehicles, even on war memorials, were effaced.

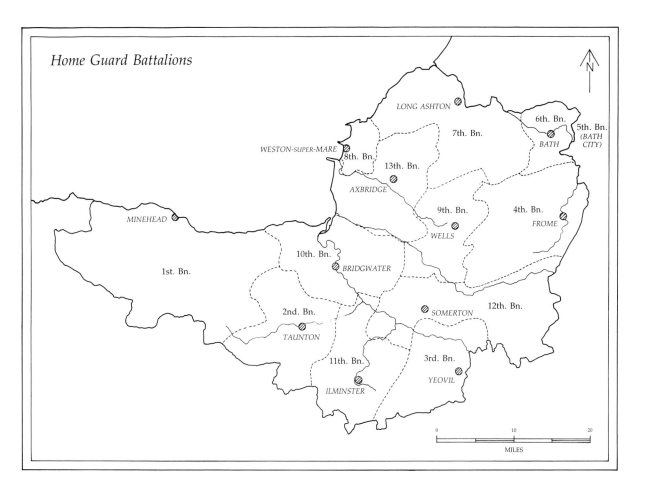

Home Guard Battalions

Poles, carts, wires, obstacles of every kind began to appear open spaces that might serve as landing grounds for enemy aircraft. Motorists were to immobilise every vehicle not actually in use. Cars left even for a short time in the streets had to be locked. The Local Defence Volunteers erected portable barricades at entrances to town and village. Every petrol station in the land was charted so that the Volunteers could deny its use to an invader, either by destruction or by the pollution of its contents.

At Taunton the LDVs spent the warm nights in points of vantage round the road blocks – every sense alert for parachutists, or for the church bells which would sound the alarm. Enemy aircraft were beginning to be seen and therefore more vital, but onerous, were the long night guards at the petrol storage depot, gasworks and other public utilities. Between these duties and daily work were sandwiched hours of drilling, fieldcraft and such firing practice as the few weapons could provide.

On 15 June the Territorial Army Association took over the administration of the Volunteers, thereby lightening somewhat the burden on the local commanders. The Group Companies were now in some cases 3,000 strong; from 1 July they were designated Battalions, retaining their former town names and each was now allowed a paid civilian administrative officer. At the same time the general scheme of command was revised. Colonel W.D. Stillwell DSO, a regular officer, was appointed Local Defence Area Commander for the Southern Area, and the county of Somerset became a zone. Colonel Gibbs now became the Somerset Zone Commander with Lieutenant Colonel C.D.G. Lyon DSO as Second in Command. The headquarters were at Taunton.

At the end of July uniforms were issued. They were of the denim type, a kind of cotton twill probably intended for use as overalls by regular troops. Field service caps and boots followed. At last the LDV began to feel and look like soldiers.

The rows of medal ribbons which now appeared on many of their comrades uniforms distinguished them as soldiers of earlier days.

Creation of the 'Home Guard'

Also at the end of July a major event happened which solved the arms problem within a few hours: 1,000,000 American-made P17 .300 rifles and 1,000 field guns with ammunition were given by the Government and people of the United States. Their assistance could not have been more timely or welcome than at this period. Special trains were waiting to carry the rifles to all the Home Guard areas and the troops worked night and day to clean them from the grease in which they had been stored. At the same time the LDV were re-christened the Home Guard and established as a fighting unit. They were now equipped and ready for battle...

Training went on apace: the 'Old Sweats' of the First War acted as musketry and bombing instructors. The Home Guard relied upon the Somerset Light Infantry to whom they were now affiliated for training, which was tough for the more elderly men, some of whom were known to be at least 70. During marching drill the Light Infantry pace of 140 paces to the minute was seldom achieved!

Despite such fears the tedium of most duties allotted to the Home Guard was great. Hours of guarding a bridge or road junction, with nothing except the night for company, must have strained the most unimaginative person's mind. On the other hand, because the county lay under the flight path of German aircraft on their way to bomb targets in South Wales, the Midlands, Bristol and the North, many hours were spent by Home Guardsmen listening to the drone of enemy bombers as they flew overhead. Perhaps the thought that some might have been part of an airborne assault and parachutists were about to drop caused the imagination to run riot whilst guarding a lonely outpost.

Amongst those who thought the Germans had landed one night was 16 year-old Eric Westman and a young colleague, both of whom were members of the Bawdrip Home Guard Platoon and were on duty on Knowle Hill:

I always will remember my first night of duty. Even though there was a blackout, the countryside looked perfect in the moonlight. All was quiet save the chiming of half a dozen church clocks, which we could hear clearly from our position overlooking Sedgemoor, where the last battle was fought on English soil. I thought of how much I had taken all these things for granted in the past, only the drone of bombers going overhead made us doubly aware of the reality of the situation. Always alert to the possibility of parachutists, imagine our alarm when we suddenly heard footsteps coming towards us on the grass: scrunch...scrunch...scrunch. Paralysed with fear, we didn't know what to do and just stood back to back – my mate clutching the 12-bore, which he didn't know how to use, and me the bandolier, which I could hardly hold – were we about to face the ultimate test? The footsteps got nearer and nearer. "Christ – the bloody Germans are on us!" I said, and was shaking like a leaf...just then a large cow loomed out of the darkness!

The Bells! The Bells!

By the end of August 1940 the Home Guard was beginning to feel confident of its ability to deal with any situation that might arise. Road blocks, consisting of concrete walls and tree trunks, had been completed, the men were well armed and knew how to deal with tanks, either using the 'Molotov Cocktails' or phosphorous 'Sip' grenades. They had studied the highways and byways, the back alleys, and even the sewers, so that they would not be taken unawares; also in the town units were beginning to know each other. In the village platoons and sections there were of course no strangers. Confidence was such that many had begun to learn the list of 'Common German Military Expressions,' which had been issued by the War Office: "*Hände hoch!*" – "Hands up"; "*Waffen hinlegen!*" – "Throw down your arms"; and "*Ergebt euch!*" – "Surrender". This was the position on 7 September 1940, the Battle of Britain at its height, when the church bells rang.

Because of the heavy concentration of invasion barges in the Channel ports, the massing of bomber aircraft and the state of the moon and tides, the General Staff thought invasion was imminent and at 20.00 on the 7th issued the pre-arranged code word: 'CROMWELL'. This code word, short, sharp and pre-emptory, coming down through Southern Command to zone and battalion, reached the outlying Somerset villages just before midnight.

It's effect upon the local Home Guard commanders was electric. In some cases they rushed to the church towers and the bells pealed out. This excess of zeal was excusable – it certainly was effective: within a short time road blocks and vulnerable points were manned by villagers, alert and ready to fight. There is no complete record of all the parishes in Somerset in which the bells, silent since June, were rung that night, but it is known that Corfe, Pitminster, Trull and Wiveliscombe were among them.

In most other areas it was realised that this was but a 'Stand to' order and church bells should not be rung until the enemy had been seen in the locality. The men therefore were called by telephone and runner. All through the night the muster went on. Sentries stopped and examined all transport and pedestrians. Boxes of grenades and ammunition were carried to strong points, while defences were brought to a state of readiness. Where there were regular troops, they stood shoulder to shoulder with the Home Guard and would so have fought had the need arisen.

Eric Westman recalls that night:

I used to guard a pillbox near the Silver Fish Restaurant at Bawdrip, near Bridgwater. I had been left alone in my parents' house and was fast asleep on a mattress in the converted coal house, which doubled as an air raid shelter, when there was a knock at the door. It was the local Home Guard sergeant, who said: "Quick – the invasion has started – they're in Bridgwater – go to the Silver Fish as fast as you can!" I asked him where they had landed and he thought somewhere near Kilve. I got dressed and pedalled off on my bike as fast as I could to the post – it was a really dark night and I couldn't see a thing. Soon I heard the clattering of a tracked vehicle coming from the Bridgwater direction – I was frightened to death. "Christ! the Germans are coming – a tank!" I said to myself. It got nearer and nearer and when it was almost on me, I made a dash into the open yard in front of the house and hid behind one of two half-barrels with oak trees growing in them, still holding my bicycle upright in the hope that they wouldn't see me. The vehicle passed – it was only one of our troop carriers!

The anti-climax came on Sunday 8 September when the Home Guard was quietly dismissed with the injunction to remain 'at the ready'. This was reinforced by the Prime Minister in a broadcast to the nation three days later.

The danger of invasion was very real as disclosed in documents captured from the Germans after their collapse in 1945. Plans were made following the fall of France. The first date chosen was 15 September 1940. Two beach-heads were contemplated, one between Folkestone and Worthing, the other at Lyme Regis. But the RAF in the Battle of Britain upset the enemy's calculations and the invasion was postponed until a later date and then until a later year. It would be too late.

In 1944 one of the defenders of Calais back in England after four years as a prisoner of war in German hands, was invited to South Somerset Home Guard Headquarters. He recounted how, on one occasion, the prisoners were ordered to remove quantities of waste paper from the officers' quarters of a crack German regiment. The paper consisted of torn up maps. Some men secreted pieces about their clothing and on return to camp reassembled the fragments after the fashion of a jig-saw puzzle. The maps were of Southern England. Alongside the towns and villages were printed the names and numbers of German divisions and the dates on which those places were to be occupied. The maps were never required. The divisions named were afterwards launched against Russia.

THE ORGANISATION

By October 1940 the Home Guard organisation in Somerset was complete. The county was divided into two groups by a line running roughly from Burnham-on-Sea south-east to Street and then eastwards to the Wiltshire boundary at Kilmington. Eventually there were in the North and South Groups seven and six battalions respectively; the strength of each battalion being stabilised at between two and three thousand men. For administration purposes, they came under the Somerset Territorial Association. As material became available the War Office issued serge battledress, greatcoats, boots, leather gaiters, respirators, gas capes and the greater part of the normal infantry equipment. Eventually staff cars and battalion trucks were supplied and more up to date weapons were issued.

The pitchfork, pike, shotgun and stave gave way to the .303 Lee Enfield rifle, Tommy Gun, Sten, Spigot Mortar, Smith Gun, the two-inch anti-tank gun, the No 73 'Woolworth' and No 74 'Sticky' bombs, which all came in their turn to make up the formidable armament the Home Guard had at their disposal.

The operational rôle of the Home Guard was often changed: official policy alternating between the need for seeking and engaging the enemy wherever he could be found and the more prosaic alternative of remaining static in defended positions and at whatever cost. As it happened the only Germans who actually appeared in Somerset were those members of the Luftwaffe shot down, but the Home Guard were often called out to render what was officially termed as 'minor assistance' to civil authorities during and after air attacks. The activities of the different battalions in Somerset were many and varied. The *esprit de corps* became very strong and the bond formed then still is plain to see amongst the survivors today.

THE COMMAND STRUCTURE

The first Somerset Zone Commander was Colonel W.O. Gibbs, ADC, with Lieutenant Colonel C.D.G. Lyon, DSO as Second in Command. Headquarters were at Taunton. This arrangement ceased on 21 October 1940 when the County of Somerset was divided into North and South Groups.

North Somerset Group/Sector

Formed on 21 October 1940 as North Somerset Group comprising 4th (Frome), 5th (Bath Admiralty), 6th (Bath City), 7th (Long Ashton), 8th (Weston) and 9th (Wells) Somerset Battalions. Commanded until March 12th 1943 by Colonel (Brigadier General retired) A.B. Incledon-Webber, CMG, DSO, with headquarters at the Drill Hall, Bridgwater. Colonel Rogers succeeded on 15 March 1943 when the headquarters were transferred to 15 Johnston Street, Bath. Colonel Rogers had commanded the Bath Garrison since 1941 and the two headquarters were now combined. The name was changed to North Somerset Sector on 30 April 1943. The 13th (Axbridge) Battalion was added on 15 May 1943. Strength at stand down: 14 officers.

South Somerset Group/Sector

Formed on 21 October 1940 as South Somerset Group, comprising 1st (Minehead), 2nd (Taunton), 3rd (Yeovil) and 10th (Bridgwater) Somerset

The South Somerset Sector Home Guard HQ at Taunton. (CRO)

Battalions. The 11th (Ilminster) and 12th (Somerton) Battalions were added in 1943. Commanded throughout by Colonel (Brigadier General retired) C.L. Norman, DSO, MVO, DL, with Headquarters first at the Territorial Hall, Taunton and from 4 October 1943 at No 6 Elm Grove, Taunton. From 8 May 1942 Colonel Norman also commanded the Taunton Garrison. The name was changed to South Somerset Sector on 30 April 1943. Strength at stand down: 12 officers.

THE BATTALIONS

1st Somerset (Minehead) Battalion

Formed in May 1940 by Colonel E.R. Clayton, CMG, DSO, who was succeeded in command by Lieutenant Colonel R.D. Alexander. The headquarters were at 'Wyncote', Minehead. The battalion area included practically the whole of Exmoor and the Brendon Hills. There were ultimately seven companies based on Porlock, Minehead, Dunster, Williton, Wiveliscombe, Dulverton and Exmoor.

The 1st Somerset (Minehead) Battalion had a mounted patrol formed to watch the broad expanse of Exmoor and this patrol is believed to have been the only Home Guard unit to which the War Office issued cavalry equipment. In the early days when there was a fear of a German invasion by way of Ireland, the 1st Battalion provided relief crews for the searchlights and the two 4-in guns on Minehead Quay. Strength at stand down: 1,367 officers and men.

Mounted patrols of the 1st Somerset (Minehead) Battalion could cover vast stretches of Exmoor. 1944. (CRO)

Local dignitaries inspect a platoon of the 1st Battalion. Note the new standard of drill as demonstrated by the sergeant on the left who is shown standing to attention at ease! (Kit Houghton)

A mounted signaller of the 1st Somerset (Minehead) Battalion tunes in his R/T. 1944. (CRO)

2nd Somerset (Taunton) Battalion

Formed in May 1940 under Major L.A. Jones Mortimer who was later succeeded by Lieutenant Colonel H.F.L. Hilton Green, DSO MC. The Battalion area covered the whole of Taunton Deane, together with the towns of Ilminster and Chard and adjacent country. The eastern part of this area was detached in April 1943 to form the 11th Somerset (Ilminster) Battalion. The companies of the 2nd Battalion were ultimately Taunton North, Taunton South, Taunton (Great Western Railway), Bishops Lydeard, Blagdon Hill, Wellington and Stoke St Mary.

In the 2nd Somerset (Taunton) Battalion there

was an independent platoon for the defence of Churchstanton (later renamed Culmhead) RAF Station. This platoon claims to have taken the first German prisoner in Somerset – a crew member from a Heinkel bomber brought down on the Blackdowns on 26 July 1940. Sergeant C. Smith, also of this platoon, was commended by the King for gallantry in rescuing the pilot of a Spitfire from RAF Churchstanton, which crashed in flames on 22 August 1941, also on the Blackdowns. Unfortunately, the Polish pilot did not survive.

For operational purposes the Taunton Companies came under the Taunton Garrison Commander. Similarly the Churchstanton Platoon came under the orders of the officer commanding the RAF station. There was a light anti-aircraft troop attached to the GWR Company for the defence of Taunton railway station. Battalion Headquarters were first at No 11 Hammet Street, Taunton and from 19 June 1942 at the Territorial Hall. Strength at stand down: 1,940 officers and men, 129 women auxiliaries.

3rd Somerset (Yeovil) Battalion.

Formed in May 1940 and commanded throughout by Lieutenant Colonel G.H.A. Ing, CMG, DSO, DL. The Battalion originally covered a wide area in the south-east corner of the county, bordering Wiltshire and Dorset. In 1943 the Somerton and Wincanton companies were detached to form the nucleus of the 12th Somerset (Somerton) Battalion. After reorganisation the companies of the 3rd Battalion were: Yeovil Borough, Ilchester, Hamdon, Crewkerne, Westland (Aircraft Factory) and Heron. Battalion Headquarters were at No 11 Summerlands Road, Yeovil.

Corporal F.A. Duke of 3rd Somerset (Yeovil) Battalion received the British Empire Medal for rescuing the rear gunner of a Wellington bomber which crashed in flames near Yeovilton on 23 January 1943. Strength at stand down: 2,112 officers and men, 34 women auxiliaries.

4th Somerset (Frome) Battalion

Formed in May 1940 and commanded throughout by Lieutenant Colonel H.G. Spencer, TD, DL. Administrative Headquarters were at the Drill Hall, Frome, where, in addition to the hall and offices, there was a miniature rifle range and a canteen. Battle Headquarters were at No 2 Mar-

A platoon of the 3rd Battalion enjoy a drink outside their unofficial 'HQ' at the Windwhistle Inn, near Chard. (CRO)

ket Place, Frome. The Battalion area included the Somerset portion of the 'Yellow' Defence Line. The companies were named: Norton St Philip, Frome, Nunney, Midsomer Norton, Radstock, Shepton Mallet and Ashwick. Strength at stand down: 2,468 officers and men, 112 women auxiliaries.

5th Somerset (Bath City) Battalion

Raised in May 1940 by Colonel G.H. Rogers, DL who later became the Garrison Commander and North Somerset Sector Commander. He was succeeded in command of the Battalion by Lieutenant Colonel L.R.E.W. Taylor, DSO. Although named Bath City, the Battalion area included Bathampton, Batheaston, Bathford, Charmy Down, Claverton, Dunkerton, Freshford, Limpley Stoke, Newton St Loe, North and South Stoke, Swainswick and Wellow. Battalion Headquarters were at No 15, Queen Square, Bath.

Very fine work during and after the severe air raids in Bath was done by the 5th Somerset (Bath City) Battalion. Nine NCOs and men were killed and seven wounded in the raid of 26/27 April 1942. For exceptional gallantry during the raids Sergeant B. Brown received the BEM. Strength at stand down: 1,765 officers and men, 143 women auxiliaries.

6th Somerset (Bath Admiralty) Battalion.

Permission to form this battalion was given on 26 May 1940 and 1,600 applications were immediately received from Admiralty personnel in Bath. Among them were a number of naval officers who, wishing to take an active part in the defence of the country, appeared as naval officers by day and LDVs at night. This procedure displeased the Admiralty, who ruled that the practice must cease. The first Commanding Officer was Commander D.C. Morrison, RN (retired), who was succeeded at Bath by Lieutenant Colonel W.C. Brown.

The 6th Somerset (Bath Admiralty) Battalion had also a good record of service in the raids. Four immediate awards were made: George Medal – Lieutenant J.A. Leslie (then a Warrant Officer); British Empire Medal – Privates N.W.S. Baker, J.M. Martell and H.D. Rees.

The City of Bath was without AA defences up to and including the April 1942 raids. Shortly afterwards the 6th Battalion was equipped with twelve 2-inch rocket projectors and eight 40mm Bofors guns. In addition five German flak guns were obtained from naval sources. But the enemy did not come again. Lieutenant Colonel Brown claimed that his command was unique in that it included both infantry and AA batteries, all part of the same unit. Strength at stand down: 960 officers and men, 77 women auxiliaries.

7th Somerset (Long Ashton) Battalion.

Admiral Sir Hugh Tweedie, KCB who commanded the 7th Somerset (Long Ashton) Battalion showed that a Somerset admiral could also make a good soldier!

The Battalion covered an area of rather more than 300 square miles, forming a semi-circle right round the south and west of Bristol City from Bath to the Bristol Channel, including the coast from the mouth of the River Yeo up to Portishead. For operational purposes the Battalion came directly under the Bristol Garrison Commander.

This battalion shared with the 1st the distinction of including both infantry and cavalry. It also helped man the 6-in guns of the coast defence battery at Portishead and the guns and rocket batteries in Bristol's anti-aircraft defence.

Enemy bombing was heavy in this area and constant help was given to the Civil Defence services. Two members of the 7th Battalion were killed and four wounded by enemy action. Eight were commended for services rendered under air attack.

Home Guardsmen 6th Battalion guarding the ruins of the Bank of England's premises in the city, after the Baedeker raids of April 1942. (Wessex Newspapers)

Members of the 7th Somerset (Long Ashton) Battalion guarding wreckage of the Heinkel 111 brought down at Failand, 25 September 1940. (John H. Moreton)

Administrative Headquarters were at Wraxall House and Battle Headquarters at the Long Ashton Research Station. There were nine companies based on Long Ashton, Keynsham, Temple Cloud, Portishead, Clevedon, Yatton, Chew Magna, Bishopsworth and Leigh Woods. Strength at stand down: 2,507 officers and men, 104 women auxiliaries.

8th Somerset (Weston) Battalion

The Weston-super-Mare Battalion formed in May 1940 at first covered a wide area to the east and north of the town. The outer area was detached in May 1943 to form the 13th (Axbridge) Battalion leaving the 8th essentially a town unit. The first Commanding Officer, Lieutenant Colonel A.H. Yeatman, DSO, DL, took over the 13th when formed, and was succeeded in the Weston Battalion by Lieutenant Colonel A.W.A. Bruce. Administrative Headquarters were at Salisbury Terrace and Battle Headquarters at the RE Drill Hall, Langford Road, Weston-super-Mare. There were finally eight companies of infantry, two light anti-aircraft troops and a bomb disposal unit.

While on duty in air attacks on its home town, two members of the 8th Somerset (Weston-super-Mare) Battalion were killed and six were wounded. In April 1944 the bomb disposal unit dealt with 78 small unexploded bombs which fell on an aircraft factory. Strength at stand down: 1,668 officers and men, 56 women auxiliaries.

9th Somerset (Wells) Battalion

Formed in October 1940 by a division of the original Glastonbury Battalion raised by Brigadier General Incledon Webber. The Wells Battalion was commanded throughout by Lieutenant Colonel J. McDonnell. Its area is adequately described by the names of its five companies which were: Wells City, Cheddar Valley, Mendip, Glastonbury and Street. Headquarters were at No 15 Union Street, Wells. In its early days the Cheddar Valley company was commanded by Captain the Reverend H.L. Walker, Vicar of Wookey. The 9th Somerset (Wells) Battalion had one unique feature – a very fine brass band. Strength at stand down: 1,248 officers and men, 42 women auxiliaries.

10th Somerset (Bridgwater) Battalion.

Throughout its existence the 10th Somerset (Bridgwater) Battalion was commanded by Lieutenant Colonel R. Chamberlin who received the OBE in recognition of his services. His work for Bridgwater did not cease with the stand-down of the Home Guard for the townsfolk promptly elected him Mayor. Headquarters were at the Drill Hall, Bridgwater. There were six companies: Headquarters, Quantock, Polden, Bridgwater, Sedgemoor and Royal Ordnance Factory. Strength at stand down: 2,266 officers and men, 177 women auxiliaries

Members of the 10th Somerset (Bridgwater) Battalion gather on the hillside above Greinton. The Home Guard and the RAF used the area for grenade and other weapons training on a range set up there. (Ann Meade)

11th Somerset (Ilminster) Battalion

Formed in April 1943 on the Ilminster and Chard Companies which, until that time, were part of the 2nd (Taunton) Battalion. There were ultimately companies at North Curry, South Petherton, Ilminster, Chard Town and Chard Rural. The Battalion was commanded throughout by Lieutenant Colonel T. Washington Metcalfe. Headquarters were at Butts Farm, Ilminster.

The central part of the Taunton Stop Line ran through this area, Ilminster and part of Chard being heavily fortified. The anti-tank ditch and defences of Ilminster had a perimeter of four miles and required a garrison of at least 750 men. After the withdrawal of regular troops less than half of the required number of Home Guards were available. The defences from that time tended to be a liability as they could not be fully manned. Strength at stand down: 1,201 officers and men, 27 women auxiliaries.

12th Somerset (Somerton) Battalion

This was an offshoot of the Yeovil Battalion and was formed in February 1943. Headquarters were at Coombe Hill House, Keinton Mandeville, the residence of the Commanding Officer, Lieutenant Colonel Sir Cecil E. Walker, Bart, DSO, MC. The Battalion covered an elongated area, with companies named from west to east – Curry Rivel, Langport, Somerton, Charlton Mackrell, Castle Cary, Bruton, Milborne Port and Wincanton. Strength at stand down: 1,676 officers and men, 96 women auxiliaries.

13th Somerset (Axbridge) Battalion

Formed in May 1943 out of the original Weston-super-Mare Battalion, it took the greater part of the area of the Weston Battalion and also its Commanding Officer, Lieutenant Colonel A.H. Yeatman, DSO, DL. He was succeeded in 1944 by Lieutenant Colonel L.M. Stevens, DSO.
The Battalion area included the western end of the Mendip Hills and the levels between the Rivers Axe and Brue. Headquarters were at Bromswald House, Axbridge. The four companies were based on Winscombe, Burnham-on-Sea, Wrington and Wedmore. Strength at stand down: 1,350 officers and men, 38 women auxiliaries.

The 15th Gloucester (Post Office) Battalion

This battalion included Post Office staff in the principal towns of Somerset and Gloucester, with headquarters at Bristol. 'A' Company, based on Bristol, had platoons at Bath, Weston-super-Mare and Shepton Mallet. 'D' Company, based on Taunton, had an additional section at Minehead. In the event of invasion all these units would have come under the operational orders of the local Somerset battalion, with whom they maintained close contact throughout. Strength at stand down: 420 officers and men (in Somerset).

22nd Devon (5th Southern Railway) Battalion

There were Somerset railwaymen in both 'A' and 'E' companies of this battalion drawn from the staff of the Southern Railway at and between the Yeovil and Chard Junction stations, and also from the staff of the Somerset & Dorset line right across the county.

Battalion Headquarters were at the Central Station, Exeter, 'A' Company Headquarters at Yeovil Town Station and 'E' Company Headquarters at Templecombe SR Station. There were light AA troops at Yeovil and Templecombe. Strength at stand down: 290 officers and men (in Somerset).

Home Guard crouch behind a hedge during an exercise with an Army Co-operation Unit of the RAF. Lysanders and Mustangs of 16 Squadron from Weston Zoyland were detailed to perform this task. (IWM)

THE ANTI-AIRCRAFT, TRANSPORT AND AUXILIARY UNITS

The gradual withdrawal of Regular units from some parts of Britain made it necessary for the Home Guard to provide its own ancillary services.

Home Guard Anti-Aircraft Units

In 1942 men from the Gloucester and Somerset Home Guard battalions were transferred to serve the Bristol anti-aircraft guns. There was at first some soul searching among the battalions as these transfers depleted their strength and necessitated the abandonment of some of the defended areas and strong points. However these difficulties were overcome and the 17th (AA) Home Guard Regiment came into being under the command of Colonel N.G. Gibson of Chew Magna, early in 1943.

A few hundred men were transferred from the 7th Somerset Home Guard Battalion, which was already manning the coastal defence guns at Portishead. Men from the Bishopsworth Company, under Captain Mainstone, entered the 71st Gloucester Heavy AA Battery and others from the Long Ashton Company were drafted into the 101st and 104th Gloucester Rocket AA Batteries. Keynsham Company provided 30 men under Captain A.A. Hitching for the 103rd Gloucester Rocket AA Battery. To the latter unit were also transferred four officers and approximately 200 other ranks of the 5th Somerset (Bath City) Home Guard Battalion.

The four Bristol rocket batteries were all sited south of the River Avon: two of them in Somerset and the others in the City of Bristol. Although they were manned mainly by Gloucester men, their action was in the county. All batteries were in action at least once, some more often, but could not confirm claims of enemy aircraft destroyed.

As previously mentioned, the City of Bath was provided with AA defences after the disastrous raids of April 1942. The somewhat unusual arrangement was made of placing the batteries under the Officer Commanding the 6th Somerset (Bath Admiralty) HG Battalion, which became both General Service and Artillery.

Light AA troops were also formed to combat low-flying attacks in daylight. They were armed with the lighter types of quick-firing guns. In some cases 'flak' towers were built of sufficient height to give a clear field of fire above the railway station roofs. Such troops were located at: Taunton: 'H' (GWR) Company, 2nd Somerset (Taunton) HG Battalion. Templecombe: 'E' Company, 22nd Devon (5th Southern Railway) HG Battalion. Weston-super-Mare: One troop each from the 'E' and 'F' Companies of the 8th Somerset (Weston) HG Battalion. Yeovil: 3rd Somerset (Yeovil) HG Battalion. Yeovil Junction 'A' Company, 22nd Devon (5th Southern Railway) HG Battalion.

Home Guard Motor Transport Units

Home Guard motor transport companies were formed in Somerset early in 1942. Their main purpose was to transport ammunition and other military stores in the event of invasion. Ordinary commercial vehicles specially earmarked would have been commandeered. Used daily for normal business purposes, these were rarely available for training.

No 2133 MT Company was formed at Taunton under the command of Major C.H. Burns, VD. This company at first included Wellington and Bridgwater, but the latter district was later detached as an independent platoon. No 2134 MT Company, under Major N.S.M. Durnford, was first located at Calne, but later had its headquarters at Frome. There was a second independent platoon based on Bristol and known as No 2136 Independent Motor Coach Platoon. Its headquarters were at the Lawrence Hill Depot of the Bristol Tramways and Carriage Co Ltd and its main function was the movement of troops, walking wounded, etc, as required.

In February 1944 the above-mentioned units were brought together under one administration as the Somerset MT Column, with Lieutenant Colonel N.S.M. Durnford in command and Captain R.T. Lancaster RASC as Adjutant and Quartermaster. Headquarters were established at 23 High Street, Wells, this being the most central point in the county.

The Auxiliary Scout Units

The nearest thing that the Home Guard had to the so called 'Churchill's Murder Bands', as Hitler had dubbed them, were the Auxiliary Scout units. Said to have come under the direct orders of GHQ Home Forces, they were certainly not attached to the normal Home Guard units in their own localities. They operated in very small cells and were organised to cover different parts of the county. Led by Captain 'Mad Dog' Ian Fenwick, their main function would have been, had the enemy overrun their district, to emerge from hiding and harass the invader by sabotaging his communications. Captain Fenwick's unique way of testing his men was to throw a two-ounce lump of primed gelignite at them.

Their organisation was a closely guarded secret, but occasionally they made their presence known during exercises by staging surprise explosions in unexpected places.

Reg Shattock was a member of the organisation:

So secret was our function that we didn't know any member of the organisation other than those in our immediate area and each individual would only maintain a communication link with an appointed local commander. I had to report directly to Colonel Ingram, who lived at Pightley House, Spaxton – he was my contact and would have issued me with orders. Our job was also to train for sabotage and as part of this I can remember we endeavoured to blow up an old tree with some explosives, but try as we might, the thing wouldn't succumb!

Fritz Coles was another member:

I only knew that Reg Shattock was in it, but knew of nobody else. We met at Pightley House, Spaxton and spent a month or two studying identification – enemy tanks, gun carriages and so on – also German regiments of the line – so we would be able to identify them easily. We had secret meeting places where we could leave messages – there was a place at the top of Enmore Hill – a couple of big stones which was our 'post box'. We never did leave any messages though! There were also underground dugouts in nearby Standards Wood, which could be used to store things like explosives. Strength at stand down: not known.

THE STAND DOWN

Three months after D-Day the Home Guard unexpectedly received its quietus on 6 September 1944 in a broadcast by the Secretary of State for War, Sir James Grigg. His words were of themselves unexceptional – simply that compulsory drills and training would be discontinued. But the unmistakable impression was conveyed that

Special Order of the Day to the Home Guard

by

General Sir Harold E. Franklyn, K.C.B., D.S.O., M.C.,
Commander-in-Chief, Home Forces

GENERAL HEADQUARTERS,
HOME FORCES.
November, 1944.

During the past few years I have had many opportunities of seeing the Home Guard in most parts of the country, including Northern Ireland. A high standard of efficiency has been reached, which has been made possible only by the keenness and devotion to duty of all ranks. I would like to emphasise the very special contribution of those who volunteered in 1940 and whose enthusiasm has never flagged since then ; they have been the backbone of their units.

The Home Guard came into being at a time of acute crisis in our history, and for over four years has stood prepared to repel any invader of our shores. The reliance that has been placed on you during these years has been abundantly justified and it has enabled our Regular troops to go overseas in sufficient numbers to give battle to the enemy with the magnificent results that we have seen.

And now as to the future. I hope that Home Guardsmen will take every opportunity of preserving the friendships and associations that you have formed during these past years. You can continue to be a real source of stability and strength to the country during what may be difficult years ahead. I hope also that you will do all in your power to help the Cadets, even if only by encouragement. Here is a way in which you can continue to render valuable service for many years to come.

I am very proud to have had the Home Guard under my command. I have enjoyed meeting and speaking to thousands of you. Now you can stand down with every right to feel that you have done your duty and contributed very materially to victory.

The best of luck to every one of you.

Well done indeed the Home Guard.

General.

On stand down, General Sir Harold Franklyn sent this congratulatory message to those under his command. (CRO)

the Home Guard was no longer wanted. Disappointed and not a little bewildered at being thus so rapidly cast aside, the Home Guard began to fade away.

On Sunday 3 December 1944 approximately 23,500 men, who formed the Somerset Home Guard, assembled for the stand down parades. While they gathered in town and village their representatives – three from each battalion – took part in the great march-past in London before the King. Beside the King stood the GOC Home Forces, General Sir Harold Franklyn, who, as commander of the 8th Corps in the stirring days of 1940, had directed from his headquarters near Taunton the building of the great defence lines of Somerset. That evening the King's broadcast to the Home Guard ended with these words:

"Officers, non-commissioned officers and men, you have served your country with a steadfast devotion. I know that your country will never

Stand down parades were held in every major Somerset town. Here members of the 2nd Somerset (Taunton) Battalion march up the High Street on 3 December 1944. (CRO)

forget that service". That, and the bonds of comradeship forged during four years of war, were probably reward enough.

ROLL OF HONOUR

The names of Somerset Home Guard members known to have lost their lives whilst on duty are as follows:

1st Battalion
Pte Robins W.J. Accident on duty
CSM Farmer J. Accidentally shot 17.12.41

3rd Battalion
2/Lt Foxwell A.G.E. Motor accident 10.1.42
Capt Hilliar J.W. Grenade accident, Binegar 9.8.42
Pte Day H. Heart failure on duty 20.9.42

5th Battalion
Pte Carter E.H. Range accident 7.10.40
Sgt Davis F.E. Killed during air raid 26.4.42
Cpl Walsh W. Killed during air raid 26.4.42
Pte Coles P.F.G. Killed during air raid 26.4.42
Pte Godwin Killed during air raid 26.4.42
Pte Kilminster L.C. Killed during air raid 26.4.42
Pte Mills T.L.G. Killed during air raid 26.4.42
Pte Park F.J. Killed during air raid 26.4.42
Pte Pearson D.C. Killed during air raid 26.4.42
Pte Self V.R.C. Killed during air raid 26.4.42
Capt Lane W. Range accident 12.8.44

7th Battalion
Pte Lovell G. On duty at Lulsgate 18.11.40

8th Battalion
Pte Raines J.C. Range accident, Worle 18.9.40

CSgt Hook S.F. Killed during air raid 28.6.42
CSM Atkins F. Range accident, Uphill 20.2.43
Pte Addicott L.C. Killed during air raid 27.3.44

13th Battalion
Pte Wills M.T. Range accident, Rowberrow 2.5.43

ECHOES OF WALMINGTON-ON-SEA:

Tales from Somerset's Dad's Army

Some of the fondest memories of the Home Guard are recalled through the good-natured humour that surrounds Britain's wartime amateur army. The BBC television series 'Dad's Army' portrayed this exceptionally well and some of the exploits of Captain Mainwaring and his men were probably nearer the truth than fiction, as most ex-members of the Home Guard will verify. The following anecdotes provide just a small insight into the goings-on in Somerset during the war years, will substantiate this.

Austin Hayter was a young contract farmer living near Templecombe and a member of the 3rd Somerset (Yeovil) Battalion Home Guard. He recalls how the Home Guard was organised and some of its successes as well as the failures – many were hilarious:

Peter Shearston, a local estate agent, formed our section of the LDV – he must have been nearly 70 at the time. I was not old enough to join at the beginning and had to get my mother's permission. There were

138

no uniforms or rifles and we just had shotguns that the farming types brought along. We didn't have any uniforms either, just armbands. Eventually we formed part of the 3rd Somerset Home Guard Battalion and Peter Shearston became our sergeant.

Our main duties were to guard bridges and to set up road blocks. We used to man the road block across the main road at Templecombe from 10 pm to 6 am – we checked everyone's passes after 10 pm. There was not much traffic at night though, so it could get pretty boring. The Milk Marketing Board moved their HQ to Templecombe House in the village in the early part of the war and one or two of their staff joined the Home Guard, one of whom was a corporal. I was on duty with him one night and on the early shift, when we saw the local policeman coming through the village – I had known him for ten years – and the corporal shouted: "Police...Halt!", made him get off his bike and asked for his credentials. I warned him that this was silly as I knew the constable well. However, the corporal insisted, checked his documents and said, "Pass friend." The policeman, who used to box in his youth, drew himself up to his full height, stared him straight in the eye and said: "I bain't no friend of yourn!"

The corporal often used to cycle up to the pub with no lights and the bobby was talking to the guards one night and caught him and said: "Friend – come here – where's your lights?" He was had up and fined 10/- by the magistrate, so the bobby got his revenge in the end – the chap was really quite upset.

One day a Polish refugee arrived out of the blue and was made known to us. He asked for volunteers to go and study guerilla warfare – I did, which meant extra parades – once you started, you were expected to carry on with the training. Altogether eight of us volunteered. We went on night exercises and had to open up culverts under the roads in the area as a means of crossing underneath – we used to plan escape routes and recce woods around the village where we might be able to dig big underground stores for provisions. We didn't actually dig any though. Then as quickly as the Polish chap had appeared, he vanished. They probably needed him for 'special duties' elsewhere. Nobody knew where he went and he was never seen again.

The most fearsome weapon in our arsenal was a Spigot mortar – it weighed about 5 cwt – it was very hard to transport and so we used a flat trailer and an old 14 hp Oxford cut up to make a tractor to pull it. This was an ideal set up and meant we could use the red petrol normally available for agricultural vehicles or lorries and not have to use the white petrol for cars, which was severely rationed. To load the mortar on this trailer was a job and we had to tie it down with a bit of string. It took five of us to man it – Peter Shearston, our sergeant, used to sit beside me on a banana box which was bolted down – the other three sat round the mortar on the back. It had no mudguards, so if we went down a hill at more than 25 mph, we used to have to use the handbrake to slow it down a bit and also if it happened to be raining they got absolutely filthy and were already well camouflaged by the time we got there! The Spigot mortar was never fired – we didn't even open the ammunition boxes which we kept in a Nissen hut up the road, so we never knew whether we had live rounds for it or not!

We held a big weekend exercise with the Guards Armoured Division and had cornered some of them in the village. They actually finished up hand to hand fighting at the bottom of Station Road. One of the defenders had got up an elder bush and was kicking at his attackers to fend them off. That's when I came in and said: "I'll soon get that bugger down," and slipped into a nearby woodshed, got an axe and cut the stick off...and down he came. They got him out in the road pinned down and were thumping him with whatever they could find, until one of the umpires came along stopped them and said: "Come on lads, I think you have had your fun."

Eric Westman was 16 years old when he joined the LDV in June 1940:

I can remember they put whacking great concrete blocks beside bridges all over the county – some of them as big as sheds – which would have been moved across to prevent tanks crossing. At these bridges, there were holes dug with a metal lid cover – these were for spider mines, which were to be placed in them. The theory was that the German tanks would go over these mines and tilt them slightly detonating them. There were tens of thousands of these placed all over Somerset, but unfortunately they found that the mines would only just fit in the holes and they had no room to tilt – none of them would have actually gone off!

ATS girls were billeted at the Silver Fish Restaurant in Bawdrip later in the war and raids were mounted on that as well. On one occasion we were armed with thunderflashes and approached the house; crept past the little bedrooms on the ground floor and saw that a window was open – it was the bathroom. One of the chaps said to me: "Fling one in there, Eric!" and I did. A few moments later it went off with a loud bang accompanied by a colossal scream. It turned out that just around the corner from the bathroom was a loo, upon which an ATS girl had been enthroned! On another occasion I managed to pinch a couple of thunderflashes to have a bit of fun with and cycled into town, where I met one of my mates. We noticed a bobby standing in the road opposite Woolworths, facing the

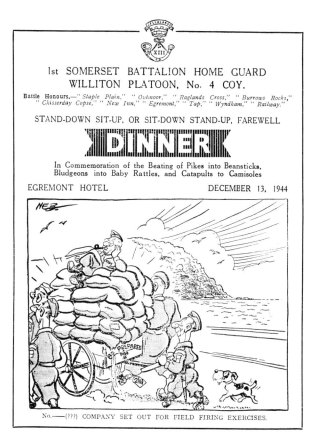

*Stand down dinners were the order of the day. This menu cover was
typical of the humour and well-being that surrounded such events.
(CRO)*

shop; we decided to give him a bit of a fright. As I
cycled past, I struck a thunderflash and threw it at
his feet, so did my mate a second or two later. They
went off with a hell of a bang. The bobby jumped a
yard in the air and belted like a scalded cat for cover
in the shop doorway! We didn't hang about and pedalled off as fast as we could into the night.

I remember that we were out on manoeuvres one
day and the whole exercise had to come to a halt –
the sergeant had lost his pipe and we all had to stop
what we were doing and search for the blessed thing!
I always reckoned that if the Germans had landed,
they would have been so paralysed with laughter, we
could have just walked up to them and taken the
weapons from their hands.

After I left the Navy in 1946 I went to live at my
parent's house in Nether Stowey. One day there was
a knock at the door and there on the step was an
ex-Home Guard NCO from our old outfit. He had a
large roll of green ribbon in his hand. "Oh Eric," he
said, "you were in the Home Guard for three years –
you've have been awarded the Defence Medal." With
that, he took out a pair of scissors and proceeded to
cut off a half-inch strip from the roll. "Here you are,"
he said, and handed me this little piece of ribbon,
then bade me goodnight, and cycled off into the darkness. He had come the 11 miles out from Bridgwater
especially to present this and now he was having to
go all the way back again – typical Home Guard!

The Home Guard and their activities around
the Midsomer Norton and Radstock area are
fondly recalled by Ron Hansford:

One day the local Home Guard were told to parade
at Pows Orchard, near Midsomer Norton, and had to
assemble to be inspected by an RSM, a regular soldier
from the Coldstream Guards – he would give them
some drill. Two dozen were lined up with pitchforks
and the RSM told them to imagine they were being
attacked by a dive bomber and react accordingly by
dispersing on hearing the whistle. The village folk
had turned out to watch the goings-on and have a bit
of a laugh. The RSM then blew the whistle and ordered
"take cover!" but all they did was to amble off in
different directions as if going to the pub for a pint.
The RSM exploded with wrath. "And what the ....
hell do you think that is – you'd all be dead before
you'd get to the .... Inn." The women had never
heard anything like it!

At a place called Clapton Woods, the Home Guard
dug underground foodstores for supplies in case of
invasion and stored some composite rations there.
They then covered these with galvanised sheeting and
sand bags. When they went back the next time, all
the biscuits were floating in the water because they
hadn't made any provision for drainage – so it was
useless as a dugout – or store!

TWELVE

The Military

THE COMMAND STRUCTURE: 8th CORPS IN SOMERSET

In the early days of the war the South Western Counties of England together formed an Army Operational Area known as 8th Corps District, under the command of Lieutenant General Sir Harold E. Franklyn, KCB, DSO, MS. This District included Bristol City and the counties of Somerset, Devon and Cornwall. From the Corps Commander's name was evolved the Corps sign of a short and plump bird on the wing, depicted on a white field within a circle. The bird was a francolin – described by ornithologists as a spur-legged partridge, in colour mottled and black, brown and white, found in Africa and South Asia and formerly in the island of Sicily. Under Lieutenant General Franklyn's command the defence of the South Western Counties was organised following the collapse of France and the isolation of the British Isles in the summer of 1940.

Corps Headquarters was at Pyrland Hall (formerly the residence of Colonel Pemberton), a stately mansion with an imposing portico, situated about two miles north of Taunton. The house is approached by a long drive across a park, bordered on the west by the Kingston Road and on the east by Cheddon Road. Today it is a preparatory school for King's College, Taunton.

On 12 January 1943 8th Corps, then commanded by Lieutenant General A.E. Grassett, left Taunton, and elsewhere played its part in the build up of the British forces for the invasion of Europe. On the departure of 8th Corps, a number of officers remained at Pyrland Hall to form the Headquarters Staff of the South Western District under the command of Major General H.M.V. Stewart, CBE, DSO, with effect from 15 January 1943. The old Corps sign was retained by the new headquarters.

The District Area remained unaltered, but to facilitate administration, was now subdivided

Pyrland Hall, HQ of the 8th Corps and the South Western District. (CRO)

into the sub-Districts of Somerset (including Bristol), Devon and Cornwall, with Headquarters respectively at Burnham-on-Sea, Crediton and Truro. At a later date Bristol Garrison area became a separate sub-District.

Troops under the new District Command included the 55th Division and a number of Home Defence battalions and Young Soldiers' battalions. By far the greater strength consisted of the Home Guard organisation of sectors incorporating 56 battalions of infantry. In addition there were Home Guard engineering units; motor transport columns; bomb disposal squads; rocket batteries; coast artillery and auxiliaries. Certain categories of army cadets also came under the District Command.

8th Corps had commenced work on an administrative scheme for the accommodation of large numbers of US Forces, the forerunners of which had already arrived in the West Country. This scheme was known by the code name of *Bolero*. It was continued by SW District and provided many problems for the staff as the US Forces grew in number from thousands to tens of thousands. By this time the District had few regular British troops under its command and these would diminish even further as the time for the launching of the Allied invasion of Europe, known as *Overlord* drew near.

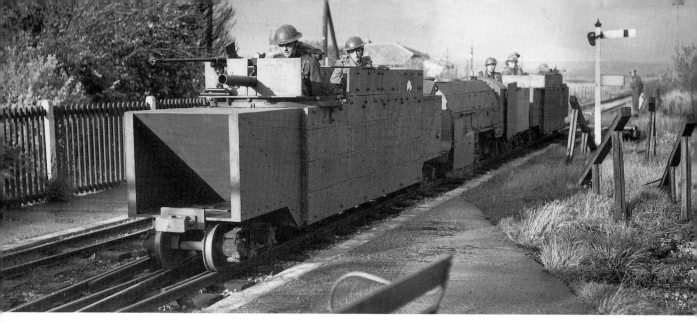

THE SOMERSET LIGHT INFANTRY

The nine battalions of the Somerset Light Infantry shared the frustrations of the first three years of the war to the full. The two regular battalions were in India and Gibraltar, the rest were at home, employed for the most part in those years of invasion scare on coastal defence duties. Thus they were compelled to watch three years of war go by before they were in action.

The 1st Battalion left the country in 1926 and were to serve overseas from then until the evacuation of India. They served in India, in the Arakan against the Japanese, and were the last British Regiment to leave Bombay in 1948. The 1st Battalion, were also back in the 13th's familiar hunting ground – the North-West Frontier – early in 1941, but like the 2nd the real job at this time was to keep an eye on the frontiers and the lines of communication open.

The 2nd served in Gibraltar from 1939 till 1943 and then went on to Italy to take part in the fighting at Cassino and the crossing of the River Gari. Transferred to Greece, they took part in the Athens fighting in December 1944 and after being engaged on frontier duty in Austria, returned to England in 1948.

The Territorial battalions in the 1939 war were the 4th and 7th, who saw action in Northwest Europe and both were heavily involved in trying to reach the beleaguered airborne troops at Arnhem, where the 7th was ordered to clear the Germans from the banks of the Rhine, enabling 2,400 men of the 1st Airborne to gain safety. The 4th had been deployed in Kent from 1940 to mid 1944 on anti-invasion duties and coastal defence.

One of the more enterprising schemes adopted as an anti-invasion measure by the 4th Battalion of the Somerset Light Infantry, was to patrol the coastline using this armoured train on the Romney, Hythe and Dymchurch Railway. The date: 14 October 1940. (IWM)

There they became well-known for the armoured train which they manned on the Romney, Hythe and Dymchurch Railway. The 7th had formed in August 1939 from the 5th Battalion, and was deployed in Somerset until they moved to Colchester in 1942. From mid '43 until the invasion of Normandy, they served in Cornwall and Berwick on Tweed.

In November 1940, three battalions – the 5th, 6th and 7th – came together to form the 135th Infantry Brigade of the 43rd (Wessex) Division. It was the first time in the Regiment's history that the Somersets had a brigade of their own. This did not last long, but the 4th later became, and the 7th remained, part of the Wessex Division, trained with them in 1943-44, and fought with them from Normandy to the Baltic. The 6th Battalion was deployed in Somerset before moving to Harwich in January 1944 and was finally disbanded in July of that year at Peacehaven, on the South Coast. Between 1940 and '44, the 5th was deployed on anti-invasion and coastal defence duties in Kent, Sussex, Yorkshire and Essex; its last two years were spent draft-finding.

Raised as a home defence battalion in 1939, the 8th's duty was to guard vulnerable points in England. In December 1941 it became the 30th Battalion and defended airfields in Somerset during 1942-3. In June 1943, it moved to Portland before overseas service in Algiers, Sicily and southern Italy, before disbanding at Rome in

January 1946.

The 9th Battalion was raised at Taunton in 1940 and initially used in the coastal defence of Somerset. Alternatively under threat with disbandment and being suggested for planned operations against the Channel Islands and the Azores, the 9th was finally broken up in 1944.

Initially raised at Ludlow in January 1940 as the 11th (Holding) Battalion, the 10th was transferred to Bridgwater in October of that year for coastal defence duties, before moving to Portland in April 1941. In November 1942, it became the 7th (Light Infantry) Battalion, Parachute Regiment, and also served in the battle for Europe.

The Depot of the Somerset Light Infantry was located at the Jellalabad Barracks in Taunton, which housed the 16th Initial Training Centre and the 3rd (Reserve) Battalion. Thousands of soldiers of the Somerset Light Infantry were trained at the barracks during the war and also at Sherford Camp in Taunton, which was constructed in 1940. Eventually the Royal Army Nursing Corps took Sherford over and it became a convalescent centre. Many of the staff came from the 8th (Holding) Battalion, of the Somerset Light Infantry. The imposing fortress-like structure of Jellalabad Barracks still stands today and houses the Regimental Museum.

The Somerset Light Infantry's remaining battalion served in Malaya post war. The Regiment lost its independence in 1959 when it amalgamated with the Duke of Cornwall's Light Infantry to become the Somerset and Cornwall Light Infantry. During the reforms and rationalisation programme of the late sixties, the Regiment became part of the Light Infantry on 10 July 1968. The Regiment lost 65 Officers and 883 Other Ranks during the Second World War. The names of the dead are recorded in the Regimental Book of Remembrance in St Mary Magdalene Church, Taunton.

During the invasion scare, many troops were stationed along the Somerset coast line at stratigic points where an attempted invasion was likely. It was the responsibility of the 'Somersets' and others to guard the coast and a 24 hour watch was kept. This duty was tedious and not much liked by the troops; boredom was the worst enemy.

Arthur Knight was a young soldier in the 'Somersets' who served his initial training at Jellalabad Barracks in Taunton:

At first, we were billeted in an old disused shop near Vivary Park which had no electric lights nor other facilities. In the July of 1940, at the beginning of the Battle of Britain, I was sent out on an extended detachment to Dunster Beach Camp, which was comprised of little more than beach huts along the sea front and four soldiers slept in each one. Facilities again were basic and even the meals were served up in a metal bath. There were no cooks as such, so everyone had to have their turn at preparing food – after all we were the Somersets! Our duties included the filling of sandbags and helping the contractors construct pillboxes along the coastline. Regular patrols of the area also used to be carried out, up to and including the seafront at Minehead, where Butlins are now.

Will Locke was with the 10th Battalion and stationed at Brean Down village on coastal defence and training duties in 1940, at the time of the invasion scare:

We were billeted in bungalows and various houses that had been commandeered. The pillboxes built along that part of the coast, for the best part, were not permanently manned by the Battalion – I think the Home Guard used them for training. Our defences consisted of sandbagged trenches that we dug in the dunes, the upper half of which was covered in corrugated iron, with further sandbags put on top. Slit lookouts were provided in order that we could practice firing a variety of weapons for training, including small bombs discharged from a grenade launcher. From our positions we could hear the ack-ack guns practising at Doniford and also the naval guns at the end of Brean Down, which used to be fired out to sea. A typical day would start with reveille at 06.00 and we would be paraded before being marched all over the place – including over to Wedmore, maybe carrying 1,000 rounds of ammunition or Bren guns, Stens – all sorts. On one occasion we were marching from Brean to Berrow and had to cross over a deep, muddy rhyne on a plank. One bloke lost his balance and fell headlong into the muddy water. He clambered out spluttering – he was covered in black slime from head to foot – and shook himself like a dog. Three or four hundred men were all standing around laughing at him and the officer said: "Where's your rifle?" He had dropped the thing and the poor chap had to go back in and retrieve it!

SOMERSET'S TERRIERS: THE TERRITORIAL ARMY

43rd (Wessex) Division

The 43rd (Wessex) Division was originally formed early in the present century in the West

Country and is still, as its name implies, intimately connected with this part of England. The Wyvern, the traditional emblem of the fighting men of Wessex, was adopted as the Divisional Sign in 1935.

During the early stages of the 1939/45 war the Division was employed in beach-defence duties in SE England, but as the threat of invasion receded, and after it became fully mobilised in 1942, the emphasis was on training. Many and varied were the exercises, and the names of 'Tiger,' 'Great Binge' and 'Spartan' are remembered by all who served in the Division in those days.

The role of the Division in the Normandy landings was that of a 'follow-up' formation and the bulk of the units were landed during the weekend June 24th – 26th. From that date onwards the 43rd Division was called upon to take a leading part in every one of the major operations launched by the British Second Army.

The battle record of the Division includes the bitterly contested fight for Hill 112, the assault of Mont Pincon, the first British assault crossing of the Seine at Vernon, the drive into Holland and relief of the Airborne at Arnhem, the Anglo-American offensive at Geilenkirchen, the clearing of the Roer Salient, the battle of the Rhineland, culminating in the breaking of the German defences before the key town of Goch and the capture of Xanten, the Rhine Crossing and the breakout northwards, finishing with the assault and capture of Bremen.

The war over, the Division was engaged in normal occupational duties with its headquarters at Celle, near Hanover. It was disbanded in July 1946, only to be reformed almost at once in the West Country with the rebirth of the Territorial Army.

The Army staged a demonstration for munitions workers on the seafront at Weston-super-Mare on 14 April 1942, in order for them to see the arms they manufactured in operation. (IWM)

A Tomahawk aircraft, probably from an Army Co-operation unit based at Weston Zoyland, gives a demonstration of ground strafing. (IWM)

The North Somerset Yeomanry

In 1803, as a result of Napoleon's invasion threat, the Frome and Selwood Troops of Volunteer Cavalry were formed, and in the following year joined forces with the Frome and East Mendip Regiment of Volunteer Cavalry. In 1814 the Regiment was given the title of North Somerset Yeomanry Cavalry.

The war gave the Regiment little chance in its mounted rôle. After one main cavalry action at Maza Ridge in the Syrian Campaign in 1941, and the realisation that mounted troops were outmoded by armoured warfare, the Regiment was chosen for conversion into 4th Air Formation Signals (NSY).

Artillery in action during the demonstration. (IWM)

In May 1942 a three day invasion exercise took place in the Southern Command and among those troops taking part were men of the Czechoslovak Independent Brigade, seen here guarding a railway strongpoint on the GWR Taunton to Chard line near Ilminster. Note the 'signalbox' is actually a pillbox. (IWM)

Under this title the Regiment provided communications between the RAF and the Army through the rest of the campaign in North Africa, through the campaign in Sicily, and up through Italy until August 1944; finally finishing the war as 14th Air Formation Signals (NSY) in North-west Europe.

255 Medium Regiment RA (The West Somerset Yeomanry)

The first record of the Regiment as the West Somerset Yeomanry is in 1850. The Regiment was embodied in September 1939 as part of the 43rd Wessex Division. They served in many parts of England until D-Day plus 21, when, as part of the Guards Armoured Division, which they had joined in 1942, they landed in Normandy. On 29 June 1944 they were first in action at Pubot en Bassin and subsequently took part in the Normandy battles, including Caripiquet Aerodrome, Caen and Miny Bocage. They took part in the Guards Armoured Division's advance from Falaise Gap to Brussels and subsequently took in the assault on the Albert and Escaut Canals. They took part in the Reichswald battle and supported the troops crossing the Rhine. They continued the advance until the final German capitulation at Cuxhaven.

After the war they went to Aachen in an occupations rôle. Thirty-four officers and men of the Regiment lost their lives during the war, and 80 were wounded. Honours awarded included 1 DSO, 6 MCs, 1 MM and 2 Croix de Guerre.

110th Field Engineer Regiment

In 1939 orders were given to bring the Divisional RE up to full war establishment strength and then to double it and form the 43rd and 45th Divisional RE. That year 1,200 men went to camp at Exmouth.

After the outbreak of war the 43rd and 45th Divisional RE were brought up to full strength with the addition of 553rd and 562nd Field Companies respectively, which were formed from militia men and a cadre from the original companies. The 43rd Division continued to be known as the Wessex and the new 45th Division became known as the West Country Division.

At the time of Dunkirk the 43rd Division was fully mobilised and ready to go to France, but instead formed a Home Forces Mobile Reserve prepared to drive off an invasion anywhere round our coasts. As more troops became available, the Division moved to the Dover area.

On 12 June 1944, following the European 'D' Day, the Wessex Engineers sailed for France commanded by Lieutenant Colonel H.E. Pike CBE DSO. During the early bridgehead days they were frequently fought as infantry and were heavily engaged, with severe casualties, in the Caen area. The first big engineering task was bridging the Seine under fire; then to Brussels and on to Arnhem.

At Arnhem they ferried across units of the Division in a desperate attempt to relieve the troops of the 1st Airborne Division, large numbers of whom they evacuated the next evening. On the following evening a gallant attempt was made to withdraw their own divisional infantry.

In the post-war organisation of the Territorial Army, Headquarters remained at Bath with outlying squadrons at Melksham, Reading and Weston-super-Mare, with a detachment at Bridgwater.

43rd Divisional Signals

Headquarters of the 43rd Divisional Signal Regiment were at Taunton, with one of the three outlying squadrons also in Somerset, at Bridgwater. The unit traces its history back to 1908 when the 43rd Divisional Telegraph Company, part of

the Corps of Royal Engineers, was formed in Exeter.

In 1939 the unit formed a second line unit for 45th Divisional Signals. In the Second World War the unit mobilised again in Wiltshire and in 1940 got as far as Dumfries on its way to Norway; but the evacuation took place before they were able to sail. For the next four years they combined shore defence with intensive training.

In June 1944 the unit landed with 43rd Division in Normandy and took part in the bitter fighting in the Bocage country. Hill 112, Mount Pincon and the Falaise Gap are names which are not likely to to be forgotten. Throughout the advance, across France into Belgium and Holland, to Aachen, the Reichswald, the Rhine Crossing and finally Bremen, the unit provided communications for the rapidly moving division. Disbanded on VJ Day in Germany, 43rd Divisional Signals was reformed in February 1947.

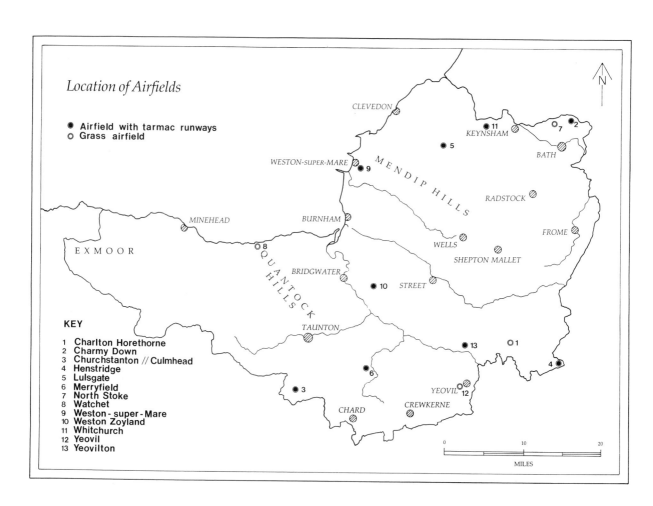

Location of Airfields

● Airfield with tarmac runways
○ Grass airfield

KEY
1 Charlton Horethorne
2 Charmy Down
3 Churchstanton // Culmhead
4 Henstridge
5 Lulsgate
6 Merryfield
7 North Stoke
8 Watchet
9 Weston - super - Mare
10 Weston Zoyland
11 Whitchurch
12 Yeovil
13 Yeovilton

THIRTEEN

Wings Over Somerset

At the outset of the war there were no operational fighter stations in Somerset, but only training establishments and those connected with the aircraft manufacturing industry or commercial flying. However, during the course of the war Spitfires and Hurricanes together with other aircraft types from front line squadrons were operating from several bases in the county and would become a familiar sight. There were a number of Royal Air Force and Fleet Air Arm training establishments set up during this period. The most active was the Fleet Air Arm base at Yeovilton, which rapidly became too small for its rôle, so satellite airfields were established at Charlton Horethorne and Henstridge.

Prior to D-Day the USAAF moved into Somerset to prepare for the assault on Europe. Both Weston Zoyland and Merryfield were handed over to them for use during this period. In addition, Charmy Down became a temporary home for USAAF units.

The price which had to be paid for air supremacy was high, as shown by Civil Defence records of the county in which no fewer than 311 crashes and forced landings of British and Allied aircraft, other than in combat, were reported between June 1940 and July 1944. Many accidents involved Royal Navy aircraft which outnumbered those of the Royal Air Force operating in the county.

In October 1940 the RAF established 67 MU at Taunton. The prime responsibility of this maintenance unit was to salvage and clear up the result of crashes and forced-landings in the south-west peninsula. They operated from a site on the Wellington Road, where large piles of aircraft wreckage could be seen.

Somerset had 13 airfields and landing grounds which were used during the war. These were: Charlton Horethorne, Charmy Down, Culmhead, Henstridge, Lulsgate Bottom, Merryfield, North Stoke, Watchet, Weston-super-Mare, Weston Zoyland, Whitchurch, Yeovil and Yeovilton. Various other landing fields dotted around the county were used by the US Army later in the war for their communications aircraft.

Some airfields remained as large grass fields, but others were constructed with concrete/tarmac runways. Apart from at Whitchurch, the Royal Navy were the first to build hard-surfaced runways. The need to practice deck landings meant that airfields like Yeovilton had four runways; Henstridge could boast five. It was not deemed necessary to practice crosswind landings as aircraft carriers operated their aircraft whilst steaming into wind, therefore Fleet Air Arm airfields were constructed with more than the the standard three-runway pattern adopted by the Royal Air Force. In the early days of the war a main runway length of 3,300 ft and a width of 150 ft was standard for fighter aircraft, but depending on the local topography, these could be longer. Yeovilton's longest was 3,480 ft and that of Culmhead 4,200 ft, but at Henstridge it was the standard 3,300 ft. Later in the war heavier aircraft meant that longer runways had to be provided and ones of 6,110 ft at Weston Zoyland and 6,000 ft at Merryfield were constructed; the latter was built in preparation for the arrival of the USAAF.

The construction of the airfield at Culmhead, which was at first called Churchstanton, was one of the monumental efforts of the war. For many months a constant stream of lorries conveying rock and ballast moved along the Blackdown Hills, those from the quarries in Devonshire coming up Wellington Hill and those conveying the pink rock of the Quantocks ascending the steep and twisting Blagdon Hill. Seven days a week this traffic went on until the wastes of Trickey Warren were transformed into a modern fighter station.

THE AIRFIELDS

Charlton Horethorne/Sigwells

Situated in King Arthur country, this grass airfield was sited on the top of an escarpment 1¼ miles north-west of the village of Charlton Horethorne and the same distance south-east of Cadbury Castle. The aerodrome was also known as Sigwells. Great attention was paid to retaining as many natural features as possible to avoid attracting the enemy's attention and living sites were widely dispersed. Initially a number of double blast pens were provided, but the airfield had few facilities for housing aircraft under cover.

The airfield was originally intended for the RAF, but no longer needed by them, became a satellite to RNAS Yeovilton and opened officially on 26 May 1942. On July 10 the first squadrons arrived, being Nos 886 and 887 with Fulmars. No 790 Squadron reformed at the airfield on 27 July and operated as the Air Direction School with Fulmars, later with Oxfords and, towards the end of the war, Fireflies and Seafires. The squadron would remain at the base until April 1945, when it moved to Zeals.

Hurricanes of No 891 Squadron moved in during August and the ignominy of the first crash to occur at the airfield happened to one of their number on the 17th, but the pilot was unhurt. On 3 September an enemy aircraft was sighted by members of the 30th Battalion Somerset Light Infantry defending the airfield, but was out of range for them to engage. It was later discovered that the aircraft was the one responsible for attacking Castle Cary Junction. Wildcats of No 893 Squadron moved in on the 9th September for a short period and were replaced by Fulmars of 897 Squadron, but they left for Old Sarum in November.

An unusual taxying accident occurred on 1 October when a Fulmar aircraft of 790 Squadron piloted by Lieutenant Commander Hodgson was in collision with a motorcycle combination ridden by postman Mr W.J. John, who was struck by the propeller of the aircraft severing his arm at the shoulder. He was taken to the RN hospital at Sherborne where he eventually recovered.

The airfield was transferred from 10 Group to the Admiralty in November and the last RAF personnel moved out in January 1943. During the year several operational squadrons, includ-

Aerial view of Charlton Horethorne taken on 3 October 1944. No fewer than 71 aircraft, a mixture of Seafires, Albacores, Fireflies and Tiger Moths can be seen around the airfield's perimeter. (FAAM)

ing Nos 884, 887 and 889 equipped with Seafires, moved in for interception training. Also Hurricanes of 804 Squadron stayed for a short while. December saw 780 Squadron with its Tiger Moth, Proctor, Harvard and Swordfish aircraft move in for pilot refresher training. No 794 Squadron took up residence during the month with Defiants and Martinets. They were engaged in target-towing and remained at the airfield until disbanded in June 1944. During this period the facilities improved on the airfield with the construction of six rudimentary Blister-type hangars and additional living quarters.

The Travelling Recording Unit (865 Squadron) equipped with Wellingtons was based at Charlton Horethorne in March 1944, but roamed widely around the country on recording duties and were only based here during the formation of the unit. No 780 Squadron moved to Lee-on-Solent in November 1944 and 790 Squadron, now equipped with Fireflies, was left as the last flying unit to remain and when they moved out on 1 April 1945 the airfield transferred back to the RAF. 42 Group Maintenance Command used it to store ammunition until it was cleared in April 1947.

Charmy Down

Built as a fighter station with three concrete and tarmac runways on a hill adjacent to the A46 road 3 miles north of Bath, Charmy Down was opened as a satellite for Colerne in November 1940, for the defence of Bristol and Bath. The first aircraft to arrive were a detachment of black-painted Hurricanes from 87 Squadron for night fighting. The rest of the squadron moved in on 11 December. Their activities were pretty abortive due to the lack of suitable equipment for interception at night and no enemy aircraft were claimed until the next May, when the CO shot down a Dornier Do 17.

No 125 Squadron arrived in August 1941 and were equipped with Defiants, also in the night fighter rôle. They were joined by 263 Squadron equipped with the locally built Westland Whirlwind. No 263 never became operational at the airfield and lost two aircraft in a collision on 9 October, resulting in the death of one pilot; the Squadron moved to Coltishall during that month. No 137 Squadron, also equipped with Whirlwinds, formed here on 20 September, the nucleus coming from 263 Squadron. They engaged in working-up on this tricky aircraft.

The Squadron's first operational sortie was made on 24 October by the CO Squadron Leader John Sample and Flying Officer Clark flying from Predannack as a forward base, who successfully attacked locomotives and fuel containers seen in railway sidings at Landerneau near Brest. Further *Mandolin* attacks were carried out in the week, but during a training flight the squadron lost their CO in a collision during formation practice on 28 October. A couple of days later another aircraft was lost in the sea following another *Man-*

Above: *Two Hurricanes of 87 Squadron at Charmy Down donated to the RAF by nurses. On the left is "Nightingale", the mount of Pilot Officer F.W. Mitchell of Ipswich, and on the right, Sergeant B. Bawden of Sydney, Australia, stands by his charge "Night Duty". Date c. 1942.* (IWM)

Left: *Control tower and underground command bunker at Charmy Down taken in 1987.* (Author)

Below: *Members of 87 Squadron gather around Hurricane "Night Duty" at Charmy Down.* (IWM)

dolin attack carried out on the railway yards at Landerneau. The pilot was Flying Officer Clark who was picked up but died from his injuries.

A number of Blister hangars were constructed around the airfield perimeter affording protection for groundcrews working out on this exposed site. A new concept in night interception was tried at Charmy Down, when a few Havocs equipped with the Helmore Turbinlite arrived in January 1942. The Havocs would illuminate the target, whilst an accompanying Hurricane shot down the enemy. The idea was fraught with difficulties, but the first patrol by a 1454 Flight Havoc and an 87 Squadron Hurricane was mounted on 24 March. There were no recorded interceptions and the Havocs were withdrawn in January 1943, along with other units thus equipped.

Several fighter squadrons, including Nos 234 with Spitfire Vbs; 245 with Hurricane IIcs and Typhoon Ibs; 417 (RCAF) with Spitfire IIs and 421 (RCAF) with Hurricanes, spent time working up at Charmy Down during the period from 1941 to 1943. In September 1942 two Boston squadrons Nos 88 and 107 were attached to the airfield. No 88 Squadron despatched six Bostons on a *Ramrod* to Le Havre and a week later No 107 carried out a raid on Cherbourg Docks setting fire to a 12,000-ton ship.

February 1943 saw the Fighter Leaders School move in from Chedworth with thirty-six Spitfire Vbs. The school gave short-sharp tactics courses to flight and squadron commanders. No 88 Squadron spent some time in April practising tactics with the FLS. The groundcrews had rather an alarming experience when the squadron was posted They were flown to Swanton Morley in two Horsa gliders towed by Whitleys of 297 Squadron as practice for the crews! 2,000 personnel from the RAF Regiment were housed at the airfield in the autumn of 1943, by which time it had been allocated to the US IXth Air Force.

In October 1944 the airfield became a satellite for South Cerney and Oxfords of 15(P)AFU used the facilities during daylight hours; these were joined by Oxfords of 3(P)AFU in November. After the hostilities ceased in Europe the airfield reverted to care and maintenance. For a period in 1946 Charmy Down was used by 92 Gliding School.

Churchstanton/Culmhead

This airfield was originally intended as an emergency landing ground and would become the busiest operational Royal Air Force fighter station in Somerset. Built with a typical three-runway pattern, the airfield, also known as Tricky Warren, opened on 1 August 1941. The perimeter was surrounded by double blast pens and ten Blister hangars were erected.

Spitfires from this station were a familiar sight over Taunton and surrounding districts. They co-operated in many Home Guard exercises and had their part in the "Wings for Victory" and other special weeks designed to stimulate the war effort.

Spitfire XIVs of 610 Squadron, Culmhead, 1944. (IWM)

The first squadrons to arrive were from No 2 Polish Fighter Wing: Nos 316 (Warsaw) and 302 (Pozan) Squadrons equipped with Hurricanes. The former stayed until the end of the year, but 302 left after a month. The Poles found that the work was dull. Their primary rôle was to defend both Bristol and Exeter, but daytime enemy activity was slight, so their duties mainly centred around convoy escort duties. They also escorted bombers during raids on the Brest Peninsula. No 316 was replaced by 306 (Torun) Squadron with Spitfires and took part in operational sweeps across the channel with other units of the Polish Wing, but it was April 1942 when the first opposition was met. In May No 154 Squadron with Spitfires joined the wing, but only stayed a month.

In February 1942 the Research Flight on detachment from RAE Farnborough arrived to conduct barrage balloon cable cutting experiments over the Pawlett Hams. No 313 (Czech) Squadron replaced the Poles in June 1942. 313 was later joined by 312 in October to form a Wing, and continued to carry out convoy patrols, which were enlivened by occasional *Ramrod* and *Rhubarb* sorties over France. In November the poachers turned gamekeepers when *Anti-*

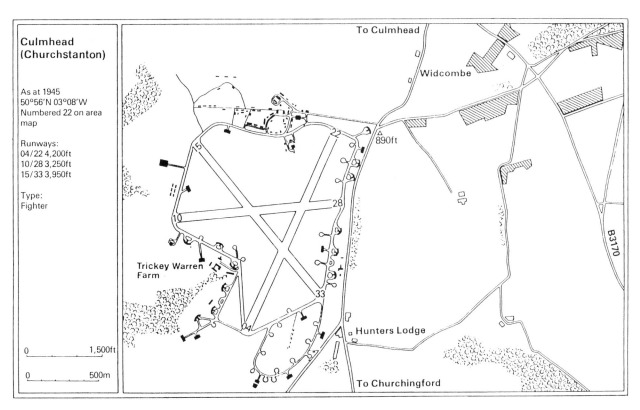

Culmhead (Churchstanton)

As at 1945
50°56'N 03°08'W
Numbered 22 on area map

Runways:
04/22 4,200ft
10/28 3,250ft
15/33 3,950ft

Type:
Fighter

0 ————— 1,500ft

0 ————— 500m

To Culmhead

Widcombe

890ft

B3170

Trickey Warren Farm

Hunters Lodge

To Churchingford

Rhubarb patrols were carried out against German fighter-bombers making hit and run raids.

The Czechs were replaced by No 66 Squadron who were joined by No 504 (City of Nottingham) Squadron in June 1943, both equipped with Spitfire Vs, who used them for deck-landing practice. During this month 234 Squadron paid a visit to the station. On 22 December the airfield was renamed Culmhead following confusion over its name with other stations prefixed by 'Church'. No 165 (Ceylon) Squadron, with Spitfire Vs and No 131 (County of Kent) Squadron with Spitfire HF VIIs were at Culmhead from December 1943 to February 1944 and made many operational sweeps. The Seafire IIIs of 24 Naval Fighter Wing, Nos 894 and 897 Squadrons, replaced them and were here for a month. Referred to as fighter defence, they actually took part in operational sweeps with Typhoons in attacks across the channel. No 165 Squadron returned in March with a later mark of Spitfire the IX and stayed for another month. These were followed in April 1944 by Squadrons 610 (Spitfire XIVs), 286 and 587 and in July 1944 when the Battle of Normandy was at its height, by Squadrons 126, 131 and 616, all Spitfire units, who conducted *Rhubarb* attacks ahead of the troop, scoring

Fighter Sweeps were carried out by Spitfires from Churchstanton over occupied Europe. No 313 (Czech) Squadron lost several pilots during such sweeps, including Flight Lieutenant M. Štušák, shot down by Focke Wulf Fw 190s over St Brieux on 8 March 1943. (John Sigmund)

many successes, particularly on locomotives and German transport. After D-Day plus seven they were landing on strips in France.

Somerset made history for it was to host the first operational RAF squadron to be equipped with jet aircraft. In July, No 616 Squadron was to receive such aircraft and two jet-propelled Meteor Mk Is arrived from Farnborough on the 2nd. The isolated location of Culmhead would ensure that prying eyes were kept to a minimum. Training got under way with the jets, but the squadron did not stay long and moved to Manston on the 21st for *Anti-Diver* operations against the V1 'Doodlebug' menace.

Nos 587 and 286 with a mixed bag of Hurricanes, Martinets and Oxfords, were engaged in Anti-Aircraft co-operation duties and returned on 22 September to Weston Zoyland and Charlton Horethorne respectively. By November 1944 the scene of battle had moved deep into the Continent and Culmhead, like many other British air stations, was placed on a care and maintenance basis. In January 1945 it again became active under Flying Training Command as a satellite to Exeter and No 3 Gliding Training School with Masters and Hotspurs until July 1945, when it again reverted to care and maintenance. 67 MU took over the aerodrome for a few months. Mobile dental equipment was stored on the aerodrome until August 1946, when Culmhead closed. Today it houses a Home Office radio station. The runways, blast pens and a few Maycrete buildings can be seen along with the forest of radio masts that now adorn the site.

Henstridge

Preparatory building work began on 355 acres of farmland, located in the extreme south-east corner of Somerset on the Dorset border, in August 1941. The progress was painfully slow and it was not until 1 April 1943 that the airfield was formally commissioned HMS *Dipper*, when No 2 Naval Air Fighter School moved in from Yeovilton. No 761 Squadron, the school's flying unit moved in with 18 Seafire 1bs, hooked Spitfire Vs and six Masters. The airfield was to become one of the busiest naval training bases in the area as Seafires practised carrier deck landings on a dummy set up on a runway.

A further 18 acres of land was acquired at Gibbs Farm for the construction of an Aircraft Rectifica-

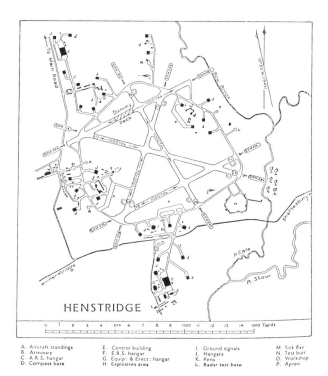

HENSTRIDGE

A. Aircraft standings	E. Control building	I. Ground signals	M. Sick Bay
B. Armoury	F. E.R.S. hangar	J. Hangars	N. Test butt
C. A.R.S. hangar	G. Equip: & Erect: hangar	K. Pens	O. Workshop
D. Compass base	H. Explosives area	L. Radar test base	P. Apron

tion Hangar and associated installations.

On 18 October 1943 Seafire IIs of No 894 Squadron disembarked from the carrier Illustrious and settled in at B Camp at Priors Down. New Seafire IIIs were received and they formed a Wing with 887 Squadron before moving to Burscough in January 1944. Following their departure No 3 Naval Fighter Wing from Lee-on-Solent moved in and worked on low-level exercises in preparation for *Operation Neptune* – bombardment spotting during the Normandy invasion. The Wing was comprised of 42 aircraft and 60 pilots from Nos 808, 885, 886 and 897 Squadrons equipped with a mixture of Seafire L IIIs, Spitfire PR XIIIs and Spitfire Vs. The Wing left at the end of March and returned to Lee.

5 June 1944 saw No 718 Squadron reform here with Seafire IIIs and Spitfire PR XIIIs as an Army Co-operation Training Unit. Henstridge was the sole Fighter School responsible for Seafire training by October 1944. No 718 Squadron and the Naval School of Army Co-operation moved out in August 1945 to Ballyhalbert in Northern Ireland, leaving No 761 Squadron the only occupant of the airfield.

The airfield continued to be used post-war; the last Royal Navy aircraft leaving in August 1952.

Barracudas of 736 Squadron, St Merryn, visiting Henstridge on 25 April 1944. Seafires of No 3 Naval Fighter Wing are seen in the background. (FAAM)

From 1953 to 1957 Air Whaling Ltd, formed by Alan Bristow, serviced its helicopters at the airfield prior to sailing to the antarctic each October. Bristow Helicopters were formed here in 1955. The airfield reopened as a satellite for Yeovilton in 1954 to practice night deck landings, much to the chagrin of local residents; this practice continued until June 1957, when Henstridge closed as a naval base. Today part of the airfield is used for private flying and a small firm operates a charter service from there. The Popular Flying Association (PFA) also hold 'fly-ins' every year at the airfield.

Lulsgate Bottom/Broadfield Down

Lulsgate Bottom opened as a relief landing ground for Tiger Moths of 10 EFTS, Weston-super-Mare in August 1940. The airfield had very few facilities but afforded a good view from the A 38 of the Tiger Moths involved in circuits and bumps.

The decision was taken to develop the site into a 10 Group fighter base and 10 EFTS stopped using Lulsgate on 10 June 1941. Work commenced on constructing a standard three-runway airfield with blast pens and Bellman hangars around its perimeter. The routine was somewhat broken on 24 July when a Ju 88 short of fuel landed on the half-built runway. At this time the airfield was known as Broadfield Down, but on recommencement of operations reverted to the name Lulsgate Bottom.

The airfield reopened to 10 Group in January 1942 as a fighter station, but no squadrons were allocated. The first unit to arrive was No 286 Squadron, an anti-aircraft co-operation unit, with Lysanders and Hurricanes, also a detachment of 116 (Calibration) Squadron with Blenheims. The latter did not stay long, but 286 remained until March, only to return again later in the month equipped with Hurricane IIcs, IVs and Defiants, being transferred to 23 Group on 1 June 1942. They departed in August.

During this time the airfield acted as a satellite for 3(P)AFU, South Cerney. The Oxfords became a familiar sight to local people. In April No 1540 (BAT) Flight was formed for 3(P)AFU training, which survived a change when Lulsgate was transferred to 3 FIS at the end of September 1943. More aircraft were allocated to the airfield from Castle Combe on 1 October and the station gradually assumed the status of a fully independent self-accounting unit. Facilities were expanded with further buildings and Blister hangars being erected.

Lulsgate was used on a number of occasions by US bombers that had been diverted due to bad weather or made emergency landings. In April 1944, no fewer than 13 BOAC aircraft from Whitchurch used Lulsgate.

3 FIS with its Masters and Oxfords continued to use the airfield until July 1945 when the unit was disbanded. The airfield became a satellite for 7 FIS, Upavon; the task was similar, but with much reduced activity from the busy days when 3 FIS used the facility. A patchy period followed until the last units left on 7 May 1946 when the airfield was reduced to Care and Maintenance. Lulsgate was relinquished in 1947, when the Ministry of Civil Aviation took it over as the future Bristol Airport, which was opened by the Duchess of Kent on 1st May 1957; a rôle it fulfils today. At the time of writing a plan to extend the airport, in order that it can handle the wide-bodied jets of the 1980s, is being considered.

Above: *Merryfield, after several years disuse, seen from the air looking north, circa 1964. Reactivated in 1972 and commissioned as* HMS Heron II, *today it is used for helicopter training.* (FAAM)

Left: *A Dakota C4 of 1315 Flight, 300 Wing, Transport Command, at Merryfield early in 1945. The control tower, fire station and a T2 hangar are visible in the background.* (Geoff Shattock)

Merryfield/Isle Abbots

Situated near the village of Ilton some $2^1/_2$ miles north-west of Ilminster, the site was selected as a bomber base in 1942. Construction commenced at the end of the year following purchase of the land from the trustees of the Baptist Church. The site was crossed by the derelict Taunton and Chard Canal, which presented some problems, but good progress was made and three tarmac runways were constructed. Three 'T2'-type hangars were also provided on the airfield perimeter. The main accommodation site between Mudge's Farm and Woodhouse Farm consisted mainly of Maycrete buildings and a few Nissen huts. A large bomb dump was also constructed on the north-west side of the aerodrome.

During the night of 27/28 March there was great excitement when a Junkers Ju 88 was attacked by a nightfighter which brought the German down a little way from the airfield. Merryfield's operational record book reported numerous spent cartridge cases and links as raining down onto the aerodrome.

The airfield, provisionally called Isle Abbots, was transferred to 70 Group control in April 1943, for administration and development as a USAAF base. The name was changed to Merryfield on 14 September, by which time the airfield was nearing completion and opened officially on 12 February 1944 as a base for the IXth Air Force, but was staffed by a number of RAF personnel. Stores arrived erratically; improvisation was the order of the day. The first aircraft to use the airfield was on 17 February, when a Beaufighter with engine trouble made a heavy landing on the unfinished north/south runway, bursting a tyre. By 27 February, the camp was equipped to house 1,500 personnel and four dispersed living sites were completed ready to receive personnel.

On 2 March a Mosquito with engine trouble landed. The pilot skilfully avoided several obstructions and men working on the runway. This aircraft, which was to spend several weeks under repair at the airfield, was just one of a number of uninvited guests to use the facilities of the freshly-laid runways.

Americans started to arrive in large numbers from 25 April 1944. The four squadrons of the 50th Troop Carrier Group (TCG), 441st Troop Carrier Wing (TCW), Nos 99th, 100th, 301st and 302nd, moved in with Douglas C-47 Skytrains and Waco Hadrian Gliders. Training for D-Day started immediately. The 61st Field Hospital was set up at the south-east side of the airfield towards D-Day and the 813rd Air Evacuation Squadron was stationed here for that period. The Americans stayed until November 1944, following the airfield's transfer to 10 Group control in August.

Merryfield was taken over by 47 Group, Transport Command on November 30th, the Dakota C4s of the newly-formed 238 Squadron having arrived a week earlier for work in Australia, but a change of plan resulted in them going to India instead. In December both No 1315 Flight and 243 Squadron arrived, also equipped with Dakotas, to form 300 Wing; they took over the Australian commitment. On 1 February 1945 No 187 Squadron formed, supposedly with Halifax IIIs, but were equipped with Dakota C4s. Halifax C8s of a development flight, an offshoot of 246 Squadron from Lyneham, attached themselves to 187 Squadron at Merryfield for servicing, but following several trips to the Middle East this flight was disbanded on 3 April.

No 187 Squadron commenced trooping flights to India in preparation for the build-up to defeat the Japanese in Burma, but left in September for Membury and were replaced by No 53 Squadron, an ex-Coastal Command Liberator squadron, from St Davids in south-west Wales. The Liberator C VIs of 53 Squadron only spent three months at Merryfield before moving to Gransden Lodge. An appalling accident occurred to one of their number on 22 November 1945 when a Liberator, fully laden with five crew and 22 passengers on their way to India, crashed at White's Farm, Broadway Pound, four miles south-west of the airfield. All 27 on board were killed. At least one of those who lost their lives was a local man serving in the Army.

The next Squadron to arrive was No 242 with Stirlings, but soon converted to Avro Yorks and

stayed here until May 1946. Oxfords of 1552 (RAT) Flight were the last to leave the airfield in September.

Reactivated in November 1951 to meet the shortage of jet pilots for the Korean War, No 208 Advanced Flying School (AFS) equipped with Vampires and Meteor T7s were stationed here. Name changes ensued and the then-called 9 FTS was disbanded in February 1955. 231 OCU with Canberras moved in two months later, but did not stay long. Westland used the airfield for testing their Wyvern carrier-borne strike aircraft from 1949 and also for flight testing repaired Meteors and Sabres. The Royal Navy used the airfield for various squadrons between November 1956 and January 1958, when Merryfield was reduced to care and maintenance status. The airfield was sold in 1960, but reopened as HMS *Heron*, RNAS Merryfield, on 22 May 1972. Today naval helicopters from both Portland and Yeovilton use it for pilot training.

North Stoke

In 1943 the turf of Lansdown Racecourse 3½ miles north of Bath was deemed ideal for use as a landing ground. The railings around the track were removed enabling an east/west runway to be laid out. Oxfords from 3 Flying Instructors School (FIS) were soon using the facilities, which could be fairly tricky, as there was a steep escarpment to the west of the landing ground which would funnel the wind between the trees, causing turbulence, making it difficult for the student pilots. An Oxford came to grief for this reason on 7 March 1945.

Only a few extra buildings were needed on the site, which was named North Stoke. Aircraft used to fly over daily from the parent station at Castle Combe. 3 FIS disbanded in July 1945 and North Stoke was transferred to 7 FIS at Lulsgate Bottom. They did not use it for long and on 22 August 1945 all flying ceased from the site and it reverted to being a racecourse.

Watchet

The Army established an anti-aircraft gunnery range at Doniford in 1925, which it was to use annually during summer months. It soon found that communications were not good with Weston Zoyland where the target-towing aircraft were based. To improve this situation a flattish

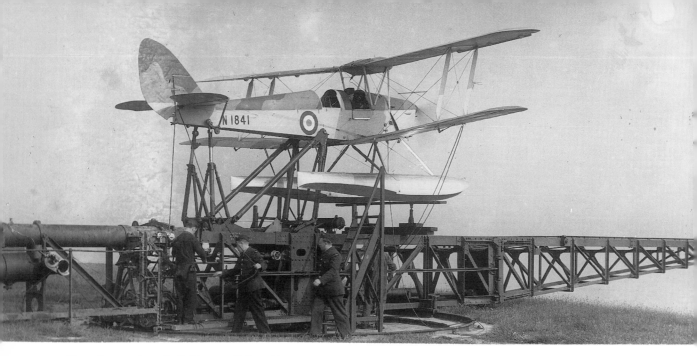

Queen Bee remote-controlled drone on its launching ramp at Watchet circa 1939/40. (Kit Houghton)

piece of land near the range was cleared for use by liaison aircraft.

Horsley drogue-towers used the strip; also, from 1929, aircraft of the Night Flying Flight, as well as Avro 504s, Tomtits and DH 60 Moths. One of the latter crashed when it hit telephone wires soon after taking off from the site on 2 July 1931.

From 1937 the pilotless radio-controlled Queen Bee, a derivative of the Tiger Moth and fitted with floats, was used as a 'live' target for the gunners. No 1 Anti-Aircraft Co-operation Unit made the first successful catapult launch of the aircraft on 3 August, but the machine was damaged landing on the water off shore. In 1938 'Z' Flight launched eight Queen Bees, but one was lost on 20 July; another was shot down in August.

Both 'X' and 'Z' Flight returned in 1939 when training continued through winter months; they both left for ranges in Wales after a year. One Queen Bee suffered an accident during this period, but four others were lost to the guns! After the Flights left all targets were towed by Henleys from Weston Zoyland, but Lysanders of 16 Squadron used the strip at Watchet, often using their 'skyhook' landing techniques.

Following the arrival of the Americans in the area from 1943, Piper L-4 Cubs used the airstrip on numerous occasions. Other communications aircraft used the facilities from time to time.

Weston-super-Mare

Weston airfield opened in 1936 for civil flying. Railway Air Services operated a Plymouth–Haldon–Cardiff–Weston–Bristol air service. In October 1938 Western Airways started the first international night services in Britain. That year RAF Locking opened as the School of Technical Training, a mile east of the airfield. A Station Flight was then established at the airport for communications and staff training; the airfield was transferred to the RAF on 1 May 1940.

Just before the war, the Ministry placed a contract with the Straight Corporation, then owners of Western Airways, for the operation of an Elementary and Reserve Flying Training School. 39 E&RFTS opened in July 1939 equipped with Magisters and Harts, but the outbreak of war forced its disbandment and the aircraft were dispersed to service Elementary Flying Training Schools (EFTS). To take its place the company was contracted to provide navigation training: 5 Civil Air Navigation School was formed on 1 September, but was renamed 5 AONS (Air Observer Navigation School) in November and continued flying Ansons on exercises over the Bristol Channel. It absorbed 3 AONS in June 1940 and with the expansion of the Empire Training Scheme 5 AONS moved to South Africa on 22 August.

At the outbreak of war all civil flying ceased and the airfield was requisitioned for the National Air Communications organisation. A limited Cardiff to Weston service restarted at the end of October for a short time. Western Airways were awarded a contract for the servicing and overhaul of countless primary trainers that flooded into the RAF.

Two shadow factories of the Bristol Aeroplane Company were established, one at Hutton and one at Old Mixon, used for the production and assembly of Beauforts and Beaufighters, which started in September, but was slow at first due to component shortages. A 4,200 ft south-west/north-east runway was constructed to prevent flight testing delays caused by waterlogging.

10 EFTS arrived at Weston from Yatesbury on September 7th 1940, equipped with Tiger Moths. Civil maintenance personnel left when 5 AONS moved abroad were absorbed by BAC to carry out service work on the Tiger Moths. Eleven of the 30 picketed Tiger Moths were badly damaged by a hurricane-force gale on 12 November despite attempts to hangar them. A burning barrage balloon struck by lightning fell on a hangar and damaged it in 1941.

Weston became very congested in June 1941, when Lulsgate was closed for flying whilst being rebuilt into a fully-fledged airfield, and 10 EFTS had to move, going to Stoke Orchard in September 1941.

Over a year passed before the RAF moved into Weston again. In October 1942 No 286 Squadron from Colerne moved in with their Hurricanes, Defiants and Oxfords, but left in April 1943 when the airfield was transferred to Technical Training Command. During July No 14 Recruit Centre was established here and the Equipment Training School (Airmen) moved in from Eastborne in August. No 286 Squadron soon returned and stayed until 29 November 1943, when it went to Weston Zoyland. A detachment of 12 Oxfords from No 116 Squadron, Croydon, replaced them and were mainly employed on the calibration of anti-aircraft gun radars all over the South-west and South Wales. Squadron personnel were billeted in huts between the Western Airways hangar and the airfield boundary with the road.

In March 1944 a detachment of an Air Torpedo Development Unit moved from Weston Zoyland to Weston to carry out dropping trials in the Bristol Channel and remained here until 1949. They were equipped with a variety of aircraft including Tempest F Vs. In July 1944 the Polish Air Staff College also moved into Weston.

Many hundreds of aircraft were constructed, or assembled and flight-tested here during the course of the war and by early 1944 the production of Beaufighter Mk Xs averaged 87 per month and continued until September 1945, when the last one came off the line.

The airfield transferred to Ministry of Civil Aviation control on 3 September 1946. BAC hoped to build the mighty Brabazon here, but the plan was abandoned. In 1955 all Bristol helicopter development and production transferred to Old Mixon. The Westland Aircraft organisation took over the division in 1960 and continued with the production of spares for the Bristol types. Three Varsity aircraft were stationed here from 1959 to 1966 and used for the Radio School at Locking. A flying club was also established but closed in the mid-seventies when the airfield went into rapid decline. The council wanted to close it, but the MOD refused and leased the whole 350-acre site to Westland. The British Rotorcraft Museum was established here in May 1978. Gliding is still carried on at the airfield by No 621 Gliding School. Westland announced extensive redundancies in 1987 and threatened closure of the works, but this was avoided. In 1988 a scheme to build a vast housing, shopping and industrial development on the site was announced, but a landing strip for executive aircraft would be retained.

Weston Zoyland

Due to its relative proximity to the anti-aircraft gunnery range Watchet the Air Ministry was attracted to this site four miles east of Bridgwater, and flying from a large field near the village started back in 1925. Summer camps were held here annually for bomber squadrons practising on nearby ranges and for target-towing aircraft used in co-operation with the gunners at Watchet. By the outbreak of war target-towing duties were being performed by Hawker Henleys and Fairey Battles.

In November 1939 a detachment of Lysanders from 16 Squadron of 70 Group Army Co-operation Command arrived for Co-op duties and in August 1940 the whole unit moved in from Follygate near Okehampton for coastal patrols and work with the Army's Western Command as well as the Home Guard. Weston Zoyland was unique because it was the only one of the AACU airfields to have an operational squadron. No 8 AACU

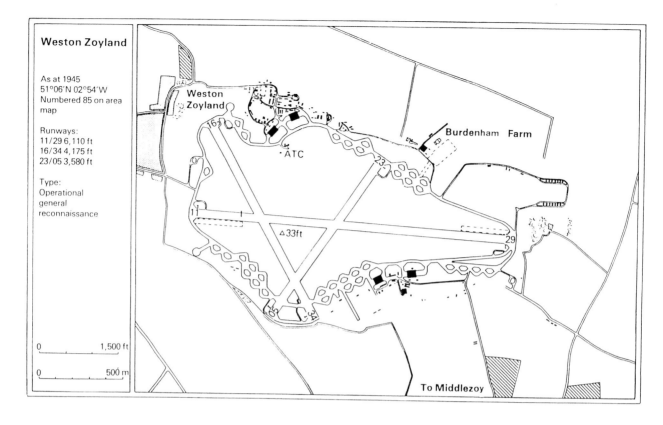

Weston Zoyland

As at 1945
51°06'N 02°54'W
Numbered 85 on area
map

Runways:
11/29 6,110 ft
16/34 4,175 ft
23/05 3,580 ft

Type:
Operational
general
reconnaissance

0   1,500 ft

0   500 m

also arrived in August from Filton for searchlight co-operation duties.

The Air Ministry made Weston Zoyland a fully-fledged self-accounting station on September 1, commanded by Squadron Leader G.A.B. Cooper. A week later all personnel were recalled from leave following an invasion alert, at which time the airfield defence was entrusted to the men of the 70th Gloucesters, who took up positions around the perimeter.

Two Lysanders and a Fox Moth of the Special Duty Flight, Christchurch, arrived in December for co-operation with the Air Defence Development Unit, which continued for a year, by which time a Henley was doing the towing.

By early 1941 the population of the camp had outgrown the temporary facilities and there was an acute shortage of accommodation with airmen billeted in Weston Zoyland, Middlezoy and Othery. Airmen had to sleep in a variety of places, including coach houses and even cheese rooms in nearby houses and farms. It was suggested that villagers relegated airmen to the worst parts of the houses, so in an attempt to improve the situation, the Police Billeting Powers were invoked. Senior officers from the station,

including the CO of 16 Squadron, enlisted the help of the Police Inspector at Bridgwater to see how this could be enforced. However, a major development scheme of the site was already underway.

Although prone to fog because of its low level, a number of aircraft diverted here when other airfields became fogbound and Weston Zoyland remained open. One instance was when a number of aircraft Gibraltar bound returned to land at Weston Zoyland short of fuel, a fact which helped to speed up development of the site. Besides runway improvements, Townsend House was taken over as the officers' mess and the village hall as a NAAFI. In April consideration was given to using the farm buildings belonging to Mr E.W. Eades and also extending the runway for use by bombers. Mr Eades died a few days later and left £2,000 for injured airmen, and as a result a 15-bed sick quarters was established in the village to cater for personnel not in need of hospitalisation.

In June 1941 No 16 Squadron suffered the loss of two Commanding Officers in as many days. On the 9th Wing Commander R.C. Hancock, visiting Roborough near Plymouth, was severely

Tomahawks of 26 Squadron were based at Weston Zoyland whilst on practice camp detachment. (IWM)

injured in a take-off accident and died the next day in hospital. Two days later returning to Weston Zoyland from Roborough after making funeral arrangements for his predecessor, Squadron Leader D. Walker's Lysander was intercepted by four Messerschmitt Bf 109s off Exmouth. His wireless operator/gunner, Corporal Perry, managed to shoot down one Bf 109, but the victory was short lived: the Lysander was despatched quickly, crashing into a house at Exmouth; both Walker and Perry were killed instantly. A few days before his death Squadron Leader Walker had selected a bombing range at Steart Flats which was to be widely used from this period on.

Airfield defence was practised regularly and a five-day exercise ended on 10 June when 600 Marines finally overcame the men from 'E' Company, 70th Battalion, The Gloucestershire Regiment, defending the perimeter. The exercise was witnessed by many 'brass hats', including Brigadier J.A.Churchill, Commander of the Western Area.

It was decided to make Weston Zoyland a major practice camp for Army Co-operational squadrons and on the 6th the first unit, No 239 Squadron, arrived with their Hurricanes. Advanced elements of the Somerset Light Infantry

arrived on 30 June to start work on the defences of the aerodrome. Various units paid visits to the station for the Practice Camp, and later in July, Nos 26 and 400 (RCAF) Squadrons with Tomahawks and 268 Squadron with Lysanders arrived. Two lame ducks in the shape of Halifaxes landed on the 24th, following a raid on Brest. In October 1492 Flight was formed to give specialist training on the Lilstock range using Lysanders, later with Martinets and Masters. During the month Nos 140 Squadron, 241 and 414 (Canadian) Squadrons spent time here for practice camp.

1942 was to see considerable activity at the aerodrome. The resident No 16 Squadron started to re-equip with Mustangs in April and also took part in operational fighter sweeps. Schoolchildren and air cadets visited Weston Zoyland on a regular basis and on 27 June No 16 Squadron played host by taking 32 cadets up on air-experience flights. The low flying antics of the Mustang pilots became legendary in Somerset, particularly when on co-op exercises with the Home Guard, which were often surprised by the sudden appearance of a Mustang from the other side of a hedge! The squadron's association with Weston Zoyland came to an end in December, when they moved to Andover. Mustangs from 170 and 63 Squadrons were stationed for a time and in September a detachment of Blenheims from 614 Squadron and two operational fighter squadrons, Nos 19 and 122, with their Spitfires arrived. Other units to visit the station during the month included 41 OTU; 13, 171 and 406 Squadrons. By the autumn 'A' and 'P' Flights of 1 AACU had become 1600 and 1601 Flights respectively; their Defiants and Henleys continuing to drone over the Watchet ranges. They were joined in January 1943 by 1625 Flight and plans were made for a reconnaissance squadron to be sited here, which were not implemented.

Work commenced by contractors to upgrade the airfield in the spring of 1943 and tarmac runways were laid over the next few months. Squadrons of the newly-formed Second Tactical Air Force used Weston Zoyland for air-firing practice from June 1943. Servicing Commando units formed from members of the RAF, Army and Navy also practised working on aircraft under field conditions, during which period there was a high turnover in squadrons and personnel. Nos 592 and 659 Squadrons were amongst the units

to use the facilities at the aerodrome.

On 18 October No 1492 Flight became 13 Armament Practice Camp. In December the towing flights became No 587 Squadron with Martinets and Henleys; for simulated attacks on gun positions, Oxfords and Hurricanes. No 286 Squadron arrived from Weston-super-Mare to join them for similar work. Two Dakotas landed from Gibraltar on 4 November due to bad weather. Among the passengers were the Regent of Iraq, Emir Abdullah, General Ismar Namiq and Lieutenant Colonel Ubaid Abdullah. No 525 Squadron formed here on 2 September with Warwick C3s as a transport unit and made some flights to Gibraltar, but moved to Lyneham in February 1944.

March 1944 saw successful trials of the M3 Radar Towed Target glider commence, undertaken by Nos 286 and 587 Squadrons. In March 2,327 hours were flown, including 455 hours of night flying by the former. They moved in April to Culmhead and Winkleigh respectively prior to the arrival of the USAAF. Drem lighting was installed at the airfield, unofficially switching on for the first time on 8 March, having a moth-like attraction for an Oxford with engine trouble which made a safe landing.

A total of 2,500 beds were set up in the barracks and hangars at Weston Zoyland in preparation for accommodating men from the 442nd Troop Carrier Group, 50th Troop Carrier Wing, IXth

When based at Weston Zoyland, Mustangs of 16 Squadron played an important rôle in RAF/Army co-operation exercises in the region. Here Flying Officer D.W. Samson prepares to fly a sortie. (IWM)

The derelict control tower photographed at Weston Zoyland in 1987. (Author)

Troop Carrier Command, USAAF. Some 2,200 personnel, 76 C-47 Skytrains and over 100 gliders of Nos 303, 304, 305 and 306 Troop Carrier Squadrons were eventually based at the airfield. During the Americans' stay Weston Zoyland was commanded by Wing Commander G.L. Blake who ensured station security was strictly observed at the time of D-Day.

The Americans moved out in October 1944, by which time No 286 Squadron had already returned, being joined by 587 Squadron in October and training resumed as normal. In February 1945 1540 Blind Approach Training Flight was established with Oxfords to operate with 6 (P)AFU, Little Rissington, replaced by 3 (P)AFU, Lulsgate Bottom in July. No 286 Squadron disbanded at the end of April but 587 Squadron continued with glider trials using Vengeance target tugs, Harvards and Masters. A number of fighter squadrons spent short periods at the airfield prior to disbandment, or a more permanent base being selected. These included No 222 Squadron who exchanged their Tempests for Gloster Meteor F3s in September 1945. No 587 Squadron disbanded in June 1946 and No 222 Squadron, being the last to use Weston Zoyland, moved out in October when the airfield was reduced to care and maintenance following the ranges' transfer to Keevil and Middle Wallop control.

The airfield was reactivated in June 1952 and 209 Advanced Flying School formed with Meteor IVs and T7s. Two years later it was renamed 12 FTS only to be changed later to No 3 All Weather Jet Refresher Squadron, which moved to Strubby in 1955. An air element of the Atomic Task Force of 76 Squadron with seven Canberras and three Varsities formed here in November 1955, joined in December by Canberra PR7s of 542 Squadron. The aircraft all left in March 1956 for sampling work during trials of the Atomic bomb in Australia. During this period guided missiles and the Jindivik flying target were stored here and the base became 'secret' for a time. The last RAF units to use Weston Zoyland were the Canberras of Nos 32 and 73 Squadrons which left in March 1957. The station reverted to care and maintenance before closing in January 1958, finally being sold by the Ministry in 1969. Today a few light aircraft and microlights use part of the airfield.

Whitchurch

Hengrove Park is the site of the Bristol Sports Centre and lies on the southern outskirts of Bristol. Until 1957 it was Whitchurch Airport when its 27-year history connected with flying came to an end. The land of two farms was purchased by the Bristol and Wessex Aero Club in 1929, which had found Filton too crowded and decided a year before that a move was necessary. The airport was constructed with the co-operation of the City Council. Work commenced and the airport was officially opened by HRH Prince Albert, Duke of York, on 31 May 1930. For the next five years it operated as a club. The year 1932 saw a number of small airlines operating summer services, but in 1935 the City Council took responsibility for the airport's development.

The Air Ministry negotiated the establishment of 33 Elementary and Reserve Flying Training School (E&RFTS) at the airport in 1938; the Reserve School at Filton had used it as a relief landing ground throughout the thirties. Operated by Gilbert Lodge and Co Ltd, it formed in December and operated 12 Tiger Moths supplemented by Hawker Harts and Fairey Battles for annual reservist training in 1939.

Facilities were considerably improved during this period: a large tarmac apron laid, hangars erected, runway lighting and a direction beacon installed. With the need to evacuate Croydon and Heston, British Airways, who had been told to produce war dispersal plans, were attracted by the facilities that the airport offered. Before the end of August 1939 the plan had become fact and, it became home for more than 60 large passenger aircraft. Many left London on Friday, 1 September and the spectacular sight they made as they flew low over the Avon Valley is remembered by many people.

All private flying ceased with the outbreak of war and the Air Ministry requisitioned the airport. 33 E&RFTS was disbanded; their aircraft used to supplement other units, leaving Whitchurch solely to be used for National Air Communications schedules, mainly to France, in autumn 1939.

The RAF made use of experienced civilian pilots, who now found themselves without work, for its hard-pressed ferrying service. The Air Transport Auxiliary was formed to meet this need and an initial batch of 30 candidates gathered at Whitchurch, undergoing flying tests on Airspeed Couriers. Women pilots were also tested at the end of the year and a number went for further training to the Central Flying School at Upavon before joining the ATA. In June 1940 B Section of No 3 Ferry Pilots' Pool (ATA) formed at Whitchurch for ferrying duties mainly concerned with aircraft produced by the Bristol Aeroplane Company at Filton.

In 1940 BOAC, then newly formed, suffered a series of setbacks. A gale on 19 March wrecked

Above: *An air stewardess welcomes passengers aboard a Frobisher airliner of BOAC at Whitchurch in 1943.* (IWM)

Below: *Veteran BOAC pilot Captain H.H. Perry in the operations room at Whitchurch, 1943.* (IWM)

two enormous HP 42W biplanes, G-AAVD and G-AAXC, which were blown together and destroyed. The second incident occurred in October when the delivery to No 271 Squadron of a DH 91 Albatross G-AEVV/AX903 was delayed by sabotage. It and another aircraft, G-AFDI, were deliberately set on fire. The third setback happened on 24 November when Bristol was heavily bombed and incendiaries dropped on Whitchurch, destroying a Douglas DC-3 Dakota and an Ensign.

Various BOAC aircraft used Whitchurch, including the Curtiss Wright CW-20 G-AGDI and the four-engined Focke Wulf Fw 200 Condor G-AGAY. Most services were flown by DC-3s to Portugal and Gibraltar across the Bay of Biscay on a timetable basis, which proved fatal on 1 June 1943, as a DC-3 was intercepted and shot down by enemy fighters over the Bay of Biscay with the loss of 17 passengers and crew, including the actor Leslie Howard. The schedules were altered accordingly and timed to arrive at Whitchurch at dawn. No more losses were recorded.

Delays caused by the delivery of Merlin engines for the Beaufighter II, resulted in airframes being transferred to Whitchurch from Filton by road in order to clear the production lines and the aircraft were completed before the ATA flew them to their allotted units.

The Bristol University Air Squadron flew Tiger Moths from July 1942, until disbanded in 1946. BOAC transferred its operations to Hurn in November 1944, following the relief of large parts of Europe, which left Whitchurch almost the sole preserve of the ATA taxi services with Ansons and Argus aircraft. BOAC used the airfield for pilot training and conversion to passenger or freight transport from June 1945, when the airfield was taken over by the Director General of the Civil Aviation Authority from the Air Ministry.

In July 1946 Great Western & Southern Airlines resumed operations and were among a number of short-lived companies trying to operate internal services from the airport. Bristol & Wessex Aero Club regained a strong foothold at Whitchurch and functioned very successfully for a number of years until the airport was transferred to Lulsgate Bottom in 1957. Until the early seventies the British Aircraft Corporation retained facilities in two hangars for the repair and re-

building of Bristol aero engine designs, such as the Hercules and Centaurus power units.

Yeovil

The Yeovil engineering firm Petters Ltd offered their services as munitions manufacturers in 1915 to the War Office and the Admiralty. The latter offered them a contract to build Short 184 seaplanes. Initially the aircraft were built at the extended factory, but were crated and sent either to Rochester or Hamble for flight testing. This was unsatisfactory so the company purchased land alongside their works at Yeovil and began to render it suitable as an airfield and completed this by April 1917, in time to test the first company-built De Havilland 4, and was extended the following year. The company was then awarded a contract to build the Vickers Vimy bomber, when new factory buildings were erected. After the First World War there was a general slump in the aviation industry and the company went through a lean period, but was saved by an order for the Wapiti, a two-seat general purpose aircraft. In 1935 the firm became Westland Aircraft Ltd, by which name it is still known today. John Brown and Co acquired a controlling interest in the thirties, and constructed a new erecting shop to cope with increased orders.

By the outbreak of war, the Lysander Army Co-operation aircraft, affectionately known to the RAF as Lizzie, was in full production, with development of the twin-engined Whirlwind fighter well advanced. The company had built 1,425 Lysanders for the RAF by the time production of the type ceased in January 1942. In addition 112 Whirlwinds were constructed for the RAF and equipped two squadrons, Nos 137 and 263. The last was built in December 1941.

The occasional air raid warning disrupted production only slightly in the first few months of the war. The company was often the intended target but only hit on two occasions, the first being on 10 July 1940. A flight shed was damaged, as was the grass surface of the airfield, but no damage was caused to the Whirlwind aircraft parked near the factory. Further attempts were made: one being on 30 September, but driven off by RAF fighters. Westland was attacked on 7 October, with only slight damage to the works, but loss of life was suffered when a civilian shelter received a direct hit.

The airfield was camouflaged against attack; dummy hedges and ditches were painted on the grass, whilst the factory was disguised to represent a row of houses. A balloon barrage was sited around Yeovil to protect the aircraft works from low-level bombing attack. Small-scale raids continued through the winter of 1940/41 and into 1942. No damage was done to the factory by them, but on one occasion a single Dornier Do 17 dropped bombs near the north side of the aerodrome on 26 March 1941, killing one person and injuring the managing director of Westland, Eric Mensforth.

The company became sub-contractors for many types of aircraft and was involved in converting ex-French orders for Curtiss Mohawk as well as de-crating, assembling and test-flying Curtiss Tomahawk and Kittyhawk fighters ordered by the RAF. In 1942/3 Westland was also contracted to produce the Fairey Barracuda Mk II carrier-borne torpedo and dive bomber, but by far the most important aircraft production carried out under contract was for Spitfires and Seafires. An initial order for Mk I Spitfires was received in 1941, but a larger one soon followed for Mk Vs – a total of 685 were built. The first Spitfire produced was rolled out on 8 July 1941. Production was switched to Seafires and the company constructed 870 Mk IIIs and 602 other marks: a total of 1,472 – the last leaving the factory in 1952. The Westland-designed high-altitude fighter, the Welkin, first flown on 1st November 1942, was eventually put into production for the RAF and from June 1945 to March 1946 some 60 were built, but they never entered operational service.

Post war production has centred around helicopters, with the exception of the awesome Wyvern turbo-prop single-seat carrier-borne strike aircraft for the Fleet Air Arm, which finally entered service in 1953, some seven years after its maiden flight, following a long gestation period fraught with difficulties. This was the company's last fixed-wing aircraft design to enter production. Since then the company has produced many excellent helicopters including the Whirlwind, Wessex, Sea King and Lynx for service with the Royal Air Force and Royal Navy, as well as many other air forces and navies all over the world. Today Westland is producing, besides their own designs, the Black Hawk S-70 tactical transport helicopter for Sikorsky, who have a large shareholding in the company. West-

Aerial view of the Westland works taken in January 1946 with Seafires, Welkins and an Oxford on the airfield. Numerous air raid shelters are seen bottom left. (Westland Helicopters Ltd)

land is also in partnership with Agusta of Italy, with whom they are currently developing the EH 101 helicopter, which will eventually replace the Sea King.

Yeovilton

Yeovilton is headquarters of the Fleet Air Arm and the largest naval air station in the United Kingdom complying to full NATO standards. Over 3,000 service and civilian personnel are employed here. Yeovilton is the home base for nine squadrons and some 120 aircraft including the Sea Harrier, Sea King, Lynx, Hunter, Canberra, and Gazelle. In addition, the Fleet Air Arm Museum at Yeovilton houses one of the finest and largest collections of historic aircraft in the world.

When the Admiralty regained control of the Fleet Air Arm in 1937, they realised that the programme for new aircraft and carriers would rapidly outgrow their training facilities. In 1938 they embarked upon a search to find suitable land on which to construct airfields in the West Country. Commander John Heath RN was despatched by the Admiralty to look for a suitable site, which he found near Ilchester and selected 417 acres of flat farm land one mile east of the village. The land was purchased in July 1939 and work started immediately on the construction of a typical training base with four tarmac runways, but progress was slow due to land drainage problems. The first hangars on the site were erected early in 1940 and on completion were handed over to Westland Aircraft Ltd as a sub-site for their Yeovil factory.

In May, with the prospect of invasion looming, the Naval Observer School moved from Ford on temporary deployment: Nos 750, 751 and 752 Squadrons arrived at Yeovilton equipped with Blackburn Sharks, Fairey Albacores and Swordfish. They left at the end of the year: 751 to Arbroath, 750 and 752 to Piarco in Trinidad.

The airfield still looked like a bomb site when it was commissioned HMS *Heron* on 18 June 1940, having officially opened on the 1st under the command of Captain H.S. Murray Smith, RN. The base continued to function despite half completed buildings and equipment scattered all over the camp. Yeovilton was bombed four times. The first occasion was on 5 July 1940 when four bombs cratered the airfield, but no damage was caused; the second was on 15 July when a small force of Junkers Ju 88s dropped 12 bombs from 900 ft, damaging a few buildings and causing some injuries. On the third occasion a lone Ju 88 dropped its bombs on the airfield on 14 August, but only slight damage was caused to a runway and fuel bowser. The last attack was made on 12 May 1941 by another lone Ju 88, but no damage nor casualties were sustained.

Yeovilton was the intended home of the Naval Air Fighting School and it remained here under various names from April 1940 to August 1972 – an impressive record. The first squadron to form was No 794 in August with Swordfish, which provided target facilities for the school and arrived on 16 September from Eastleigh. Apart from a short detachment to Warmwell in March, they remained until July 1943 before moving to Angle and flew a mixture of aircraft including Swordfish, Roc, Skua, Martinet and Defiant.

The flying elements of the Fighter School, comprising of Nos 759 and 760 Squadron, started to assemble on 16 September. No 759 Squadron with a motley collection of aircraft including Blackburn Rocs, Skuas and Sea Gladiators flew in from Eastleigh; adding Masters, Fulmars and Martlets, followed by Sea Hurricanes in June 1941 and later Spitfires, Seafires, Blenheims, Wildcats and Oxfords to its inventory. The squadron became the Advanced Flying School component of No 1 Naval Air Fighting School in April 1943, and by May had a complement of 66 Sea Hurricanes, 8 Spitfires, 24 Fulmars and 15 Masters on strength. The No 1 Fleet Fighter Pool, 760 Squadron, had been similarly equipped as 759 on arrival and also added Masters to the collection, followed by Hurricanes in October 1941, on which they standardised, until temporarily disbanded on 31 December 1942. The school got down to the business of producing fighter pilots for the numerous first-line squadrons being formed.

Meanwhile the Westland (Ilchester) Works had already become a major repair centre for damaged Spitfires and started modification work on the ex-French contract Mohawks and Tomahawks. The works undertook the conversion of Lysanders for covert operations to fly SOE agents to and from enemy held territory, but the main activity would be centred on Spitfires for the rest of the war.

The first front line squadron to be formed at Yeovilton was No 827 on 15 September with Albacores; they moved to Crail on 2 November for

YEOVILTON

SCALE OF YARDS
0   500   1000   1500   2000

A. Aircraft standings
B. Armoury
C. A.R.S. hangar
D. Compass base
E. Control building
F. E.R.S. hangar
G. Equip. & Erect. hangar
H. Explosives area
I. Ground signals
J. Hangars
K. Pens
L. Radar test base
M. Sick bay
N. Test butt
O. Workshop
P. Apron

Above: *Pilots of 807 Squadron with their Seafire L.IIcs at Yeovilton in July 1942.* (IWM)

Below: *Somerset could boast having the first operational jet squadron, No 616, which converted to the type at Culmhead in July 1944. This early example of a Meteor is seen at Yeovilton the same year.* (FAAM)

work-up, before moving south in May 1941. In December No 807 Squadron arrived with Fulmars but did not remain long and left in February 1941 before joining HMS *Furious* in March.

On 5 March 1941 787 Squadron formed from ex-804 Squadron aircrew as the Fleet Fighter Development Unit and was equipped initially with Sea Gladiators, Sea Hurricanes, Fulmars and Martlets, before moving to Duxford on 18 June. No 761 Squadron formed here on 1 August, and operated as an Advanced Training Squadron with Fulmars and Sea Hurricanes before moving to Henstridge on 10 April 1943, following the airfield's commissioning as HMS *Dipper* ten days before.

Further front line squadrons formed or worked up at Yeovilton during 1941 including No 804 in February, who equipped with Sea Hurricanes and Fulmars for duty on board catapult-armed merchant (CAM) ship, as convoy protection against attacks by Fw 200 Condors. No 883 Squadron formed on 10 October with six Sea Hurricanes, but left in February for duty with 14 Group RAF at Peterhead, before embarking on

HMS *Avenger* for Russian convoy escort work. Most of the 12 Bellman hangars had been completed by this time and large sections of the base had been camouflaged. No 885 Squadron re-formed at the beginning of December with six Sea Hurricanes and joined HMS *Victorious* in June.

The accommodation sites of Nissen and Maycrete huts were still insufficient, but expanding rapidly. Further property and land was requisitioned in surrounding villages, mainly for the accommodation of WRNS. Other dispersal areas were taken over at Manor Farm, Specklington Farm, also land at Bridgehampton and Podimore. Seven Mains hangars were built at these locations.

No 802 Squadron reformed with six Sea Hurricane IBs on 1 February 1942 and after an extensive work-up, embarked on HMS *Avenger* in September for convoy protection work. 762 Squadron formed on 23 March as an Advanced Flying Training School squadron equipped with Fulmars; it moved to St Merryn in April, but arrived back on 8 September and equipped with Sea Hurricanes. The base was rapidly reaching saturation point in 1942 and with the advent of American Lease-Lend aircraft it became necessary to build satellites at Charlton Horethorne and Henstridge.

Charlton Horethorne opened in May becoming HMS *Heron II* and 790 Squadron formed there in July, attached to the Fighter Direction School, thus relieving Yeovilton of some pressure. No 887 Squadron arrived on 1 June with their Fulmars, but moved to Charlton Horethorne on 10 July. The other satellite at Henstridge did not open until April 1943, when No 2 NAFS was formed there. These two airfields concentrated on the training of Wildcat, Martlet and Corsair pilots as well as housing the Fleet Requirements Unit, the Twin Conversion Unit, No 762 Squadron and the Advanced Flying School 761 Squadron. Approximately 150 cranked-wing Corsairs were on strength in 1945, but with the ending of Lease-Lend, they disappeared and were replaced by Seafires.

A Fighter Controller School was started in rudimentary form here in 1941. A Direction Centre was established at Specklington Manor where from a glasshouse built on top trainee controllers learnt their trade by directing Wrens pedalling radio-equipped ice cream tricycles around the airfield dispersals! The formation of 790 Squadron would give them a chance to direct the real thing.

In April 1943 No 748 Squadron, the fighter pool, arrived from St Merryn with Fulmars and Martlets staying until October 1944, when it went to Dale. 736 Squadron re-formed in May as the School of Air Combat, but left for St Merryn with their Seafires and Wildcats in September because of the overcrowding at Yeovilton, to become the School of Naval Air Warfare. On 7 September 882 Squadron arrived from Lee-on-Solent with their Barracudas and stayed at Yeovilton until November when the squadron moved to Tain in Scotland. No 825 Squadron with Swordfish and Sea Hurricanes were here for a few days in September. The first Firefly RNVR squadron to be formed at Yeovilton was No 1770 on 1 October, followed in February 1944 by No 1771 with 12 of the aircraft before moving on 4 March to RNAS Burscough in Lancashire.

In April 1945 RNAS Zeals in Wiltshire opened as another satellite airfield for Yeovilton and trained Corsair pilots as part of No 1 Naval Air Fighter School, Yeovilton, but it was no longer needed after the war and closed down in February 1946. With the end of the war and the subsequent run-down of the Fleet Air Arm, most of the squadrons still left at Yeovilton were disbanded, leaving No 759 Squadron and the resident Fighter Direction School as the only occupants of Yeovilton. The school went to Kete in South Wales in 1945 and the airfield was left at a low ebb. No 759 Squadron (No 1 Fighter School) disbanded in March 1945, thus ending a long association with Yeovilton.

Yeovilton's future was secured in November 1951 when it was decided that the station would be the shore base for the Fleet's all-weather fighters and with the advent of jet aircraft, work started in the summer of 1952 on lengthening the runways. Many front line and training squadrons continued to be based here, over the years and the airfield has seen a great variety of aircraft, including Seafire 17s, Sea Furies, Sea Vampires, Sea Venoms, Seahawks, Scimitars, Sea Vixens, Phantoms, Wessex and latterly Falcons of the civilian operated Fleet Requirements Unit, besides those it currently operates.

The Spitfire Mark II, presented by the citizens of Weston-super-Mare, seen here at the Castle Bromwich factory in early 1941. (Avon County Library)

SOMERSET'S SPITFIRES

The presentation aircraft

The Battle of Britain brought home to most people the urgent need for fighter aircraft. Lord Beaverbrook, as Minister of Aircraft Production, was charged with the responsibility of maximising output from factories producing these fighters. The Government had mentioned in May 1940 a nominal round figure of £5,000 as being the sum required for the purchase of a fighter aircraft. Apart from the patriotic individuals of means, who donated a Spitfire themselves, 'Spitfire funds' started up all over the United Kingdom so all could contribute, including children who could donate their pocket money, to a worthy cause.

Somerset soon had several set up: Bath's fund had passed £5,000 by 18 August 1940 – only 11 days after the appeal was launched and enough to purchase 'their' Spitfire, with funds still coming in. Bath's presentation Spitfire Mk 1 X4906 was photographed, complete with the City's coat of arms emblazoned on the fuselage, and appeared in the local paper on 5 March 1941 to provide tangible evidence to its citizens of their proud contribution.

Bridgwater Borough and Bridgwater District raised £6,427 7s 9d for the Spitfire fund. This purchased Spitfire Mk 1 R7163, which was taken on charge with 24 MU on 4 March 1941. Allocated

This Whirlwind of 137 Squadron at Charmy Down was presented to the RAF by Mr and Mrs Ellis of Fiji. The pilot is Pilot Officer E.L. Musgrave of Sydney, Australia. (IWM)

to 452 (RAAF) Squadron, Kirton-in-Lindsey on 24 April and on 10 May to No 313 (Czech) Squadron at Catterick, it did not last long. Whilst being flown by Sergeant Gutvald on 27 May it crashed at Uckerby, near Scorton, killing the pilot. Bridgwater has commemorated its contribution by mounting a plaque in the foyer of its council offices at the Priory in the town. During the War Weapons Week, which ended in February 1941, the collection was £208,808 – more than double the target and enough to purchase ten bombers, 40 Spitfires or 60 tanks!

Other towns in the county set up funds and purchased Spitfires; Weston-super-Mare contributed and their Spitfire Mk II P7925 rolled off the Castle Bromwich production lines at about the same time.

FOURTEEN

The Royal Observer Corps

For nearly six years the Royal Observer Corps maintained a constant watch upon the skies of Britain. They were the 'Eyes and Ears' of the Royal Air Force. The organisation was also essential for the efficient working of the air-raid warning system throughout the country. There were 29 observer posts in Somerset, covering the whole of the county. The network of posts covering the whole of Britain was completed just in time for the opening phases of the Battle of Britain.

There was at first no uniform and observers on duty wore the same striped armlet as is usually worn by the Police, but with the words 'Observer Corps' superimposed in red letters. In April 1941 the valuable services of the Corps were officially recognised by the grant of the title 'Royal'. In 1943 there was a complete reorganisation when official ranks were introduced for the first time, but the ROC remained unique: being composed of civilians, paid by the Air Ministry, and controlled by Fighter Command. The arrangement under which some of the personnel were full-time and others part-time volunteers was continued. Uniforms began to be issued in 1941: the officers' service dress was similar in pattern and colour to those of the Royal Air Force, but with special ROC titles and buttons. Women observers were similarly attired, but with the choice of skirt or trousers. The Corps had its own cap badge depicting a watcher of Armada days holding aloft a flaming torch.

The function of the Corps was to identify, track and report all aircraft, whether friendly or hostile. Each post was manned by two observers at a time; the full establishment for a Post was 21, including a Chief and Leading Observer. The posts were sited on high hills, on the tops of buildings, or at any vantage point where the terrain offered a wide field of vision. Posts, grouped in clusters of three or four, were connected together and to the operations room at observer centres by 'open' telephone lines; each Group consisting of some 36 to 40 posts.

Observer centres were planned on somewhat similar lines to the RAF operations rooms. The plotters sat around a large table, each connected to three or four posts. There were thus normally 12 plotters on duty at each centre. The table had a large map of the area and as the reports came in, the aircraft tracks were plotted onto it. This was done by the use of movable symbols so that the tellers, looking down from a raised dais, could pass onto the nearest RAF operations room a continuous picture of all air activity. The type and number of aircraft, the direction and height at which they were flying was also indicated. The plotters also passed on to the table supervisor information received from the posts such as weather reports and other matters of operational value.

Of the observer posts in Somerset, those in the south of the county, 19 in all, formed part of No 22 Group centred on Yeovil. This Group was formed in March 1939. The posts were located at Porlock, Dunster, Exford, Exton, Glastonbury, Holford, North Petherton, Burnham-on-Sea, Chilton Polden, Marston Magna, Lydeard St Lawrence, Wellington, Chard, Templecombe, Bruton, Langport, Hatch Beauchamp, Ham Hill and Crewkerne.

There were ten observer posts in the northern part of the county. They formed part of No 23 Group with headquarters at Bristol. This was an older group, having been formed in 1937. The Somerset posts in this group were located at Winscombe, West Harptree, Keynsham, Westbury-sub-Mendip, Clevedon, Radstock, Weston-super-Mare, Shepton Mallet, Long Ashton and Frome. No 23 Group 'stood to' for one week during the Munich crisis in 1938. The next call came on 24 August 1939 and from that day until the end of the war in Europe, a constant watch was kept.

Outstanding events for the Observer Corps in Somerset were the engagements during the Bat-

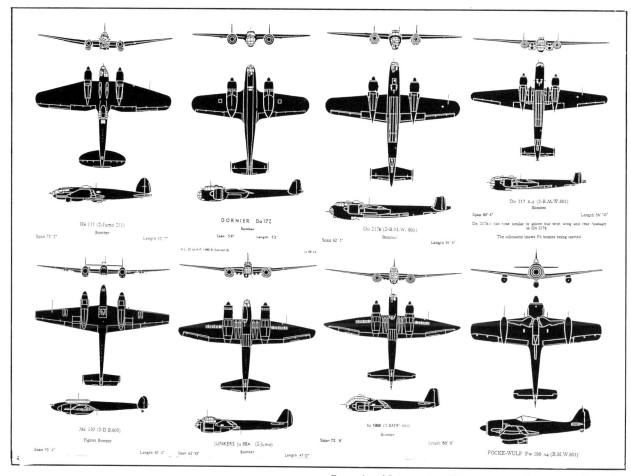

Examples of German aircraft types known to have operated over the county. All, with the exception of the Focke Wulf Fw 190, were lost by the Luftwaffe in Somerset. (Author)

tle of Britain, followed by the blitz raids on Bristol and on Somerset towns. Large numbers of enemy aircraft passed over the county during the German raids on Northern, Midland and South Wales cities, often for continuous periods of 12 or 13 hours. The courses of all these aircraft were methodically 'told forward' thereby giving the defenders accurate information as to the probable weight and duration of the attacks. A glance at a map shows that lines drawn from the Cherbourg Peninsular to Bristol, Cardiff, Swansea, Liverpool, Glasgow and Belfast, all pass over Somerset.

There was also the ever-increasing activity of our own aircraft going out to the attack and returning in the early hours of the morning. The culminating point was reached on D-Day when thousands of British and American aircraft crossed the Somerset skies. A number of observers from Somerset took an active part in the naval operations in connection with the invasion of Normandy.

On 10 May, 1945, the Royal Observer Corps 'stood down' from war duties. Today their rôle has changed: no longer are they responsible for the tracking of aircraft; now the ROC would be mainly concerned with monitoring nuclear fall-out in time of war. A number of ROC posts are kept active in Somerset, but a great many closed during the radical changes that took place in the late sixties.

Ivo Peters was in the Royal Observer Corps for many years and was awarded a BEM in recognition of his services to the Corps. In the latter part of the war he was Chief Observer of the ROC post at Keynsham:

Our post was K1 (King 1) and came under 23 Group, whose HQ was in Bristol. 23 Group Operations Room controlled North Somerset, South Gloucestershire, West Wiltshire and Bristol itself. The 'King' cluster of posts were spread around the City: K1 at Keynsham;

The derelict Observer Corps Post at Porlock photographed in 1987.
(Author)

K2 at West Harptree; K3 at Avonmouth and K4 north of Filton. All four posts were linked by continuous telephone circuit and also to the operations room.

For medical reasons, at first I had difficulty in being accepted for service in the ROC, but eventually joined the Corps on 1 January 1942; they were very well organised by then. The 'Centre' crews varied considerably in efficiency; the outstanding one at Bristol was 'F' Crew which mainly consisted of barristers, accountants, solicitors – all professional types – they were right on the ball. The posts also varied in efficiency. I had a wonderful selection of people at K1. Two of my best observers were a Methodist parson and a farmhand. We had every type – from all walks of life and social classes.

There were normally only two on duty at the post at any one time; No 1 was in charge and No 2 acted as telephonist and plotter. Many of us had to do a day's work and could only do evenings, nights or early mornings, except at weekends, but the Methodist parson was ideal for weekdays, as were retired people. We were expected to do a certain number of hours duty, and I tried to do at least 24 a week.

After the Battle of Britain there weren't many sightings of enemy aircraft during the daytime, but on one occassion we caught a brief glimpse of a Ju 88 that had come in under low cloud. An aircraft was reported as approaching our post from the north, which was thought to be a Blenheim – there was great excitement when we reported it to be a Junkers 88. It had apparently successfully attacked Parnell's at Yate, a factory making gun turrets for bombers. Although it was rare to see a hostile in daylight, it was not uncommon for single aircraft to come over under cloud cover to

Members of the Royal Observer Corps Post No. L2 at North Petherton c. 1940. Arthur Spender is third from right in back row.
(Arthur Spender)

appear suddenly over a target, giving our defending forces little chance of interception. At night, the only time we saw a German aircraft was if one had been picked up in a beam of a searchlight, but we could hear them as we were under the flight path from northern France to the Midlands.

One of the more spectacular scenes I ever witnessed whilst on duty, was when Bomber Command were practicing for a low-level daylight attack on the west coast of France. They had to practice flying at nought feet – literally to follow the contours of the ground, so as to be under the German's radar screen. We had received no warning from the ops room Plotter of aircraft approaching from the east, when we heard a growing crescendo of sound and were surprised by the fact we couldn't see anything at all at first. Then quite suddenly we saw the most fantastic sight: first one, then two – three – four – perhaps a score or more Lancasters appeared over the top of Lansdown. They swooped down over the hill to follow closely the line of the valley and we were actually looking at the upper sides of their wings as they did so. They flew right over our post and were so low that the grass was actually bending with the slipstream. Then others followed – wave after wave of them went by – possibly 90 or more. I think they might have been on a practice run before attacking St Nazaire – it was just before the Normandy invasion.

Arthur Spender joined the Somerset Special Constabulary in 1937 and within a year joined the Observer Corps and was a member of the North Petherton post, situated on Dancing Hill:

In the beginning we had no facilities at all – we just sat in deckchairs armed with binoculars and a telephone. Most of the time it was routine work and fairly monotonous. We used to plot Lysanders going in and out of Weston Zoyland more than any other type. However, every aircraft movement in our area had to be plotted. We had a direct telephone line to No 22 Group at Yeovil. Our post was L2; Holford L1; Burnham L3; Chilton Polden L4, which were all linked to each other.

One day we had a visit from a plain clothes policeman and thought he was a spy – it was a bit of a snap visit on his part. He offered his ID card, but we said, that was all right, and he then started asking some questions about this and that and we naturally became suspicious of him, so one chap telephoned Group HQ at Yeovil whilst the others kept him chatting. Yeovil then contacted the Police who sent the local bobby up on his bike. He was exhausted by the time he got to us and was puffing like anything – I don't think he had had so much excitement in years. The plain clothes policeman's identity was confirmed, but he was very peeved about it, so we made a pot of tea to pacify him!

PART IV

THE PEOPLE'S WAR

A long way from home. (H.H. Hole via Local History Library)

FIFTEEN

Somerset: A Safe Haven

Government Evacuation Scheme

As the Germans marched into Poland on 1 September 1939 the evacuation of children and old people from the cities to the comparative safety of the countryside was set in motion. For several days almost all normal train services were withdrawn so that the railways could concentrate upon their "errands of mercy." It could not be foreseen in those early days that the collapse of France would place the whole of her Channel coastline in enemy hands. Somerset therefore was thought to be a safe area. Somewhat surprisingly Bristol was placed in the same category and became the "not so quiet" retreat for a considerable part of the country's broadcasting system.

The arrival of large numbers of children marked the first visible impact of war upon Somerset. In their wake came expectant mothers, the blind, the aged and the infirm. They were warmly welcomed in their temporary homes, but country life was vastly different from life in the cities. Many of the children remained in the country throughout the war years and have returned to renew the links forged in those difficult days.

For all those officially evacuated a small billeting fee was paid to the householders week by week from Government funds. The scheme was administered by Billeting and Welfare Officers appointed by the local authorities. It required great tact and patience and on the whole worked well.

In April 1939, the Ministry of Health had appointed county district councils in Somerset as reception authorities for evacuees from London. On the outbreak of war the evacuation of children from the capital went smoothly, but they gradually returned home as there was no sign of danger from bombing in the early months and children were homesick. When the bombing of London did commence in the late summer of 1940, there was a mass exodus of women and children, which overloaded the authorities trying to arrange a speedy and smooth departure from the capital. Many women and children returned to the billets allocated to them in September 1939, only to find them full. In consequence, the Regional Commissioner and County Council officials in the South West set up co-ordinating bodies in conjunction with the Ministry of Health and district councils for the reception of evacuees.

The scheme worked well on the whole, despite occasional hiccups. So many train-loads of evacuees were signalled to Dulverton – almost on a nightly basis – that it became known to the locals as the 'Rabbit Run'. Things, however, did not always go to plan. At Williton the authorities were expecting a train load of school children and their teachers. The 12-coach train duly arrived at the station; the waiting official stared in disbelief – instead of the expected load, it was full of mothers-to-be, mothers with babies and toddlers! Plans that had taken months to prepare, had gone awry at one stroke. Harassed reception officials passed the news to the waiting villages, where billeting officers had to start again from scratch. They did a fantastic job, compressing months of work into a few hours. By midnight everyone on that train was accommodated.

The reception committees and billeting officers continued to perform miracles during this phase of the war. There were countless stories of trains arriving unexpectedly at destinations, or with loads of evacuee children accompanied by their teachers. In many cases these children arrived clutching a few personal belongings – maybe in a brown paper parcel or a small suitcase – and would be carrying their gasmasks. They would be bewildered, confused and tired after a long journey – and very homesick: a heart-rending sight to those who had to cope in these situations.

In the summer of 1940 there was a further influx of people when the enforced evacuation of some of the south-east coast 'invasion' towns

Evacuees from London arrive at Williton Station the first weekend of war. This train was one that brought in an 'unexpected' load. (H.H. Hole via Local History Library)

was carried out. Taunton became host to a large number of the displaced inhabitants of Hastings. Four trainloads arrived without warning during the night and were all billeted within 48 hours – a truly remarkable achievement by all concerned.

Three female welfare workers were appointed by the County Council during the war to look after the welfare of the evacuees. They operated from Taunton, Glastonbury and Ubley, near Bristol.

A Billeting Officer's lot

Life was not always easy for the billeting officers. Many people objected to being asked to accommodate evacuees and invented excuses. The late Ray Waddon, a well-known Somerset journalist, was a billeting officer who wrote of his experiences. He was surprised to find many people suffered from 'heart' trouble in Somerset: " I can't take any, sir" said one woman. "Of course I'd

like to, but 'tis me 'eart, you see. 'Ees that bad 'e do go pit-a-pat all day long and never do stop." One lone bachelor when asked how many bedrooms there were in his house said: "I'm not sure sir, I'd best go and 'ave a look...'tis either one or two." On discovering he had two he added: "I've always led a straight-forward life sir, and I'm not having any woman in *my* house."

A vicar's wife said her house was haunted, whilst the officers themselves were sometimes accused of currying favour with their friends in high places by not imposing evacuees on those in positions of influence or power. This often brought about the comment: "What about they in the big 'ouse, then? Why can't they take any more?"

Life-styles often clashed: the street-wise youngsters from the East End of London found life very different in a rural county and the values of their country cousins were often poles apart in temperament, outlook and domestic habits, but on the whole the majority fitted in remarkably well, considering the trauma to which they and their hosts had been subjected.

As the bombing intensified, particularly on the principle cities of Bristol, Southampton, Portsmouth and Plymouth, individual evacuees found their own way into Somerset. Most made their way to Taunton, where they were rested and fed before being directed to billets in the surrounding districts. Great strain was put on the organisers in the Borough, but they coped admirably and the method of distribution was largely successful.

Schools

Close liaison was maintained with the Chief Education Officer and the Ministry of Labour with the object of keeping the schools together as much as possible. Primary school children started to arrive from London on Friday, 1 September 1939, from when on all schools in Somerset were closed for instruction until further notice.

At the outbreak of war there were 487 separate primary schools in the county; by the end of the war there would be an additional 451 premises taken over for primary school instruction. In spite of this, it was often necessary to work a 'double shift' system – evacuees would be taught in the morning and local children in the afternoon, or vice versa.

Under the first evacuation scheme children from East Ham, Barking and West Ham were received in Somerset. By October the numbers had risen to 15,674 pupils and 1,107 teachers, a figure which by May 1941 had more than doubled.

During this period the majority of the children came from Acton, Barking, Bristol, Croydon, Ealing, East Ham, Essex, Hornsey, Ilford, Leyton, London, Southampton, Surrey, Walthamstow, West Ham and Willesden.

The staffing of schools could be difficult, particularly as in some cases the proportion of teacher to pupil was low, a fact not helped by some teachers being recalled to their own areas.

The same problems occurred with secondary school children. A number were evacuated en bloc to Somerset and allocated to the following areas:
1. The Poplar School of Navigation and Engineering (104 pupils) to Dr Morgan's School, Bridgwater and the Bridgwater Technical Institute. 2. The Hammersmith Technical School (124 pupils) used the premises of the Burnham Technical Institute and the Old County Library Depot. 3. Cooper's Company Secondary School, Stepney (314 pupils) used the old huts formerly used by the Frome Grammar School. 4. Regent Street Polytechnic (317 pupils) shared the premises and hall of the Minehead Grammar School. 5. South East Essex Technical College (313 pupils) shared the premises of Elmhurst Grammar School, Street. 6. Coborn School for Girls, Poplar (199 pupils) occupied the old premises of Bishop Fox's School in Staplegrove Road, Taunton. Bishop Fox's School moved to new premises on kingston Road in October 1939. 7. The Regent Polytechnic Craft Day School (109 pupils) used the premises of Sidcot School and Winscombe Woodborough Elementary School. 8. Barking Abbey School, Essex (344 pupils) shared the Weston-super-Mare Grammar School, but returned to London following the Girls' Grammar School being blitzed in 1942. 9. Charles Edward Brook School for Girls (156 pupils) shared with Yeovil Technical Institute the old premises of the Yeovil School, which had been vacated for a short while before the outbreak of war.

Further children were evacuated during the V-1 'Doodlebug' and V-2 rocket attacks on London and the South East during the summer of 1944 into an already overcrowded county.

Evacuation figures

The number of evacuees as on 1 August 1940 were: unaccompanied children 24,776; Mothers 472; accompanied children 970; teachers 1,340; helpers 254; others 15 – a total of 27,527. By 11 January 1941, the number of evacuees had increased to 62,874, plus 56,682 war workers – an all time high, which gradually reduced as the pressures on the cities lessened.

A secure home in time of need

The late Mary Wallbridge had several evacuees to stay during the war and recalled, shortly before her recent death, what it was like to have children from the poorer parts of London:

Our evacuees were obtained through Mr Clatworthy, the Evacuating Officer, and we were given a choice of boys or girls. I requested two girls but my husband said he wanted boys and wouldn't have girls in the house because of war going on a long time and he didn't want responsibility of teenage girls. Bill and

Members of the Wallbridge family in 1939: (L to R) Elizabeth, Arthur and Mary, with twin evacuees Bill and Len Brown from Plaister. (Author)

Len Brown,twins aged 9½, arrived at the outbreak of war, in September 1939, and they only had what they stood upright in – shabby grey shorts, shirts, no underclothes at all. Their father was in Trinity House on the Nore lightship – their mother was an ordinary London Eastender from Plaister. They arrived at lunchtime and came into the dining room and queried the use of the table napkins set at their places. The mother asked whether I took in washing as there was a lot on the line and I explained it was the family's washing and not a bag wash as had been suggested! She said she sent all hers to the laundry and had it washed in a bag – it was never taken out and washed like that and returned...cheapness, I suppose.

I worked very hard for the twins, and Len said to me in appreciation one day, that he was going to buy me a deckchair when he became Prime Minister so I could sit outside Downing Street all day long and do nothing! I was so touched that I cried. The twins were given sixpence each pocket money – to buy stamps, 3d. a week and the other 3d. they could spend on what they liked, and so they bought a bar of chocolate for my daughter and me.

Bill and Len had only been with us for a fortnight and we were sitting down to lunch, when there was a knock at the door – their father had arrived. He came into the dining room and tears were running down his cheeks – I reassured him that the boys were happy, but he said he thought he would never live to see the day when his children were sitting down properly to lunch at the table. Each of the twins slept in a brass bed – they had never slept in any bed before – only underneath one and had a bath once in a blue moon if they went to the Public Baths.

One Saturday there was a knock at the door and there to greet me was a woman with an old leopardskin coat – arms akimbo – and a pansy-boy in a light-blue overcoat, winklepicker shoes and long black hair – one beautiful girl with a real silk dress, and another one who was not so pretty. The woman said they were the twins' relations and they had come to stay. I said they couldn't possibly do so and the boys came out and also said exactly the same. They asked where they could go for lodgings and even offered to share my bed, if I didn't mind.

The authorities paid 7/9 a week for each twin, which was supposed to cover pocket-money and clothing, which was really a joke – it in no way covered what we actually had to spend on them. Later on in the war I asked for some sheets when we had a 'bedwetter' to stay and was offered one of the heavy canvas sheets instead! The evacuees were not fed at school – we gave them breakfast, lunch, tea and supper. There were also restrictions: I was told I couldn't hit them in any way but I said if they were coming to me they would be brought up as my own, and given a hiding if the occasion arose...but I never had to. I never saw any list of rules or guidelines, but I gather that there was such a publication – anyway, our billet was considered the best in the village!

The twins eventually left us and got into trouble straight away – we had treated them as our own grandchildren – both went to old ladies in North Petherton who couldn't cope with them at all. I met Bill in the village one day who told me he was going to the police courts – he said he had watched the farmer planting willows and when he had gone, he pulled them up – he was going to be famous and get his name in the papers. Bill asked what my husband would say and I told him he would be very upset and that he had let us both down after all our hardwork – he then burst into tears. On another occasion, I saw a crowd around a pylon in Dawes field and someone coming up the lane said: "It's one of the evacuees up a pylon." – it was Bill...of course!

A Sanctuary for the Nation's Treasures

On the evening of 22 August 1939 a lorry drove quietly into the precincts of the disused prison at Shepton Mallet. Its consignment of mysterious cardboard containers was unloaded. Other lorries followed day by day all through the months of September, October and November, by which time the cells and the basement of the prison held about 10,000 containers.

Seven years passed before it became known

that Somerset had given sanctuary to the most ancient and valuable of the nation's archives from the Public Record Office. They included the Domesday Book, the financial Records of the Exchequer from the 12th to the 14th centuries, early Chancery Records, Journals of the House of Commons, Registers of the Privy Council, the early records of the King's Court and the courts of law which grew out of it, State Papers and Treaties from the 12th century on to the present time.

The resident staff consisted of an assistant keeper and a repairer. Arrangements for the protection of the building and its contents in the event of danger were made with the National Fire Service and the British and American Military Authorities who successively occupied the remainder of the prison. The building escaped damage throughout the whole war. Despite the improvised and unaccustomed conditions of storage it was claimed that any one of the of the tens of thousands of documents could be found and produced at short notice.

The continued bombardment of London made necessary a dispersal of the priceless possessions of the Victoria and Albert Museum. For some of these the choice of the authorities fell upon Montacute House near Yeovil. Here, in the months of September and October 1941 were deposited some of the most valuable exhibits from the V & A. Thus for four years the old house was closed to visitors. Happily Montacute House escaped damage and when the war was ended all these objects were safety returned to the Museum.

The chief office of the Central Council for the Care of Churches was located at Dunster. It is not surprising therefore that so many of the priceless things entrusted to the care of the Council found a temporary home in Somerset. Amongst the items stored in the dry stone-vaulted crypt of Wiveliscombe church was the Gospel Book of St Chad from Lichfield. Church plate was stored in the vaults of a Taunton bank and in the cellar of a farmhouse high up on Exmoor. Other irreplaceable church possessions stored in Somerset include a thirteenth century reredos from Thornham Parva in Suffolk, a mediaeval paten from Cliffe-at-Hoo in Kent, the Jacobean pulpit from Odiham in Hampshire, and the model of the ship "Mary Rose" from Portsmouth Cathedral.

Twenty-nine lorry loads of furniture and fittings from the London city churches were sent into Somerset. Some found a temporary home at Wiveliscombe. Others were stored in the vaulted cellars and outbuildings of St Audries School. They included reredoses, screens, pulpits, fonts, churchwardens' pews, doorcases and two whole organs. They came in all from twenty-one city churches, among them such well-known buildings as St Mary-le-Bow, St Stephen Walbrook, St Peter's Cornhill, St Helen Bishopsgate, St Katherine Cree and St Andrew Undershaft. Some of these fitments became homeless when their churches were destroyed or damaged by enemy action.

London church bells also came to Somerset. Many were stored in the cloisters of Cleeve Abbey. They came from St Bartholomew the Great, St Bartholomew the Less and from St Andrew Undershaft in Leadenhall Street.

SIXTEEN

Civil Defence

ORGANISATION

The men and women of the Civil Defence began to train themselves in air raid precaution duties at a time when 'appeasement' was the order of the day. When the inevitable war came, the nucleus of a comprehensive Air Raid Precaution service was fortunately in being, trained and capable of rapid expansion. Under the ARP Act of 1937 county councils became the responsible authorities and planning began on a wider basis. This was put into effect in Somerset in June 1938 when the administrative county was divided into eight areas, each with its own organiser and staff.

The ARP areas were as follows:

No 1 (Clevedon) Area:
> Clevedon, Portishead and Long Ashton Rural District.

No 2 (Bathavon) Area:
> Keynsham, Radstock and Midsomer Norton, Frome and the Rural Districts of Bathavon, Frome and Clutton.

No 3 (Weston-super-Mare) Area:
> Weston-super-Mare and Axbridge Rural District.

No 4 (Bridgwater) Area:
> Bridgwater, Burnham-on-Sea and Highbridge, and Bridgwater Rural District

No 5 (Wells) area:
> Wells, Glastonbury, Shepton Mallet, Street and the Rural Districts of Wells and Shepton Mallet.

No 6 (Yeovil) Area:
> Yeovil, Chard, Wincanton, Ilminster, Crewkerne and the Rural Districts of Langport, Wincanton, Yeovil and Chard.

No 7 (Taunton) Area:
> Taunton, Wellington and the Rural Districts of Taunton and Wellington.

No 8 (Minehead) Area:
> Minehead, Watchet and the Rural District of Williton (including Williton and Porlock).

To these must be added the independent City of Bath, making nine in all.

With the outbreak of war, recruitment and training went on apace. Separate services to cover rescue work, first aid, demolition, etc., gradually took shape. On 2 September 1941 the ARP became merged into the Civil Defence General Service and the gold letters CD with a crown above were substituted for ARP on all badges. The whole Service was broadly conceived on the lines of an Army ready for battle. There was this difference – the Civil Defence Army rarely had to move into battle, it was always in the field. Only when particular areas were under heavy attack were reinforcements sent from one area to another.

The Somerset County Civil Defence control room was located in the basement of the County Hall, Taunton. In this room was a large wall-map on which all air raid incidents were plotted. Here decisions were taken for the reinforcement of hard-pressed towns within the county, or of more distant places in need of help. Thus at different times Somerset men and women were to be found on Civil Defence duty in London, Bristol, Exeter, Plymouth, Sherborne and elsewhere. This control room, of course, was manned continuously throughout the war.

THE SERVICES

Police

The work of the police was closely linked to that of the CD services. Their normal peace-time work continued as before, except that it was greatly increased. They were assisted by temporary full-time men known as Police War Reserves and also by the Special Constabulary. The duties of the latter, like most of the war-time voluntary services, were mostly performed at night or at weekends. Their work was often monotonous and unobtrusive: not always receiving the recog-

The Weston-super-Mare Auxiliary Fire Brigade with their Coventry Climax 'Godiva' pump. (Weston Museum)

An ATS officer takes the salute from Women Post Office Messengers during a parade of the services and trades in Weston-super-Mare. (Avon County Library)

nition which it deserved.

The City of Bath had its own Police Force and Special Constabulary. The latter suffered heavily during the *Baedeker* raids on the city in April 1942 when eight of their number were killed. Their names are recorded on a memorial plaque at the City Police Headquarters. Also commemorated is Constable Kenneth Snook of the County Constabulary who was killed on duty in the city at the same time.

National and Auxiliary Fire Service

Included in 'Civil Defence' was the National Fire Service which was formed in August 1941 by the amalgamation of all the fire brigades in the country, together with the Auxiliary Fire Service. It played a great part in minimising the effects of the enemy's incendiary bombs. Its success may be judged by the fact that the wholesale destruction of property by fire in London and many provincial cities in the raids of 1940 did not occur again on anything approaching the same scale. Organised on a nationwide basis, the National Fire Service was able to move reinforcements wherever they were needed most.

Fire Watchers, WVS, Messengers, Bomb Disposal

To defeat German fire attacks it became neces-sary to maintain a watch on every building. The challenge was met by the organisation of a Fire Guard, composed of householders, of factory and office workers. The volunteers included men and women of every age and status. In 1942 when the Compulsory Service Orders came into full effect practically every able-bodied person not already in the Home Guard Civil Defence or

Just prior to the Baedeker raids, the Combe Down Rescue and Decontamination Parties parade with their equipment. (Bath Reference Library)

other Service was drawn into the net.

The Women's Voluntary Service also played a very important part in the Civil Defence scheme and the Home Guard was also included in the forces mobilised against attack from the air.

An army of male and female ARP messengers were employed to maintain vital communication links with the rescue services in the event of air raid damage to telephone lines.

No account would be complete without mention of the bomb disposal units, both naval and military, which dealt with the great numbers of unexploded bombs and mines the Luftwaffe left in its trail. The work was arduous and hazardous in the extreme. It required more than ordinary courage.

Rescue, Mutual Assistance and Gas Decontamination Squads; First Aid Parties; Wardens' Service; Ambulances

Somerset had 39 rescue parties with a unit strength of seven and an establishment of 21 personnel. There were 26 decontamination squads with similar manning levels. In addition 107 first aid parties with a unit strength of five and an establishment of 15 personnel were provided. Due to manpower shortages later in the war, it was decided to form 94 combined first aid and rescue parties. From September 1944, as the situation allowed, this reduced to 37.

Reinforcements in the form of rescue squads were sent to neighbouring towns when these received severe bombing, notably Bristol. When the London services required assistance due to the 'V' weapon attacks volunteers from Somerset answered the appeal.

Each area had a Chief, a Divisional, Group and Head wardens. The number of wardens were allocated on a population basis: ranging from 10 to 4 per thousand according to local risk.

Somerset was allocated 108 ambulances, each of which had a driver and an attendant. An ambulance driver was attached to each Party. It was the intention for an ambulance and a first aid party should move as on unit and that the personnel should work and train as a team.

Rest and Feeding Centres

In the autumn of 1939, the Government asked Public Assistance Committees to make arrangements for emergencies which might arise through persons being made homeless as a result of bombing. Food was obtained, stored and a quantity of blankets secured. Though a small scheme at first, it was later extended in order that the northern part of the county might be

181

able to meet emergency conditions in the Bristol area leading to a large number of evacuees coming to Somerset.

As conditions altered and the West of England came in to the target area, the scheme was further extended, and by December 1941, over 1,000 rest centres had been arranged, an immense amount of equipment accumulated and distributed. In addition, some 15,000 voluntary helpers were enrolled for service.

The Rest and Feeding Centres Scheme operated on six occasions in 1941, but none of these could be regarded as major operations. In 1942, however, there were the *Baedeker* raids on Bath and Weston-super-Mare; in both places the scheme went into operation. Following the Bath air raids, numerous rest centres were opened in the north of the county and thousands of people were sheltered and fed. Meals were cooked and distributed to the rest centres from institutions at Clutton, Frome and Keynsham. After the raids on Weston-super-Mare, cooked meals were provided from institutions at Axbridge and Bridgwater.

For a time there was a continual stream of refugees from London, arriving mainly at Taunton, and in the summer of 1940, a rest and reception centre was operating there day and night. Some institutions were used as reception centres for evacuees on arrival: meals and temporary accommodation was provided. Some aliens were also received at these institutions. The scheme was highly successful and withstood every strain imposed upon its services.

DEFENCE AND INVASION COMMITTEES

During the war the complicated system of local government in the county was interlocked with a number of wartime services, as for example, Police, Fire Service, Air Raid Precautions, Women's Voluntary services and the British Red Cross. It was recognised that in an emergency, there was a possibility these individual authorities and organisations might work in watertight compartments, therefore lack knowledge of each other's duties – perhaps there might even be jealousies between them.

With this in mind, in July 1941 defence committees were formed in each town and village in the county. The aims of these were to ensure that the plans of the military and civilian services in the area covered by the committee were formulated and properly dovetailed into a local defence scheme. To quote a contemporary circular on defence committees: "...in the event of an invasion, and a town or village being isolated, there will be ready at hand a body of people trained to act together, to give every assistance to the military and to sustain the civil population in its ordeal...".

The members of such defence committees were drawn from councils, military commands, civil defence services (ARP, Police and Fire), gas, water, electricity, medical services and from representatives of the Ministries of Health, Food, Labour and Information. Each member of the defence committee learned the duties of the other members and under the direction of the chairman (usually the Mayor, Chairman of the Council or ARP controller), overlapping and confusion of orders was eliminated. Almost every possibility was envisaged by the committees and plans for local action were drawn accordingly.

ARP RECORD OF OPERATIONS SUMMARY

Compared with other parts of the country, it can be said that Somerset suffered comparatively little damage and proportionately few casualties from enemy raids; apart from the two notable ones on Weston-super-Mare; several sharp raids on Yeovil and the devastating trilogy of raids on Bath. Those aside, it would appear that no actual heavy bombing, apart from 'hit and run' raids, was directed against any place in the county. However, due to the proximity of Bristol, to cities and towns in South Wales as well as others in the north, and to the routing of enemy planes over the county to these targets, a comparatively large number of missiles were unloaded over Somerset: fortunately the majority of these dropped on the extensive open ground, causing proportionately little damage and few casualties.

According to records the first bomb (high explosive) was dropped at 09.15 on 18 June 1940 at Flax Bourton near Bristol. This was followed the next day by four HEs at Thornfalcon and West Hatch near Taunton: on this occasion the Nags Head Inn was damaged. There were no casualties at the time the bombs fell but a woman died later of shock.

The last bombs were dropped on 15 May 1944 and consisted of 23 HEs – of which four did not

Women at War

There was hardly any field of activity in which women were not engaged – they stood side by side with the men on gun sites, in the dockyards, on the airfields, in Civil Defence, in the Fire Service, in the factory and on the farm – and especially the care of the sick and the wounded.

The Women's Voluntary Service

The work of the Women's Voluntary Service for Civil Defence was more diversified and its members more numerous than any other of the wartime women's organisations. County Headquarters were set up at 29 Oxford Street, Weston-super-Mare immediately prior to the outbreak of war in 1939. As the work extended, a move was later made to more commodious premises at 24 Beach Road, Weston-super-Mare. Here the activities of the Service were directed by Mrs Orr-Ewing as County Organiser, with Miss D. Alston as County Secretary. There were assistant organisers for the many activities of the Service and Centre Organisers in almost every town and rural district in Somerset.

The Service was conceived primarily to assist the Civil Defence services. The WVS Housewives' Service helped the air raid wardens by making lists of residents and their next of kin,

Members of the Women's Land Army make up the greater proportion of the cast at the East Coker Young Farmers' concert party in 1944. (Mildred Matthew)

Wrens work on a Seafire at RNAS Henstridge (HMS Dipper) in November 1944. (FAAM)

thereby providing information of essential value in the bombed towns and villages. They shopped and cooked for bombed out people, took in homeless children, traced the missing and worked in the Emergency Feeding Centres. Many women undertook a course in basic ARP training, particularly as to decontamination after gas attack. Cards in house windows indicated those housewives who had thus qualified.

Other work for Civil Defence included the Queen's Messenger Food Convoy. The vehicles were staffed by WVS and at Weston-super-Mare driven by them as well. Clothing depots were operated which proved invaluable to people who had lost all under the enemy's attack. In many

towns the rest centres were staffed by the WVS. The volunteer car pool was of immense value in a land short of motor vehicles due to stringent petrol rationing. At Weston-super-Mare the WVS ran a Services' hostel at Ashbrooke, Ellenborough Park North, which from its opening in August 1941 to the end of December 1945 provided beds for no fewer than 54,961 men. The WVS 'British Welcome Clubs' were opened in many districts where there were large numbers of American troops and were much appreciated by them.

The WVS made camouflage netting for the Fighting Services, knitted woollen comforts, assisted in British Restaurants and school canteens,

An ATS exhibition was held at Taunton on 20 December 1941 and seen here are girls representing, to quote the official caption, 'types' in the service. (IWM)

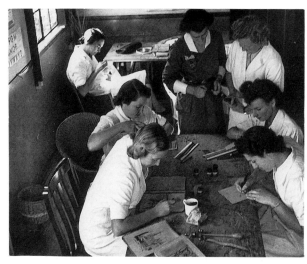

An occupational therapy centre was set up in 1941 at Middleway Camp, Taunton, to train instructors for the rehabilitation of injured servicemen. This was a six month course. This scene shows women undergoing training in a leatherwork class at the centre in September 1942. (IWM)

ran county market produce stalls, assisted in salvage collection and in the National Savings movement. Somerset 'adopted' the Borough of Lambeth and did much in the collection of furniture and utensils to re-establish those in Lambeth whose homes had been destroyed. During the period of the flying bomb and rocket attacks on London in 1944-1945 Somerset WVS volunteers went to London to relieve the hard-pressed women there who were in turn entertained and given much-needed rest in Somerset.

The City of Bath had its own WVS, but its activities corresponded with those elsewhere, except that Bath 'adopted' Streatham, London and sent four vanloads of furniture and household equipment to those who had lost home and belongings in air attacks.

Women Home Guard Auxiliaries

From the first days of the Local Defence Volunteers, there were always women prepared to cook for them should the Force be embodied within their ranks. Others helped in the various headquarters as telephonists and clerks. In some places the women, by a rota system, stood by in the church belfries so that the bells could be instantly rung in the event of invasion. Many of these early volunteers were members of the WVS.

The War Office was somewhat tardy in recognising the women's part in the Home Guard, but eventually did so. With due solemnity they laid down conditions of service for 'Nominated Women'. The origins of this strange title are obscure. Objection was so widespread that the authorities gave way and pronounced in favour of the more acceptable title of "Women Home Guard Auxiliaries". In the years 1943 and 1944 when the Home Guard was completing its signals organisation, the number of women auxiliaries greatly increased. They were recruited in the towns and in the villages for duty as telephonists and signal clerks, and at the time of the stand down in December 1944 there were rather more than a thousand Women's Home Guard Auxiliaries in the county.

No uniform was provided for the women auxiliaries, there were however, enthusiasts who adapted men's denim blouses for their own use and converted issue trousers into skirts. In one battalion women signallers were to be seen in men's battledress complete with shoulder titles and flashes. The women signallers undertook regular duties. The cooks were seen less often as, with the exception of exercises, their services were not required.

Two Wrens working on Seafires at Henstridge in November 1944.
Top: *Wren Donahue (AMO) attends to a cannon's mechanism.*
Bottom: *P/O Wren Lyon carries out a radio check in non-working rig for the benefit of the camera.* (FAAM)

Women's Auxiliary Police Corps

With one exception members of the Women's Auxiliary Police Corps in Somerset undertook full-time duties throughout the war years. Many acted as telephone operators, clerks, typists and secretaries. All did a certain amount of patrol work each day. They always patrolled in pairs and did valuable work in connection with crimes and misdemeanours concerning women and children. The Corps had its own Inspector who was attached to the County Constabulary Headquarters at Taunton.

It was the auxiliary policewomen who operated the air raid sirens in many towns. They also had the task of passing the air raid warnings to RAF stations in the vicinity and to all outlying districts. The City of Bath had its own Women's Auxiliary Police Corps under the Chief Constable.

Toc H Services Canteens

Toc H is a men's movement, but it has a women's section and it was upon the women that a great part of the work fell of running the many Services' canteens up and down the country. Over 60% of Toc H men went into the Forces. Of the few who remained many assisted in the Services' canteens on the administrative side, but the greater number of workers were women.

The largest of these Toc H Services' clubs in Somerset was at Bath. It was founded in January 1939 and ran for seven years. It had a canteen, lounge, rest room, billiards room, recreation hall, dormitories and a chapel. The club provided in all 44,610 beds and just short of one million meals for Servicemen. It was honoured on 4 October 1941 by a visit from HM Queen Mary and on two occasions by the Founder Padre the Reverend P.B. (Tubby) Clayton.

Not all the Toc H Services' clubs in Somerset were or could be on the same scale as that at Bath but each unit did its best in accordance with its opportunities. The idea was simply to provide a touch of home. The clubs, both large and small,

were situated at; Axbridge, Bath, Bridgwater, Castle Cary, Crewkerne, Ilminster, Langport, Minehead, Portishead, Stoke-under-Ham, Taunton, Wellington, Werescot Camp (near Sampford Arundel), Weston-super-Mare and Winscombe.

Mobile Canteens

The people of the United States did much to help the people of the West Country. Taunton, Massachusetts presented its English namesake with a mobile canteen in 1941 and at Vivary Park, Taunton, formally presented on 3 July "this rolling kitchen with the best wishes of your namesake in America". Later the British War Relief Society added a second 'rolling kitchen' to the first.

These vehicles did good work. They served the inhabitants of Bridgwater who were temporarily rendered homeless by unexploded mines in 1941. The canteens were at Weston-super-Mare during the air raids of 1942. In 1943 they served a large body of workmen preparing the great supply depot at Norton Fitzwarren for the use of the US Forces. They were also used in Taunton for the many invasion exercises of the Home Guard and Civil Defence services, not to mention the great parades which were a feature of the "War Weapons," "Salute the Soldier," "Wings for Victory," and other National Savings campaigns of the war years. These mobile canteens were manned by members of the Taunton Corporation staff, the majority of them women, in their spare time and in a voluntary capacity.

Girls' Training Corps

The Girls' Training Corps, the pre-Service training organisation, was noted for its smart appearance, the girls wearing white blouses, navy blue skirts and berets. They were eager to assist the war effort to the fullest possible extent and were to be found in various auxiliary capacities. They made efficient telephone operators and took regular duties in some of the Home Guard signals offices, Bridgwater being a notable example.

Above: *Pictured at Filton during the Battle of Britain, Hurricane P3021 of 504 Squadron which crash-landed in the Yeovil area following an action over the south-west coast on 30 September 1940. The aircraft was repairable, but was lost totally in a crash at Almondsbury in October 1941.* (Via Mrs Teresa Tutt)

Below: *A crew member snaps his nine colleagues standing atop their 351BG B-17 Flying Fortress, having crash-landed near the lighthouse on Burnham sands on 31 December 1943. The B-17 had been one of 31 despatched by the Group to attack Cognac airfield; seven were lost and 14 were damaged.* (Via Mrs I. Drinkwater)

Appendices

APPENDIX 1

ALLIED AIRCRAFT LOSSES/ACCIDENTS AND CREW CASUALTIES IN SOMERSET: 1939-1945

Date	Type	Location	Unit/Base	Crew state/Names
8.6.39	Queen Bee	Watchet AA Gunnery ranges	1 AACU, (Det)	pilotless drone
5.8.39	Queen Bee	Watchet AA Gunnery ranges	1 AACU, (Det)	pilotless drone
15.8.39	Queen Bee	Watchet AA Gunnery ranges	1 AACU, (Det)	pilotless drone
18.9.39	Blenheim P4861	Crashed on take-off, Weston	82 Sqdn	not known
26.9.39	Henley L3345	Overshot on landing, Yeovil	1 AACU, Weston Zoyland	not known
28.11.39	Anson N5084	On Exmoor	148 Sqdn, Harwell	5K
18.12.39	Hind K4641	Cheddar	19 MU	pilot safe (P/O S.N. Johnson)
20.12.39	DH84 G-ACJT	Crashed on take-off, Weston	Western Airways, Weston	1K (L.I. Arnott)
2.1.40	Battle L5277	Undershot landing, Weston Zoyland	207 Sqdn	not known
15.1.40	Anson K8819	Crashed Castle Cary	School of Air Navigation	1 safe (F/O Richardson), 1 inj (P/O Bain)
5.2.40	Henley L3314	Crashed on landing, Weston-s-Mare	1 AACU, Weston Zoyland	not known
19.3.40	HP42W G-AAUD	Blown together in gale - damaged	Imperial Airways	not involved
19.3.40	HP42W/3 G-AAXC	beyond repair at Whitchurch	Imperial Airways	not involved
7.4.40	Gladiator N5623	In sea off Portishead	263 Sqdn, Filton	1K (Sgt K.T. Vickery)
17.5.40	Hind K6777	Shepton Mallet	1 FTS (FAA), Netheravon	pilot safe (Sub-Lt M.G. McKendrick RN)
14.7.40	Hind K6658	Pylle, nr Evercreech	1 FTS (FAA), Netheravon	1k (LA I. Farquhar) 1 safe (Sub-Lt D. Phillips)
22.7.40	Queen Bee P4684	Shot down off Watchet (AA range)	1 AACU (Det)	pilotless drone
30.7.40	DH85 G-ADBH/AV986	Forced-landed, Houndstone Camp	RAC Duties	pilot safe
1.8.40	Spitfire K9879	Smokey Hole field, South Brewham	1 PRU, Heston	1K (Lt Cmdr G.B. Kingdon RN)
16.8.40	Defiant L7010	In sea, St Audries	5 OTU, Aston Down	2K (Sgts J.D. Gwynne & W.C. Munro)
19.8.40	Anson N5132	Littleton Lane, Wellow	5 AONS, Weston	4K (P/O F.J.A. Cameron; LACs R.T. Howard, J.A. Hodgson; AC2 W.H. Howard), 2 injured LACs H.P. Wigg, I. MacInnes)
27.8.40	Hurricane	Chelvey, nr Brockley	not known	Polish pilot safe
12.9.40	Battle N2148	Excleave, Dulverton	12 OTU, Benson	3K (Sgts Jooris, Long & Mitchell)
17.9.40	Albacore L7118	Sparkhayes Beach, Porlock	827 Sqdn, RNAS Yeovilton	crew safe
18.9.40	Lysander P1687	Forced-landed, Banwell	16 Sqdn, Weston Zoyland	pilot safe (P/O G.R. Goudge)
18.9.40	Magister	Forced-landed Mells Road Station	not known	pilot safe
23.9.40	Tiger Moth	Forced-landed, Chew Stoke	not known	crew safe
25.9.40	* Spitfire L1008	Belly-landed S Moor, Glastonbury	609 Sqdn, Warmwell	pilot safe (Sgt J. Hugh-Rees)
25.9.40	* Spitfire X4177	Forced-landed, Newton St Loe	152 Sqdn, Warmwell	pilot safe (S/Ldr P.K. Devitt)
25.9.40	* Spitfire N3173	Church Farm, Woolverton	152 Sqdn, Warmwell	1K (Sgt K.C. Holland)
25.9.40	* Hurricane P3222	In field near Mells Road Station	238 Sqdn, Middle Wallop	pilot safe (Sgt D.S. Harrison)
25.9.40	* Hurricane N2957	Forced-landed on Charmy Down	238 Sqdn, Middle Wallop	pilot safe (Sgt F.A. Sibley)
26.9.40	Master N7675	Braddick's Field, Martock	RNAS Yeovilton	2K (Mid D.S.T. Wells; Sub-Lt H.W. Richarson)
29.9.40	* Hampden X2914	West House Farm, Chilton Polden	106 Sqdn, Cottesmore	3K (Sgts Shelfer, Harvey, Boyne), pilot injured (Sgt Huggins)
30.9.40	Wellington R3168	½m W Simonsbath (Challacombe Rd)	75 (NZ) Sqdn, Feltwell	1K 5 safe
30.9.40	* Hurricane P3021	Crash-landed Yeovil area	504 Sqdn, Filton	pilot safe (Sgt B.M. Bush)
30.9.40	* Hurricane P3774	Forced-landed S of Yeovil area	504 Sqdn, Filton	pilot safe (Sgt W.H. Banks)
30.9.40	* Hurricane	Crashed 1½m S Priddy Church	not known	pilot safe
1.10.40	Hurricane P1653	Bennet's Field, 2m W Congresbury	5 OTU, Aston Down	pilot safe (Sgt S.A. Harker)
1.10.40	Battle K9223	Cokerhurst Farm, Wembdon, B'water	RAE (Det Exeter)	1K (R.O. Tipple), 1 safe (S/Ldr C.H.A. Coleman)
3.10.40	Hart K6469	1,000 yd SE Bathford Church	9 FTS, Hullavington	2 badly injured
10.10.40	Vega Gull X9435	Fitzroy, nr Taunton	8 AACU, Weston Zoyland	2K (Sgt V.N. Buchan; AC2 L.C. Kell)
12.10.40	DH91 G-AFDI	Damaged by arson (w/off 12.12.40)	BOAC, Whitchurch	not involved
12.10.40	DH91 G-AEVV	Damaged by arson (repaired)	BOAC, Whitchurch	not involved

Date	Type	Location	Unit/Base	Crew state/Names
15.10.40	Henley L3423	Crash-landed (wheels up)	1 AACU, Weston Zoyland	crew safe (pilot on a charge)
16.10.40	Blenheim Z5964	C-landed nr Brfd-o-Avon - Bath Rd	4 FPP, Kemble	not known
16.10.40	Anson R3395	Clutton Hill, Farmborough	3 FPP	pilot safe (Capt L.A. Wilkins ATA)
16.10.40	Hurricane R4174	Forced-landed in pond, Whitchurch	504 Sqdn, Filton	pilot safe (P/O R.E. Tongue)
16.10.40	Hurricane N2603	Between Clapton & Old Down Inn	5 OTU, Aston Down	pilot injured (Sgt W. Wieraszka [Polish])
17.10.40	Albacore	Broad Hill, nr East Chinnock	827 Sqdn, RNAS Yeovilton	crew safe
8.11.40	Tiger Moth	Ducks Hill, Pibsbury, Langport	not known	1K, 1 safe
13.11.40	Henley L3252	Kilton (slight damage to 'plane)	1 AACU, Weston Zoyland	crew safe
14.11.40	Hurricane	F-landed Lower Hill Fm, Butleigh	not known	pilot safe
15.11.40	Henley L3442	Crashed into pillbox on aerodrome	1 AACU, Weston Zoyland	crew safe (F/Lt G.C. Hyde; Sgt G. Russell)
19.11.40	Martlet	Alford Halt, 2m W Castle Cary	RNAS Yeovilton	pilot safe
24.11.40	Ensign G-ADTC	Damaged during raid, Whitchurch	BOAC	not involved
24.11.40	DC3 G-AGBI	Damaged during raid, Whitchurch	BOAC (owned by KLM)	not involved
25.11.40	Magister	Nunney Woods, nr Frome	not known	pilot safe
2.12.40	Tiger Moth	Beckington	not known	pilot safe
4.12.40	Leopard Moth	F-landed ½m E Wiveliscombe Church	not known	pilot safe
7.12.40	Lysander	Crash-landed, Woolavington 352418†	16 Sqdn, Weston Zoyland	pilot safe
9.12.40	Tiger Moth	Creech St Michael	10 EFTS, Weston	crew safe
12.12.40	Tomahawk	Crash-landed near Norton-s-Hamdon	Westland Aircraft, Yeovil	pilot injured (H.J. Penrose)
12.12.40	Whirlwind P6980	Sand Bay whilst air/ground firing	263 Sqdn, Exeter	pilot reported drowned
12.12.40	Tiger Moth T5442	In sea 1½m S Brean Down	10 EFTS, Weston	crew drowned
16.12.40	Lysander	Crashed on aerodrome	16 Sqdn, Weston Zoyland	2K (F/Lt Rust; Sgt Hancock)
17.12.40	Henley L3424	Blackmoor Lane, Cannington	1 AACU, Weston Zoyland	crew safe
17.12.40	Beaufort N1108	Higher Stolford Fm, Brendon Hill	No 8 Ferry Pilots School	1K (F/O B. Walker)
17.12.40	Hurricane	Valles Farm, The Leaze, Frome	not known	pilot safe
24.12.40	Hurricane P8083	Bristol Plain Farm, nr Priddy	247 Sqdn, Roborough	1K (F/O J.W. Hamill)
29.12.40	Hurricane	Stockwood Hill, Keynsham	87 Sqdn, Charmy Down	pilot safe
31.12.40	Hurricane	In field, 300 yd S Sidcot School	not known	pilot safe
1.1.41	Henley L3442	Crashed on landing (salvaged)	1 AACU, Weston Zoyland	not known
2.1.41	Fulmar	Lattisford, Wincanton	RNAS Yeovilton	1K
5.1.41	Oxford L9702	Forced-landed, Chewton Mendip	3 SFTS, South Cerney	crew safe
6.1.41	Oxford	Wellow	not known	crew safe
12.1.41	Magister	Greenore, Wells	32 Sqdn, Kemble	1K (Sgt R J.K. Gent)
16.1.41	Tiger Moth R5120	Higher Pipps, Priddy	10 EFTS, Weston	crew safe (P/O H.M. Cooch + 1)
17.1.41	Tiger Moth	Bleadon Wharf, nr Weston-s-Mare	10 EFTS, Weston	2 injured
17.1.41	Hurricane	½m W Norton St Phillip Church	not known	pilot safe
25.1.41	Battle P6764	Town Quarry, Weston-s-Mare	1 SFTS, Netheravon	1K (F/Lt T.P. De La Rue)
4.2.41	Harvard	200 yd NE Rode Church	not known	2 crew safe
4.2.41	Albemarle P1360	Boscombe, Crewkerne	RAE/AAEE	3 crew safe
4.2.41	Hurricane	Seymour's Court Farm, Beckington	not known	pilot safe
4.2.41	Leopard Moth	Combe Down, Bath	not known	crew safe
6.2.41	Hart	Berkley, near Frome	not known	crew safe
11.2.41	Wallace K8701	2m SW Walton Gt Common Pool Moor	1 Signals School	crew safe
13.2.41	Whirlwind	Swang Farm, 1m NW Charlynch	263 Sqdn, Charmy Down	pilot safe (Sgt R.B. Skellon)
20.2.41	Shark K8503	Cameroons Paddock, Keynsham	No 1 AGS, WorthyDown	2k (P/O J.W. Ridler; POA E.W. Buxton)
20.2.41	Defiant N3446	Cottage Farm, Bannerdown	256 Sqdn, Colerne	1K (Sgt D. Rees)
22.2.41	Anson N5295	½m W Clutton Parish Church	1 FPP 4	crew safe
26.2.41	Master N7776	Home Farm, Somerton Erleigh	RNAS Yeovilton	1K (Sub-Lt J. Stafford-Clark) 1 safe (Sub-Lt J.E. Scott)
26.2.41	Magister	Charlton Mackerell	not known	1K, 1 injured
7.3.41	Battle	Forced-landed, Red Road, Berrow	not known	1 injured 1 safe
19.3.41	Roc L3105	Fergrove Farm, Woolston	760 Sqdn, RNAS Yeovilton	2K (Sub-Lt W. Derbyshire; LAM J.W.J. Howes)
20.3.41	Gipsy Moth	Forced-landed nr Gas Works, W-s-M	not known	1 safe
21.3.41	Master T8449	Forced-landed Townend, E Harptree	9 FTS	pilot safe (Cpl R.A. Cooper)
24.3.41	Hart	F-landed 1m SE Wells Police Stn	not known	1 safe
28.3.41	Tiger Moth R5127	Crashed at Long Ashton	10 EFTS, Weston	1 seriously injured (LAC Villa)
28.3.41	Tiger Moth	W Broadmore Hlt, Kingston Seymour	10 EFTS, Weston	1 seriously injured
30.3.41	Wellington R1043	Manor Farm, Mudford	103 Sqdn, Honington	1K, 5 injured
2.4.41	Boston	Forced-landed, Tricky Warren	not known	crew safe
6.4.41	Blenheim L9252	Crashed on landing, Weston-s-Mare	272 Sqdn, Chivenor	not known
10.4.41	Defiant N3390	Spun in on approach, 3m NE Bath	307 Sqdn, Colerne	2K (P/Os J. Dziubek, M. Frychel [Polish])
18.4.41	Beaufighter	Duredown Farm, Simonsbath	not known	1 safe (baled out)
19.4.41	Hurricane	Holton X Roads, nr Wincanton	RNAS Yeovilton	pilot safe
27.4.41	Halifax L9501	Crash-landed, Weston Zoyland	35 Sqdn, Linton-on-Ouse	crew safe
2.5.41	Audax K3103	F-landed, Milton Hill Fm, W-s-M	1 SFTS, Netheravon	crew safe
2.5.41	Lysander T1551	Castlehill Wood, Croscombe	16 Sqdn, Weston Zoyland	2K (P/O D.R. Watts; AC2 G.F. Owen)

Date	Type	Location	Unit/Base	Crew state/Names
2.5.41	Beaufighter	Yeovil Aerodrome	not known	crew safe
8.5.41	Magister	F-landed Taswell's field, Holway	not known	pilot safe
11.5.41	Hurricane	Pinksmoor Lane, Rockwell Green	not known	pilot baled out
12.5.41	Hurricane	Globe Farm, Hazelbury Plucknett	not known	pilot injured (burns)
17.5.41	Hurricane P5203	River Parrett, Langport	759 Sqdn, RNAS Yeovilton	pilot drowned (Sub-Lt J.N.W. Parish)
19.5.41	{ Oxford L4565	Curland	3 SFTS, South Cerney	pilot safe (LAC R.C. Thompson)
	{ Oxford L4578	Barrington Hill, Broadway	3 SFTS, South Cerney	pilot safe (LAC J.G.A.N. Fitt)
19.5.41	Magister	Churchstanton airfield	not known	crew safe
20.5.41	Tiger Moth N9274	Hit vehicle on landing	10 EFTS, Weston	not known
20.5.41	Henley L3442	Crashed on Tow Target practice	1 AACU, Weston Zoyland	2K
21.5.41	Hurricane P3152	Hazelgrove House, Sparkford	759 Sqdn, RNAS Yeovilton	1K (Lt J.P. Eustace RNVR)
1.6.41	Proctor	½m W Churchill Church	Navy a/c not known	2 injured 1 safe
10.6.41	Spitfire P8143	Shiplate Court Farm, Bleadon	501 Sqdn, Colerne	1K (Sgt C.J. Barton)
12.6.41	Hampden	In sea, believed off Brean	106 Sqdn, Finningley	4K (Sgts H.W. White & G.T. Corbett + 2)
13.6.41	Hurricane P2878	Near Ilchester	759 Sqdn, RNAS Yeovilton	1K (Sub-Lt M. Westerman RNVR)
14.6.41	Fulmar	Ashington, near Yeovil	RNAS Yeovilton	pilot safe
17.6.41	Albacore	Cars Cliff Farm, Cheddar Gorge	not known	3 injured
20.6.41	Tiger Moth R5122	Brean Down (in field)	10 EFTS, Weston	1K (P/O C.R. Greenhill) 1inj (LAC Kilpatrick)
20.6.41	Henley L3423	In sea, 5m NNW Watchet	1 AACU, Weston Zoyland	2K (Sgt D.A. Frost; LAC H. Blundred)
30.6.41	Spitfire	F-landed on Golf Links, Minehead	not known	pilot safe
3.7.41	Shark	Near Crewkerne	RNAS Yeovilton	2 safe
6.7.41	Tiger Moth	F-landed Wallmarsh Farm, Rodden	not known	pilot safe
6.7.41	Fulmar N4068	Near Yeovilton aerodrome	759 Sqdn, RNAS Yeovilton	2K (Sub-Lt T. Duncan RNVR; AMech B.E. Randle)
10.7.41	Anson L7957	Charlton Horethorne	3 AONS	crew safe
11.7.41	Moth Minor	Near Sparkford	Impressed a/c	2 safe
14.7.41	Hurricane T9520	East Lydford, Keinton Mandeville	317 Sqdn, Exeter	pilot safe (Sgt P. Roscik [Polish])
26.7.41	Spitfire	Forced-landed, Porlock	not known	pilot safe
27.7.41	Wellington	Yeovil Aerodrome	not known	crew safe
4.8.41	Magister	⅝m S Mells Church	not known	crew safe
9.8.41	Tiger Moth R4783	Hutton, Weston-s-Mare	10 EFTS, Weston	crew safe (F/O F.P. Davis + 1)
10.8.41	Beaufort	1m S Mark Church	not known	crew safe
11.8.41	Spitfire	Stogursey	not known	pilot injured
12.8.41	Whirlwind	Yeovil Aerodrome	Westland Aircraft	pilot safe
13.8.41	Spitfire	Yeovil Aerodrome	Westland Aircraft	pilot safe
14.8.41	Tiger Moth	Brent Knoll	not known	crew safe
15.8.41	Fulmar	Chilthorne Dormer	RNAS Yeovilton	crew safe
16.8.41	Defiant N3499	Upper Langridge Farm, Charlecombe	125 Sqdn, Charmy Down	1K (Sgt H.L. Learning)
19.8.41	Hart K4949	½m SE Claverton Church, nr Bath	1 SFTS, Netheravon	2K (ActLA R.G. Watson & E.S. Ingle)
22.8.41	Spitfire	Merry Harriers Inn, Churchstanton	302 Sqdn, Churchstanton	1K (Sgt E. Kropiwnicki [Polish])
2.9.41	Hurricane Z3576	Kingsdown, Bath	87 Sqdn, Charmy Down	not known
2.9.41	Hurricane P2953	Hulkshay Farm, North Petherton	759 Sqdn, Yeovilton	1K (Mid J.F. Williams RNVR)
3.9.41	Dragonfly X9389	Penwood Farm, Chedzoy	8 AACU, Pengam Moors	2K (F/Lt R.M. Sales; Sgt H.W. Bellingham)
8.9.41	Blenheim V5377	Mells Park, Mells	13 OTU, Bicester	3K (Sgts J.L. Nyman, C.M. Pratt, J.L. Rodwell)
18.9.41	Hurricane	Yeovilton	RNAS Yeovilton	pilot safe
19.9.41	Beaufighter T4659	Blackland Hill, Exford	OADU, Kemble	2K (Sgt H.C. Fox + 1)
19.9.41	{ Lysander	Collided on take-off	16 Sqdn, Weston Zoyland	crew safe
	{ Tomahawk		400 Sqdn, Odiham	crew safe
20.9.41	Magister P2459	600 yd SE Alford Church	BACorp, White Waltham	pilot safe
25.9.41	Tiger Moth T6617	Overturned on landing	10 EFTS, Weston	not known
25.9.41	Fulmar N4129	Near West Camel	RNAS Yeovilton	1K (Sub-Lt D. Simmonds RNVR)
1.10.41	Hurricane Z3839	NE Wellow Church, nr Radstock	87 Sqdn, Charmy Down	pilot baled out, Radstock (Sgt W. Shimmons)
2.10.41	Henley L3384	Crashed on take-off	1 AACU, Weston Zoyland	not known
7.10.41	Hurricane	1m SE Hazelbury Plucknett	RNAS Yeovilton	pilot safe
9.10.41	Hurricane L1789	Godney, near Meare	9 SFTS, Hullavington	pilot injured (P/O R.I. Tibbenham)
9.10.41	{ Whirlwind P6968	GWR Goods Yard, Saltford	263 Sqdn, Charmy Down	1K (P/O O.J.H. Hoskins)
	{ Whirlwind P6999	Bowling Green, Weston, Bath	263 Sqdn, Charmy Down	pilot safe (F/O H.J. Coghlan DFC)
16.10.41	Hurricane V7675	Yeovilton Airfield	759 Sqdn, RNAS Yeovilton	1K (Sub-Lt A.C. Scott RNVR)
16.10.41	Spitfire	Forced-landed Otterford, Taunton	not known	pilot safe
17.10.41	Magister	Stoke Lane, Shepton Mallet	not known	crew safe
22.10.41	Tiger Moth	F-land Old Flying Ground, Berkley	not known	pilot safe
23.10.41	Hurricane R4220	3m NE Cheddon, near Taunton	52 OTU	pilot safe (P/O J.W. Williams)
25.10.41	Magister	Impens Farm, North Newton	8 AACU, Pengam Moor	2K (F/Sgt T.A. Maslen; Sgt R. Bedkowski)

Date	Type	Location	Unit/Base	Crew state/Names
28.10.41	{ Whirlwind P7053	Manor Fm, Englishcombe, Bath	137 Sqdn, Charmy Down	1K (S/Ldr J. Sample DFC)
	{ Whirlwind	Slight damage - returned to base	137 Sqdn, Charmy Down	pilot safe (Sgt M.J. Peskett)
3.11.41	Tiger Moth	West Horrington, Wells	not known	crew safe
5.11.41	Tiger Moth	Masbury, Dinder	not known	crew safe
13.11.41	Magister	Crashed, Weston-super-Mare	not known	crew safe
15.11.41	Lysander	Bishops Lydeard	16 Sqdn, Weston Zoyland	crew safe
17.11.41	Hurricane	F-landed ½m W Norton St Philip	not known	pilot safe
20.11.41	Magister	Buckland Denham	not known	crew safe
20.11.41	Magister	Near Frome	not known	crew safe
20.11.41	Hawk	Bristol Plain, Rodney Stoke	White Waltham	1K (2nd Off ATA R. Baker)
20.11.41	Mohawk	1½m West of Priddy Church	39 MU, Colerne (?)	1K
21.11.41	Hurricane	Postlebury Farm, Cloford	RNAS Yeovilton	1K (Sub-Lt C. Don RNVR)
1.12.41	Beaufort N1044	Court Hill, Exford	5(C)OTU, Chivenor	4K (P/O R.W. Hopkins [Aus]; Sgts Smart, S.G. Boyle & R. Masters)
16.12.41	Magister	Chilton Cantelo	not known	2 injured
22.12.41	Anson N1337	Wanstrow	3 AOS 2	injured (Sgt Foster + 1)
24.12.41	Magister L8280	Forced-landed, Godminster Manor	not known	crew safe
25.12.41	Magister	Near Shepton Mallet	not known	crew safe
28.12.41	Whitley Z9297	In field near Electcy Wks, W-s-M	OADU, Honeybourne	crew safe
2.1.42	Spitfire P8071	Lulsgate	417 Sqdn, Charmy Down	pilot safe (Sgt D.C. Goudie [Can])
5.1.42	Whitley Z6979	Steart Flats	10 OTU, Abingdon	crew safe (Sgt G.B.C. Miller + 4)
5.1.42	Hurricane	Ashington Wood, near Yeovilton	RNAS Yeovilton	1K
6.1.42	{ Spitfire P7983		17 Sqdn, Charmy Down	not known
	{ Spitfire P7544	Hit Spitfire P7544 on aerodrome	417 Sqdn, Charmy Down	not known
17.1.42	Magister	Woodbarn Fm Bishops Sutton	not known	crew safe
20.1.42	Beaufort	Woobine Farm, Watchfield	BAC (?)	crew safe
20.1.42	Lysander	In field NW Trull Church	not known	crew safe
25.1.42	Tiger Moth	Tenett's Field, Newton St Loe	not known	not known
26.1.42	Havoc AW395	Crashed twix Colerne/Charmy Down	1454 Flt, Charmy Down	2K (J. Armanowski; S. Gasak [Polish])
5.2.42	Spitfire X4232	Forced-landed, Timberscombe	53 OTU, Llandow	pilot injured
8.2.42	Hurricane BD941	Naish Farm, Clapton-in-Gordano	87 Sqdn, Charmy Down	1K (Sgt J.R. Keith RCAF)
10.2.42	Tomahawk	In field at Manmoor, Stogursey	239 Sqdn, Weston Zoyland	pilot injured
12.2.42	Anson W2641	Near Full Quart Inn, Hewish	32 MU	4 safe
13.2.42	Hurricane	Dead Woman's Ditch, Crowcombe	not known	1K
17.2.42	Hurricane	Manor Farm, Englishcombe, Bath	not known	pilot safe
20.2.42	Harvard	West Hill Gardens, Radstock	USAAF	not known
20.2.42	Lysander	Near Wincanton Racecourse	Old Sarum	crew safe
20.2.42	Harvard	West Hill Garden, Radstock	not known	pilot safe
22.2.42	Wellington AD638	Forced-landed, Porlock	1443 Ferry Flight	crew safe
23.2.42	Magister T9884	Near Wincanton Racecourse	Old Sarum	2K (P/Os D.G. West & E.W. Bright)
27.2.42	Magister	400 yd S Orchard Portman	41 OTU	2K
8.3.42	Tiger Moth T8192	Forced-landed, Porlock	'D' Flt, 1 AACU	pilot safe (Sgt A.W. Chute)
8.3.42	Lysander V9742	Broomfield, North Petherton	16 Sqdn, Weston Zoyland	crew safe (P/O D.A. Grenville-Herongate)
8.3.42	Spitfire AA857	F-land nr Queen's Head, Willsbrge	2 FPP, Whitchurch	pilot safe (1st/Off E.D. Iredale [Fem/ATA])
8.3.42	Tiger Moth N6932	Crashed on take-off from base	87 Sqdn, Charmy Down	2 injured (Sgts Harding & Alexander)
8.3.42	{ Hurricane BN228	Collided with Havoc on co-op duty	87 Sqdn, Charmy Down	pilot baled out (Sgt E.L. Banks [Can])
	{ Havoc	Landed at base - damaged controls	1454 Flt, Charmy Down	pilot safe (P/O A.L. Barge) Op baled out (Sgt Matthews)
12.3.42	Spitfire AD189	Near Crewkerne	602 Sqdn, Perranporth	pilot injured
13.3.42	Hurricane BN864	Tripp Farm, Clatworthy. Brendon	239 Sqdn, Gatwick	1K (P/O J.J.J.Grevatt RNZAF)
24.3.42	Wellington P9210	Pawlett Hams, 1m W Pawlett Church	RAE, Farnborough (Det)	pilot injured (S/Ldr C.R.J. Hawkins DFC)
25.3.42	Hurricane	Yeovilton	RNAS Yeovilton	pilot safe
25.3.42	Hampden P5329	Sparks Farm, Watchfield	455 Sqdn, Wigsley	4K (P/O A.H. Metcalfe + 3)
26.3.42	Spitfire	Near Churchstanton Church	Polish FW, Churchstanton	pilot badly injured
1.4.42	Hurricane Z3779	Bridgwater Road Farm, Dundry	87 Sqdn, Charmy Down	1K (Sgt R.W. Marshall)
2.4.42	Henley	Crash-landed, Blue Anchor	not known	crew safe
3.4.42	Hurricane	Chew Magna	not known	pilot safe
6.4.42	Hampden P1299	Near RAF Locking Camp	16 OTU, Upper Heyford	4K (Sgts A.B. McKeith, W.B.M. Wilson, H.G. Stalker & F.A. Dann)
8.4.42	{ Spitfire P8366	Golf Links, Minehead	53 OTU, Llandow	pilot injured (Sgt R.H. Orlebar)
	{ Spitfire P8249	Returned to base	53 OTU, Llandow	pilot safe
8.4.42	Battle	1m SE West Buckland	not known	crew safe
8.4.42	Anson N5182	On farm, Upton Noble 5m SW Frome	10 OTU	pilot safe (P/O D.O. Hornsey)
8.4.42	{ Hurricane Z7125	Bindle's Field, West Camel	760 Sqdn, RNAS Yeovilton	1k (Sub-Lt H.W.H. Perry)
	{ Hurricane P3398	Bower's Field, West Camel	759 Sqdn, RNAS Yeovilton	1K (Mid G.D. Cook)
8.4.42	Tiger Moth N6857	Pound Copse, Gaer Hill	Abingdon	1K (P/O J.C. Jones), 1 injured (P/O Johnson)

Date	Type	Location	Unit/Base	Crew state/Names
13.4.42	Proctor	Wayford	not known	pilot safe
15.4.42	Spitfire	Collided with lorry on airfield	Polish FW, Churchstanton	not known
16.4.42	Hurricane	Norton Manor Farm, Limington	RNAS Yeovilton	pilot safe
18.4.42	Hurricane N2631	Kings Field, Stoke Trister	759 Sqdn, RNAS Yeovilton	pilot safe
18.4.42	Hurricane	Pylle	759 Sqdn, RNAS Yeovilton	pilot injured
18.4.42	Spitfire	Crash-landed, Churchstanton	Polish FW, Churchstanton	not known
22.4.42	Hurricane Z7080	Bower Hinton Farm, Martock	759 Sqdn, RNAS Yeovilton	1K (Temp [A] Sub-Lt R. Macmillan)
25.4.42	Hurricane Z2461	Kewstoke, Weston-s-Mare	87 Sqdn, Charmy Down	pilot safe (F/Sgt K.K.B. Gildner RCAF)
25.4.42	Hurricane	Near Somerton	87 Sqdn, Charmy Down	pilot baled out
25.4.42	Hurricane BE566	Near Charmy Down	87 Sqdn, Charmy Down	pilot baled out (P/O R.J. McNair)
26.4.42	Hurricane	Somerton	not known	pilot injured
27.4.42	Spitfire AD553	200m from Axbridge rlwy station	312 Sqn, Fairwood Common	1K (F/Lt R. Rohacek [Czech])
27.4.42	Shark	Horsington	RNAS Yeovilton	crew safe
1.5.42	Hurricane	1m SW Ilchester Church T 95042T†	RNAS Yeovilton	pilot safe
1.5.42	Master T8849	Henstridge O 170403†	9 (P)AFU	crew safe (Sgts V. Hennessy, T. Schofield)
3.5.42	Wellington X3756	Sand Bay, Kewstoke	57 Sqdn, Methwold	crew baled out (Sgt Preston + 5)
7.5.42	Proctor BV553	Crashed on airfield	Churchstanton	crew safe
8.5.42	Oxford	Heathfield	not known	crew safe
8.5.42	Spitfire	Wrecked in hillside crash	Polish FW, Churchstanton	not known
10.5.42	Tiger Moth	Crashed near Radstock	not known	crew safe
4.6.42	Boston BD115	Undershot on landing	1454 Flt, Charmy Down	not known
5.6.42	Hurricane Z7161	Bindle's Field, W Camel, O 17458†	759 Sqdn, RNAS Yeovilton	1K (Lt J.C. Luke)
7.6.42	⎰ Fulmar	Collision on landing	RNAS Yeovilton	1K (Lt D.H.B. Carlisle RNVR)
	⎱ Fulmar		RNAS Yeovilton	1 safe (Sub-Lt A.R. Street)
8.6.42	Hurricane	2m S Glastonbury	not known	pilot safe
24.6.42	DH Moth	Corston	not known	crew safe
24.6.42	Tiger Moth	Ston Easton	not known	crew safe
26.6.42	Magister N3831	Crashed at Bishops Lydeard	Churchstanton	2 injured
29.6.42	Mustang	Pawlett Hams	16 Sqdn, Weston Zoyland	pilot safe
30.6.42	Hurricane	1m SW Bruton Church	not known	pilot safe
30.6.42	Mustang AG551	On foreshore, Stolford	16 Sqdn, Weston Zoyland	1K (P/O G.P.D. Young)
1.7.42	Glider (Hotspur)	1m SE Withycombe Church	296 (Glider) Sqdn, Netheravon	8 injured
1.7.42	Hector K8108	Croydon Hall, Roadwater	Netheravon	crew injured (W/O J.A. Burcher + 1)
3.7.42	Tomahawk	Dinder, Wells	41 OTU, Oatlands Hill	1K (P/O T.M. Horsefall)
5.7.42	Blenheim R3912	Pawlett Hams, Bridgwater	13 OTU, Bicester	3K (Sgts A. Hogg, G.I. McBoyle, J.F. Anderson)
5.7.42	Beaufighter EL235	Crashed on take-off, Weston	No 2 Ferry Pilots School	pilot safe (1st/Off S.E. Mitchell [Fem ATA])
6.7.42	Magister	Orchard Portman	not known	crew safe
12.7.42	⎰ Spitfire P8148	Collision W-s-M, crashed Draycott	52 OTU, Aston Down	pilot baled out
	⎱ Spitfire P8278	Returned to base	52 OTU, Aston Down	pilot safe
13.7.42	Whitley BD534	Crashed on take-off, W Zoyland	296 Sqdn, Netheravon	1K (Sgt L.E. Fairchild) 3 safe
13.7.42	Taylorcraft HL534	Critchell Farm, near Frome	651 OAP Sqdn	crew safe (T/Capt Carmichael)
30.7.42	Hurricane HL779	St Catherine's, Charmy Down	87 Sqdn, Charmy Down	1K (F/Sgt S. Bocking [Canadian])
2.8.42	Oxford BG599	Crashed on aerodrome	Weston Zoyland	crew safe
2.8.42	Mustang AG538	Crashed into Henley L3257 on a/f	16 Sqdn, Weston Zoyland	pilot safe (P/O A.S. Collins RCAF)
4.8.42	Defiant DR865	Crashed into perimeter of 'drome	1 AACU, Weston Zoyland	2K (F/Lt M.W. Hamlyn; Cpl C.H. Odle)
11.8.42	Tiger Moth T7733	Crash-landed on aerodrome	Churchstanton	not known
12.8.42	Whitley G-AGDU	Damaged beyond repair	BOAC, Whitchurch	not known
17.8.42	Spitfire EP640	Crash-landed on aerodrome	Churchstanton	not known
17.8.42	Hurricane	Crash-landed on aerodrome	891 Sqdn, C.Horethorne	pilot safe
23.8.42	Magister	Frome	not known	crew safe
26.8.42	Spitfire AP500	Crash-landed on aerodrome	66 Sqdn, Churchstanton	not known
8.9.42	ME 108	Crashed on landing	Weston Zoyland	pilot safe
12.9.42	Audax	Crashed on aerodrome	Weston Zoyland	crew safe
16.9.42	Henley L3406	Crashed near aerodrome	1 AACU, Weston Zoyland	not known
17.9.42	Magister	Butleigh	not known	2K
18.9.42	Hurricane AG259	Poundsford Park, Pitminster	RAE	pilot safe (F/Lt J.T.L. Shore)
18.9.42	Master III	Crashed near Street	16 Sqdn, Weston Zoyland	2K (Sgt Adcock; Sgt Bate RE)
19.9.42	⎰ Mustang AG438	Collided, ION Yeovil	41 OTU	not known
19.9.42	⎱ Fulmar N4126		RNAS Yeovilton	not known
22.9.42	Oxford W6610	Crashed into tree Lulsgate Bottom	3 (P)AFU, Lulsgate	2K (P/O N.L. Casely, Sgt J.N. Harvey RAAF)
22.9.42	Oxford	Burrington	3 (P)AFU, Lulsgate	2K
22.9.42	Mustang	Crashed when overshot perimeter	16 Sqdn, Weston Zoyland	pilot safe
4.10.42	Wellington R1400	Cucklington, nr Wincanton	22 OTU	crew safe (P/O R.G. Tithe + 4)
6.10.42	Fulmar	2m NE Montacute Station	not known	1K
11.10.42	Tiger Moth	Milborne Port	not known	crew safe

Date	Type	Location	Unit/Base	Crew state/Names
12.10.42	{ Mustang AM197 { Dominie X7140	Struck Dominie on take-off	16 Sqdn, Weston Zoyland 614 Sqdn	pilot safe (P/O D.B. Williams) pilot safe (S/Ldr A.G. Parnall)
15.10.42	{ Fulmar N4079	Collided over Lusgate, crashed	761 Sqdn, Yeovilton)	1K (Sub-Lt Shorte)
15.10.42	{ Fulmar N4008	top of Cheddar Gorge	761 Sqdn, Yeovilton)	Pilot safe (Sub-Lt Starkey)
15.10.42	Shark	Near Cannington	not known	crew safe
19.10.42	Proctor	Near Templecombe	not known	2 safe
23.10.42	Tiger Moth T8177	Crashed, Watchet landing ground	'P' Flt, AACU, W Zoyland	crew safe (F/Lt W. Lock + 1)
28.10.42	Fulmar	Chilton Cantelo	RNAS Yeovilton	1K
29.10.42	Wellington BK310	Holford, flew into hill rtng/ops	150Sqdn, Kirmington	1K, 4 injured
29.10.42	B-24 Liberator	Porlock Marshes	USAAF	11K (L.C.Reiss, W. Duffleman, W.J. Williams, T.W. Lewis, J. Dimuzo, E.R. Purdy, J.D. Odell, C.G. Sorrel, S.D. Wardney, J.G. Simpson + 1)
30.10.42	{ Master { Spitfire	Pines Garage, Broomfield 211326† Broomfield	53 OTU, Llandow not known	2K (Sgts I.W. Storey & H. Josephs) 1K (P/O B.W. Andrews)
1.11.42	Hurricane '3151'	In fld, Green Ditch Lane, Clapton	'Delivery' to Colerne	pilot safe (from 2 Sqdn)
8.11.42	Hurricane	West Camel	RNAS Yeovilton	pilot injured
13.11.42	Henley L3319	crashed Weston Zoyland	1601 Flt, Weston Zoyland	not known
14.11.42	Hurricane Z5153	Crashed 2m W Charmy Down	245 Sqdn, Charmy Down	1K (F/O D.A. Dawson RCAF)
16.11.42	Halifax DT588	Mells, nr Frome	158 Sqdn, Rufforth	crew safe (P/O G. Herbert + 6)
16.11.42	Hurricane	Crashed at Langridge, 3½m N Bath	not known	not known
23.11.42	Mustang	Crash-landed near Bridgwater	16 Sqdn, Weston Zoyland	pilot safe (P/O B.N. Cooke)
24.11.42	Mustang	Caught fire on aerodrome	16 Sqdn, Weston Zoyland	pilot safe
26.11.42	Martinet HN960	Forced-landed, Sedgemoor	1601 Flt, Weston Zoyland	pilot injured (P/O F.S. Salter)
26.11.42	Martlet	Babcary	762 Sqdn, RNAS Yeovilton	1 injured
26.11.42	Martlet	Hambury Farm, Ilchester	762 Sqdn, RNAS Yeovilton	1K (Sub-Lt W. O'Bryen RNVR)
27.11.42	Whitley EB294	Crashed near Ilchester	299 Sqdn, Keevil	crew safe (P/O J.V. Snell + 4)
27.11.42	Master	Sutton Mallet	not known	1 injured
27.11.42	Master	Crashed at Chew Magna	not known	not known
2.12.42	Tiger Moth BB694	F-landed, Hobbs Wall, Farmborough	not known	pilot safe (2nd Battn, Glider Pilot Regt)
5.12.42	{ Hurricane Z4702 { Hurricane AE977	Mid-air collision, Godney 970630† Godney 906615†	759 Sqdn, RNAS Yeovilton 759 Sqdn, RNAS Yeovilton	pilot safe (Mid [A] J.S. Byrd RNVR) pilot safe (Lt D.T. Keene RNVR)
6.12.42	Proctor BV548	1½m SW Charlton Horethorne Church	TAG School, Worthy Down	pilot slightly injured
17.12.42	Oxford L9695	Durbin's Farm, Nailsea 95906†	286 Sqdn, Locking	3K (pilot-Sgt Hammond + 2)
21.12.42	Blenheim L8438	Crash-landed, Combe Down, Bath	307 Sqdn, Exeter	not known
28.12.42	Martlet 'No 563'	F-landed, 1½m NW Buckam Weston	748 Sqdn, RNAS Yeovilton	pilot safe
30.12.42	Wellington HX745	Crastley Farm, Beckington	1443 (F) Flight, Harwell	1K, 2 seriously injured
4.1.43	Wellington W5613	Orchardleigh, Frome	21 OTU	2K, 1 injured, 2 safe
11.1.43	Defiant AA443	Crashed near Bleadon Church	286 Sqdn, Weston Zoyland	crew safe (F/Lt J.P. Joyce + 1)
23.1.43	* B-17 F.Fortress	Crash-landed, Lulsgate	303BG, Molesworth	1K (Sgt Stanner) 4 inj (2nd Lts C.L. Herman, S.B. Sinopoli; Sgts M. Levin, E.T. Yannie, C.E. Craft), 5 safe (1st Lt J.A. Castle; 2nd Lt K.M. Fitzsimmons; Sgts Loll, J.S. Klasnick, M. Semonick)
23.1.43	Wellington	Between Yeovilton & Limington	15 OTU, Hampstead Norris	4K (P/O G.W. Lean [Nav] +3) 1 injured
26.1.43	{ Spitfire P8208 { Spitfire P8207	In Bristol Channel off Portishead Returned to base (?)	52 OTU, Aston Down 52 OTU, Aston Down	pilot safe pilot safe
8.2.43	Oxford	Henstridge	not known	crew safe
10.2.43	Hurricane	East Pennard	not known	pilot injured
12.2.43	Proctor HM294	South Petherton No 2	Radio Sch, Yatesbury	crew safe (Sgt C. Coulson + 1)
13.2.43	Oxford	River Axe, Brean	not known	1K, 1 injured (Polish pilot rescued)
13.2.43	{ Halifax W1182 { Wellington BL460	Langport, mid-air collision	158 Sqdn, Rufforth 166 Sqdn, Kirmington	7K (Sgts E.W. King, K.W. Scott, C.W. Steadman + 4) Pilot crash-landed a/c (F/Sgt G. Ashplant), rest of crew baled out
17.2.43	Leopard Moth	Leighton, Wanstrow	not known	crew safe
21.2.43	Hurricane	Charlton Mackerell	not known	pilot injured
3.3.43	Piper Cub	West Cranmore	US a/c	crew safe
8.3.43	Wellington X3219	Barton St David	21 OTU	5K
10.3.43	Magister	Fitzhead	not known	crew safe
12.3.43	Magister	Stoke St Mary	not known	crew safe
29.3.43	Halifax HR688	Maundown Hill, Wiveliscombe	502 Sqdn, St Eval	not known (Capt of aircraft reported safe)
31.3.43	Hurricane	Weston Bampfylde	not known	pilot injured
2.4.43	Spitfire	Churchstanton	313 Sqdn, Churchstanton	pilot injured
4.4.43	Whitley EB285	1m E Highbridge	42 OTU	2 injured, rest safe
5.4.43	Hurricane	South Berrow	not known	pilot injured

Date	Type	Location	Unit/Base	Crew state/Names
5.4.43	{ Spitfire EP660 { Spitfire AR518	Collided whilst taxiing	313 Sqdn, Churchstanton 313 Sqdn, Churchstanton	pilot safe pilot safe
6.4.43	Spitfire	Nollis Hill, near Taunton	not known	not known
8.4.43	Spitfire P9541	Abandoned over Haycombe, Bath	52 OTU, Aston Down	pilot safe (Sgt G. Ashworth)
10.4.43	Martinet	Crashed on take-off	1492 Flt, Weston Zoyland	not known
12.4.43	Mosquito DD727	Oakhill, nr Bath	264 Sqdn, Colerne (?)	2K
13.4.43	Tiger Moth DE672	Kewstoke, Weston-s-Mare	10 GP Communications Flt	crew safe (F/Lt V.A. Carter + 1)
14.4.43	Fulmar	Milborne Port	RNAS Yeovilton	crew safe
7.5.43	Proctor	South Marksbury	not known	1 injured
8.5.43	Mustang AG519	Stockland Bristol	4 Sqdn, Odiham	pilot safe (F/Lt G.L. Huntley)
13.5.43	Fulmar	Queen Camel	RNAS Yeovilton	2K
15.5.43	Tiger Moth	Coleford	not known	crew safe
15.5.43	Hurricane V6760	Downside Abbey cricket field	759 Sqdn, RNAS Yeovilton	1K+9K (Sub-Lt A.C.H. McCraken & 9 schoolboys)
21.5.43	Hurricane	Muchelney	759 Sqdn, RNAS Yeovilton	pilot injured
27.5.43	Hurricane	Oakhill, Shepton Mallet	759 Sqdn, RNAS Yeovilton	1K
27.5.43	Piper Cub	Freshford	US a/c	1 injured
30.5.43	Mustang AM108	Crashed on landing at base	170 Sqdn, Weston Zoyland	1K
4.6.43	Lysander P1691	Blown over in gale	8 AACU, Weston Zoyland	not involved
4.6.43	Spitfire AR512	Into train near Bradford-on-Tone	313 Sqdn, Churchstanton	1K (F/O J. Čermák [Czech])
9.6.43	Beaufighter	Locking Airfield (Weston)	BAC (?)	crew safe
10.6.43	Hurricane	Marston Magna	RNAS Yeovilton	pilot safe
11.6.43	Halifax EB132	Ashley Coombe, Porlock Weir	295 Sqdn, Holmsley South	4K, 2 injured
15.6.43	Oxford	Butcombe	not known	1K
27.6.43	Hurricane	Burtle	not known	pilot injured
27.6.43	Spitfire	Ilton	not known	1K
1.7.43	Hurricane	Yeovilton	RNAS Yeovilton	pilot safe
5.7.43	Hurricane	Bruton	RNAS Yeovilton	pilot safe
13.7.43	Martinet HP182	Forced-landed, Watchet (salvaged)	1600 Flt, Weston Zoyland	2 injured (Sgt G.R. Hunt + 1)
22.7.43	Anson	Mark	not known	crew safe
25.7.43	Spitfire Vb BL291	Crashed at Yatton	504 Sqdn, Ibsley	pilot safe (P/O P.J. Doyle RNZAF)
27.7.73	{ Spitfire EP726 { Spitfire BL928	Jumped chocks on Charmy Down and collided - destroying 2nd a/c	52 OTU, Aston Down 52 OTU, Aston Down	not involved not involved
28.7.43	Wellington	In sea, Brean Sands	not known	not known
2.8.43	Oxford LX218	Quarry Farm, Redhill	not known	1K (Sgt R.N.P. Brown RAAF)
2.8.43	{ Hurricane { Hurricane	Mid-air collision - Bolders Hill Clanville, nr Castle Cary	RNAS Yeovilton RNAS Yeovilton	1K pilot injured
2.8.43	Magister L6911	Higher Holbrook Farm, Wincanton	not known	2 safe
5.8.43	Oxford	Backwell, Brockley	3 (P)AFU, Lulsgate	2K
10.8.43	Hurricane	Bristol Channel, 7m N Lilstock	RNAS Yeovilton	pilot missing
16.8.43	Spitfire	Winsford Hill	not known	pilot safe
20.8.43	Wellington MP652	Flew into hillside, Broomfield	407 Sqdn, Chivenor	5K, 1 injured
20.8.43	Boston	Dinder, Wells	US a/c	4K
21.8.43	Wellington LA986	Toms Hill, Exford	3 (C)OTU	6 injured
23.8.43	Oxford AB771	Crashed on take-off, Lulsgate	3 (P)AFU, Lulsgate	2K
25.8.43	Tiger Moth T6526	Frome	22 EFTS	2 injured (F/Sgt Sawyer + 1)
6.9.43	Martinet	Brent Knoll	Weston Zoyland	1 injured, 1 safe
7.9.43	Wellington	Near Chard	not known	3K, 2 injured
13.9.43	Shark	Heathfield	not known	2 injured
16.9.43	Martinet	Brean Down	Weston Zoyland	1 injured, 1 safe
16.9.43	B-17 F.Fortress	Long Holcombe, Simonsbath	388BG, Knettishall	2K, 9 injured
23.9.43	'Secret'	Barwick, Exmoor	not known	1 safe
25.9.43	Spitfire MH674	Ilton	165 Sqdn, Churchstanton	pilot safe (F/O K.W. Evans)
30.9.43	Hurricane	Westover Farm, Drayton	not known	Polish pilot injured
7.10.43	Beaufighter V8470	Dunkerton, nr Bath	301 Ferry Training School	1K
8.10.43	Martinet HN952	Crashed in sea off Watchet	1492 Flt, Weston Zoyland	2K (F/O D.M. Joss [?]; Sgt J. Hall)
10.10.43	'Secret'	Ilchester	not known	2 injured
11.10.43	Henley L3361	Crashed Weston Zoyland	1 AACU, Weston Zoyland	not known
12.10.43	L-4 Cub	Ringwell, Norton St Phillip	USAAF	pilot safe
24.10.43	Spitfire	Churchstanton	RAF Churchstanton	pilot injured
25.10.43	Henley L3442	Crashed on landing	1601 Flt, Weston Zoyland	not known
26.10.43	Henley L3266	Crashed on landing	1601 Flt, Weston Zoyland	not known
28.10.43	Master	Crashed at Wellow, nr Bath	not known	1 injured, 1 safe
28.10.43	Beaufighter MM849	Corthorne Farm, Exford	125 Sqdn, Fairwood Common	2 injured
5.11.43	Spitfire EE615	Pitney	610 Sqdn, Churchstanton	pilot safe (Lt A.A. Nido [American])
11.11.43	Beaufighter ND206	West Pennard, Glastonbury	301 Ferry Training School	crew safe

Date	Type	Location	Unit/Base	Crew state/Names
12.11.43	Glider (target)	Near airfield perimeter	Weston Zoyland (Det)	crew safe (P/O Breheny; AC Sigall)
15.11.43	Hurricane	Thurloxton	not known	1K
15.11.43	Glider (target)	Crashed into house near 'drome	Weston Zoyland (Det)	crew safe (W/Cmdr Blake; AC Radford)
25.11.43	Mosquito	Almarny Farm, Muchelney	not known	crew safe
25.11.43	Martlet	Charlton Horethorne	RNAS Sigwells	1K
30.11.43	Tiger Moth T6463	Churchstanton	Stn Flt, Churchstanton	pilot safe (W/O W.S. Maskery)
2.12.43	Martinet	Mendip View Fm, Kingston Seymour	Weston Zoyland	2K
5.12.43	Seafire	Shipham	not known	pilot safe
13.12.43	Martinet EM411	Crashed at Woolavington	587 Sqdn, Weston Zoyland	2K (Sgt R. Wellsby + 1)
15.12.43	Martinet	Porlock	587 Sqdn, Weston Zoyland	crew safe
16.12.43	Spitfire BS491	Chelvey Farm, Backwell	541 Sqdn, Benson	1K (P/O R. Johnson)
19.12.43	Martlet	Cloford	not known	1K
20.12.43	Martinet	Wedmore	Weston Zoyland	crew safe
24.12.43	Hurricane	Draycott	not known	1K
31.12.43	* B-17 F.Fortress	Burnham-on-Sea, in mud	351BG, Polebrook	11 safe
1.1.44	Tiger Moth	West Doulting, Shepton Mallet	not known	crew safe
14.1.44	Oxford	Crashed at West Harptree	not known	1K (F/Sgt J.J. Cleary RAAF)
15.1.44	Beaufighter	Crashed at Bleadon	not known	crew safe
18.1.44	Piper Cub	Bruton	US a/c	crew safe
20.1.44	{ Spitfire MH796 { Spitfire MH822	Landing accident on airfield	165 Sqdn, Culmhead 165 Sqdn, Culmhead	pilot injured 1K (F/O E.H. Francis)
21.1.44	* Wellington LN667	Crashed at Shapwick	30 ADU	4K (F/O R.D. Fearns; F/Sgt R.J. Letcher + 2)
27.1.44	Stirling EH933	Bridgetown, Exmoor	1660 CU, RAF Swinderby	8K (Sgt R.A. Partridge +7)
31.1.44	Martinet EM412	Buncombe Wood	587 Sqdn, Weston Zoyland	2K (Sgt J.W. Barcikowski + 1)
4.2.44	Spitfire	Crashed on landing	616 Sqdn, Culmhead	1K
5.2.44	Piper Cub	Dunster	US a/c	2 injured
9.2.44	Magister T9872	Bratton Seymour	not known	2 inj (W/Os E.F. Crosswell, W.S. Maskery)
14.2.44	Piper Cub	Dulverton	US a/c	crew safe
15.2.44	Oxford LW776	Crashed 1m W Whitchurch	3 FIS, Lulsgate	2K (F/Lt F.J. Garvey DFC; F/O L.W.R. Rogers)
19.2.44	Mosquito	Ston Easton	not known	2K
22.2.44	Welkin	Bunford Bridge (GWR)	Westland Aircraft	pilot safe (H.J. Penrose?)
14.3.44	Liberator	Hazel Manor Farm, Compton Martin	US Navy, Dunkeswell (?)	5K, 5 injured
20.3.44	Martlet	Till Bridge, Ilchester	RNAS Yeovilton	1K
20.3.44	B-17 F.Fortress	Dulverton	not known	1K 9 safe
23.3.44	Oxford HN203	Crashed into ditch, Whitchurch	3 FIS, Lulsgate	crew safe
24.3.44	Oxford	Forced-landed, Blue Anchor	not known	crew safe
27.3.44	DH 82	Crashed at Mells	not known	crew safe
29.3.44	Piper Cub	Crashed at Tintinhull	US a/c	crew safe
4.4.44	Oxford V3511	U/C collapsed due to pilot error	3 FIS, Lulsgate	crew safe
8.4.44	Piper Cub	South Brewham	US a/c	crew safe
7.5.44	Tiger Moth	Marksbury	not known	crew safe
8.5.44	Master EM355	F-landed ½m W Bleadon/Uphill Stn	3 FIS, Lulsgate	2 safe
11.5.44	Martinet	West Quantoxhead	587 Sqdn, Weston Zoyland	1K
25.5.44	US aircraft	Crashed at Bathampton	USAAF	not known
30.5.44	Oxford V3862	Hit hedge landing in bad weather	3 FIS, Lulsgate	2 safe (F/O A.G. Mayfield, P/O D.T. Cook)
3.6.44	Spitfire	Crashed soon after take-off	126 Sqdn, Culmhead	pilot safe (F/Lt Owen)
6.6.44	Oxford L4616	Waggon & Horses Inn ½m N Lulsgate	3 FIS, Lulsgate	2K (F/Lt P.M. Cadman; F/O H.H.V. Roots)
19.6.44	* Spitfire	C-landed on return from patrol	126 Sqdn, Culmhead	pilot safe (F/Sgt Hinton)
19.6.44	Glider (unident)	Stolford	believed Weston Zoyland	not known
25.6.44	B-17 F.Fortress	Higher Ilbere, Kingston	457BG, Glatton	crew baled out
25.6.44	* B-17 F.Fortress	Snag Farm Yard, Wincanton	91BG, Bassingbourn	9K
8.7.44	Mosquito MM129	Weston-super-Mare	692 Sqdn, Graveley	not known
10.7.44	Mosquito HK500	Pen Mill, Pen Selwood	410 Sqdn, Colerne	2 safe
10.7.44	UC 64A Norseman	Hillcombe Farm, South Brewham	USAAF	3K
10.7.44	{ Master W9067 { L-5 Sentinel	Collided on approach to land at Whitchurch Both a/c destroyed	3 FIS, Lulsgate USAAF	crew injured crew injured
17.7.44	Glider (unident)	Forced-landed near Wedmore	believed Weston Zoyland	occupants safe
22.7.44	Oxford	Crashed at Hutton	not known	not known
31.7.44	Oxford BG245	Hit Drem lighting pole ½m E drome	3 FIS, Lulsgate	2 crew injured
18.8.44	Widcat	Ashington	RNAS Yeovilton	not known
21.8.44	Master AZ605	In sea Langford Grounds, Clevedon	3 FIS, Lulsgate	2 crew missing (RNVR & RNZVR)
26.8.44	Wellington LN293	Uplands Lane, Keynsham	12 OTU, Chipping Warden	6K (W/O J.C. Harvey; Sgts Patterson, Martin, Hankin, Evans & Blewitt)

Date	Type	Location	Unit/Base	Crew state/Names
17.9.44	Horsa RJ113	Farrington Gurney	'D'Sqdn, Glider Pilot Rgt	23K (Sgt R.A. Fraser; L/Sgt R.H. Allen + 21)
11.10.44	Tiger Moth BB863	Blown over whilst picketed	587 Sqdn, Weston Zoyland	not involved
14.11.44	Oxford P8899	Crashed on landing, Lulsgate	3 FIS, Lulsgate	status n/a (F/Os J.A. Newbury, J.A. Kennedy)
23.11.44	Halifax LL126	Parsonage Farm, Long Ashton	1662 HCU, Blyton	7K (F/O J. Kisieliwicz; P/O J.T. Malowski F/Sgt W. Rucinski; Sgts J.S. Radonski, S. Jurka, F Kruszczak, S Jaquszcak)
7.3.45	Oxford	Crashed at North Stoke	3 FIS, Lulsgate	not known
12.4.45	Mosquito NS586	In field adj W Zoyland airfield	A&AEE, Boscombe Down	2K (F/Lt J.R. Smith, STO [civ] G. Douglas)
26.4.45	Oxford BM777	Caught fire on approach at Weston	1335 CU, Colerne	crew safe
3.7.45	Lancaster SW278	In sea, 5m NW Kewstoke Church	166 Sqdn, Kirmington	7K (F/O Doyle, P/O Barlow; Sgts Butler, Edge, Sullivan, Gitson; F/Sgt A.R. Kirschener)
5.7.45	Beaufighter	Crashed at Queen Charlton	not known	pilot (Robert Paynes) injured
7.7.45	Corsair	Steart Island	not known	not known
3.9.45	Beaufighter RD558	Crashed at Withypool	151 RU(A)	2K (F/O A. Besschkops + 1)
10.9.45	Halifax RG380	Crowcombe Park	517 Sqdn, Brawdy	9K (F/Os Hobden, McMillan; P/O K.G. Proverbs; P/O Bee; F/Sgts Everett, Vinton, Cartwright; Sgts Groves, Gordon)
22.11.45	Liberator KH126	White's Farm, Broadway Pound	53 Sqdn, Merryfield	27K (F/Lt L. Mielecki; F/O G.J. Myers; F/O S. Kleybor; F/O A. Wize; F/Sgt J. Brzezinski + 22 pass)

Other aircraft were lost or damaged operating outside Somerset whilst based at airfields in the county; the following are examples:

Date	Type	Location	Unit/Base	Crew state/Names
9.6.41	Lysander	Crashed on take-off, Roborough	16 Sqdn, Weston Zoyland	pilot died of injuries (W/Cmdr R.C. Hancock)
11.6.41	* Lysander	Shot down by Me 109s, Teignmouth	16 Sqdn, Weston Zoyland	2K (S/Ldr Walker; Cpl Perry)
1.10.41	Hurricane	Crashed near Wolverhampton	316 Sqdn, Churchstanton	not known
28.10.41	Whirlwind	Wheels-up landing at Colerne	137 Sqdn, Charmy Down	pilot safe (Sgt Brennan)
30.10.41	* Whirlwind P7091	In sea following attack nr Brest	137 Sqdn, Charmy Down	pilot died of injuries (F/O Clark)
24.2.41	Hurricane	Hit HT wires on Army co-op excrse	87 Sqdn, Charmy Down	1K (F/Lt Roscoe)
28.4.42	Spitfire	Crash-landed at Exeter	Polish FW, Churchstanton	not known
1.5.42	Magister L8201	Forced-landed nr Cullompton	Stn Flt, Churchstanton	not known
28.6.42	Tiger Moth	Crashed nr E Carlton, Northants	87 Sqdn, Charmy Down	2K (P/O Sainsbury; Sgt Turnbull)
18.10.42	Mustang	Crashed near Warmwell	16 Sqdn, Weston Zoyland	pilot killed
18.11.42	* Spitfire	In sea after attk on Lanion	313 Sqdn, Churchstanton	1K (Sgt J. Hloužek [Czech])
15.1.43	{ *Spitfire	Collided 15km NW Cap de la Hague	313 Sqdn, Churchstanton	1K (F/Sgt J. Bláha [Czech])
	{ * Spitfire VB546		313 Sqdn, Churchstanton	1K (F/O B. Krátkoruký [Czech])
27.2.43	* Spitfire	In dog-fight with FW 190s, Brest	313 Sqdn, Churchstanton	1K (F/Lt M. Štušák [Czech])
8.3.43	* Spitfire	Shot down by FW 190 nr St Brieux	313 Sqdn, Churchstanton	1K (F/Lt B. Štefan [Czech])
14.5.43	* Spitfire EP539	Attacking 'E'Boats, St Peter Port	312 Sqdn, Churchstanton	1K (F/O J. Novák [Czech])
24.6.43	Martinet HN908	Crashed 1 mile S Greenham Common	1492 Flt, Weston Zoyland	not known
9.5.44	* Seafire	Hit by flak, f/landed nr Vannes	894 Sqdn (FAA), Culmhead	pilot safe (Lt Meakin)
10.5.44	* Seafire	Ditched in sea on *Instep* patrol	894 Sqdn (FAA), Culmhead	pilot rescued safe (Lt Van Wijk)
12.5.44	* Seafire	Lost in attack on St Malo harbour	887 Sqdn, Culmhead	pilot missing (Lt King)
1.6.44	* Spitfire	Hit by flak attacking train	131 Sqdn, Culmhead	pilot missing (W/O Atkinson)
7.6.44	* Spitfire	On *Rhubarb* 273, crashed into sea	126 Sqdn, Culmhead	pilot missing (Sgt Webster)
10.6.44	* Spitfire	On *Rhubarb* 275, ditched in sea	616 Sqdn, Culmhead	pilot rescued slightly injured (F/Lt Graves DFC)
12.6.44	* Spitfire	Shot down attacking Laval airfield	616 Sqdn, Culmhead	1K (F/Lt Harrison)
12.6.44	* Spitfire	In sea returning from *Rhubarb*	616 Sqdn, Culmhead	pilot rescued (F/Lt Cleland)
19.6.44	* Spitfire	Crashed in sea off St Malo	616 Sqdn, Culmhead	pilot missing (W/O Hart [Australian])
21.6.44	* Spitfire	Crash-landed at Bolt Head	131 Sqdn, Culmhead	pilot injured
27.6.44	* Spitfire	Forced-landed, Cardonville (Fr)	131 Sqdn, Culmhead	pilot safe (F/O Roberts)
11.7.44	* Spitfire	Hit by flak - returned to base	616 Sqdn, Culmhead	pilot injured (F/O Cooper)
25.8.44	Spitfire	Crashed twix Manston & Culmhead	131 Sqdn, Culmhead	1K (F/Lt Bearman)
16.4.45	Vengeance	Crashed at Burton-on-Trent	587 Sqdn, Weston Zoyland	pilot injured + 5K (civilians)

Undated or unconfirmed aircraft crashes, including 'eyewitness' accounts:

1944	Halifax	Crashed on landing at Whitchurch	not known	one injured, rest of crew safe

The following reports of aircraft crashes and forced-landings are taken from extracts of the Somerset County Council ARP Area Reports; scant details only are given and do not identify the type, or as in most cases, the fate of the crew. However, they can be taken as confirmed incidents:

Date	Type: Hostile/Friendly	Location	Crew state
27.11.40	Unidentified friendly	Priston Road, Marksbury, nr Bath	pilot safe
3.12.40	Unidentified friendly	Redhill, nr Bristol	not known
13.1.41	Unidentified friendly	Nr X Rds S-Sub-Hamdon/Martock/Ilminster	pilot slightly hurt
3.3.41	Unidentified friendly	Berrow	not known
24.3.41	Unidentified friendly	Forced-landed ½m SW Somerton	not known
26.3.41	Unidentified friendly	½m N Creech Paper Mills	crew safe
3.10.41	Unidentified friendly	½m SE Paulton Church	not known
29.10.41	Unidentified friendly	In sea, 3-4m NW Porlock Weir	not known
23.11.41	Unidentified friendly	Berrow sands	not known
16.1.42	Unidentified friendly	Chew Magna	1 safe
30.4.42	Unidentified friendly	1m SE Henstridge (Dorset?)	not known
29.6.42	{ Unidentified friendly	Corfe, nr Taunton – possible collison	not known
	{ Unidentified friendly	Cotlake, nr Taunton	not known
16.10.42	Unidentified friendly	Crewkerne	not known
23.4.43	Unidentified friendly	'Training plane' S of Coxley Church	not known
20.8.43	Unidentified friendly	'Trainer' South Brewham	crew safe
2.5.44	Unidentified friendly	US aircraft, Kittisford, Wellington	1 injured
15.8.44	Unidentified friendly	Porlock (Plane wrecked)	crew safe

Not all of the local ARP records have survived and therefore it has been impossible to produce a definitive list of losses. The County Record Office, Taunton, holds all the remaining files, but it is quite possible that the Royal Observer Corps might have wartime documents that would verify, or otherwise, these details. In addition, the ARP register of incidents log books from July 1940 - April 1943 have entered at least one hundred other unsubstantiated reports of crashed aircraft that cannot be connected with either of the above lists, therefore they are unlikely to be an accurate total of the allied losses suffered in Somerset, but only as a guide to illustrate the many hazards of wartime flying and flying training.

NOTES:

1 Most of the above losses or accidents were due to other reasons than through combat, but those known to be damaged or lost either on operations or due to enemy action are marked thus: *
2 Some aircraft that forced-landed incurring only slight damage were dismantled at the crash site and removed to be repaired to fly again.
3 Major losses in the county are given for 1939 before the outbreak of war and beyond VE/VJ Day and up to the end of 1945.
4 With a great deal of research it would be possible to establish the various Squadrons with which all above aircraft were on strength at the time of the incidents, but where there is little or no local evidence as to their origin, 'not known' has been entered. Further information regarding these losses can be obtained from the Air Historical Branch, Ministry of Defence.
5 Grid references marked thus † are for the Military Grid system based on 500, 100, 10 and 1km squares, which, according to the scale, were overprinted on maps. It is likely that the ARP services would have used 1 inch to 1 mile maps with 1km grids printed thereon.
6 Aircraft collisions, or possible incidents of this nature, are noted by bracketing as appropriate.
7 Culmhead airfield was renamed as such on December 22 1943, having previously been called Churchstanton.

APPENDIX 2

LUFTWAFFE LOSSES IN SOMERSET: 1939-45

Time/Date	Type	Ident	Unit	Location	Cause	Des	Name	State
1750/14.8.40	HEINKEL He 111P	1G+NT	9/KG27	Charterhouse, Cheddar	F (92Sqdn)	(F)	Oltn Ernst Ohlenschlager	(P)
						(B)	Uffz Kurt Sulzbach	(P)
						(Bf)	Uffz A. Blumenthal	(P)
						(Bm)	Fw Nickolaus Jug	(P)
						(Bs)	Gfr Kurt Kupsch	(P)
1800/14.8.40	HEINKEL He 111P	1G+?T	9/KG27	Bridgwater Bay	F (92Sqdn)	(F)	Hptmn J. Riedel	(M)
						(B)	Uffz A. Witt	(M)
						(Bf)	Uffz Hans Dolata	(K) *WS

Time/Date	Type	Ident	Unit	Location	Cause	Des	Name	State
						(Bm)	Fw E. Haumann	(M)
						(Bs)	Gfr E. Wolf	(M)
1805/14.8.40	HEINKEL He 111P	1G+OT	9/KG27	Puriton, Bridgwater	F (92Sqdn)	(F)	Ltn Otto Uhland	(P)
						(B)	Uffz Joseph Krenn	(P)
						(Bf)	Uffz Edo Flick	(P)
						(Bm)	Ogfr Hans Ramstetter	(P)
						(Bs)	Gfr Gerhardt Rother	(P)
1150/25.9.40	HEINKEL He 111P	G1+DN	5/KG55	Failand, Portbury	AA(236Bty)	(F)	Oltn Gottfried Weigel	(P)
						(B)	Ofw Alfred Narres	(P)
						(Bf)	Ofw Georg Engel	(P)
						(Bm)	Uffz Karl Gerdsmeier	(P)
						(Bs)	Gfr Karl Geib	(P)
1200/25.9.40	HEINKEL He 111P	G1+EP	6/KG55	Woolverton, Frome	F(152Sqdn)	(F)	Hptmn Helmut Brandt	(P)
						(B)	Ofw Gunter Wittkamp	(K)
						(Bf)	Ofw Rudolf Kirchoff	(K)
						(Bm)	Uffz Hans-Fritz Mertz	(K)
						(Bs)	Gfr Rudolf Beck	(K)
0945/27.9.40	JUNKERS Ju 88A-5F	4U+RL	3/(F)123	Porlock Beach	F (152Sqdn)	(F)	Fw Helmut Ackenhausen	(P)
						(B)	Obltn Willi Rude	(P)
						(Bf)	Ofw Erwin Riehle	(P)
						(Bm)	Ogfr Wilhelm Reuhl	(K) *PL
1145/27.7.40	MESSERSCHMITT Bf 110C-4	U8+CL	3/ZG26	Haydon, Radstock	F (504Sqdn)	(F)	Ltn Joachim Koepsell	(P)
						(Bf)	Uffz Johann Schmidt	(K)
2330/16.10.40	DORNIER Do 17Z	7T+HK	2/KüFlGr606	Maesbury, S. Mallet	AA	(F)	Fw Heinrich Faupel	(K)
						(B)	Obltn z See Erwin Blanck	(K)
						(Bf)	Ogfr Wilhelm Schnake	(K)
						(Bm)	Fw Gerhard Steppat	(K)
1412/22.2.41	HEINKEL He 111H-5	1G+GM	4/KG27	Mud flats, Portbury	AA (236Bty)	(F)	Ltn Berndt Rusche	(P)
						(B)	Fw Alfred Hanke	(K)
						(Bf)	Fw Georg Jankowiak	(K)
						(Bm)	Uffz Heinrich de Wall	(K)
						(Bs)	Gfr Erich Steinbach	(K)
2245/4.4.41	HEINKEL He 111H-5	1H+ED	StabIII/KG26	Hewish, Weston-s-Mare	NF(604Sqdn)	(F)	Ofw Herbert Rose	(P)
						(B)	Fw Georg Fietzek	(P)
						(Bf)	Ofw Erich Blüher	(K) *WS
						(Bm)	Fw Ernst Groschel	(P)
						(Bs)	Gfr M. van Kaldenkerken	(K) *WS
2250/3.5.41	HEINKEL He 111P-2	1G+IT	9/KG27	Corton Denham, Yeovil	NF(604Sqdn)	(F)	Oltn Hans Zollner	(P)
						(B)	Uffz Erwin Ehlers	(P)
						(Bf)	Fw Florian Piechota	(P)
						(Bm)	Fw Albert Amode	(K)
2330/3.5.41	JUNKERS Ju 88A	M7+AH	1/KGr806	½m N Stoke St.Michael	NF(600Sqdn)	(F)	Ofw Fritz Schäfer	(P)
						(B)	Ltn Gottwald Gerlach	(P)
						(Bf)	Helmut Soland	(P)
						(Bm)	Fw Walter Kramer	(P)
0100/4.5.41	HEINKEL He 111H-5	1H+BH	1/KG26	Crowcombe Heathfield	NF(604Sqdn)	(F)	Ofw Richard Gemar	(K)
						(B)	Fw Hans Kopp	(K)
						(Bf)	Uffz Herbert Muller	(P)
						(Bm)	Uffz Wilhelm Ditz	(K)
2328/7.5.41	HEINKEL He 111P-2	1G+DR	7/KG27	Andersea, Bridgwater	NF(604Sqdn)	(F)	Fw Heinz Laschinski	(P)
						(B)	Fw Heinz Schier	(K) *BW
						(Bf)	Ofw Otto Willrich	(P)
						(Bm)	Fw Fritz Klemm	(K) *BW
2355/7.5.41	HEINKEL He 111P-2	1G+NA	StabsSt/KG27	1m SW Wrington	NF(600Sqdn)	(F)	Ofw Heinrich Ronge	(P)

Time/Date	Type	Ident	Unit	Location	Cause	Des	Name	State
						(B)	Oltn Johannes Maron	(P)
						(Bf)	Fw Heinz Dietrich	(P)
						(Bm)	Uffz Heinrich Eggert	(P)
						(Bs)	Ogfr Helmut Hilger	(P)
0107/5.7.41	HEINKEL He 111H-5	1H+FR	7/KG26	Great Elm Estate, Frome	NF(604Sqdn)	(F)	Ltn Siegfried Baden	(P)
						(B)	Fw Ernst Witt	(P)
						(Bf)	Gfr Ludwig Kugel	(P)
						(Bm)	Ogfr Eduard Köppl	(K)
0610/24.7.41	JUNKERS Ju 88A-4	4D+DL	3/KG30	Landed at Lulsgate	PE	(F)	Uffz Wolfgang Hosie	(P)
						(B)	Fw Paul Zimmermann	(P)
						(Bf)	Ogfr Franz Sander	(P)
						(Bm)	Ogfr Robert Riemann	(P)
2112/28.10.41	JUNKERS Ju 88A-4	4D+MR	7/KG30	Wembdon, Bridgwater	NF(604Sqdn)	(F)	Ltn Helmuth Haakh	(P)
						(B)	Ofw Walter Lehnhoff	(P)
						(Bf)	Gfr Bernhard Unruh	(P)
						(Bm)	Gfr Hubert Mayer	(K)
2215/1.11.41	DORNIER Do 217	not known	not known	In sea, St.Audries Bay	NF	(F)	not known	(K)
						(B)	not known	(K)
						(Bf)	not known	(K)
						(Bm)	not known	(K)
0325/18.5.43	JUNKERS Ju 88A-14	3E+EH	1/KG6	Timberscombe, Minehead	NF(151Sqdn)	(F)	Ltn Horst Hahn	(K)
						(B)	Ogfr Fritz Sagemüller	(K)
						(Bf)	Uffz Albert Wurtz	(P)
						(Bm)	Fw Otto Bök	(P)
0300/18.5.43	DORNIER Do 217E-4	U5+EK	2/KG2	Woodspring Bay, Weston	PE	(F)	Uffz Joachim Tröger	(P)
						(B)	Uffz Wilhelm Schmidt	(K)
						(Bf)	Uffz Werner Grothe	(K) *WS
						(Bm)	Uffz Erich Gratz	(K)
0300/18.5.43	DORNIER Do 217E-4	U5+DL	3/KG2	Woodspring Bay, Weston	PE	(F)	Ltn Emil Holthaus	(M)
						(B)	Uffz Fritz Richter	(K)
						(Bf)	Uffz Heinrich Schumacher	(K)
						(Bm)	Uffz Willi Petzke	(K)
2350/27.3.44	JUNKERS Ju 88A-14	B3+BL	3/KG54	Isle Brewers, Ilminster	NF(456Sqdn)	(F)	Ofw Hans Brautigams	(P)
						(B)	Ogfr Kurt Chalon	(P)
						(Bf)	Uffz Robert Belz	(K)
						(Bm)	Obgfr Alfred Malezki	(P)
2355/27.3.44	JUNKERS Ju 88A-4	B3+UA	Stab/KG54	Tadham Moor, Wedmore	AA	(F)	Ltn Wolgang Fritz	(P)
						(B)	Ogfr Gunter Baermann	(P)
						(Bf)	Uffz Heinrich Schink	(K) *WS
						(Bm)	Ogfr Heinrich Schweizer	(P)
0005/28.3.44	JUNKERS Ju 88A-4	B3+SK	2/KG5	Upper Cheddon, Taunton	NF(219Sqdn)	(F)	Ltn Friedrich Kerkhoff	(K)
						(B)	Uffz Gunter Pfauder	(P)
						(Bf)	Uffz Rudolf Teisman	(P)
						(Bm)	Ogfr Werner Decho	(P)
0010/28.3.44	JUNKERS Ju 188E-1	U5+EN	5/KG2	Coxley, Wells	NF (68Sqdn)	(F)	Ltn Werner Siebert	(P)
						(Kb)	Uffz Klaus Holst	(P)
						(Bf)	Uffz Matthias Josephs	(P)
						(Bs)	Fw Hermann Sagel	(P)
						(Bs)	Gfr Marcel Rozycki	(P)
0230/15.5.44	JUNKERS Ju 188A-2	3E+LK	2/KG6	Inwood, Henstridge	NF(488Sqdn)	(F)	Ltn Gerhard Wentz	(P)
						(Kb)	Uffz Karl Fritz	(P)
						(Bf)	Uffz Hilmar Kqrf	(K) *HY
						(Bs)	Uffz Karl Hoyer	(P)
						(Bs)	Gfr Gerhard Büttner	(K) *HY

Time/Date	Type	Ident	Unit	Location	Cause	Des	Name	State
0230/15.5.44	DORNIER Do 217K	U5+MR	7/KG2	Camel Cross, Yeovilton	NF(488Sqdn)	(F)	Ltn Johannes Domschke	(K)
						(B)	Uffz Emil Chmillewski	(P)
						(Bf)	Uffz Waldemar Jungke	(P)
						(Bs)	Uffz Otto Schott	(P)
							Totals:	43K
								5M
								72P

F = Fighter(s); NF = Nightfighter; AA = Anti-aircraft fire; PE = Pilot error; K = Killed; M = Missing; P = Prisoner of War
* Aircrew who remain interred in the county: BW = Bridgwater; HY = Haycombe, Bath; PL = Porlock; WS = Weston-super-Mare

Several members of German Aircrew that were once buried in the county have since been exhumed and moved to the German Military Cemetery at Cannock Chase, Staffordshire. These include: Ltn Horst Hahn (Timberscombe 18.5.43); Obergfr Fritz Sagemüller (Timberscombe 18.5.43); Ltn Friedrich Kerkhoff (Upper Cheddon 27.3.44); Uffz Robert Belz (Isle Brewers 27.3.44), were buried at Taunton and then moved to Cannock Chase on 12/13 March 1963. Gfr Hubert Mayer (Wembdon 28.10.41) and Ltn Johannes Domschke (Camel Cross 15.5.44) were buried at Bridgwater and similarly moved to Cannock Chase as were the entire crew of the Dornier (Maesbury 16.10.40), who had been buried at Wells. There are also six other crew members of German aircraft that were not shot down in Somerset, but who are buried in Haycombe Cemetery, Bath. All the graves are well tended.

NOTES

1 German Aircrew terms
Flugzeugführer (F): Pilot; *Beobachter* (B): Observer; *Bordfunker* (Bf): Wireless Op/Air Gunner; *Bordmechaniker* (Bm): Flight Mechanic/Air Gunner; *Bordschütze* (Bs): Air Gunner; *Kampfbeobachter* (Kb): Group Observer.

2 Luftwaffe ranks with their approximate RAF equivalents

Officers		**Non-Commissioned Officers (NCOs)**	
Generalfeldmarschall:	Marshal of the Royal Air Force	*Stabsfeldwebel:*	Warrant Officer
Generaloberst:	Air Chief Marshal	*Oberfeldwebel:*	Flight Sergeant
General der Flieger:	Air Marshal	*Feldwebel:*	Sergeant
Generalleutnant:	Air Vice Marshal	*Unteroffizier:*	Corporal
Generalmajor:	Air Commodore		
Oberst:	Group Captain	**Other Ranks (ORs)**	
Oberstleutnant:	Wing Commander		
Major:	Squadron Leader	*Obergefreiter:*	Leading Aircraftsman (LAC)
Hauptmann:	Flight Lieutenant	*Gefreiter:*	Aircraftsman First Class (AC1)
Oberleutnant:	Flying Officer	*Flieger:*	Aircraftsman Second Class (AC2)
Leutnant:	Pilot Officer		

3 Élite Luftwaffe *Geschwader* (Operational Units) that suffered losses over Somerset
KG27: *Boelcke* (WW1 fighter ace); 3/(F)123: *Eiserne Dritte* (Iron Third); ZG26: *Horst Wessel* (Hitler Youth Leader); KG54: *Totenkopf* (Death's Head); KG55: *Greifen* (Griffons); KG26: *Löwen* (Lions); KG2: *Holzhammer* (Woodhammer/Mallet).

4 Notation of German Operational Units
Gruppe(n) = Wing(s); *Staffel(n)* = Squadron(s); *Kampfgeschwader* (KG) = Bomber Group; *Zerstörergeschwader* (ZG) = Long Range Fighter Group; *Jagdgeschwader* (JG) = Fighter Group; *Fernaufklärungs* (F) = Long Range Reconnaissance (squadron); *Küstenfliegergruppe* (KüFlGr) = Maritime wing originally part of the German Navy (*Kriegsmarine*) absorbed by the Luftwaffe as conventional bomber unit:

5 Examples of Luftwaffe Units
II/ZG26 = II Wing, Long Range Fighter Group 26; 9/KG27 = No 9 Squadron of Bomber Group 27; 3/(F)123 = No 3 (Long Range) Squadron of Reconnaissance Group 123; Stab/KG54 = HQ Staff of Bomber Group 2; StabIII/KG26 = HQ Staff of III Wing, Bomber Group 26; 2/JG26 = No 2 Squadron of Fighter Group 26; Erprobungs Gruppe 210 = Experimental Test Wing 210; 2/KüFlGr606 = No 2 Squadron of Maritime Luftwaffe Wing 606; 1/KGr806 = No 1 Squadron of Independent Bomber Wing 806.

NB: Gruppen (normally three in *Geschwader* [Group]) always indicated by Roman numerals; *Staffeln* (numbered 1 to 9) in Arabic numerals

APPENDIX 3

LOCATION OF PILLBOXES AND FIXED DEFENCES IN SOMERSET

NB: These are known locations of the thousand or so pillboxes built between 1940/42

COASTAL DEFENCES:

Grid ref	Location	Grid ref	Location	Grid ref	Location
SS		**ST**		**ST**	
865481	Porlock Weir Harbour	005431	A39, NW Carhampton	292527	Berrow Beach (Church)
865481	Porlock Weir Harbour	005444	Dunster Beach	292532	Berrow Beach
885480	Porlock Bay	005446	Dunster Beach	293523	Berrow Beach (Church)
891484	Porlock Bay	007439	GW Rly, nr Dunster Beach	293524	Berrow Beach
911483	Bossington Hill, Minehead	008436	GW Rly, Ker Moor, Dunster	293539	Berrow Beach (Church)
984464	Warren Point, Minehead	009437	GW Rly, Ker Moor, Dunster	294524	Berrow Beach (Church)
984464	Warren Point, Minehead	008441	Dunster Beach	294525	Berrow Beach
985464	Warren Point, Minehead	009441	Dunster Beach	294533	Berrow Beach
996445	Marsh Street, Dunster	009442	Dunster Beach	295523	Berrow Beach (Church)
996445	Marsh Street, Dunster	014435	Ker Moor, Blue Anchor	296524	Berrow Village
997454	Dunster Beach	022434	Blue Anchor Station	299523	Dunster Village
		071435	Loopholed wall, Watchet	331657	Sand Bay, Kewstoke
ST		074434	Watchet	332648	Sand Bay, Kewstoke
		071454	Lilstock	332653	Sand Bay, Kewstoke
021435	Blue Anchor Station	312587	Uphill Beach	464775	Woodhill, Portishead
004445	Dunster Beach	292526	Berrow Beach(Church)		

INDIVIDUAL POSITIONS: surrounding airfields [not command bunkers], railway/road strongpoints and other military installations which also usually had defensive positions built within perimeter

Grid ref	Location	Grid ref	Location	Grid ref	Location
ST		**ST**		**ST**	
039344	Raleighs Cross	342605	Weston Airfield	373593	Elborough, Locking
197234	Rumwell, Taunton	347595	Weston Airfield, Hutton	375593	Locking
201258	Norton Fitzwarren Camp	347597	Weston Airfield, Hutton	448100	Crewkerne
204256	Norton Fitzwarren Camp	348596	Weston Airfield, Hutton	449101	Crewkerne
205257	Silk Mills, Norton Fitzwarren	351401	Bawdrip S&D/A39	541239	Yeovilton (A303)
216230	Sherford, Taunton	351609	A371, Weston Airfield	542239	Yeovilton (A303)
330401	Bawdrip (pumping station)	352608	A371 Weston Airfield	543240	Yeovilton (A303)
331400	Bawdrip (King's Sedge Drain)	353602	Weston Airfield	548149	A30, Yeovil (SW)
338602	Weston Airfield	355597	Locking	739676	Lansdown Hill, Bath
340604	Weston Airfield	355604	A371, Weston Airfield	798676	GWR/A4, Batheaston
341605	Weston Airfield	355605	A371, Weston Airfield		

TAUNTON STOP-LINE: Chard Junction/River Axe to mouth of River Parrett (Including defences around adjacent towns and vital points, viz: Chard, Ilminster and Cogload Junction)

Grid ref	Location	Grid ref	Location	Grid ref	Location
ST		**ST**		**ST**	
250258	Bathpool Bridge, Bathpool	298233	T&CC, Lillsdon	307289	Cogload Junct, Outwood
270251	Ruishton	298235	T&CC, Lillsdon	307291	Cogload Junct, Outwood
270256	B&TC, Creech St Michael	299232	T&CC, Lillsdon	307368	Bridgwater Station
271250	Ruishton	299232	T&CC, Lillsdon	307385	R Parrett, Bridgwater
271250	Ruishton	300375	R Parrett, Bridgwater	307389	R Parrett, Bridgwater
271252	B&TC, Creech St Michael	300377	R Parrett, Bridgwater	307397	R Parrett, Horsey
271253	B&TC, Creech St Michael	301371	R Parrett, Bridgwater	307475	R Brue, Burnham
271254	B&TC, Creech St Michael	301372	River Parrett, Bridgwater	308224	13 A/TBs, Wrantage
271256	B&TC, Creech St Michael	301373	River Parrett, Bridgwater	308224	Wrantage
272249	T&CC, Ruishton	301373	River Parrett, Bridgwater	308229	Wrantage
272250	T&CC, Ruishton	301408	R Parrett, Dunball	308285	Cogload Junct, Outwood
272250	T&CC, Ruishton	301414	R Parrett, Dunball	308293	Cogload Junct, Outwood
273246	Ruishton	302231	Hammonds Farm, Wrantage	308296	Cogload Junct, Outwood
274255	Creech St Michael	302276	Cogload Junc (x 3)	308354	B&TC, Somerset Bridge
275245	T&CC, Ruishton	302368	R Parrett, Bridgwater	308368	Bridgwater Station
275255	B&TC, Creech St Michael	302374	R Parrett, Bridgwater	308376	Bath Road, Bridgwater

276256	B&TC, Creech St Michael	302378	R Parrett, Bridgwater	308378	Bath Rd, Bridgwater
277253	B&TC, Creech St Michael	302382	R Parrett, Bridgwater	308380	Bristol Rd, Bridgwater
278252	B&TC, Creech St Michael	303229	Hammonds Fm, Wrantage	308384	Bristol Rd, Bridgwater
280243	T&CC, Lower Fm, Thornfalcon	303277	Cogload Junction	308402	R Parrett, Horsey
282243	T&CC, Lower Fm, Thornfalcon	303389	R Parrett, N Bridgwater	309223	T&CC, Wrantage
282258	B&TC, Creech St Michael	303396	R Parrett, N Bridgwater	309223	T&CC, Wrantage
283259	B&TC, Foxhole, Creech	304229	Hammonds Farm, Wrantage	309224	T&CC, Wrantage
283430	Pawlett Hams	304280	Cogload Junction	309224	T&CC, Wrantage
284434	Pawlett Hams	304308	B&TC, North Newton	309279	Cogload Junct, Outwood
285259	B&TC, Foxhole, Creech	304309	B&TC, North Newton	309282	Cogload Junct, Outwood
285429	Gaunt's Farm, Pawlett	304309	B&TC, North Newton	309283	Cogload Junct, Outwood
286242	T&CC, Thornfalcon	304361	B&TC, Hamp, Bridgwater	309285	Cogload Junct, Outwood
287426	Gaunt's Farm, Pawlett	304364	B&TC, Bridgwater	309299	B&TC, Hedging
287431	Pawlett Hill	304392	R Parrett, N Bridgwater	309300	B&TC, Hedging
288262	B&TC, Charlton	305228	T&CC, Wrantage	309300	B&TC, Hedging
289429	Gaunt's Farm, Pawlett	305281	B&TC/Rly, Outwood	309315	B&TC, Hedging
289431	Pawlett Hill	305289	B&TC, Outwood	309357	Bridgwater Station
289433	Pawlett Hill	305304	B&TC, North Newton	309362	B&TC, Somerset Bridge
290242	T&CC, Thornfalcon	305312	B&TC, North Newton	309368	Bridgwater Station
290429	Gaunt's Farm, Pawlett	305356	B&TC, Somerset Bridge	309371	Colley Lane, Bridgwater
290431	Pawlett Hill	305358	B&TC, Somerset Bridge	309374	Bridgwater Station
291265	B&TC, Charlton	305374	Rly, Bath Rd, Bridgwater	309383	Rly, Sydenham, B'water
291434	Pawlett Hill	305408	R Parrett, Dunball Wharf	309408	R Parrett, Dunball Wharf
292271	B&TC, Charlton	306227	T&CC, Wrantage	310228	T&CC, Wrantage
293267	B&TC, Charlton	306282	Cogload Junction, Outwood	310280	Cogload Junct, West Lyng
293435	Pawlett Hill	306313	B&TC, North Newton	310281	Cogload Junct, West Lyng
293435	Pawlett Hill	306359	Somerset Bridge, Bridgwater	310352	B&TC, Huntworth
296236	T&CC, Lillsdon	307226	T&CC, Wrantage	310359	Rly, Somerset Bridge
297234	T&CC, Lillsdon	307280	Cogload Junction, Outwood	311227	Wrantage
297234	T&CC, Lillsdon	307281	Cogload Junction, Outwood	311278	Cogload Junction
311357	Rly, Somerset Bridge	307284	Cogload Junction, Outwood	311279	Cogload Junction
312225	Wrantage	332086	Chard (S), railway line	343139	Rly/Herne Hill, Dowlish Ford
312283	Cogload Junction	332094	Chard Station	343140	Rly/Herne Hill, Dowlish Ford
312351	B&TC, Huntworth	334092	Nr Chard Station	343141	Rly/Herne Hill, Dowlish Ford
312411	Dunball	334096	Chard Reservoir	343172	Railway line, Ilton
312411	Dunball	334194	Near Merryfield, Ilton	344020	Holditch Court, Holditch
313219	Crimson Hill, Wrantage	335085	Chard (S), railway line	344137	Rly/Herne Hill, Dowlish Ford
313220	Crimson Hill, Wrantage	335090	Chard (E)	345071	Horn Moor, nr Chard
313350	B&TC, Huntworth	336084	Chard (S), railway line	345073	Horn Moor, nr Chard
314216	Curry Mallet	336090	Chard (E)	345144	Cold Harbour, Ilminster
314220	Crimson Hill, Wrantage	336184	T&CC, Merryfield, Ilton	345152	R/Isle/A303, Ilminster
314222	Crimson Hill, Wrantage	337053	Rly line, Perry St, Chard	346129	Sea, Ilminster
314350	B&TC/Rly, Huntworth	337055	Rly line, Perry St, Chard	346145	Cold Harbour, Ilminster
315216	Curry Mallet	337084	Railway line, nr Chard	346152	R Isle/A303, Ilminster
315415	Railway Br, Dunball	337084	Railway line, nr Chard	346171	T&CC, Ilton (SW)
315416	Railway Br, Dunball	337086	Railway line, nr Chard	346172	T&CC, Ilton (SW)
316314	B&TC, Whites, North Newton	338056	Perry Street, nr Chard	346174	T&CC, Ilton (SW)
317216	Curry Mallet	338058	Perry Street, nr Chard	347129	Sea, Ilminster
317319	B&TC, North Moor	338083	Chard (S), railway line	347143	Herne Hill, Dowlish Ford
317410	Puriton Hill	338087	A30, Chard	347143	Herne Hill, Dowlish Ford
317410	Puriton Hill	338089	Oaklands, Chard	347151	Rly/A303, Ilminster
318230	Newport, Wrantage	339046	R Axe/SR, Chard Junction	347166	T&CC, Ilton (SSW)
318280	GWR, West Lyng	339046	R Axe/SR, Chard Junction	348131	Sea, Ilminster
318280	GWR, West Lyng	339048	R Axe/SR, Chard Junction	348149	Rly/A303, Ilminster (W)
318316	B&TC, North Moor	339055	Perry Street, nr Chard	348150	Rly/A303, Ilminster (W)
318345	B&TC, Huntworth	339056	Perry Street, nr Chard	348151	Rly/A303, Ilminster (W)
318367	Colley Lane, Bridgwater	339057	Perry Street, nr Chard	348171	Cad Green, Ilton
319214	Curry Mallet	339081	Chard (S), railway line	349161	T&CC/Rly, Ilminster (NW)
319319	B&TC, North Moor	339120	Railway line, Peasmarsh	350155	Rly, Winterhay Green Ilm,
319342	Rly/B&TC, Huntworth	339123	Railway line, Peasmarsh	353085	Lydmarsh, Chard (E)
320333	B&TC, Hay Moor	340057	B3167, Perry Street	353087	Lydmarsh, Chard (E)
321337	B&TC, Hay Moor	340061	Rly line, Perry Street	353149	A303, Ilminster Town
322210	Curry Mallet	340079	Chard (S), railway line	354147	Shrubbery Hotel, Ilminster
322325	B&TC, Fordgate	340081	Chard (S), railway line	355145	Ilminster Town (SW)
322328	B&TC, Fordgate	340103	Rly line, Chard reservoir	358154	Beacon Hill, Ilminster
323209	T&CC, Beer Crowcombe	340113	Rly line, Manor Fm, Chard	359139	A3037/Herne Hl, Ilminster
323209	T&CC, Beer Crowcombe (A/TBs)	340123	Railway line, Peasmarsh	360144	Ilminster, nr town centre
323210	T&CC, Beer Crowcombe	341064	Rly line, White Gate	360155	Beacon Hill, Ilminster
		341071	Rly line, Forton, Chard	361137	A3037, Ilminster (S)

Grid ref	Location	Grid ref	Location	Grid ref	Location
325205	T&CC, Beer Crowcombe (A/TBs)	341073	Rly line, Forton, Chard	361152	Beacon Hill, Ilminster
326205	T&CC, Beer Crowcombe	341112	Rly line, Manor Fm, Chard	363137	Dillington, Ilminster
326207	T&CC, Beer Crowcombe	341124	Peasmarsh, Ilminster	365148	Ilminster Town (N)
328204	T&CC, Beer Crowcombe (A/TBs)	342109	Rly, Woodhouse Fm, Chard	366149	Ilminster Town
329087	Chard (S), railway line	342109	Rly, Woodhouse Fm, Chard	367139	Pretwood Hill, Ilminster
329201	T&CC, Beer Crowcombe	342131	Rly line, Sea, Ilminster	368146	A303, Ilminster (E)
331087	A30, Chard	342139	Whitney Bottom, Horton	372177	R Isle, Ilford Bridges
331090	Chard	342140	Whitney Bottom, Horton	373153	Dillington, Ilminster
331091	Chard	342173	Railway line, Ilton	375152	Dillington, Ilminster
331093	Chard	343048	R Axe/SR, Chard Junction	376151	Dillington, Ilminster
331094	Chard	343070	Railway line, Horn Moor	377135	Kingstone, nr Ilminster
331095	Chard	343138	Rly/Herne Hl, Dowlish Ford	377146	Nott Oak/Dillington, Ilm
331196	T&CC, Nr Merryfield	343138	Rly/Herne Hl, Dowlish Ford	377152	Nott Oak, Ilminster

GHQ STOP-LINE GREEN: Highbridge to Freshford nr Bath

Grid ref	Location	Grid ref	Location	Grid ref	Location
ST		**ST**		**ST**	
323468	R Brue/Rly St, Highbridge	441443	B3151, Westhay Moor	629511	S&D, Old Down (PB+A/TBs)
323470	R Brue/Rly St, Highbridge	444426	nr Westhay Bridge	649515	S&D, Chilcompton (A/TBs)
328463	R Brue, Brent Fm, Highbridge	448100	R Whitelake, Westhay	651516	S&D, Chilcompton Bank
331463	R Brue, Brent Fm, Highbridge	448425	R Whitelake, Westhay	651523	S&D, Chilcompton Tunnel
334462	R Brue, Hackness, Highbridge	471419	R Whitelake, Godney	707556	S&D Rly, Writhlington
337457	Hackness, Highbridge	483422	R Whitelake, Godney	708555	S&D Rly, Writhlington
337460	R Brue, Hackness, Highbridge	486422	R Whitelake, Godney	716559	S&D/Wellow Brook, Foxcote
340459	R Brue, Bason Bridge (W)	491429	Upper Godney	718560	S&D/Wellow Brook, Single Hill
343456	East Huntspill	492428	Upper Godney	721562	S&D/Wellow Brook, Single Hill
351456	R Brue, Bason Bridge (E)	505434	Fenny Castle, North Moor	729565	S&D/Wellow Brook, S Littleton
355455	R Brue, Bason Bridge (E)	561455	A371, Wells (S)	729565	S&D/Wellow Brook, S Littleton
355455	R Brue, Mark Moor	561455	A371, Wells (S)	733568	S&D Railway, Wellow
371451	R Brue, Mark Moor	563454	Nr King's Castle, Wells	735568	S&D Railway, Wellow
373451	R Brue, Mark Moor	566454	King's Castle	745582	Wellow Brook, Wellow
374450	R Brue, Mark Moor	576453	Sharcombe Park, Dinder	750583	S&D/Wellow Brook, Wellow
376450	R Brue, Mark Moor	576453	(x 15 anti-tank blocks)	753583	S&D/Wellow Brook, Wellow
377450	R Brue, River Br, Mark Moor	581451	Dinder Wood, Dinder	755586	S&D/Wellow Brook, Wellow
379448	R Brue, River Br, Mark Moor	585454	N Dinder Wood, Dinder	757592	S&D/Wellow Brook, Twinhoe
380447	R Brue, River Br, Mark Moor	588456	NE Dinder Wood, Dinder	764597	B3110/Wellow Brook, Midford
382446	R Brue, River Br, Mark Moor	589461	Chilcote Manor, nr Wells	766593	B3110/Wellow Brook, Midford
402447	R Brue, Tadham Moor	591453	Chilcote Manor, nr Wells	773596	Hinton Abbey, nr Midford
405455	North Drain, Tadham Moor	596466	ESE East Horrington	774595	Hinton Abbey, nr Midford
415440	R Brue, Tadham Moor	596466	ESE East Horrington	783596	Sharpstone, nr Freshford
418438	R Brue, Tadham Moor	604468	S&D Railway, Masbury	783597	Sharpstone, nr Freshford
422435	R Brue, Tadham Moor	605469	S&D Railway, Masbury	786595	R Frome, Sharpstone
427432	R Brue, Westhay Level	611481	S&D Railway, Masbury	786598	R Frome, Sharpstone
431431	R Brue, Westhay Level	612488	S&D Railway, Binegar	788598	R Frome, Woodside
435428	R Brue, nr Westhay Bridge	621507	S&D Railway, Moorwood	793599	R Frome, Woodside
439426	R Brue, Westhay Bridge	622500	S&D Rly, Gurney Slade	794601	R Frome, Freshford

GHQ STOP-LINE YELLOW: *Freshford to Witham Friary (River Frome)*

Grid ref	Location
ST	
777453	Blatchbridge Fm, S Frome
778456	Blatchbridge Fm, S Frome
783500	Oldford Hill, N Frome
788515	Bonnyleigh Hill, Beckington
794517	Bonnyleigh Hill, Beckington
795535	Shawford, Woolverton
804579	Farleigh Hungerford

ABBREVIATIONS

A/TBs	Anti-Tank Blocks
B&TC	Bridgwater & Taunton Canal
Fm	Farm
GW Rly	Great Western Railway
Junct	Junction
PB	Pillbox
Rly	Railway (railway lines are GWR, unless otherwise stated)
R	River
S&D Rly	Somerset & Dorset (Joint) Railway
SR	Southern Railway
St	Station
T&CC	Taunton & Chard Canal

APPENDIX 4

PRISONER OF WAR CAMPS IN SOMERSET

The following is a list of the main PoW camps compiled from German records; no similar British records exist in the Public Record Office:

CAMP No	ADDRESS
37	Colley Lane, Bridgwater
44	Halswell House, Goathurst Camp, Nr Bridgwater
107	Penleigh Camp, Wookey Hole, Nr Wells
403	Brockley Camp, Brockley, Nr Bristol
405	Barwick House Camp, Barwick, Nr Yeovil
665	Cross Keys Camp, Norton Fitzwarren, Nr Taunton
666	Stoberry Park, Wells
1022	Norton Fitzwarren, Nr Taunton

Note:

The main influx of PoWs came after the fall of Tobruk, when thousands of Italians were taken in North Africa and eventually brought to this country. They accounted for the majority of PoWs in Somerset for the best part of the war. It was not until after D-Day that large numbers of German prisoners were seen in the county. The majority of prisoners worked on farms; some even boarded with their employers, rather than in the camps. PoWs were not an uncommon site in local towns - they were allowed to visit cinemas and other selected amenities towards the end of the war, but had to be back in camp before pub closing time. Many had local girlfriends. Some settled in the county after the war and became British citizens.

From the Other Side of the Fence: A Prisoner of War's View

Nunzio Notaro was in the Italian Engineer Regiment (Genio) and captured at Tobruk in 1941 when the Australians overran the Italian Garrison. From North Africa he was sent to a PoW camp in South Africa at Sondervander, where his guards were Zulu warriors. He was eventually shipped to Great Britain in the *Orbitor*. Landing at Liverpool, he was sent to a holding camp in Oldham, Lancashire. The camp was an old converted soap factory several stories high which could hold many hundreds of prisoners. The facilities were rudimentary. Many prisoners were ill or unfit, generally through lack of food - internment in South Africa had not been kind to them. Notaro should have gone with his colleagues to

This stained glass window and others in East Chinnock church were made, donated and installed by an ex-Luftwaffe gunner, Herr Gunther Anton of Leonberg, Germany, in grateful memory of the help and comfort he found in prayer here. As a PoW at Houndstone, Yeovil, he worked on a local farm during the latter part of the war. (Author)

The memorial to Romulus and Remus erected by the side of the A39 road not far from West Horrington, near Wells. It was constructed by an Italian stonemason, a PoW working and living in the area during the war, in recognition of the kindness shown to him by local people. (Author)

Scapa Flow to work on the defences, but he was ill and sent to Goathurst Camp near Bridgwater. He describes camp life and working on the land:

My first impressions of the camp were not too bad. The buildings at Goathurst were mostly of wooden construction with a proper roof, but some of the buildings were of corrugated iron. The huts were 20 yd long with bunks spaced every 4 ft - there were 64 of us accommodated in each. No personal locker or cupboard was provided - we didn't need storage space because we had no belongings and only one change of clothes.

Security at Goathurst consisted of high fencing all the way round, but there were no watchtowers. Officers guarding us were billeted at Halswell House, and other ranks were in a barrack hut outside the compound.

We did our own washing with very hard soap, but we were not allowed hot water, although there was plenty available for personal hygiene with showers and baths provided. There were 700 prisoners in the camp at first, so one was lucky to get one bath a week. The billets had proper electric lighting and heating with a tortoise stove in the middle - some billets had two. There was plenty of coal available for them, but the billets got very cold in winter. However because so many people slept in each one it was not too cold! We had to sleep in our underwear because we were not issued with pyjamas. Bedding provided was one bolster and one blanket but no sheet. Some of us had an extra blanket though. We supplemented our bedding with an overcoat. Our uniform was dark brown with diamond patches, one on the right leg and one on the back. On some uniforms the patches were circular.

Although food was very short, we were treated quite well. Rations did improve: instead of one loaf of bread for 16 it was shared by eight - twice as much as we got before in South Africa, although there was not enough to go round - we were still hungry. We didn't like eating potatoes and preferred bread - it was part of our staple diet. We had pasta, a few potatoes and a little meat. It was supplied by the Army. We just wanted bread by itself and complained about the lack of it. If we ate bread in the morning we didn't get any more until the evening. 1lb of margarine was issued for 20 people, but we didn't eat it and arranged a swop for more bread. We had a 2oz cheese ration once a week - depending on the cookhouse dishing it out!

There was no communication with my family after being captured - they didn't know for ten months whether I was alive or dead. We were allowed to write one letter every three weeks in Africa, but in the UK we could write as often as we liked. No stamp was required - the Red Cross saw to that. We took our letters to the Sergeant Major's office and he arranged to post them. It took another four months for my family's reply to reach me.

The Commandant had only one arm - he was wounded at Tobruk - but was good man and had a lot of tolerance towards us PoWs. He was sympathetic and, if one had a complaint, you could go and see him. Few of us had complaints though. If a PoW misbehaved he would spend a few days or weeks in the prison camp jail - sentenced was passed by him. The brick-built prison was just outside the camp by oak tree and you couldn't escape from it. One PoW was the Commandant's driver and used to go all over the place ferrying him about but we were eventually allowed out of camp to work once we could be trusted. The British were very suspicious at first.

We were allowed to work on the farms straight away - gangs of 20/25 used to be picked up by bus and taken to work which included loading coal, spreading earth dug out from a river, or cleaning beaches. There was one guard armed with a rifle to each gang. Buses came in every day to pick us up and dropped us off where we were needed. The guard used to stand at doorway of the bus with his rifle which was quite frightening. The local people would give us funny looks and stare at us, but they got used to seeing us around.

Farmers used to phone the camp and make arrangements for prisoners to work on their farm. If a farmer just wanted one or two men, it was his responsibility to collect them and was responsible for their security.

When things got better we had more freedom. We caught fish from a local river, built a little fire, cooked and ate them there and then. We used to take some back to the camp in the bus. The guards didn't mind and everybody in the camp ate fish! We had to be back by four o'clock for tea at 4.30. We had our own kitchen and cooked for ourselves.

I worked on a farm and stayed there from 1943. The authorities asked for PoWs to be billeted on the farm if the farmers agreed. Many of us did. The camp still had 500 living in and about 200 living out on farms locally. If a PoW was living on a farm, the farmer deducted - say £1 - from the money due to the Government for keeping the PoW on the farm, rather than in the camp to cover the cost of keep. I lived in the farmhouse with a proper bedroom and was fed as part of the family. I got up at 6.00 to collect the cows and milked them. If one wished for a transfer to another farm the staff sergeant at the camp would see to it. We were paid every fortnight for working on a farm and got 3 shillings a week, but the farmer paid 8 shillings a day to the authorities for 16 hours work! We had to go back to the camp and sign the register to pick up our pay.

We had quite a lot of freedom and could go back to the camp to see our friends or go to church if we wished. There was a chapel in the camp with an Italian padre, also an Italian doctor came to the camp every day. PoWs were allowed to go to the local cinema during the war. I often used to bicycle in to the Odeon from the farm. We weren't allowed to go into the pubs though - anyway, we didn't have much money - but used to buy fish and chips costing 2/- or 3/- a time. I earned extra money from shooting rabbits and sold them in Glastonbury for 3d each. The farmer supplied the cartridges. I used to get 6d for a hare. By the time I went to Mr Ebsary's farm, I had earned £20.

Others in the camp used to make all sorts of things, including jewellery from old bits of aluminium. There was one chap who used to work for Alfa Romeo before the war. He was brilliant and could make marvellous rings from a half-crown coin. PoWs used to make and sell all sorts of things to the locals or make toys to give to the kids.

There was another camp at Colley Lane in Bridgwater with a similar number of prisoners. All Italians were moved to Brymore in Cannington when German PoWs started coming in from July 1944. Brymore Camp was smaller, but most PoWs were living on farms by then.

I stayed in the UK until repatriated in 1946. After the war ended PoWs could apply to stay in UK, which I did and arrived back in September 1947.

APPENDIX 5

HM SHIPS WITH SOMERSET NAMES AND ASSOCIATION

Name	Class	Type	Tonnage	Remarks
HMS *Kilmersdon*	Kil Class	Patrol Gunboat	890	Class built: 1917-19, Some used as minesweepers
HMS *Yeovil*	Hunt Class	Minesweeper	800	Class built: 1918-19
HMS *Nunney Castle*	Castle Class	Corvette	1,010	Class built: 1943-44
HMS *Bridgwater*	Hastings Class	Sloop	1,045	Built: 1928
HMS *Weston*	Hastings Class	Sloop	1,045	Built: 1932
HMS *Wellington*	Grimsby Class	Sloop	990	Built: 1934
HMS *Exe*	River Class	Frigate	1,370	Class built: 1941-43
HMS *Frome*	River Class	Frigate	1,370	Class built: 1941-43
HMS *Parrett*	River Class	Frigate	1,370	Class built: 1941-43
HMS *Dulverton*	Hunt Class	Escort Destroyer	1,050	Class built: 1940-42, Bombed and sunk in Aegean Sea 13.11.43
HMS *Exmoor*	Hunt Class	Escort Destroyer	907	Built: 1940, sunk by U-Boat Feb '41. *Burton* renamed *Exmoor*
HMS *Mendip*	Hunt Class	Escort Destroyer	907	Built: 1940
HMS *Quantock*	Hunt Class	Escort Destroyer	907	Built: 1940
HMS *Bath*	Town Class	Destroyer	1,020	American lease-lend (WW1 four-stacker)
HMS *Burnham*	Town Class	Destroyer	1,020	American lease-land (WW1 four-stacker)
HMS *Churchill*	Town Class	Destroyer	1,020	American lease-lend (WW1 four-stacker)
HMS *Wells*	Town Class	Destroyer	1,020	American lease-lend (WW1 four-stacker)
HMS *Dunkery*	Hills Class	Trawler	–	Minesweeping/anti-submarine
HMS *Lorna Doone*	Paddlesteamer	Minesweeper	–	Built: 1891 Scrapped 1949

APPENDIX 6

BRITISH ARMY REGIMENTS, BATTALIONS & UNITS IN SOMERSET

The following list obtained from local records provides a sample of the regiments, corps and units known to have been stationed in Somerset or for training on ranges in the county. It cannot be deemed as definitive, since a great number only spent short periods of time in Somerset and were widely dispersed, mainly in billeted or sometimes tented accommodation:

REGIMENT	BATTALION/UNIT	LOCATION/TRAINING AREAS	DATES
Royal Warwickshire Regiment	2nd Battalion	Burnham	1940/1
Royal Warwickshire Regiment	8th Battalion	West Luccombe	1940/1
Green Howards	4th Battalion	Bridgwater, Cannington	1941/1
Green Howards	5th Battalion	Brean, Bruton, Cheddar	1940/1
Grenadier Guards	1st Motor Battalion	Winsford	1942
Grenadier Guards	2nd Battalion	Bruton	1940
Coldstream Guards	1st Battalion	Radstock	1940
Coldstream Guards	4th Battalion	Frome	1942
7th Guards Brigade		Charlton Musgrove	1940
1st Guards Armoured Division	HQ	Cucklington/ Milborne Port	1940
Parachute Regiment	1st Battalion	Exford	1942
Parachute Regiment	4th Battalion	Exmoor	1945
Worcestershire Regiment	8th Battalion	Bruton	1940
94th LAA Regiment RA	323/324 Batteries	Yeovil, Misterton	1942
42nd (Searchlight) Regt RA	368 Battery & others	Yeovil	1944
66th (Searchlight) Regt RA	447 Battery & others	Yeovil	1940
76th (Searchlight) Regt RA	493 Battery & others	Yeovil, Brendon Hills etc	1940
220th (Searchlight) Regt RA	129 Battery & others	Houndstone	1940

23rd Field Regiment RA	89 Battery	Yeovil	1942
30th Field Regiment RA		Stoke-sub-Hamden	1940
87th Medium Regiment RA		Dunkery Range	1945
21st Training Regiment RA		St Audries	1945
208th LAA Regiment RA		Houndstone	1940/1
Royal Engineers	835 Bomb Disposal Coy	As required	1940/1
Royal Engineers	148 Field Squadron	Stoke-under-Ham	1942
Royal Engineers	930 Port Construction Repair Coy	Steep Holm, Flat Holm	1940/1
42nd Armoured Division Sigs		Cucklington	1943
Military Pioneer Corps (Aux)	55th Coy	Preston Park, Yeovil	1941
70th Gloucestershire Regiment		Yeovilton, Weston Zoyland	1941
225th Light Field Ambulance		Beckington	1941
147th Essex Yeomanry	511 Battery	Frome	1943
Royal Northumberland Fuslrs	4th Battalion	Shepton Mallet	1941
Independant Czech Brigade		Yeovil, Ilminster	1942

NB: The above list does not include The Somerset Light Infantry Battalions, which are covered elsewhere in the text, together with other known units and regiments.

Selected Index

216